HANDBOOK FOR THE TRIAL OF CONTRACT LAWSUITS:
Strategies and Techniques

HANDBOOK FOR THE TRIAL OF CONTRACT LAWSUITS: Strategies and Techniques

Edward J. Imwinkelried, J.D.

Prentice-Hall, Inc., Englewood Cliffs, New Jersey

Prentice-Hall International, Inc., *London*
Prentice-Hall of Australia, Pty. Ltd., *Sydney*
Prentice-Hall of Canada, Ltd., *Toronto*
Prentice-Hall of India Private Ltd., *New Delhi*
Prentice-Hall of Japan, Inc., *Tokyo*
Prentice-Hall of Southeast Asia Pte. Ltd., *Singapore*
Whitehall Books, Ltd., *Wellington, New Zealand*

This publication is designed to provide accurate and authoritative information with regard to the subject matter covered. It is sold with the understanding that the publisher is not engaged in rendering legal, accounting, or
other professional advice. If legal advice or other expert assistance is required, the services of a competent professional person should be sought.

*—From a Declaration of Principles jointly adopted by a Committee of the
American Bar Association and a Committee of Publishers and Associations.*

Library of Congress Cataloging in Publication Data

Imwinkelried, Edward J.
    Handbook for the trial of contract lawsuits.

    Includes bibliographical references and index.
    1. Contracts—United States—Trial practice.
2. Trial practice—United States.   I. Title.
KF8925.C58I45   346.73'02'0269   81-7330
ISBN 0-13-382606-6   347.30620269   AACR2

Printed in the United States of America

About the Author

Edward J. Imwinkelried has broad experience as a teacher, writer, and practitioner in the field of law.

He practiced several years with a legal services program and the government. His practice with the legal services program was in the consumer field; and as a government attorney, he had experience administering public contracts.

During the past eight years, he has taught both Contracts and Evidence and has lectured on Evidence to practicing attorneys in over 20 states in continuing legal education programs.

His writing credits include an Evidence hornbook for West Publishing Company, and a book entitled *Evidentiary Foundations* for Michie Publishing Company. He is in the process of co-authoring a new Evidence casebook for Michie Publishing Company.

Currently, Mr. Imwinkelried is a Professor of Law at Washington University in St. Louis.

DEDICATION

I would like to dedicate my work on this handbook to

my parents, John and Enes Imwinkelried;
my parents-in-law, Mary Jane Clark and the late
   Lyman (Brownie) Clark;
and to Cindy, Darth, and Morgan.

A Word from the Author

Who are the master Contract litigators? Do they know some secret, Druidic lore that sets them apart from other attorneys? The truth is that these masters are so successful because they understand Contract litigation as "a seamless web." They are outstanding litigators because they have a command of three bodies of learning (Contract law, Evidence law, and Trial Techniques), and they know how to integrate all three bodies of learning into their trial presentations.

They did not learn how to integrate those three bodies of learning in law school. Most law schools present those bodies of learning to their students in three separate courses—with little or no attempt to interrelate the courses. Even after graduating from law school, it is difficult for an attorney to learn how to integrate the three subjects. Most commercially available texts focus on only one of the subjects. It is almost impossible for the typical practitioner to find the time to teach himself or herself how to integrate the three subjects. If you are primarily a business advisor, your law office work keeps you more than busy. You are occasionally forced into combat in the courtroom, but you cannot find time in your hectic schedule for an in-depth study of Evidence and Trial Techniques. Even if you are engaged in general litigation practice, you do not have time to study Contract law intensively. In January you try a personal injury case, in February you defend a felony prosecution, and now in March you have to litigate a construction contract dispute.

The purpose of this handbook is to help the typical, busy practitioner who cannot afford the luxury of devoting hours to studying Contracts *and* Evidence *and* Trial Techniques. This book attempts to break down the barriers between those three bodies of learning and show you how the master Contract litigators use all three bodies of learning together. Having taught Contracts *and* Evidence *and* Trial Techniques for several years, I have written this handbook to show you how to integrate the Contract law, Evidence law, and Trial Techniques that a commercial litigator must know. Step by step, the book reviews each major stage of the trial: voir dire examination, opening statement, the examination of witnesses, and closing argument. At each step, it attempts to accomplish four objectives.

First, the book explains the governing, substantive Contract law. It discusses the common law and the Uniform Commercial Code. Although the book does not cover all Contract doctrines, it reviews the doctrines commercial litigators most frequently encounter. The discussion of abstract Contract theory is kept to a minimum. For attorneys interested in more detailed, sophisticated analyses of the theories, I have included legal research references to the texts I have found most useful: J. Murray, *Contracts* (2d rev. ed. 1974) (hereinafter cited as Murray) and J. White & R. Summers, *Uniform Commercial Code* (2d ed. 1980) (hereinafter cited as White & Summers). This handbook converts each Contract theory into a list of concrete facts to prove at trial; the text lists the historical facts the trial attorney must prove to use the Contract doctrine. This part of the handbook tells the trial attorney *what* facts to prove.

Second, the handbook analyzes the controlling Evidence law. It mentions the common law and the new Federal Rules of Evidence. Again, the discussion of theory is minimal. Attorneys interested in more thorough treatments of Evidence law will find this handbook interspersed with legal research references to the most popular Evidence hornbook, C. McCormick, *Handbook of the Law of Evidence* (Cleary ed. 1972) (hereinafter cited as McCormick). This handbook dissects each Evidence doctrine into a list of elements to prove at trial; the book converts each Evidence theory into a checklist for laying the foundation at trial. This part of the handbook tells the attorney *how* to prove the facts necessary to invoke the Contract doctrine in the courtroom.

Third, the handbook gives a sample line of questioning that is both complete and correct—*complete* in the sense that the content of the line of questioning satisfies all the requirements of substantive Contract law and *correct* in the sense that the form of the questions complies with Evidence law. This part of the book should give the trial attorney new confidence that his or her foundation meets the requirements of both Contract and Evidence law.

Finally, the handbook explains how the trial attorney uses a theory and theme at each stage of the trial. To be appealing to a jury, your case must have simplicity and continuity; and perhaps the essential point of this handbook is that the attorney can best achieve those qualities by developing a theory and theme. Chapters 5 through 9 analyze the essential elements of most plaintiffs' theories: contract formation (Chapter 5), contract interpretation (Chapter 6), the satisfaction of the conditions to the defendant's duty (Chapter 7), the defendant's breach of duty (Chapter 8), and the plaintiff's remedies (Chapter 9). While Chapters 5 through 9 approach the problem of developing a theory and theme from the plaintiff's perspective, Chapters 12 through 15 take the defendant's perspective. Those chapters give the reader an overview of the possible defense theories, and review the four basic defense theories or lines of defense. Again and again the handbook harks back to the message that the commercial litigator must use a theory and theme to unify the case for the jurors.

It is my hope that by reading this handbook, more and more lawyers will move into the category of attorneys who have mastered the skill of developing persuasive theories and themes. In criminal cases, the courts are making the sixth amendment guarantee of effective representation more meaningful. The problem of ineffective counsel is just as acute in civil cases. As one trial judge recently told me, many attorneys trying Contract cases "don't even know how to handle the document the contract is written on." The judicial system must produce justice in both civil and criminal cases, and justice in civil cases cannot be assured until we raise the level of trial advocacy in civil suits, including Contract actions.

Edward J. Imwinkelried

ACKNOWLEDGMENTS

I would first like to thank my research assistants, Mr. Theodore Blumoff and Ms. Judith Leenov. They did all the preliminary research for this handbook, edited the entire manuscript, and made several suggestions that substantially improved the final product. I would also like to thank Ms. Lucy Karl who assisted with the editing.

Finally, I would like to thank the Washington University Law School typists who prepared this manuscript: Ms. Jane Bettlach, Ms. Bobette Buster, Ms. Sharon Frank, Ms. Patricia Heuermann, Ms. Beverly Jarboe, and Ms. Mary Ellen Powers.

Table of Contents

Part IV: The Post-Evidence Stages of the Trial

CHAPTER 1

The Overriding Importance of the Theory and Theme in a Contract Lawsuit—The Winning Strategy

Sec.

Sec. 1-1. The Necessity of Mastering the Facts in the Case File

A trial judge once lamented about the difficulty of becoming a competent litigator: "In law school, they teach you theory for three years, and then they have the audacity to expect you to practice facts for the rest of your life." This lament reflects the importance of facts in the practice of law. In reality, every rule of law is a conditional imperative: If ultimate "facts" *A* (mutual assent) and *B* (consideration) concur, legal consequence *C* flows (a contract is formed). To trigger the legal consequence, the attorney must prove the existence of the conditioning facts.

The facts are especially important to the trial attorney. Without sufficient facts, the attorney will suffer a pretrial summary judgment or a directed verdict at trial. Moreover, if the attorney does not present the facts persuasively, the attorney will be unable to motivate the jury to want to find for the attorney's client.

Sec. 1-2. The Secret of Success as a Trial Attorney—Developing a Theory and Theme for Your Case

Given the critical importance of facts at trial, a competent litigator will gather a mass of facts before trial; the litigator uses informal techniques such as interviews and formal discovery devices including depositions and interrogatories to collect factual ammunition. The end result of these discovery efforts is an extensive compilation of letters, deposition transcripts, invoices, tape recordings, experts' reports, and other relevant material.

The danger is that the attorney will be tempted to present to the jury virtually every fact gathered in discovery. That temptation can be very strong; if you paid $1,000 for an expert's report, there is an understandable inclination to use the report at trial. However, presenting all the facts would overwhelm and confuse the jury. You may be intimately familiar with the most minute facts in the case file because you have lived with the file for months or years, but the jurors are absolute strangers to the fact situation. The attorney must be selective. Before trial, the attorney must select a theory and a theme; and at trial, rather than deluging the jury with all the facts, the attorney must have the discipline to single-mindedly develop the theory and theme.

The Theory

A "theory" corresponds roughly with a cause of action or count in the complaint. For example, the first count in a Contract complaint might generally allege that the defendant breached an express, oral contract. More specifically, the count alleges that the plaintiff and the defendant formed the contract at a particular time and place; that the defendant breached by refusing to deliver; and that the breach caused certain damage, entitling the plaintiff to relief. The "theory" includes all the specific facts (formation, performance, and damages) that condition the legal consequence (the plaintiff's entitlement to relief) in this conditional imperative. As we noted in the Foreword, Chapters 5 through 9 discuss the five basic elements of most plaintiffs' theories: The parties formed a contract (Ch. 5); the contract created certain conditions for the plaintiff to fulfill and a duty for the defendant to perform (Ch. 6); the plaintiff satisfied the conditions (Ch. 7); the defendant breached the duty (Ch. 8); and the plaintiff is entitled to a remedy (Ch. 9). Chapters 12 through 15 analyze the four most common defense theories: The parties never formed a contract (Ch. 12); the contract is unenforceable (Ch. 13); the defendant did not breach (Ch. 14); and the plaintiff is not entitled to the particular remedy he or she is seeking (Ch. 15).

The Theme

The "theme" is your strongest argument on the critical element of your theory. For example, suppose that the defendant responded to the complaint by filing a general denial. By the end of discovery, you know that contract formation (element #1) will be the pivotal, disputed issue in the case; when the defendant deposed your client, 90% of the questions related to contract formation. If you cannot prove contract formation, the jury will reject your theory; but if you can, it will be relatively easy to show breach and damage. Before trial, you deposed the superintendent of the defendant's shipping de-

partment. The deponent admitted that he had begun labeling boxes for shipment to the plaintiff and that the defendant "ordinarily does not do so until
after striking a firm bargain to sell." Your theme should be to stress the defendant's habitual shipping practice and to argue that "actions speak louder
than words": The defendant may now deny contract formation, but its actions indicated that even the defendant thought there was a contract. It is
ideal if you can capsulize your theme in a short, catchy expression such as
"actions speak louder than words" or "the case of the boxes labeled for
plaintiff." If you can reduce your theme to a short phrase, you can impress
it upon the jury by repeating it several times during the course of the trial.

Sec. 1-3.   The Use of Pretrial Proceedings to Select the Theory and Theme

How do we arrive at this theory and theme? We use the pretrial pro-
ceedings to identify them.

a.   The Theory

Assume that when the plaintiff filed his or her complaint, the complaint
contained three counts or theories: express, oral contract; express, written
contract; and promissory estoppel. The litigation process is like a funnel that
is constantly narrowing. At the beginning of the process, when we file the
complaint, all three theories seem possible.

We first enter the pleading stage. In this stage, the defendant can eliminate the plaintiff's theories that lack legal merit by demurring or moving to
dismiss. The demurrer and motion challenge the theories' legal sufficiency.
In effect, the defendant contends that even if the plaintiff proves the alleged
facts, the plaintiff is not entitled to relief. The legal consequence C does not
flow from the alleged facts, A and B. Assume that count #3 invoked promissory estoppel to enforce a vague promise to sell by the defendant. In many
jurisdictions, promissory estoppel is only a consideration substitute. In these
jurisdictions, even if there is detrimental reliance on a promise, the promise
itself must satisfy the normal definiteness standards for contract promises.[1]
If the judge thought that the promise alleged in count #3 was fatally ambiguous, the judge would sustain a demurrer to count #3.

After the pleading stage, we enter the discovery stage. The funnel narrows further, and we now eliminate the pleaded theories that lack factual
merit. At the outset, the attorney believed that it would be possible to prove
count #2, an express, written contract. However, discovery shows that the
documents exchanged between the parties never specified a quantity term. A
court will ordinarily not imply a quantity term.[2] Given the state of the available documents, the defendant might well obtain a summary judgment on
count #2. Even if the defendant does not file a summary judgment motion,
prudence dictates that the plaintiff abandon count #2. The trial theory
must be consistent with all the facts you do not intend to dispute; like a sci-

entific hypothesis, a theory must account for all the available data. If you urge a theory inconsistent with the undisputed facts, you play into the opponent's hands; you have created a strawman whom the opponent can easily destroy.

The pleading and discovery stages thus serve as a negative process of elimination; we abandon the theories lacking either factual or legal merit. The negative process helps us select the final theory to be urged at trial.

However, the discovery stage also serves the affirmative function of providing the attorney with factual data. When there is more than one theory with legal and factual merit, this data aids us in choosing the theory for trial. The strongest theory is usually the theory supported by the most high-quality corroborating evidence—documentary or physical proof or the testimony of disinterested witnesses. When the possible theories have roughly the same amount of corroboration, consider two factors in making your choice of a theory. First, choose a theory based on substantial justice rather than on technical legal rules. For example, a fraud defense has much more jury appeal than a Statute of Frauds defense. Second, choose a theory that casts your client in a role the jurors can readily identify with. If the defendant is a buyer, the plaintiff's breach of warranty is a good defense theory; the defense casts the defendant in the role of consumer, and most jurors can readily think of themselves in the same role.

b.   The Theme

Moreover, on the basis of the discovery data, the attorney should be able to identify (1) the most critical, disputed part of the theory of the case; and (2) the attorney's strongest argument on that part of the theory. The identification is especially easy if there has been a pretrial conference. More and more trial judges are using the conference to narrow the issues and force as many stipulations as possible. In our hypothetical, after carefully reviewing the discovery work product and pretrial order, the attorney concludes that (1) proving contract formation will be the key to prevailing on the remaining theory, count #1; and (2) based on the testimony of the superintendent of the defendant's shipping department, an "actions speak louder than words" argument will be the strongest theme for the plaintiff. "Actions speak louder than words" is a short expression that you can repeat several times during the trial and that the jury should have little difficulty remembering. A Perry Mason devotee might dub this theme "the case of the boxes labeled for the plaintiff." As we shall see in Chapter 17, your theme can relate to (1) which witness the jurors should believe; (2) which inferences the jurors should draw; or (3) how the jury should apply a legal standard.

Sec. 1-4.   The Use of the Theory and Theme at Trial

Simply stated, at trial everything the attorney does should relate to the theory, and the attorney's emphasis should be on the theme. The attorney must use the theme as a unifying, recurring motif at trial.

If the judge permits you to make brief preliminary remarks before beginning the voir dire questioning, devote a sentence or two to stating your theory: "Ladies and gentlemen, as Judge Lopardo just explained, we've asked you here today to help us decide a dispute between my client, Mr. Grant, and the defendant. Mr. Grant contends that the defendant orally promised to sell him some air conditioners and that the defendant later broke that promise. I'm going to ask you a few questions now to help us to determine whether you can give Mr. Grant and the defendant a fair, impartial trial." During the voir dire questioning of the prospective jurors, attempt to insinuate your theme. You want to lay the groundwork for the argument that the defendant's habitual practice is to label boxes for shipping only after contract formation:

Q[3] Ms. *X*, when you hear the word "habit," what do you think of?
Q   Do you think that businesses can have habits just as people do?

During opening statement, explicitly describe your theory of the case and emphasize the theme. Label your theory: "The evidence will show that the defendant broke an oral promise to sell 20 air conditioners to Mr. Grant (the plaintiff). This gives Mr. Grant the right to collect money damages from the defendant." Then describe the facts showing formation of the oral contract, breach, and damage. You can describe the breach and damage allegations in slightly greater detail than you used in the complaint. But you should go into much greater detail on the critical element of contract formation. Spend at least twice as much time discussing that issue, mention the anticipated testimony of the superintendent of the defendant's shipping department, and at least once voice your "actions speak louder than words" theme.

During the evidentiary presentations, your theory of the case and the opponent's theory establish the standard of relevance. It is a serious mistake to include all the evidence logically relevant to the general "subject matter" of the action or even to the pleadings. You should ask a question only if the answer is logically relevant to proving your theory. Every other fact in the case should be disregarded or, at most, saved for rebuttal. Further, in the course of eliciting the testimony, devote the most time to your theme. Use your most attention-getting voice and demeanor when you are eliciting the testimony bearing upon the theme. In terms of time and tone, the highlight of your evidentiary presentation should be the testimony of the superintendent of the defendant's shipping department.

During closing argument, after the amenities, repeat your theory of the case. Then point out to the jury that the breach and damage parts of your theory are relatively undisputed. Briefly show the jury that the opponent has explicitly or tacitly conceded those elements of your theory. Next tell the jurors that the critical issue in the case is formation. Argue that issue by developing your theme. Voice your theme once: "But, ladies and gentlemen, I'm confident that you'll find that there was a contract because actions speak louder than words—and the defendant's own actions show that the defendant believed there was a contract." Review the testimony of the superintendent of the defendant's shipping department. Directly quote key passages from that person's deposition and trial testimony. Before concluding and asking for your verdict, repeat the theme, perhaps converting it into a rhetorical question: "And ladies and gentlemen, when you go back into the jury room to deliberate, I'd like you to ask yourselves just one question: Weren't the defendant's acts the acts of someone who believed and knew that he or she had entered into a legally binding contract with Mr. Grant? The defendant's acts speak, and those acts say clearly that there was a contract."

Finally, request jury instructions that state your theory and highlight your theme. For example, some jurisdictions have instructions on the weight of habit evidence or the impeaching value of conduct inconsistent with a person's statements. The plaintiff should request those instructions because they will reinforce the theme in the jury's mind.

The comments in this chapter are a variation on an old adage: "You've got to tell 'em you're going to tell 'em; tell 'em; and then tell 'em you've told 'em." In the opening statement, tell the jurors what your theme is. During the witnesses' testimony, prove the facts supporting the theme. In the summation, remind the jury of the theme. Employ the theme to give your trial presentation simplicity and continuity.

CHECKLIST FOR PLANNING AND USING A THEORY AND THEME

____ During the pleading stage, abandon your theories that lack legal merit.
____ During the discovery stage, abandon your theories that lack factual merit.
____ Choose your strongest theory.
 ____ The theory must be consistent with all the undisputed facts.
 ____ There is quality, corroborating evidence for the theory.
 ____ The theory is based on substantial justice rather than on a technical legal rule.
 ____ The theory casts your client in a role the jurors can readily identify with.
____ Identify the element of your theory that will be most sharply disputed at trial.
____ Identify your strongest argument on that element of your theory—your theme.
____ Reduce your theme to a short, memorable phrase.
____ Use the theory and theme to unify your case at trial.
 ____ During voir dire, mention your theory and insinuate your theme.
 ____ During opening statement, explain your theory and stress the evidence relating to your theme.

___ During your evidentiary presentation, offer only evidence that develops your theory.

___ During your evidentiary presentation, stress the theme.

___ Obtain jury instructions that discuss your theory and theme.

___ During summation, repeat your theory, identify the disputed part of your theory, and argue that part of your theory by stressing the theme.

FOOTNOTES

[1] J. Murray, Contracts §92 (2d rev. ed. 1974).

[2] J. Calamari & J. Perillo, The Law of Contracts §2-13 (2d ed. 1977).

[3] "Q" represents "question" throughout this text.

PART I

The Pre-Evidence Stages of the Trial

CHAPTER 2

Jury Selection as Part of the Winning Strategy—Exposing the Theory and Indoctrinating on the Theme

Sec. 2-1. Voir Dire Examination of Prospective Jurors

Chapter 1 explained how the trial attorney uses the pretrial stages to select the theory and theme. This chapter explains how the attorney goes about implementing the theory and theme at trial.

If the action is a jury trial, the jury selection phase is critical. Depending upon the jurisdiction's procedure and the judge's discretion, the jury selection procedure may afford the attorneys the first opportunity for significant, personal contact with the prospective jurors (veniremen). This is your only chance to converse with the jurors in two-way communication. Common sense and several of the available studies of jury behavior tell us that in trial work, as in many other activities, the initial impression is lasting and important.

a. The Preliminary, Opening Remarks

The judge and attorneys often make preliminary remarks to the prospective jurors before beginning the actual voir dire questioning. The preliminary remarks accomplish three purposes. First, the remarks explain the purpose of the voir dire examination to the veniremen: "Now, ladies and gentlemen, this is called the voir dire questioning. During this questioning, the opposing counsel and I will ask you some questions about your background. I want to apologize in advance if any of my questions offends you. I'm not trying to pry into your private lives. I simply want to make sure that both parties receive a fair trial from an impartial jury." Second, during the remarks, the venire is introduced to the various trial participants, especially the parties and their counsel. Refer to your client by name but always refer to the opponent as "the plaintiff" or "the defendant." Third, the remarks expose the jurors to the parties' theories of the case. If the judge permits you as plaintiff's counsel to make preliminary remarks, seize the opportunity to introduce your *theory*: "The parties, my client and the defendant, are asking you to resolve their dispute. Mr. Nash (the plaintiff) contends that the defendant orally agreed to sell Mr. Nash some seed. Mr. Nash contends that the defendant broke that promise and now owes Mr. Nash $9,000. The defendant denies that he owes Mr. Nash any money."

Many judges prefer to make the opening voir dire remarks themselves. If the judge does not make the remarks, the plaintiff's counsel should; and by using a friendly demeanor and conversational tone during the remarks, the plaintiff's counsel can begin building rapport with the venire.

b.   The Voir Dire Questions—The Four Types of Questions to Ask

After the preliminary remarks, counsel begin the voir dire questioning or examination. When you question, try to refer to each venireman by name. Have a chart depicting the jury box; and as the bailiff calls out each venireman's name and the venireman takes a seat in the box, write the name on your chart. The questions themselves serve four different purposes.

1.   To gather information that may be a basis for challenge for cause.

This is a proper purpose for voir dire questions in all jurisdictions. In commercial litigation, the questioner should stress questions about family and occupational data. If the venireman or a member of the venireman's immediate family has a close personal or business relationship with a party to the lawsuit, the venireman may be challengeable. You want to learn the venireman's current job and past employment history.

Questions posed for this purpose should be non-leading, but they should at least specify the topic:

Q   Mr. *A*, how, if at all, are you related to the defendant?

The questions should be non-leading to encourage the veniremen to talk at some length and give you a feel for their personalities.

2.   To gather information that will help you intelligently exercise peremptory challenges.

Jurisdictions differ on whether this is a legitimate purpose of voir dire questions. In some jurisdictions, you may pose such questions as of right; but in other jurisdictions, you may do so only in the judge's discretion. In a Contract suit, the counsel should inquire about the venireman's prior jury service and the occupational and associational background of both the venireman and the members of the venireman's immediate family. Even if the occupational or associational relation to a party is not close enough to be ground for challenge for cause, you may want to peremptorily strike the venireman.

If the venireman has served on a jury before, learn the type of action; you may want to strike the venireman if he or she has already sat as a juror in a Contract case.

You also probably want to strike the venireman if the venireman or an immediate family member works in the industry involved in the suit. If the suit involves a mining contract and the prospective juror's husband is a miner, there is a danger that the venireman will consult her spouse about the case.

An attorney representing a corporation or other large business entity will want to probe for economic prejudice; the attorney may want to strike a venireman who is a member of a militant union or consumer group or the proprietor of a small business such as a corner grocery that competes on a daily basis with larger business entities. Conversely, the attorney for a natural person plaintiff suing an entity may want to strike a venireman with a background in manufacturing, wholesaling, or retailing; that type of venireman can too readily identify with the defendant.

Questions posed for this purpose should be non-leading and relatively open-ended:

Q   Ms. Z, in your own words, tell us something about yourself.
Q   The evidence in this case will show that my client is a fairly large business, employing 10,000 people and doing $15,000,000 in business every year. How do you feel about large businesses?

An open-ended question will force the venireman to talk at some length and give you some insight into his or her personality. The more extensively they talk, the more likely they are to betray any prejudice. You cannot ferret out prejudice by asking leading questions, eliciting yes or no answers.

THE DISCLOSURE OF AN INKLING OF PREJUDICE

How should you proceed when a question eliciting background information about cause or peremptory challenges discloses an inkling of prejudice? Suppose that you represent a private builder, suing the city on a construction contract. When your contractor walked off the work site, the mayor held a press conference and castigated the contractor. The media publicized the conference. You have just asked whether any venireman had read anything in the newspapers about the case. Figure 2-1 illustrates the flow of the voir dire questioning.

1. If there is no inkling of any prejudice, proceed with your planned voir dire questions. For example, your next topic might be prior jury service.

2. If there is an inkling of prejudice, explore the inkling with the juror. If exposing the other veniremen to the information might taint them, first ask the judge to temporarily excuse them.

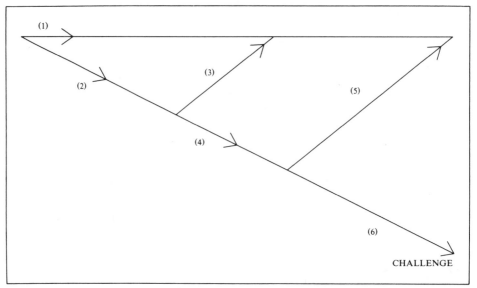

Figure 2-1: THE PLANNED VOIR DIRE QUESTIONS

3. If after exploring you are convinced that there is no real prejudice, return to your planned voir dire examination.

4. If after exploring you think that there is a possibility of prejudice, teach the venireman that the prejudice should not affect the jury deliberations and give the venireman an opportunity to assure you of his or her fairness.

5. If the prospective juror gives you a convincing assurance, return to your own planned voir dire questions. Before doing so, you might want to question the other veniremen to ensure that they understand what you taught the venireman you were questioning. (Notwithstanding the venireman's verbal assurance, you still may want to strike that person.)

6. If the venireman does not give you a satisfactory assurance, disqualify that venireman past any possible rehabilitation. You want to force the judge to excuse the venireman for cause; you do not want to have to use one of your precious peremptory strikes to remove the venireman.

In other words, if your questioning ends at step 1, 3, or 5, proceed to your next planned voir dire topic such as a prior jury service. However, if the questioning proceeds from step 2 to step 4 and finally to step 6, you will want to remove the venireman from the jury.

Apply this model to our construction contract hypothetical involving the newspaper reports of the mayor's press conference.

1. No venireman raises his or her hand. There is no inkling of prejudice. Proceed to your next, planned question—prior jury service.

2. A juror raises her hand. You should explore. First ask the judge to excuse the other veniremen. Then ask exploratory questions such as:

Q   What did you read?   [EXPLORING]
Q   When did you read it?   [EXPLORING]
Q   What did the article say about this case?   [EXPLORING]

3. The venireman may answer that the article said only that the case was going to trial; as far as she can remember, the article said nothing about the merits of the dispute. Return to your planned voir dire examination.

4. The venireman answers that the article reported that the mayor had criticized your client for walking off the work site. Teach the venireman and give her an opportunity to assure you of her fairness:

Q   Now, as you understand, you can't consider the mayor's statement as evidence?   [TEACHING]
Q   Do you understand that you have to base your decision in this case on the evidence presented in court?   [TEACHING]
Q   Do you understand that you have to put that article out of your mind?   [TEACHING]
Q   Can you promise me that you'll put that article out of your mind and give Mr. Nelson a fair trial, based only on the evidence in court?   [SOLICITING THE ASSURANCE OF FAIRNESS]

5. The venireman assures you that she will put the article out of mind. Return to your planned voir dire questions. If you have conducted this questioning in the presence of the other veniremen, you might want to put a few teaching questions to them before you ask your next, planned question. Even if the venireman gives you the verbal assurance you solicited, you still may decide to strike her. Her nonverbal conduct (stuttering, noticeably labored breathing, lateral eye movement, or tense body posture) may lead you to suspect that the assurance is not as firm as the verbal statement makes it out to be.

6. The juror does not give you a flat assurance of fairness. For example, even after the teaching questions, the juror says "Maybe." You probably want to remove this venireman. You do not want to have to spend one of your strikes to do so; use very leading questions and try to disqualify the venireman beyond any possible rehabilitation to set up a challenge for cause:

Q   I appreciate your honest answer. Now you're telling me that you're not sure you could completely disregard the article?
Q   I suppose that you honestly fear it might influence you—at least subconsciously?
Q   You think it might somewhat affect you during your deliberation in this case?
Q   So there's a real possibility that it would affect you?

Note that the questioner encouraged the disqualifying answers by thanking the venireman for "your honest answer." Verbally reward the venireman for candid answers. Do not use the perjorative words "prejudice" or "bias." Try to appeal to the venireman's own sense of fairness. Some attorneys attempt to induce the venireman to admit that there is an appearance of un-fairness:

> Q   If you were Mr. Nelson, wouldn't you feel uncomfortable knowing that someone who read that article was sitting as a juror?
> Q   Do you think you would feel more comfortable sitting on some other case that you didn't know anything about?[1]

When you are pursuing purposes #1 and 2, information is flowing from the veniremen to you. If you pursue purposes #3 and 4, the flow reverses; you are giving the veniremen information.

3.   *To indoctrinate the jury on the facts supporting your theme.*

You do not have a right to ask such questions in any jurisdiction. However, these questions are often asked in the judge's discretion. Affirmatively, introduce your *theme.* You might pose the voir dire questions about habit evidence that were mentioned in Chapter 1 to support the "actions speak louder than words" theme. Negatively, expose the factual weaknesses in your case and solicit the veniremen's promise that they will not decide against you on that ground. For example, during his deposition, your client's general manager may have made a foolish, prior inconsistent statement. You should expose this factual weakness at the first opportunity. The weakness will sound much worse if your opponent is the first to mention the problem to the jury. Worse still, the jury may suspect that your were hiding the facts from them.

These questions should be mildly leading. First introduce the problem, "There may be evidence that our general manager, Ms. Wilson, made some statements inconsistent with her testimony today." After broaching the problem, get the veniremen to promise that they will not "automatically" or "necessarily" disbelieve Ms. Wilson's testimony "merely" or "simply" because of the prior inconsistent statement.

4.   *To indoctrinate the jury on the legal doctrines favoring your theory and theme.*

Again, you do not have a right to ask such questions, but you may do so with the judge's tolerance. For example, the Contract plaintiff should make certain that the venire realizes that the burden of proof is a mere preponderance rather than proof beyond a reasonable doubt.

There are two sorts of rules of law that you should emphasize during voir dire. First, mention rules that may surprise the jury. If you want to hold business entity #2 liable for business entity #1's contracts, mention the vicarious liability doctrine. Make certain that the jury understands from the outset that if you establish certain facts, they can hold corporation *B* liable for corporation *A*'s breach of contract. Second, mention disfavored rules of law. A Contract defendant relying on a technical defense such as the

Statute of Frauds should attempt to explain the defense and solicit the veniremen's promise to follow the judge's instructions even if they disagree with the rule of law.

The questions serving this purpose should be blatantly leading:

Q   Do you realize that in a civil suit such as this case, the plaintiff's burden of proof is only a preponderance of the evidence and not proof beyond a reasonable doubt?

Your tone and inflection should suggest the correct answer to the venireman; and you can incorporate leading language such as "as you know" and "as you realize" into your questions. If you ask the venireman a non-leading question about a rule of law, you may force the venireman to confess ignorance—and thereby both embarrass and irritate the venireman.

Indoctrinating questions should incorporate some of the key wording of the anticipated jury instructions. If the judge will probably give a habit evidence instruction using the wording "business practice," employ that precise wording in your question. By using this wording in your voir dire, opening statement, direct examination, and summation, you can create an "echo" effect. At the end of the trial when the judge finally instructs the jury, the instruction will *sound* as if the judge is echoing—and reinforcing—your theory and theme.

Sec. 2-2.   Removing Prospective Jurors by Challenge

a.   The Procedures for Exercising Challenges—Effective Phrasing for Passes and Strikes

The procedure for exercising challenges varies from jurisdiction to jurisdiction. Under the traditional method, the attorneys challenge in the jurors' hearing. In these jurisdictions, if the attorney is satisfied with the panel, you often hear the attorney say, "We pass for cause." It is a sounder tactic to announce, "We are happy with the present panel." That remark not only ingratiates the attorney with the venire; it also makes it more difficult for the opponent to challenge. On the other hand, if the attorney wants to challenge, the attorney sometimes says, "We challenge (or strike) venireman *X*." It is better to use this expression, "We would like to excuse venireman *X* and thank him for his time today."

b.   Whom Should You Challenge

For decades, the bar has used simplistic stereotypes of the kinds of venireman each attorney should challenge. These stereotypes have been especially prevalent in the criminal and personal injury bars. For example, the conventional wisdom is that the civil plaintiff strikes northern Europeans, Germans, and Englishmen, while the civil defendant challenges southern Europeans. These stereotypes should be taken with several grains of salt, but there are several useful propositions the commercial litigator should be familiar with.

Both parties ordinarily want to remove a venireman if that venireman or a member of the venireman's immediate family works in the industry involved in the case. There is an intolerable risk that such a venireman will become the self-appointed expert and leader during jury deliberations. You also want to remove a venireman if the venireman is likely to have an economic bias in your opponent's favor. Suppose, for instance, that a real estate broker is suing a homeowner for commission. The homeowner's attorney should strike salespersons from the venire; even if they do not deal in real estate, they are likely to identify with the plaintiff.

As a general proposition, the plaintiff wants a homogeneous group of persons; the more homogeneous the group, the stronger the probability that they will concur and attain the majority required for a plaintiff's verdict. If liability is close, the plaintiff should strike persons with very precise mental habits, such as accountants, engineers, and cabinetmakers; they may disregard the judge's instructions and demand more than a mere preponderance of the evidence. If the plaintiff wants substantial damages, the plaintiff's attorney should move most retired and elderly people; they may be too conservative in fixing the amount of recovery.

In contrast, the defendant usually prefers a heterogeneous group; the more heterogeneous the group, the greater the likelihood of disagreement.

SCIENTIFIC JURY SELECTION

Fortunately, the folklore of challenge strategy is now being replaced by serious social science. Any trial attorney should be familiar with two research projects on jury selection. One is the National Jury Project. In 1979, the Project released *Jury Work: Systematic Techniques*. Rather than classifying persons on ethnic or occupational grounds, the text classifies veniremen on the basis of the roles they will probably play during jury deliberation: leaders, fillers, negotiators, and holdouts. The text gives a rough, psychological profile of each type of venireman and helps the attorney categorize each venireman during the voir dire.

Another important project is the Law-Psychology Graduate Training Program at the University of Nebraska—Lincoln. Two researchers in the program published *Using Communication Cues to Evaluate Prospective Jurors During the Voir Dire*, 20 Arizona Law Review 629 (1978). The article guides the attorney in interpreting the verbal, paralinguistic, and kinesic cues veniremen unknowingly give the trial attorneys during voir dire. Rather than relying on stereotypic notions and inarticulate hunches, the attorney should capitalize on the growing body of excellent literature on the psychology of jury selection.

JURY SELECTION CHECKLIST

____ During the preliminary remarks, introduce your theory.

____ During the voir dire questioning itself.

     ____ Ask non-leading questions to elicit data to determine whether to challenge for cause.

     ____ Ask non-leading, open-ended questions to elicit data to determine whether to challenge peremptorily.

         ____ Questions about prior jury service

         ____ Questions about occupational background

         ____ Questions about associations

     ____ Ask mildly leading questions to indoctrinate on the facts.

         ____ Suggest your theme.

         ____ Expose your weaknesses and solicit the venireman's promise not to decide the case against you because of the weakness.

     ____ Ask blatantly leading questions to indoctrinate on legal doctrines.

         ____ Legal doctrines that may surprise the veniremen

         ____ Disfavored legal doctrines

____ Decide which veniremen to challenge.

     ____ Challenge veniremen with technical knowledge relevant to the case.

     ____ Challenge veniremen whose occupational or associational background makes it easy for them to identify with the opposing party.

     ____ Challenge veniremen with whom you do not feel personally comfortable.

____ Announce your strikes and passes.

     ____ If you decide to strike a venireman, ask that the venireman be "excused" and thank the venireman for his or her time.

     ____ If you decide to pass, state that you are "happy" with the jury.

FOOTNOTE

[1] McElhaney, *Trial Notebook — Voir Dire*, 5 Litigation 37, 42, 50 (Spring 1979).

CHAPTER 3

Opening Statement as Part of the Winning Strategy—Telling a Story That States Your Theory and Emphasizes Your Theme

Sec.

Sec. 3-1.   Introduction

Like jury selection, the opening statement is a telling stage in the trial process. If the trial judge follows the common federal practice and does all the voir dire questioning, the opening statement is your first opportunity for personal contact with the jury. The studies by the Chicago Jury Project show that in 80% of the cases, the jurors eventually return the same verdict that they would have returned if they had voted immediately after the opening statements. Moreover, this is a significant opportunity for advocacy because this is the part of the trial the attorney has the most control over. Since opposing counsel rarely object during opening, the opening is a unique opportunity to talk to the jurors with little risk of interruption.

Sec. 3-2.   Should You Deliver an Opening Statement?

The emphatic answer is yes. Surprisingly, many commercial litigators waive opening statements in bench trials (without a jury). Waiver is a serious mistake. The judge knows far more law than a lay juror would, but the judge may be absolutely ignorant of the facts of the case. No matter how simple the fact situation seems to you, the trier of fact is a complete stranger to the facts. Further, an opening statement enables you to present your *theory and theme*. You may think that you have planned a logical, orderly evidentiary presentation, but the trier of fact will be much better able to follow your presentation if you alert the trier to your theory and theme.

Sec. 3-3.   When Should You Deliver Your Opening Statement?

The defendant faces the only difficult choice: Should I deliver the statement immediately after the plaintiff's opening, or should I delay until the beginning of my case-in-chief? Of course, the problem disappears if there are several defendants, for example, a contractor and the contractor's surety. The defense attorneys should coordinate; one should deliver an opening statement immediately after the plaintiff's, and the other should delay opening until the beginning of the defense case-in-chief.

What if there is only one defendant? The temptation is to delay the opening until you have heard the plaintiff's evidentiary presentation; if you immediately follow the plaintiff, you may tip your hand too early or prematurely commit yourself to a theory or theme that will become untenable. However, the prevailing norm is that the defense should deliver the opening immediately after the plaintiff's opening. The reasoning underlying the norm is that the first impression is so lasting and critical. As the Chicago Jury Project shows, the jurors tend to adhere to their initial impression formed after the openings. If the defense gives the plaintiff an uninterrupted opportunity to present the plaintiff's theory to the jury, many jurors' minds will be made up before the defense presents any evidence.

There are three exceptional situations, however, in which experienced litigators deviate from the norm and delay their opening until the defense case-in-chief. First, the plaintiff's opening may be very weak. There is little need to immediately counter a weak opening statement. Second, the defendant may have a surprise defense theory or theme. If you have a surprise witness to the plaintiff's economic duress or fraud and your general denial permits you to raise that defense theory, you probably do not want to reveal the witness or defense before the plaintiff's case-in-chief; the revelation will be more dramatic and the plaintiff will have less chance to prepare to rebut the defense if you defer your opening. Finally, you may want to defer the opening if you anticipate a lengthy plaintiff's case-in-chief. If the plaintiff's case will consume weeks or months, the jury may forget the defense opening by the time the defense case-in-chief begins.

Even if the defense attorney decides to defer the opening, there is a tactic for interrupting the flow of the plaintiff's case. Immediately after the plaintiff's opening, in the jury's hearing request that the judge give the jury preliminary instructions on the plaintiff's burden of proof and the juror's obligation to keep an open mind until they have heard all the evidence. Merely making the request in the jury's hearing interrupts the plaintiff's case. Further, if the judge grants the request, the instructions serve many of the same functions that an early defense opening would serve.

Sec. 3-4.   How Should You Structure an Opening Statement?

In the final analysis, the structure of the opening is a matter of the attorney's personal taste and style. However, the following format is usually effective for a Contract suit.

a.   Introduction

In your introductory remarks, attend to the amenities. Introduce yourself and your client. Always refer to your client by name, "Mr. Grant" or "Acme Corporation" (later simply "Acme"); personalize your client and make it easier for the jury to identify with your client. By the same token, refer to the other counsel as "the opposing counsel" and to the opposing party as "the plaintiff" or "the defendant."

Next, if you are the plaintiff, state that the opening is not evidence. As Professor Jeans has pointed out, this statement is a bit silly; in effect, you tell the jury not to attach any weight to your opening statement. However, the real reason why the plaintiff should make the statement is that if the plaintiff does not, an astute defense counsel will promptly point that out to the jury: "The plaintiff's attorney neglected to tell you. . . ."

The tactics are different for the defense attorney. If the basic defense theory is the weakness of the plaintiff's factual showing, the defense should probably emphasize that the opening is not evidence. However, if the defense has a strong factual case, it is inadvisable for the defense attorney to reiterate that the opening is not evidence.

b.   The Statement of the Issues

The next component of the opening is the statement of the issues. The approach to this component depends upon whether you are plaintiff or defendant.

If you are plaintiff, from the very outset try to simplify the issues for the jury. "During the next few days, you're going to hear a lot of witnesses and see a lot of letters and records. The case at first may seem complex. But I want you to realize that this is really a very simple case." Next, slowly describe all the elements of your *theory*: "Mr. Grant contends that he and the defendant entered into an agreement (contract formation); that the defendant later broke that agreement (contract breach); and that the defendant's act of breaking the agreement caused Mr. Grant a loss of $37,000 (remedy)." Finally, identify the central, disputed element of the theory: "Ladies and gentlemen, the real issue in this case is whether Mr. Grant and the defendant entered into a contract." If you alert the jurors to the pivotal issue, they can concentrate more effectively on the evidence relating to that element.

If you are the defense attorney, in your statement of the issues, try to defuse those that may generate emotional sympathy for the plaintiff. If there is going to be no real dispute over certain issues, seriously consider conceding them during opening: "Ladies and gentlemen, we don't deny that Acme refused to accept those air conditioners. We also don't deny that the plaintiff eventually sold those air conditioners for $60,000—and not the $97,000 the plaintiff quoted to Acme." When appropriate, convey your sense of sympathy to the jury; if the plaintiff's attorney stated in his opening that because of the loss, the plaintiff had to lay off workers, respond by saying, "Acme is sorry that the plaintiff didn't receive the $97,000 it wanted, and we certainly sympathize with the workers who were laid off." But then remind the jury of the real issue in the case: "But the real issue in this case is whether Acme and the plaintiff entered into a contract. Our position is that there was no contract. And for that reason, as regrettable as the loss and the layoffs are, Acme simply isn't legally liable for the loss."

c. Preview the Evidence

The preview consists of two parts:

1. *The background of your client.*

Although the character evidence rules limit your ability to tell the jurors about your client's personal history, most judges will permit you to briefly describe your client's background: "The evidence will show that Mr. Grant has been a general contractor in this area for the past 17 years. He was born in Iowa, but his family moved here when he was very young. He attended State College, got his civil engineering degree there, and began working as a contractor right after graduation." If your client is a business entity, you can say something along these lines: "The evidence will show that Acme has had its headquarters here in town for the past 30 years. Acme has 800 local employees, and they manufacture refrigerators for sale throughout the United States." Begin personalizing and humanizing your client to help the jury identify with your client.

2. *The historical merits of your theory.*

After describing your client's background, preview the evidence on the historical merits. What are the DO's and DON'Ts of the preview?

DON'T preface every statement with "The evidence will show. . . ." The repetition becomes monotonous and boring. Make it clear once that you are simply previewing the evidence, and then make positive declarative statements about the historical facts and events.

DON'T overstate or exaggerate. An overstatement will come back to haunt you. Some jurors not only listen carefully; they also take notes. A few years ago my father served as a juror in a Contract lawsuit. By the end of the trial, he had 30 pages of single-spaced, handwritten notes about the trial! An attentive juror may remember that you did not deliver on evidence you promised during opening. An astute opposing attorney will remind the jury during closing of your overstatement during opening. The opposing attorney may even have the court reporter prepare an interim transcript of your statement during opening; the opposing counsel will quote the overstatement to the jury and ram it down your throat.

Some experienced litigators even favor deliberately understating the case in opening; the jury can then be pleasantly surprised at the strength of your case. New trial attorneys should probably avoid that strategy; as we previously noted, the jurors' initial impression of your case is often lasting, and an inexperienced attorney's attempt to use the sophisticated stratagem of understatement may backfire. But whatever other rhetorical devices you use, never overstate in opening.

The most important DO in an opening statement is this: *Tell a simple, interesting story that states your theory, exposes your weaknesses, and emphasizes your theme.*

"*A simple story.*" As previously stated, the jurors are complete strangers to the fact situation. Until the trial began, they may have never heard the parties' names, and they may not even be familiar with the names of the locations of key events. If the suit is a breach of warranty action based on defective quality, there may be references to technical terms the jurors have never heard before. Do not go into great detail. Tell a simple story in the Hemingway tradition. In this respect, the defense has a significant advantage. The plaintiff must devote a good deal of his or her opening to acquainting the jury with the suit's basic factual setting. Rather than reiterating those facts, the defense can concentrate on the pivotal issue in the case. A short, forcefully delivered defense opening can project confidence to the jury.

If the facts are complex, with the judge's permission, use audio-visual aids during opening. If a contract formation issue turns on the jury's understanding of an exchange of several letters between the parties, prepare a chart listing the various letters. If an anticipatory repudiation issue turns on the sequence of the repudiation, retraction, and election, use a chart of the key dates and events. Use a diagram or photograph of the product involved in a breach of warranty case.

"*An interesting story.*" The attorney delivering an opening statement is like a storyteller. You have to arrest the jury's attention; and if you can sustain that attention throughout the story, you have taken a giant step toward persuading the jury to believe your theory of the historical merits. There are several effective techniques for arresting and sustaining attention.

Use vivid diction—the sort of diction you find in the writing of William Faulkner. Faulkner uses concrete nouns and verbs. He packs the action and visual imagery into his nouns and verbs rather than prolonging and weakening his sentences by overloading them with adjectives and adverbs. When you refer to contract formation, say that "they shook hands"—not "they agreed." Similarly, when you refer to a breach of warranty, say that the machine "sputtered and then fell silent"—not "the machine did not conform to specifications." This is the sort of diction that helps a jury "picturize" your theory of the case.[1]

Emphasize the human dimension of the historical merits. Your client did not demand a written acceptance because he "trusted" the defendant. Your client was "surprised and shocked" when the defendant refused to deliver the truck. The defendant "screamed and swore" at your client when your client asked about the delivery of the merchandise. Rather than "sustaining damages," your client "suffers losses."

Dramatize the key testimony by acting it out. Suppose that you want to stress the testimony about contract formation. Just before you reach that part of the opening, pause, take a few steps to the center of the jury box, and change your voice tone, volume, and pace. Act out the gesture of shaking hands with the defendant. Shift to the first person: "My client will testify, 'I shook the defendant's hand'. . . ." Help the jury visualize your theory of the case. If you bring that other sense into play, other things being equal, the jury is much more likely to accept your theory of the facts.

"*A story that states your theory.*" There are several organizational formats to choose from.

You can review the facts on the historical merits in a narrative, chronological order. Some counsel prefer not to refer to the names of specific witnesses; at the last moment, an anticipated witness may become unable to attend the trial, or you may have to call the witness out of the anticipated order. Chronological sequence is usually the easiest for the jury to follow.

Or you can organize your opening statement as a list of witnesses you intend to call. List the witnesses in the order in which you intend to call them, and briefly summarize each witness' expected testimony. Some counsel prefer this format when they foresee that the case will boil down to a swearing contest between the witnesses on the two sides.

Or you can organize the opening statement in terms of the essential elements of your cause of action or *theory of the case*. For the Contract plaintiff, this format overlaps with the chronological format: first in point of time contract formation, then the satisfaction of conditions, next breach, and finally in point of time the injury caused by the breach. Reviewing the elements of your theory is probably the best organization for the opening in the typical Contract lawsuit.

As in the case of the phrasing of your voir dire questions, try to work the key language of some of the anticipated jury instructions about your theory into the opening. Do not tell the jury that you are quoting the anticipated instructions; it is unnecessary to do so, and the judge may find it objectionable. Simply incorporate the anticipated language in the hope that you can create the "echo" effect we previously discussed.

"*A story that exposes your weaknesses.*" Pre-empt your opponent's references to the weaknesses in your case. The weakness may be a prior inconsistent statement by your client's general manager. It is far better for you to mention that statement in a passing reference than for the jury to learn about it for the first time in a statement the opposing counsel makes in a highly accusatory tone of voice. Or the weakness may be the seemingly astronomical amount of damages you are praying for in the case. Mention that figure as soon as possible. If the jurors hear that large figure for the very first time in summation, they may be overwhelmed and return a small verdict. After mentioning their case's weaknesses, some attorneys like to add: "Ladies and gentlemen, during this trial we're going to show you the good parts of our case. And we'll show you the bad parts of our case. To put it simply, we're going to show you the truth."

"*A story that emphasizes your theme.*" You must state your entire theory in the opening, but hit hardest at your theme. Signal that the jury should pay special attention to this part of the opening: "Ladies and gentlemen, then you will hear Mr. Nerney's testimony that the defendant actually boxed the air conditioners and labeled them for shipment to Mr. Grant. Please pay special attention to this evidence." Even if you decide not to name most of your witnesses, you may want to name the witness who will give the strongest testimony on your theme. Go into more detail about the facts relating to your theme, and devote more time to the theme than to the other parts of your theory of the case. Pause before you reach that subject, take a step or two, and emphasize the importance of the topic by changing the pace, tone, and volume of your voice. As in the case of the discussion of your overall theory of the case, incorporate the key wording of some of the anticipated jury instructions on your theme.

d. Conclusion

Before concluding, express confidence in your theory and especially in your theme: "When you've heard all the evidence in this case, I'm confident you'll conclude that there was a contract, that the defendant breached the contract, and that that breach cost Mr. Grant $37,000. When all the evidence is in, you'll be convinced that the defendant's actions speak louder than words, and that the actions prove that there was a contract." Lastly, tell the jury the precise verdict they should return at the end of the case: "After you've heard all the evidence, I'll speak to you again. That's the closing argument in the case. At that time, I'll ask you to return the only just verdict in this case—a verdict for the plaintiff, Mr. Grant, in the amount of $37,000."

Having concluded your opening, you are now ready to move into the evidentiary stages of the trial.

CHECKLIST FOR OPENING STATEMENT

_____ Introduce yourself and your client. Immediately begin personalizing your client.

_____ Explain the function of opening statement. If you are the plaintiff, add that the opening statement is not evidence.

_____ Tell the jury that the case will prove to be relatively simple.

_____ Mention all the elements of your theory.

_____ Highlight the element of your theory that you expect will be most hotly disputed.

___ Preview the evidence.
___ Describe your client's personal background.
___ Describe your version of the historical merits in a storytelling fashion.
   ___ Keep the story simple and short.
   ___ Make the story interesting.
   ___ State your theory in the course of telling the story.
   ___ Mention your most glaring weaknesses.
   ___ Stress the element of your theory that the theme relates to.
___ Express confidence in your theory.
___ Verbalize the short, catchy expression you have reduced your theme to.
___ Conclude by mentioning the precise verdict you will want the jury to return at the end of the case.

FOOTNOTE

[1] T. Mauet, Fundamentals of Trial Techniques 65 (1980).

PART II

The Plaintiff's Evidence

CHAPTER 4

How to Structure the Plaintiff's Case-in-Chief to Present Your Theory and Underscore Your Theme

Sec. 4-1.   The Steps in Planning Your Evidentiary Presentation.

After the opening statements, the parties make their evidentiary presentations. The evidentiary presentations must be carefully planned. In planning a case-in-chief, the attorney must answer four questions: (1) Which witnesses and documents should I include in the case-in-chief? (2) In what sequence should I call the witnesses? (3) How should I organize the direct examination of each individual witness? and (4) How should I draft the individual questions to be asked during the direct examination?

Sec. 4-2.   Step #1: Deciding Which Witnesses and Documents to Include in the Case-in-Chief

The theory of the case dictates the answer to this question. You should include something in your case-in-chief only if it is relevant to proving your theory or disproving the opponent's theory. To have maximum persuasive effect, your evidentiary presentation must have continuity and simplicity; and you can attain those two qualities only if you force yourself to exclude material that is (1) relevant to the case's subject-matter or pleadings but (2) irrelevant to your theory of the case. Either resolve not to present such material at all, or at least exclude the material from your case-in-chief and save it for rebuttal.

Suppose that after pretrial discovery, the defense attorney concludes that there is a strong argument that there was no final bargain and a weak argument that the defendant was guilty of some fraud in concluding the bargain. Experienced defense attorneys would select as their theory of the case the stronger contention that there was no contract. It will be tempting to present the weak evidence of fraud during the defense case-in-chief, but it would be inadvisable to do so. A weak fraud defense might backfire; a fraud argument is a form of character assassination, and the jury might resent the defendant for making the argument without strong factual support. Moreover, including the fraud argument in the defense case-in-chief will detract from the case's continuity and credibility. The law permits you to argue alternatively and even inconsistently: There was no contract; even if there was a contract, there was no breach; even if there was a breach, there was no damage, etc. But it is difficult to sell inconsistent defenses to a jury; when a lay juror hears the defense counsel say, "Even if . . . ," the juror may easily misinterpret that as an admission. Select your theory of the case; and have the courage to exclude from the case-in-chief material that does not contribute to the theory even if that material is marginally relevant to the case.

You do not even have to present all the evidence relevant to your theory. "Overproving" your theory can be counter-productive. A lengthy case-in-chief often bores the jury. On most elements of your theory, content yourself with your client's testimony plus some quality corroboration: one document, object, or disinterested witness. The only element of your theory that warrants more detail is the pivotal issue that your theme relates to. On that issue, present as much quality corroboration as possible within reason.

Sec. 4-3.   Step #2: Deciding the Sequence of the Witnesses in the Case-in-Chief

The next step in structuring the plaintiff's case-in-chief is deciding the sequence in which you present material during the case. It is ideal if the judge agrees to give an opening instruction on the substantive law governing your case (your "theory" instruction) at the very beginning of your case-in-chief. A 1976 Pennsylvania bar study indicated that an opening instruction significantly increases the jury's understanding of the plaintiff's evidence. Some judges now routinely give an opening instruction to the jury, and other judges will do so upon request. After the judge's opening instruction, you present your evidence. There are two schools of thought on the proper sequence of your evidence.

One school is of the persuasion that you should almost always call the witnesses in strict, chronological sequence: the plaintiff's salesman who formed the contract with the defendant, the plaintiff's vice-president who received the defendant's telephone call announcing a breach, and finally the head of the plaintiff's sales department who unsuccessfully attempted to resell the merchandise on the open market. This school has a substantial following among commercial litigators because Contract law lends itself so nicely to chronological analysis: formation, then breach, and finally damage.

However, the second school of thought is probably the prevailing sentiment. The second school is sometimes referred to as the "sandwich" theory: Sandwich your case between two strong witnesses—start with a strong, attention-getting witness and end with a strong, appealing witness. This school has a sound basis in the psychological principles of primacy and regency: In a lengthy series of points, a person is most likely to remember the first point and the last point.

The second school dovetails with our previous discussion of the theory and theme. The theory gives the jury a framework or overview for understanding your case. It is ideal to begin your case-in-chief with a witness who can testify to the entire theory. If your client is a sole proprietor or the active partner in a small partnership, the client may be a good, first witness; the client is likely to have personal knowledge of most of the facts relating to formation, breach, and damages. Lead off with the "theory" witness; and, if possible, at least introduce the theme during that witness' testimony. If the superintendent of the defendant's shipping department told your client that the boxes had been labeled for shipment to the plaintiff, introduce that statement as a vicarious admission during your client's direct examination. Your client's direct examination then exposes the jury to both your theory and your theme.

Finish your case with your strongest witness on the theme of your case. If your assessment is that the superintendent of the defendant's shipping department is a relatively honest person, you might want to call the superintendent as your last witness. A majority of jurisdictions now follows the approach of Federal Evidence Rule 611(c); since the superintendent is legally identified with the defendant, you could call the superintendent as an adverse witness and both lead and impeach. When you resort to 611(c), let the judge and jurors know what you are doing; when you call the witness, announce: "Your honor, we next call the defendant's shipping superintendent, Mr. Nerney, as an adverse witness." You can end your case-in-chief on a high note underscoring your theme: The witness will either admit preparing the boxes for shipment to your client or be forced to acknowledge his statements to that effect in the deposition transcript.

The best possible witness to conclude your case-in-chief with is an apparently disinterested witness who can testify to the facts supporting your theme. If an impartial third party had been present in the defendant's warehouse and noticed the boxes prepared for shipment to plaintiff, that third party should be the plaintiff's last witness.

Sec. 4-4.   Step #3: Planning and Presenting the Direct Examination of Each Individual Witness

a.   Planning the Direct Examination

After you have decided the gross sequence of witnesses, you must decide the sequence of topics in each witness' direct examination.

1.   The witness' personal background.

One point of agreement among experienced litigators is that the first topic you cover should be the witness' personal background. As previously stated, the character evidence rules limit the extent of your description of the witness' personal history, but many judges will permit a brief inquiry. Covering this topic first helps to relax the witness. If the person has never testified before, covering this topic first will put the witness at ease; their own personal history is the subject witnesses feel most comfortable and confident about. Further, the description of the witness' background gives the witness stature in the jurors' eyes. The jurors will get a feel for the witness' intelligence and honesty. If you try to go into too much detail about the witness' background, the judge will cut off the line of questioning; but spend a few minutes describing the background before you rush to the historical merits of the case.

2.   The historical merits

Many attorneys use a mechanical, chronological sequence for presenting the witness' testimony on the historical merits. To be sure, a chronological sequence is usually the easiest for the jurors to follow. However, more and more attorneys reject this approach.

Perhaps a substantial minority of attorneys prefer to *begin* the direct testimony on the merits with an attention-getting topic rather than with the first event in point of time. Professor Hegland subscribes to this view: "Corbin never said that you had to begin at the beginning. Neither did Williston. So why do beginners almost invariably begin there and flail away until they eventually reach the bloody end? The problem with this approach is that it's boring . . . and totally without pizazz."[1]

In the *middle* of the direct, try to pre-empt the cross by exposing the witness' weaknesses. If your client had a few drinks before a critical conversation, elicit that fact on direct. Do not wait for the opposing attorney to elicit that fact on cross to impeach your client's memory. The fact will seem less damning and you will seem more candid if you anticipate the cross. In the past, some judges precluded this type of direct on the ground that you may not impeach your own witness. However, Federal Evidence Rule 607 now reads that "[t]he credibility of a witness may be attacked by any party, including the party calling him."

A majority of experienced litigators also deviate from chronological sequence to *end* on a high note. This practice is eminently sound. Suppose that the plaintiff is suing for breach of warranty on some drums of liquid fertilizer. To prove the breach, the plaintiff calls the analyst from a testing laboratory. The analyst ran two chemical tests on randomly selected drums from the shipment; the first test tended to show a breach of warranty, but the second test was inconclusive. As the previous paragraph indicates, if you call this witness at all, you should elicit the testimony about both tests on direct. If you do not mention the inconclusive test on direct and the opponent forces the admission on cross, the jury will conclude that you were trying to hide the facts. If you are going to mention both tests, you certainly should not follow strict chronological sequence. The analyst's testimony will harm your case if the testimony concludes with a description of the inconclusive test. Always end on a high note even if doing so requires departing from chronological order.

Try to end the direct well before the next scheduled morning or afternoon recess. Force the opponent to begin cross-examination before the recess. This timing has two advantages. First, you pressure the opposing counsel to rush the cross and end before the recess. The opposing counsel will not want a dramatic cross interrupted by a recess. Second, you prevent the opposing counsel from using the recess to refine the planned cross-examination. Make the opponent's cross as impromptu as possible.

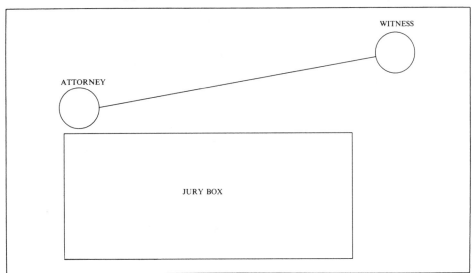

Figure 4-1: THE PROPER POSITION FOR THE DIRECT EXAMINER

b. Presenting the Direct Examination

If the judge permits, position yourself at the end of the jury box. Figure 4-1 illustrates the proper position. If you can hear the witness, the jury can. Positioning yourself there also forces the witness to look in the jurors' direction. Jurors are impressed if the witness looks them straight in the eye while the witness is testifying. If the witness is so frightened that he or she fixes his or her stare on you, preface your question with, "Please tell the jurors. . . ."; and at the same time, gesture towards the jury. Stand two or three feet to the side of the jury railing. That position allows you to view the jurors' facial expressions during the witness' answers. If the jurors' faces register disinterest or confusion during a critical answer, go back and elicit the answer more emphatically and clearly.

Give your profile to the jurors. If there are two actors on a theatre stage—one in an open or frontal position and the other in profile—the audience tends to focus on the first actor. If you are properly positioned, the witness will be giving the jurors an open or frontal view. If you assume a relatively inconspicuous profile position, the jurors will tend to focus their attention where it belongs—on the witness. In direct examination, you are the director, but your witness is the star.

Punctuate the direct examination verbally and physically. The witness may be testifying about several elements of your theory: contract formation, breach, and damages. You want to highlight the organization of the direct for the jurors. Introduce each new subject with a topic, declarative sentence: "Ms. Burton, you've been telling us about the signing of the contract. Now let me ask you a few questions about the delivery of the transistors." Between topics, pause, take a step or two, and change the tone or volume of your voice.

Listen carefully to the answer. Your natural tendency is to ask the next planned question immediately after the witness' answer. However, the witness may not give the expected answer, and the unexpected answer may necessitate that you re-ask the question or move to a new line of inquiry. It seems obvious that you should listen to the answer, but in truth listening is one of the most difficult tasks for the trial attorney. The neophyte attorney's nervousness makes it difficult to listen carefully; if you are nervous about your own performance, the temptation is to think about your next question rather than listen to the witness' answer to the question you have already asked. Your pretrial preparation also makes careful listening difficult. If you are well prepared, if you have reviewed the proposed testimony with your witness several times, you have an expectation as to what the answer will be; and psychological studies document that, unfortunately, we tend to "hear" what we expect to hear rather than what the speaker actually says.

Pause before asking the next question. This is another trap that a well-prepared attorney can fall into. If you know the proposed direct too well, you tend to anticipate the end of the answer and ask the next question too quickly. If you do, the jury may suspect that the direct is a well-rehearsed act and less than the truth. The direct examination should proceed naturally and spontaneously. Count to two, let the answer sink into the jurors' minds, and then ask the next question.

Sec. 4-5.   Step #4: Drafting the Individual Questions for the Direct Examination

The norm is that the direct examiner should use short, plainly worded, open-ended, non-leading questions that echo the anticipated instructions on the theory and theme.

"*The norm.*" This is not a categorial rule. An experienced trial attorney knows when to depart from the norm. For example, if your witness does not have a pleasant personality, you will not want to use open-ended questions. The more the witness talks, the more of his or her personality is exposed to the jury, and the less the jury will like the witness.

"*Short questions.*" The shorter the question, the easier it will be for the witness and jurors to understand the question. Reading psychology experts tell us that in writing, sentences ordinarily should not exceed 25 words in length; reader comprehension drops off markedly when the sentence exceeds 25 words. In speaking, the sentences should be even shorter. Try to limit your questions to 15 or fewer words.

"*Plainly worded questions.*" In direct examination, the attorney should display communicative skill rather than vocabulary. Use "before" and "after" rather than "previously" and "subsequently." Drive to the defendant's office in a "car" rather than a "motor vehicle." "Walk up" or "down" stairs to get to the contract-signing ceremony rather than "ascending" or "descending" the stairs.

"*Open-ended questions.*" If you have a good witness (a witness whose demeanor evidences intelligence and honesty), do not ask narrowly phrased questions. The witness is your best exhibit, and you must put the exhibit on display. Let the witness talk at some length, and give the jurors a feel for the witness' personality. The jurors will not learn much about the witness as a person if you force the witness to consistently answer yes or no. Moreover, recent studies at Duke University suggest that when an attorney asks narrowly phrased questions on direct, the jurors often infer that the attorney is doing so because the attorney lacks confidence in the witness.[1] Once they draw that inference, the jurors tend to discount the witness' testimony.

"*Non-leading questions.*" The primary form problem for the direct examiner is the use of leading questions.

Federal Evidence Rule 611(c) continues the received orthodoxy that leading questions are generally forbidden on direct examination. However, the general prohibition against leading questions on direct is riddled with exceptions. By way of illustration, the direct examiner may use leading questions to question a hostile witness, to assist a witness who is not fluent in English (an increasing occurrence because of the growing frequency of international business transactions and contracts), to establish preliminary facts, and to refresh a witness' recollection.

Using leading questions on direct is not only objectionable under evidence law; it is bad trial advocacy. If you have prepared the witness properly by reviewing the contract documents and deposition transcripts, the witness usually does not need the crutch of a leading question. More importantly, leading questions are almost always narrowly phrased; and they restrict the witness' opportunity to display his or her honesty and intelligence to the jury. A non-leading question is a much better vehicle for putting a good witness on display during direct examination.

On a cautionary note, though, remember that you should not use exclusively non-leading questions on direct. Sometimes you do not want to ask a question at all; as previously stated, you can punctuate the direct with declarative, topic sentences such as, "Now let me ask you some questions about your attempts to reach the defendant's vice-president that afternoon." To elicit the witness' background, you may use imperative sentences such as, "Tell us about your educational background." Some of your questions on preliminary, relatively unimportant facts can be mildly leading. However, most of the attorney's statements on direct should be non-leading questions.

The practical challenge then is to learn how to consistently phrase non-leading questions. A good rule of thumb is that you should begin your questions with words such as "what," "who," "when," "where," "how," "which," and "why." These are natural interrogatory words.

It would be leading to ask, "Did the defendant have money in his hand?" You could ask, "*What* did the defendant have in his hands?"

It would be leading to ask, "Was the defendant the person who answered the telephone?" You could ask, "*Who* answered the telephone?"

It would be leading to ask, "Did the defendant hand you the sheet of paper after you said you wanted to buy the car?" You could ask, "*When* did the defendant hand you the sheet of paper?"

It would be leading to ask, "Was the defendant standing in the accountant's office when the defendant said that?" You could ask, "*Where* was the defendant standing when he said that?"

It would be leading to ask, "Did the defendant deliver the shipment in one of his own trucks?" You could ask, "*How* did the defendant deliver the shipment?"

It would be leading to ask, "Did the plaintiff point to the blue model?" You could ask, "*Which* model did the plaintiff point to?"

It would be leading to ask, "Did you reject the shipment because it did not conform to the contract specifications?" You could ask, "*Why* did you reject the shipment?"

"*Questions that echo the anticipated instructions on the theory and theme.*" Even before trial when you are drafting your questions, you should have a good idea of the wording of the final jury instructions. As in the case of your voir dire questions and opening statement, try to incorporate key expressions from the anticipated instructions about your theory and theme. The probable instruction on your "actions speak louder than words" theme may be a habit evidence charge using the phrase "business practice." Incorporate that expression directly into one or more of your direct questions developing your theme.

LEGAL RESEARCH REFERENCE:
McCormick §§5-6

CHECKLIST FOR PLANNING THE PLAINTIFF'S CASE-IN-CHIEF

____ Decide which witnesses and documents to include in the case-in-chief.

     ____ Exclude evidence that does not contribute to your theory.

     ____ For most elements of your theory, include your client's testimony and one piece of quality corroboration.

     ____ For the key element of your theory that the theme relates to, include as much corroboration as possible within reason.

____ Decide the sequence of the evidence in your case-in-chief.

     ____ The first witness should be the witness who can give the jurors the best overview of your theory.

     ____ In the middle of your case, call the witnesses in roughly chronological sequence.

     ____ The last witness should be the strongest witness on your theme.

____ Decide the sequence of the topics in each witness' direct examination.

     ____ First have the witness briefly describe his or her personal background.

     ____ Then have the witness testify about the historical merits.

         ____ Start with an attention-getting topic.

         ____ In the middle of the direct examination, cover the material in roughly chronological sequence.

         ____ End on a high note, ideally an item of testimony relating to your theme.

____ Draft the direct examination.

     ____ Introduce each major division of the direct examination with a topic, declarative sentence.

     ____ Use imperative sentences to elicit the witness' testimony about his or her personal background.

     ____ When you elicit the witness' testimony on the historical merits, use

         ____ short questions (15 or fewer words)

         ____ plainly worded questions

         ____ non-leading questions (questions beginning with "what," "who," "when," "where," "how," "which," and "why")

         ____ questions that incorporate key expressions from the anticipated jury instructions on your theory and theme.

FOOTNOTE

[1] Douglas, *More Effective Courtroom Technique*, Trial Diplomacy Journal 10, 12 (Winter 1979).

CHAPTER 5

The Methods of Proving Contract Formation—The First Element of the Plaintiff's Theory

Sec. 5-1. An Overview of the Plaintiff's Theory of the Case—A Preview of Chapters 5 Through 9

In the last chapter, we discussed in general terms planning the case for the plaintiff. What are the essential elements of the typical plaintiff's theory? In most jurisdictions, the plaintiff must sustain the initial burden of going forward and the ultimate burden of proof[1] on the following issues to prevail:

—The plaintiff and defendant formed a valid contract.

—The contract should be construed as creating certain conditions for the plaintiff to fulfill and a duty for the defendant to perform.

—All the conditions to the defendant's duty were either fulfilled or excused.

—The defendant breached the duty.

—Any additional facts conditioning the particular remedies the plaintiff seeks.

These are the five ultimate facts that usually comprise the plaintiff's theory. They serve as a checklist for presenting the plaintiff's case. We shall discuss contract formation in this chapter, the construction of the contract in Chapter 6, conditions in Chapter 7, breach in Chapter 8, and remedies in Chapter 9.

Sec. 5-2. Contract Formation—Mutual Assent and Consideration

To prove contract formation, the plaintiff must establish mutual assent and consideration:

—The plaintiff and defendant manifested mutual assent to a sufficiently definite bargain, and
—The plaintiff gave the defendant legally sufficient consideration to make the defendant's promise enforceable, or there is some substitute for consideration such as a promissory estoppel.

Sec. 5-3. Mutual Assent—Substantive Contract Doctrine

Most Contract formation problems lend themselves to the offer-acceptance model; to determine whether there was a valid contract, the court searches for an offer followed by a matching acceptance. To establish mutual assent under this model, the plaintiff must demonstrate that one of the parties (the plaintiff or defendant) first prepared a valid offer for the other party; the first party then communicated the offer to the other; and the second party accepted the offer.

a. The Offer

An offer is a definite, conditional promise, manifesting the intent to enter a legally binding, final agreement.

"*A conditional promise.*" The offeror makes a promise conditioned on a return promise or performance by the offeree. Suppose that a vendor offers to sell a microwave oven for $1,100. The proposal is a promise to sell the oven, and the promise is conditioned on the offeree's payment of $1,100.

"*Manifesting intent to enter a legally binding agreement.*" The proposal may explicitly provide that it contemplates a legally binding agreement, or the proposal may explicitly provide to the contrary. What if the proposal is silent on the subject? In that circumstance, most courts use rebuttable presumptions of the parties' intent. If the proposal was made in a business context, the courts usually assume that the parties intended a legally enforceable bargain. In contrast, if the proposal was made in a family or social context, the courts ordinarily presume that the parties desired a gentlemen's agreement which could not be enforced in court.

"*Manifesting intent to enter a final agreement.*" Finality of the bargain is one of the most important requirements for finding an offer. Unfortunately, there are no hard-and-fast rules a court may use to determine mechanically whether the proposal manifests finality. Rather, the courts weigh five factors in making the decision:

—The language used. It is ideal if the proposal uses the term of art, "offer." The use of "quote" cuts against finding an offer, but its use is not dispositive.
—The definiteness of the terms in the proposal. The more specific the terms, the more confidently we may infer that the bargain was final.

—The size of the group of addressees. The larger the group the proposal is addressed to, the less likely the court is to hold that the proposal is an offer. For that reason, courts treat most advertisements as invitations for offers rather than offers.

—The degree of formality. What if the proposal refers to the subsequent execution of a formal, written contract? Does that reference preclude the formation of a valid contract until the writing's execution? Most jurisdictions now answer that question in the negative, although the reference is still a factor cutting against treating the proposal as an offer.

—The surrounding circumstances. The addressee may know that the proposer is negotiating with third parties for the sale of the same property mentioned in the proposal. The proposer would ordinarily not be foolish enough to expose himself or herself to liability on two or more contracts. Thus, this surrounding circumstance may prompt the court to refuse to characterize the proposal as an offer.

"*A definite promise.*" The proposal's definiteness is not only a factor in deciding whether the proposal looks to a final bargain; definiteness is also a separate requirement for an offer.

At common law, to qualify as an offer, the proposal must specify the identity of the contracting parties, the subject matter, quantity, quality, purchase price, terms of payment (lump sum or installments), and delivery. The courts were willing to imply some terms such as quality or purchase price because the courts could look to the custom or rate prevailing in the market to fill in the proposal's gap. However, the courts would not fill in the quantity term. Moreover, if the parties fixed a material term ambiguously or reserved it for future mutual determination, the courts would not treat the proposal as an offer.

Uniform Commercial Code 2-204(3) relaxes the standard for definiteness:

> Even though one or more terms are left open, a contract for sale does not fail for indefiniteness if the parties have intended to make a contract and there is a reasonably certain basis for giving an appropriate remedy.

The Code's language still requires finality ("the parties have intended to make a contract"), but the Code's only definiteness mandate is that the proposal be specific enough to permit the judge to frame a remedy for breach. Chapter 9 discusses remedies.

LEGAL RESEARCH REFERENCE:
Murray §§18-30
White & Summers §§1-1 & 1-3

b. Communicating the Offer

The offeror must communicate the offer to the offeree. The proposal does not become effective as an offer until the offeree receives the communication. The offer is then open for acceptance.

c. The Acceptance

An acceptance occurs when a proper offeree, with knowledge of the offer's existence and the intent to accept, makes the requested return unconditionally.

"*A proper offeree.*" As a general proposition, only the addressee may accept the offer. The most notable exception to the general proposition is that an offer embodied in an option contract is ordinarily assignable.

"*With knowledge of the offer's existence.*" Suppose that two identical offers ("I offer to buy your home for $120,000" and "I offer to sell my home to you for $120,000") cross in the mails. Does that form a contract? The traditional view is that the cross-offers do not form a contract; one of the parties must still accept the other party's offer.

Or suppose that a person performs an act without knowledge that the offeror has announced a reward to the act's performance. Is the person entitled to the reward? Since the person did not know of the reward's existence, most courts deny recovery.

"*With intent to accept the offer.*" If the offeree says in so many words that he or she is accepting, the courts readily find this element. If the offeror requested a return promise and the offeree gave that promise, the intent to accept is certainly present.

The more difficult question is this: When does the offeree's silence adequately manifest intent to accept? The general norm is that silence is ineffective as acceptance. However, in some exceptional cases, the courts equate silence with acceptance. If one business solicits an offer from another and the first business then retains the offer for an unreasonably long time, the courts infer acceptance from silence; the courts reason that by soliciting the offer, the offeree assumed the burden of communicating any rejection within a reasonable time.

Another exceptional situation is the case in which the past pattern of dealings between the parties gives rise to an inference that silence means acceptance. In several transactions, the course of dealing between the parties was that the offeree received the offer and, after a time lapse, performed without ever making a formal acceptance. This course of dealing makes it reasonable for the offeror to conclude that silence means acceptance.

Finally, if the parties' initial understanding is that the offeror's delivery of goods to the offeree is a sale on approval under Uniform Commercial Code 2-326 and 2-327, silence accompanying retention of goods for a substantial time period effects an acceptance.

"*Makes the requested return.*" Uniform Commercial Code 2-206(1)(a) provides that "[u]nless otherwise unambiguously indicated by the language or circumstances, an offer . . . shall be construed as inviting acceptance in any manner . . . reasonable in the circumstances." Thus, under the modern view, the offer may expressly or impliedly give the offeree more than one method of acceptance.

However, some courts still begin their analysis with the traditional assumption that an offer authorizes *a* method of acceptance. Although the Code and the second Restatement of Contracts abandon the terminology, the "bilateral"-"unilateral"-"reverse unilateral" contract distinction is still useful in identifying the proper method of acceptance. An offer looking to a bilateral contract usually invites the offeree to accept by making a return promise. An offer looking to a unilateral contract generally invites acceptance by a return act. Reverse unilateral contracts are extremely rare; in offers looking to a reverse unilateral contract, the offeror manifests willingness to perform an act immediately in exchange for a return promise. This distinction is helpful in deciding whether the offeree has made the requested return. In making this decision, the judge analyzes three questions.

First, must the offeree communicate a return promise? If the offer looks to a unilateral contract, the offeree ordinarily does not have to communicate acceptance. The courts assume that in the routine course of events, the offeror will learn of the offeree's performance of the act. A communicated acceptance is necessary only when the act is relatively private and the offeror is unlikely to learn of its performance. On the other hand, the offeree generally must communicate to effectively accept offers looking to bilateral and reverse unilateral contracts. The offeror may expressly or impliedly dispense with communication, but the judge will begin with the assumption that communication was necessary.

Second, did the offeree use an authorized means of communication? The earliest common-law stance on this issue was that the offeree had to use the same means of communication the offeror used; if the offeror made the offer by telegram, the offeree had to accept by telegram. The courts then moved to the view that the offeree was authorized to use the same means or a faster means; if the offeror used a letter, the offeree could resort to a letter or a telegram. The modern view, embraced by Uniform Commercial Code 2-206(1)(a), is that the offeree may employ any reasonable means of communication.

Finally, if communication is necessary, when is the contract formed—at the time of dispatch or the time of receipt? The prevailing, "mailbox" rule is that the contract is formed at the instant the offeree properly dispatches the acceptance by an authorized means. The Uniform Commerical Code takes a bold step beyond the common law; by virtue of Uniform Commercial Code 1-201(38), even if the offeree uses an unauthorized means of communication, the contract is formed at the time of dispatch so long as the acceptance arrives "within the time at which it would have arrived if properly sent. . . ."

"*Unconditionally.*" The common law rigorously insisted on an exact match between the terms of the offer and the purported acceptance—the so-called "mirror image" rule. If the offeree insisted upon any differing terms in the purported acceptance, the purported acceptance was ineffective to create a contract.

Uniform Commercial Code 2-207 makes a dramatic break from the common-law doctrine. U.C.C. 2-207(1) and (2) govern contracts formed by writings, and 2-207(3) controls contracts formed by the parties' conduct.

CONTRACTS FORMED BY WRITINGS

U.C.C. 2-207(1) answers the question whether the parties' writings form a contract. This subsection states the general rule that either "(a) definite and seasonable expression of acceptance or a written confirmation . . . sent within a reasonable time operates as an acceptance. . . ." The subsection explicitly abolishes the mirror image rule; the subsection announces that the general rule applies "even though (the document) states terms additional to or different from those offered. . . . " There is only one exception to the general rule: The document operates as a counter-offer when its "acceptance is expressly made conditional on assent to the additional or different terms." To invoke this exception, the document should (1) red flag the additional or different provisions, and (2) state in no uncertain terms that there is a contract only if the original offeror agrees to these terms.

If the court finds a contract under subsection (1), the court proceeds to subsection (2). This subsection answers a different question: What are the terms of the contract? In general, the terms are the terms of the original offer. *Different* terms stated in the purported acceptance become part of the contract only if the offeror assents to them.[2] If either or both of the parties are not "merchants" as defined by U.C.C. 2-104(1), an *additional* term becomes part of the contract only if the offeror assents. Finally, if both parties are merchants, additional terms presumptively become part of the contract; between merchants, the additional terms are excluded only if, in the statute's words:

(a) the offer expressly limits acceptance to the terms of the offer;
(b) they materially alter it; or
(c) notification of objection to them has already been given or is given within a reasonable time after notice of them is received.

CONTRACTS FORMED BY THE PARTIES' CONDUCT

If the parties' writings do not form a contract, the judge turns to subsection (3) of the statute.

The first sentence in subsection (3) answers the question whether the parties' conduct forms a contract. Their conduct has that effect if their acts "recognize the existence of a contract"; both parties are behaving as if there is a contract between them (for example, the seller delivers and the buyer accepts a shipment).

The subsection's second sentence addresses the issue of the terms of the contract. The terms include (1) "those terms on which the writings of the parties agree," and (2) "any supplementary terms incorporated under any other provision of this act," such as the implied warranties set out in U.C.C. 2-314 (merchantability) and 2-315 (fitness for a particular purpose).

LEGAL RESEARCH REFERENCE
Murray §§44-52, 54-57
White & Summers §§1-2 & 1-4

d.   Related Substantive Doctrines

In addition to substantive Contract law, the commercial litigator must be familiar with agency, partnership, and corporation law.

Assume that the plaintiff is a business entity such as a corporation. Before the court recognizes the plaintiff's capacity to contract or sue, the court may require that you demonstrate *de facto* or *de jure* corporate status. You can usually demonstrate that status through the testimony of one of the plaintiff's directors or officers.

Or assume that the plaintiff dealt with someone other than the defendant himself or herself. The plaintiff must then prove the third party's actual or apparent (ostensible) authority to represent the defendant. In the typical case, you can readily prove apparent authority by establishing the third person's title and the manner in which the defendant's other employees treated the third party, for example, by referring questions and decisions to the third party.

Agency, partnership, and corporation law are beyond the scope of this short text. However, we would be remiss if we did not point out that in planning the plaintiff's case, the commercial litigator must take into account substantive rules other than Contract doctrines.

Sec. 5-4.   Mutual Assent—Related Evidentiary Doctrine

How do we use these substantive Contract doctrines in the courtroom? Evidence law supplies the answer to that question. We shall use a number of different fact situations to illustrate the most common methods of proving mutual assent and the evidentiary problems presented by each method.

a.   Face-to-Face Oral Negotiation

The simplest method of proving mutual assent is establishing an agreement reached in face-to-face oral negotiations. To satisfy Federal Evidence Rule 602, the witness must base his or her testimony on personal or first-hand knowledge. Under Evidence Rule 701, the witness should generally restrict the testimony to statements of observed fact. However, in the course of describing the negotiations, the witness may properly express lay opinions on such subjects as the identity of the other negotiating person.

LEGAL RESEARCH REFERENCE:
McCormick §§10-11

The witness' references to the opposing party's statements are not subject to a hearsay objection for two reasons. One is that the statements are not being used for a hearsay purpose. Under the objective theory of mutual assent, it is logically relevant that the statements were made; the statements are operative facts and exempt from the hearsay definition under Federal Evidence Rule 801(c). The second is that the statements will almost always qualify as a party-opponent's admissions and, hence, be exempt under Evidence Rule 801(d)(2).

LEGAL RESEARCH REFERENCE:
McCormick §§249 & 262

Consider a simple hypothetical. The plaintiff, Blanton, sells automobiles. The plaintiff alleges that on Monday, he offered to sell a car to the defendant, Nadler, and that on Tuesday, Nadler accepted.

Q   Mr. Blanton, where[3] were you on the afternoon of January 12th?
A[4] In my office at the car dealership.
Q   What happened then?
A   Someone came in to look at the cars.
Q   Who was that person?
A   The defendant, Theodore Nadler.
Q   Where is he now?
A   In the courtroom.
Q   Specifically, where is he sitting?
A   At the end of the table over there.
Q   How is he dressed?
A   He's wearing a blue suit and a red tie.
Q   Your honor, please let the record reflect that Mr. Blanton has identified the defendant.
J[5] It will so reflect.
Q   What happened after the defendant arrived?
A   First we spent about half an hour checking out cars.
Q   What happened after you checked out the cars?
A   I could see that he was interested in the Mazda GLC station wagon, so I decided to make an offer to him.
Q   What did you promise to do for Mr. Nadler?   [OFFER—CONDITIONAL PROMISE][6]
A   To sell him the car he'd been looking at.
Q   What did you ask him to do in return?   [OFFER—CONDITIONAL PROMISE]
A   To pay me $5,800.
Q   How did you describe this proposal to Mr. Nadler?   [OFFER—FINALITY]
A   I told him that I was making him a firm offer.
Q   How many people did you make this proposal to?   [OFFER—FINALITY]

A   Only the defendant.

Q   What did you propose to sell him?   [OFFER—FINALITY AND DEF-
INITENESS]

A   The red Mazda GLC wagon he had looked at.

Q   What, if anything, did you tell him about its condition?   [OFFER—FI-
NALITY AND DEFINITENESS]

A   I told him that it was in good condition and if he bought it, he'd get the
normal factory warranty.

Q   What purchase price did you mention to him?   [OFFER—FINALITY
AND DEFINITENESS]

A   As I said, $5,800.

Q   How precise was the figure you mentioned to him?   [OFFER—FINAL-
ITY AND DEFINITENESS]

A   Exact. I told him that I'd sell it to him for that precise amount—an even
figure.

Q   What terms of payment did you mention to him?   [OFFER—FINALI-
TY AND DEFINITENESS]

A   A lump sum 30 days after he accepted the offer. He had said he knew he
had enough money in his checking account.

Q   When did you promise to deliver the car?   [OFFER—DEFINITENESS]

A   When he paid the money in 30 days.

Q   Where did you promise to deliver?   [OFFER—DEFINITENESS]

A   At my dealership.

Q   How did the defendant respond to your offer?

A   He said that he wanted to think it over very seriously. He assured me
that he'd come back the next day.

Q   What happened the next day?

A   He came back.

Q   Who came back?   [ACCEPTANCE—PROPER OFFEREE]

A   The defendant.

Q   What happened when he came in?

A   We talked about the offer I had made him.

Q   What did he say?   [ACCEPTANCE—INTENT TO ACCEPT—RE-
QUESTED RETURN]

A   He told me he'd thought it over and wanted to buy the car.

Q   Precisely what words did he use?   [ACCEPTANCE—REQUESTED
RETURN]

A   Nothing fancy. He just said something like, "I want to accept your offer."

Q   What terms of the offer, if any, did he ask to change?   [ACCEPTANCE
—UNCONDITIONALLY]

A   None.

Q   What new terms, if any, did he want to add to the bargain?   [ACCEP-
TANCE—UNCONDITIONALLY]

A   None.

Q   What happened after he said that he accepted your offer?

A   I told him that that was great. Then I said come back in 30 days with the
money, and the car's yours.

This hypothetical exemplifies *the double conversion process* that is the key to using Contract doctrine in the courtroom. You start with an abstract Contract concept such as the offer. First, convert that doctrine or concept into a list of factual elements. As we have seen, the offer concept breaks down into factual elements such as conditional promise, finality, and definiteness. Second, convert each factual element into one or more short, plainly worded, non-leading questions. For example, the definiteness element of the offer doctrine converted into the questions:

Q What did you propose to sell him?   [SUBJECT-MATTER, QUANTITY]
Q What, if anything, did you tell him about its condition?   [QUALITY]
Q What purchase price did you mention to him?   [PRICE]
Q How precise was the figure you mentioned to him?   [PRICE]
Q What terms of payment did you mention to him?   [TERMS OF PAYMENT]
Q When did you promise to deliver the car?   [DELIVERY DATE]
Q Where did you promise to deliver the car?   [PLACE OF DELIVERY]

We shall use the same process in the next subsection.

b. Defendant's Personal Admission of the Formation of a Contract

Federal Evidence Rule 801(d)(2)(A) authorizes the introduction of personal admissions. In pertinent part, the Rule states that the plaintiff may introduce a statement when "[t]he statement is offered against a party and is . . . his own statement, in either his individual or a representative capacity. . . . " The foundation for a personal admission is straightforward. The foundation requires that the plaintiff prove that

1. The witness on the stand heard a person make a statement.
2. The witness identifies the person as the defendant.
3. The statement is inconsistent with the defendant's position at trial. If the defendant has denied contract formation, any statement expressly or impliedly acknowledging the contract's formation will qualify.

The following line of questioning lays a proper foundation for a personal admission. The witness is one of the defendant Nadler's acquaintance:

Q Where were you on the afternoon of January 13th?
A At my office.
Q What were you doing?   (1)[7]
A I was just having a conversation with a friend.
Q Who was that friend?   (2)
A The defendant.
Q What is his name?   (2)
A Theodore Nadler.
Q Where is he now?   (2)
A He's in the courtroom.
Q Where is he sitting?   (2)
A At the end of that table over there.

Q   How is he dressed?   (2)

A   He's wearing a blue suit and a red tie.

Q   Your honor, please let the record reflect that the witness has identified the defendant.

J   It will so reflect.

Q   What, if anything, did he say during this conversation?   (3)

A   He said he's just come back from Joe Blanton's car dealership on Lindbergh Road.

Q   What else did he say?   (3)

A   He said he's just bought a Mazda station wagon from Blanton.

LEGAL RESEARCH REFERENCE:
McCormick §262

c.   **Vicarious Admissions by the Defendant's Agents About the Formation of a Contract**

The common law recognizes vicarious admissions as well as personal admissions. In some cases, if the declarant is the defendant's agent, the law will impute the agent's statement to the defendant. The common law applies this doctrine when the defendant has authorized the declarant to serve as the defendant's spokesperson. Federal Evidence Rule 801(d)(2)(c) codifies this doctrine; the Rule admits a statement made "by a person authorized by him (here the defendant) to make a statement concerning the subject." The vicarious admission doctrine necessitates the following foundation:

1.   The declarant was the defendant's agent.
2.   The defendant authorized the declarant to make the particular statements. The general manager of a business usually has such implied authority.
3.   The statement expressly or impliedly acknowledges the formation of the contract.

Assume that in our last hypothetical, the roles were reversed. Nadler is now the plaintiff. Blanton had refused to deliver the car when Nadler tendered the purchase. Blanton now denies the formation of the contract. The witness is Clark, another Blanton customer who was interested in the same car:

Q   Where were you on the morning of January 14th?

A   I visited the Blanton car dealership on Lindbergh.

Q   What happened when you arrived there?

A   I met a Mr. Graham.

Q   Who was he?   (1)

A   An employee of the dealership.

Q   What was his position?   (2)

A   He was the sales manager.

Q   How do you know that?   (2)

A   That was the title on his office door.

Q How did the other employees treat him?   (2)
A They sort of treated him like their superior or boss. While I was talking to him, several employees asked for decisions on several things. For example, they'd ask him for permission to make an offer under the sticker price for a car. That sort of thing.
Q What did you and Mr. Graham discuss?   (3)
A I was interested in a red Mazda station wagon that was sitting in the floor room.
Q What, if anything, did you tell Mr. Graham about this car?   (3)
A I said I was very interested in it.
Q How did he respond to your statement?   (3)
A He said he was sorry, but only the day before they had sold that same car to a Mr. Nadler. He said he could let me have that car only if Mr. Nadler didn't come up with the money in a month.

There is growing sentiment for a broader vicarious admission exception. Many jurisdictions now hold that the declarant need not be a spokesperson; these jurisdictions extend the doctrine to any of the defendant's agents so long as the declaration relates to the agent's employment duties. Under the emerging view, the foundation is simpler:

1. The declarant was one of the defendant's agents.
2. The declarant made the statement at a time when he was one of the defendant's agents.
3. The declaration relates to the agent's employment duties. Elicit testimony about the agent's occupational duties.
4. The declaration expressly or impliedly acknowledges the existence of the contract.

Slightly revise the hypothetical. The car dealership is still the defendant, denying the formation of a contract. In this variation of the hypothetical, the sale was made by an employee salesman rather than by the owner of the dealership. The witness is still Clark:

Q Where were you on the morning of January 14th?
A I visited the Blanton car dealership on Lindbergh.
Q What happened when you arrived there?
A I met a Ms. Cornbleet.
Q Who was she?   (1)
A One of the salespeople.
Q How do you know that?   (1)
A She told me that.
Q How was she dressed?   (1)
A She was wearing one of those red jackets that all the Blanton salespeople wear.
Q Where did you talk with her?   (1)
A First in the showroom and then in her office.
Q What sign, if any, was on the door to her office?
A As I recall, it read, "Susan Cornbleet, Salesperson."

Q   What happened after you met Ms. Cornbleet?
A   She showed me some cars.
Q   Which cars?
A   A couple that were on the floor, including a blue station wagon that really impressed me.
Q   What, if anything, did you say to Ms. Cornbleet about this car?   (3)
A   I said I was interested in it.
Q   How did she respond?   (4)
A   She told me she was real sorry. She said that she had sold that very car to a Mr. Nadler the day before.
Q   When did Ms. Cornbleet make this statement?   (2)
A   Right while I was on the premises of the dealership.

It is arguable that the salesperson's statements would not qualify as vicarious admissions under the traditional view, limiting the doctrine to spokespersons. However, under the expanded doctrine, Ms. Cornbleet's statements acknowledging contract formation are admissible.

LEGAL RESEARCH REFERENCE:
McCormick §267

d.   Identification of a Voice at the Other End of a Telephone Conversation by a Witness Familiar with the Voice

The offeror may make the offer by telephone, or the offeree may accept by that medium. To authenticate the telephone conversation, the plaintiff must identify the speaker. One recognized authentication method is the voice's identification by a person familiar with the voice. Federal Evidence Rule 901(b)(5) sanctions this technique. The foundation requires proof that

1. The witness heard a voice at a particular time and place.
2. The witness recognized the voice as the voice of a specific person.
3. The witness is familiar with that person's voice.
4. The witness explains the basis for the familiarity.

Assume that the plaintiff is Mr. Giles, who sells stationery. Mr. Hillary is one of Mr. Giles' regular customers. Giles is suing Hillary for breach of a contract to purchase a large quantity of envelopes. Giles has already testified that he offered to sell the stationery to Hillary for $460:

Q   Where were you on the morning of February 9th?   (1)
A   In my office.
Q   What happened while you were there?   (1)
A   I received a telephone call.
Q   Who was the caller?   (2)
A   The defendant, Mr. Hillary.
Q   How do you know that it was Mr. Hillary?   (3)
A   I recognized his voice.
Q   How did you become familiar with his voice?   (4)
A   He's been a regular customer for a long time.

Q   How long have you known him?   (4)
A   At least six years.
Q   How frequently do you see him?   (4)
A   At least once a week. Sometimes two or three times. He owns a big department store in town, and he merchandises a lot of stationery.
Q   What did Mr. Hillary say when he called you?
A   He told me that he wanted to accept the offer at the $460 price I had mentioned to him. He said he'd checked around town, and no one was willing to beat the $460 figure I had quoted him.

LEGAL RESEARCH REFERENCE:
McCormick §226

e.   Identification of a Voice at the Other End of a Telephone Conversation by the Telephone Directory Doctrine

The courts understandably assume that the telephone directory accurately lists telephone numbers. Given that assumption, they have developed the telephone directory technique for authenticating a telephone conversation. Federal Evidence Rule 901(b)(6) states the doctrine: The plaintiff can authenticate the defendant's

> [t]elephone conversation, by evidence that a call was made to the number assigned at the time by the telephone company to [the defendant], if . . . in the case of a person, circumstances, including self-identification, show the person answering to be the person called. . . .

To lay this foundation, the plaintiff must show that

1. The telephone directory lists a particular number for the person.
2. The witness dialed that number.
3. The witness requested the person the number is listed for.
4. The person answering identified himself or herself as the requested person.

In the previous hypothetical, assume that Mr. Giles made the offer to Hillary but Giles asked his new clerk, Mr. Folsom, to contact Hillary to learn whether Hillary accepted the offer. Folsom has never spoken with Hillary before. Folsom is the witness:

Q   Where were you on the morning of February 9th?
A   In my office at work.
Q   What happened while you were there?
A   As he always does, Mr. Giles stopped by to give me my assignments for the day.
Q   What assignments did he give you that day?
A   Several, including phoning Mr. Hillary.
Q   What did you do then?   (1)
A   As soon as the boss left, I phoned Hillary.
Q   How did you learn the defendant's telephone number?   (1)

A   I checked it out in the local telephone directory.
Q   What did you do after you found the number in the directory?   (2)
A   I dialed it.
Q   What response did you get?   (3)
A   Somebody answered.
Q   What did you say then?   (3)
A   I said I wanted to talk to Mr. Hillary.
Q   What did the person at the other end of the telephone say?   (4)
A   He said something like, "You're talking to him. I'm Hillary."
Q   What did you say then?
A   I told him that Mr. Giles wanted to know whether he was going to take the envelopes for $460.
Q   What did the defendant say?
A   He told me he had decided to accept the boss' offer. He said he'd checked around town, and no one was willing to beat the $460 figure the boss quoted him.

LEGAL RESEARCH REFERENCE:
McCormick §226

f.   The Authentication of a Writing by Someone Who Witnessed the Writing's Execution

When the parties do not have offices in the same city, they often negotiate by correspondence. When this is the case, proving mutual assent often requires authenticating documents exchanged between the parties. The plaintiff can use direct, authenticating evidence in the form of the author's acknowledgment to the testimony of a person who witnessed the writing's execution. The common law sanctions this method, and Federal Evidence Rule 901(b)(1) also recognizes authentication by "[t]estimony that a matter is what it is claimed to be." To present the testimony of a witness to the writing's execution, the plaintiff should show

1.   Where the person witnessed the writing's execution.
2.   When the person witnessed the writing's execution.
3.   Who was present.
4.   What occurred—the writing's execution.
5.   That the person recognizes the exhibit as the writing previously executed.
6.   How the witness recognizes the document.

Suppose that Hillary had decided to accept Giles' offer by letter. Ms. Collier is a friend of Hillary. She was present in Hillary's office when he wrote a letter of acceptance to Giles:

Q   Ms. Collier, where were you on the afternoon of February 9th?   (1), (2)
A   I was in Jack Hillary's office.
Q   Who was there in the office?   (3)
A   Just me and Jack. We were shooting the breeze.

Q   What, if anything, happened while you were there?   (4)
A   Jack was writing out a letter. He apologized for doing it while I was there, but he said he wanted to get it into the mail quickly.
Q   Your honor, I request that this be marked plaintiff's exhibit number one for identification.
J   It will be so marked.
Q   Please let the record reflect that I am showing the exhibit to the opposing counsel.
J   It will so reflect.
Q   I request permission to approach the witness.
J   Permission granted.
Q   Ms. Collier, I now hand you plaintiff's exhibit number one for identification. What is it?   (5)
A   It's the letter Jack was writing out.
Q   How do you recognize it?   (6)
A   I was sitting right by the desk while Jack was writing it.
Q   How close were you to the letter while the defendant was writing it?   (6)
A   A foot or two away.
Q   How good is your vision?   (6)
A   Perfect. 20-20.
Q   How well could you see the letter as the defendant was writing?   (6)
A   Very clearly. There weren't obstructions or anything else in the way.
Q   What characteristics of the exhibit are you relying on as the basis for your identification?   (6)
A   I remember the layout of the letter, the handwriting style, and some of the contents.
Q   Your honor, I now offer plaintiff's exhibit number one into identification as plaintiff's exhibit number one.
J   It will be received.
Q   I request permission to hand copies of the exhibit to the jurors for their inspection.
J   Permission granted.
Q   Ms. Collier, please read the first paragraph of this exhibit to the jurors.
A   It reads: "Dear Mr. Giles. I've thought about your offer to sell me the envelopes for $460.00. I've decided to accept. . . ."

LEGAL RESEARCH REFERENCE:
McCormick §219

g.   The Authentication of a Writing by Someone Familiar with the Purported Author's Handwriting Style

The plaintiff sometimes does not have the good fortune of finding a witness who observed the writing's execution. As an alternative, the plaintiff may present the authenticating testimony of someone familiar with the purported author's handwriting style. At common law, the courts admit this testimony as a proper form of lay opinion. Federal Evidence Rule 901(b)(2) expressly allows "[n]onexpert opinion as to the genuineness of handwriting, based upon familiarity not acquired for purposes of litigation." The plaintiff must prove that

1. The witness on the stand recognizes the handwriting.
2. The witness is familiar with the handwriting of the author.
3. The witness specifies the basis for the familiarity.

Assume that Ms. Collier was Hillary's friend but that she had not seen him write the letter of acceptance to Giles. She has already testified that she is Hillary's long-standing friend:

Q   Your honor, I request that this be marked plaintiff's exhibit number two for identification.
J   It will be so marked.
Q   Please let the record reflect that I am showing the exhibit to the opposing counsel.
J   It will.
Q   I request permission to approach the witness.
J   Granted.
Q   Ms. Collier, I now hand you plaintiff's exhibit number two for identification. What is it?
A   It seems to be some letter.
Q   Who wrote this letter?   (1)
A   I would say that the author was Mr. Hillary.
Q   How can you tell that?   (2)
A   I know his handwriting style. I can recognize it. It's quite distinctive.
Q   How long have you known him?   (3)
A   I'd say easily thirteen years.
Q   How well do you know him?   (3)
A   We're very close friends. As I previously testified, we're friends of long standing.
Q   How often have you seen him write on a document?   (3)
A   Maybe hundreds of times over the years.
Q   Your honor, I now offer plaintiff's exhibit number two for identification into evidence as plaintiff's exhibit number two.
J   It is admitted.
Q   I request permission to hand copies of the exhibit to the jurors for permission.
Q   Ms. Collier, please read the first paragraph of this exhibit to the jurors.
A   Yes. Let's see. It says: "Dear Mr. Giles. I've thought about your offer to sell me the envelopes for $460. I've decided to accept. . . ."

LEGAL RESEARCH REFERENCE:
McCormick §221

h.   The Authentication of a Writing by the Reply Letter Technique

This doctrine is analogous to the telephone directory doctrine. The courts assume that the mails are reliable just as the courts presume the accuracy of the telephone directory. The plaintiff sends a written offer to the defendant's address. In the regular course of mail, the plaintiff receives a response. The response is purportedly signed by the defendant, and the letter's contents are responsive to the plaintiff's letters. This fact situation gives rise to a circumstantial inference that the defendant authored the second letter. In our illustration, the reply letter is an acceptance, but it could just as easily be an offer. The foundation includes these elements:

1. The plaintiff drafted a letter.
2. The plaintiff placed the letter in a properly stamped envelope.
3. The plaintiff addressed the envelope to the defendant.
4. The plaintiff mailed the letter to the defendant.
5. The plaintiff received a letter.
6. The letter reached the plaintiff in the regular course of mail.
7. The second letter referred to the plaintiff's letter.
8. The second letter was purportedly authored by the defendant.
9. The plaintiff recognized the exhibit as the second letter.
10. The plaintiff explains why he or she recognizes the exhibit.

In this variation of the hypothetical, assume that Giles and Hillary resided in different cities.[8] Giles now mails the offer to Hillary, and Giles is testifying to authenticate Hillary's letter of acceptance. Giles has already authenticated his written offer. Giles has just testified that he had talked to Hillary by phone and discussed the sale of the stationery in general terms:

Q   What did you do after you hung up?   (1)
A   I wrote Hillary a letter making him the offer. That's that first exhibit you had me identify a few moments ago.
Q   How did you prepare your letter, exhibit 1?   (1)
A   I personally typed it and signed it.
Q   What did you do after signing the letter?   (2), (3), (4)
A   I placed it in an envelope. I put the postage on the envelope, addressed it to the defendant, and then put it in the mail chute in our office building.
Q   Where does the chute go?   (4)
A   It leads right to the regular postal letter box on the ground floor.
Q   How did you learn the defendant's address?   (3)
A   We have a telephone directory for the city where he has his store.
Q   When did you mail your letter to him?   (4)
A   February 9th.
Q   What happened then?   (5)
A   In a few days I received a response letter.
Q   When did this letter arrive?   (6)
A   As best I remember, it arrived on February 15th.
Q   How often have you exchanged letters with people in Chicago?   (6)
A   Lots of times. Many of our best and biggest customers have their headquarters there.
Q   How long does it normally take to get a response from Chicago?   (6)
A   Maybe six days, give or take a day.
Q   How much time passed between when you mailed your letter to the defendant and when you received the second letter?   (6)

A   Six days on the nose.

Q   Why did you refer to this letter as a response letter?   (7)

A   I called it that because it responded to my letter. I mean that it even referred to my letter. It started with a sentence like, "I am in receipt of your letter dated February 9th."

Q   Whose name appeared on the bottom of the letter?   (8)

A   The defendant's.

Q   Your honor, I request that this be marked plaintiff's exhibit number two for identification.

J   It will be so marked.

Q   Please let the record reflect that I am showing the exhibit to the opposing counsel.

J   The record will reflect that.

Q   I request permission to approach the witness.

J   You may do so.

Q   Mr. Giles, I now hand you plaintiff's exhibit number two for identification. What is it?   (9)

A   It's the letter I've been describing for the last couple of minutes.

Q   How do you recognize it?   (10)

A   The defendant has a distinctive signature, and I can recall the contents of the letter very clearly.

Q   Your honor, I now offer plaintiff's exhibit number two for identification into evidence as plaintiff's exhibit number two.

J   It will be received.

Q   I request permission to have the witness read the first paragraph and signature block to the jury.

J   Permission granted.

Q   [*To the witness.*] Please read the first paragraph and signature block to the jury.

A   Right. It says, "Dear Mr. Giles. I am in receipt of your letter dated February 9th. As you may recall, in that letter, you offered to sell me the stationery for $460. I have decided to accept your offer. I have checked around, and I now know that $460 is a good price for the quantity and quality of envelopes you offered in your letter. Very truly yours, John Hillary."

Q   I request permission to hand copies of the exhibit to the jurors for their inspection.

J   Permission granted.

In the hypothetical, the plaintiff personally mailed the letter. In a large business, the draftsman of the letter rarely mails the letter personally. The plaintiff usually presents testimony about the business' mail handling routine.[9] Some employee familiar with the routine testifies to the use of out-going mail baskets, the role of the mail clerk, the functions of the mail room, the use of mail bags, and delivery of the bags to the post office. Federal Evidence Rule 406 liberally admits evidence of business' habitual practices; and the habit evidence has sufficient probative value to support a finding that on the occasion in question, the business followed its normal mail handling practice.

LEGAL RESEARCH REFERENCE:
McCormick §225

i. The Authentication of a Writing by a Questioned Document Examiner

We have already discussed the use of lay opinion testimony identifying the author's handwriting style. In addition, the plaintiff may use the testimony of an expert questioned document examiner. Federal Evidence Rule 901(b)(3) provides that a document may be authenticated by a "[c]omparison by . . . expert witnesses with specimens which have been authenticated."

Before calling the QD expert, the plaintiff authenticates exemplars or samples of the defendant's handwriting. The plaintiff may use any authentication technique other than expert comparison to prove the samples' genuineness. The trial judge rules finally on the samples' authenticity. The plaintiff then calls the expert. The expert compares the questioned document with the exemplars and ventures an opinion as to whether the same person who wrote the exemplars authored the questioned document. To satisfy this foundation, the plaintiff must show these elements:

1. The exemplars are authentic.
2. The witness qualifies as an expert on document examination.
3. The expert compares the exemplars with the questioned document.
4. The witness specifies the basis for his or her opinion, that is, the points of similarity between the exemplars and the questioned document.

Now suppose that Giles calls Mr. Kelly to give expert testimony authenticating Hillary's letter of acceptance. Giles has already authenticated and introduced two other letters by Hillary. Those exemplars are plaintiff's exhibits numbers one and two. The letter of acceptance is plaintiff's exhibit three for identification:

Q   Where do you work?   (2)
A   I work at the Marshall Forensic Laboratory on B Street downtown.
Q   What type of work does the laboratory do?   (2)
A   We're a private laboratory. We run scientific analyses on a commercial basis. We do lots of work for lawsuits.
Q   How long have you worked there?   (2)
A   Roughly six years.
Q   What are your duties at the laboratory?   (2)
A   My field of specialization is questioned documents.
Q   What does a questioned document examiner do?   (2)
A   My primary task is figuring who wrote documents. I try to identify the author.

Q   What is your educational background?   (2)

A   I possess a B.S. degree from Washington University in St. Louis.

Q   What other training have you had in questioned document examination?
    (2)

A   I've gone to lots of short courses—one- or two-week seminars—through-
    out the country on the subject.

Q   How many short courses have you attended?   (2)

A   At least ten of them during the past six years.

Q   What professional organizations, if any, do you belong to?   (2)

A   I am a member of the American Society of Questioned Document Exam-
    iners and the Forensic Sciences Foundation.

Q   How often have you testified as an expert?   (2)

A   Maybe 150 or 200 times.

Q   How many times have you testified as an expert on questioned document
    examination?   (2)

A   On each occasion that I've appeared in court, I've testified on that sub-
    ject.

Q   I now hand you plaintiff's exhibits numbers one and two and plaintiff's
    exhibit three for identification. What are they?   (3)

A   They're some letters purportedly signed by John Hillary.

Q   How many times have you seen these letters?   (3)

A   Once before at my lab. Your clerk brought them over for me to study.

Q   What did you do when my clerk gave them to you?   (3)

A   I examined them carefully.

Q   How did you do that?   (3)

A   First I analyzed them by my unaided eye. Then I brought them under a
    high-powered microscope.

Q   How can you recognize these exhibits as the letters you previously stud-
    ied?   (3)

A   I recognize the handwriting. In my line of work, you become very atten-
    tive to even small peculiarities in people's handwriting styles.

Q   Do you have an opinion whether the author of exhibits one and two also
    wrote plaintiff's exhibit three for identification?

A   Yes.

Q   What is your opinion?   (4)

A   I'm certain that there is common authorship.

Q   What is the basis for your belief?   (5)

A   There are numerous peculiar characteristics present in all documents.
    There are peculiarities in line alignment, spacing between letters, writing
    slant, and the way some of the vowels are written.

Q   Your honor, I now offer plaintiff's exhibit number three for identification
    into evidence as plaintiff's exhibit three.

J   It will be introduced.

Q   I request permission to have the witness read the first paragraph and sig-
    nature block to the jury.

J   You have my permission.

Q   [*To the witness.*] Please read that to the jury.

A   O.K. It reads, "Dear Mr. Giles. I am in receipt of your letter dated February 9, 1981. As you may recall, in that letter you offered to sell me the stationery for $460. I have decided to accept your offer. I have checked around, and I now know that $460 is a good price for the quantity and quality of envelopes you offered in your letter." The signature block says, "Very truly yours, John Hillary."

Q   Your honor, I request permission to hand copies of all three exhibits to the jurors.

J   Permission granted. Go right ahead.

LEGAL RESEARCH REFERENCE:
McCormick §205

j.   Authentication of a Business Writing by Proof of Proper Custody

The standards for authenticating business records are very lax. To authenticate a business record, the plaintiff may use any authentication technique available for the authentication of private writings. However, there is an additional technique: proof that the record came from proper custody. The witness vouches that he or she knows the plaintiff's filing system, took the record from the proper files, and recognizes the exhibit as the record removed from the file. The foundation includes these elements:

1.   The witness is familiar with the plaintiff's filing system.
2.   The witness took the record from the right file.
3.   The witness recognizes the exhibit as the record taken from the file.
4.   The witness specifies the reason why he or she recognizes the exhibit.

Assume that Giles made a written offer to Hillary and that Giles was unavailable at trial to personally authenticate the written offer. The witness is Ms. Martinez, the head of Giles' Records Department:

Q   Ms. Martinez, what is your occupation?   (1)

A   I head up Mr. Giles' Records Department.

Q   How long have you held that position?   (1)

A   I've had that job for nine years and three months.

Q   What are your duties?   (1)

A   I supervise the preparation, maintenance, retention, and destruction of all the company's records.

Q   How well do you know the plaintiff's filing system?   (1)

A   I'm thoroughly familiar with it. I probably know more about it than anyone, even Mr. Giles.

Q   Ms. Martinez, where were you this morning?   (2)

A   I was at our office.

Q   What were you doing there?   (2)

A   I was removing some records from the files for use at trial.

Q   Where did you get these records?   (2)

A   From the February 1981 file. We assign a drawer to each year, and then there are big files in the drawer for each month.

Q   Which file did you remove these records from?   (2)

A   The one with the label "February 1981."

Q   Your honor, I request that this be marked plaintiff's exhibit number one for identification.

J   It will be so marked.

Q   Please let the record reflect that I am showing the exhibit to the opposing counsel.

J   The record will so reflect.

Q   I request permission to approach the witness.

J   Granted.

Q   I now hand you plaintiff's exhibit number one for identification. What is it?   (3)

A   It's the letter I removed from the file this morning.

Q   How can you recognize it?   (4)

A   I certainly know Mr. Giles' handwriting, and I can generally recall the letter's contents.

Q   Why do you recall the contents of the letter?   (4)

A   I read it carefully when I removed it from the file this morning. I wanted to be 100% sure that I had the right letter.

Q   Your honor, I now offer plaintiff's exhibit number one for identification into evidence as plaintiff's exhibit number one.

J   It will be received.

Q   I request permission to hand copies of the letters to all the jurors for their inspection.

J   Granted.

Q   Ms. Martinez, whom is this letter addressed to?

A   The defendant.

Q   Who sent the letter?

A   Mr. Giles.

Q   What is the date on the letter?

A   February 19th.

Q   Please read the first paragraph of the letter to the jurors.

A   All right. It reads, "Dear Mr. Hillary. As you undoubtedly recall, yesterday over the phone we discussed your purchase of some stationery from my firm. I thought about your proposal last night, and I am now prepared to offer you the stationery for $460. . . ."

LEGAL RESEARCH REFERENCE:
McCormick §224

k.   The Authentication of a Tape Recording of a Relevant Conversation

If the parties distrust each other or are simply exceedingly cautious, they may tape record conversations during the negotiations. To prove mutual assent, the plaintiff may have to introduce a tape recording of a conversation between plaintiff and defendant. At first, the courts were very skeptical of tape recordings. The courts thought that tapes could easily be tampered with; and consequently, the courts prescribed a very strict foundation for the authentication of a tape. Many jurisdictions adhere to the strict view even today. Under that view, the foundation requires proof that

1. The person operating the equipment was competent.
2. That person recorded a conversation between plaintiff and defendant.
3. The operator used certain equipment to record the conversation.
4. The equipment was in working order.
5. The operator used correct operating procedures.
6. At the time it was made, the tape faithfully reproduced the conversation.
7. The operator accounts for the custody of the tape between the time when it was made and the time of trial.
8. The operator identifies the exhibit as the tape recording.
9. The operator vouches that the tape is still an accurate reproduction of the conversation.

Suppose that Messrs. Giles and Hillary had held a negotiating session at Giles' offices. They decided to tape record the conversation. Giles ordered one of the personnel from his security division to record the conversation. The operator was Mr. Vernon:

Q What is your occupation? (1)

A I worked in Mr. Giles' security department.

Q How long have you worked there? (1)

A Maybe three years.

Q What are your duties? (1)

A I do general security work. I also do a lot of the internal security planning for the firm, including electronics and tape recording.

Q How long have you worked with tape recorders? (1)

A I guess about ten years.

Q When did your interest in that field begin? (1)

A When I was in the service. I had some military police and radar experience, and that experience just naturally led me to this job.

Q What training have you had in the electronics field, especially tape recording? (1)

A In the Air Force, I took a course that lasted two months, and I've attended lots of seminars since then.

Q Where were you on the morning of February 18th? (2)

A I went to Mr. Giles' office. He had asked me to stop by with some recording equipment.

Q What did you do while you were at his office? (2)

A I recorded a conversation between Mr. Giles and the defendant.

Q Who was the other party to this conversation? (2)

A The defendant, Hillary.

Q Where is he now? (2)

A In the courtroom.

Q Specifically? (2)

A He's sitting at the end of that table over there on the right.

Q How is he dressed? (2)

A He's wearing a blue leisure suit and black shoes.

Q You honor, please let the record reflect that the witness has identified the defendant.

J It will so reflect.

Q What equipment did you use to make this recording?   (3)

A I used a Sony recorder with microphone and some Panasonic tape.

Q How often have you used this equipment before?   (3)

A Very frequently. I've found these products to be quite trustworthy.

Q What condition was the equipment in when you made this recording? (4)

A Excellent.

Q How do you know that?   (4)

A I have a checklist to make certain that all the machinery is working right. I went through the whole checklist; and as icing on the cake, I test recorded some conversation between Mr. Giles and the defendant. I played it back, and the test recording was just fine. ·

Q How did you use the equipment to record the conversation between Mr. Giles and the defendant?   (5)

A To begin with, I plugged in the recorder and attached the mike. After the test recording, I turned the reel over and threaded it.

Q What did you do then?   (5)

A I told Mr. Giles and the defendant that they could begin, and they did. I guess they talked about 45 minutes.

Q What did you do next?   (6)

A I replayed the whole conversation to make sure that I got it all.

Q What was the quality of the recording?   (6)

A Just about perfect. I got everything they said, and it was real easy to understand everything they said.

Q What did you do after you replayed the whole tape?   (7)

A I took the tape off the recorder and stuck it in our safe in security.

Q How many people know the combination to the safe?   (7)

A Only three people.

Q Who are they?   (7)

A Mr. Giles, the head of security, Mr. Marsen, and myself.

Q What happened to the tape after you placed it in the safe?   (7)

A As far as I know, with only one exception until today, it's been in the safe.

Q What was the exception?   (7)

A About three weeks ago, you and I removed it from the safe to listen to it.

Q Who was present at that time?   (7)

A Just you and me.

Q Where were you while I was listening to the tape?   (7)

A I was there the entire time.

Q What did you do after I listened to the tape?   (7)

A I stuck it right back in the safe.

Q Where has the tape been since then?   (7)

A I would think that it's been in the safe until this very morning. I didn't remove it, and there's been no indication that anyone's even touched it since you and I played it that day.

Q Your honor, I request that this be marked plaintiff's exhibit number one for identification.

J It will be so marked.

Q Please let the record reflect that I am showing this to the opposing counsel.

J The record will duly reflect that.

Q I request permission to approach the witness.

J Go right ahead.

Q Mr. Vernon, I hand you plaintiff's exhibit number one for identification. What is it? (8)

A It's the tape I made of the conversation.

Q How do you know that? (8)

A I made some markings on the reel. I can easily recognize them.

Q What condition is the tape in? (9)

A Good condition.

Q How do you know that? (9)

A When I took it out of the safe this morning, I replayed it. It sounded as good as ever.

Q Your honor, I offer plaintiff's exhibit number one for identification into evidence as plaintiff's exhibit number one.

J It will be admitted into evidence.

Q I request permission to play the exhibit for the jurors.

J Permission granted.

If the tape is lengthy, you may want to prepare a transcript of it. Have the witness testify that the transcript is an accurate record of the tape's contents. In the judge's discretion, you may distribute copies of the transcript to the jurors to help them follow the tape.

The above foundation is time-consuming. Today, many courts have relaxed the test for admitting tape recordings. In the final analysis, verifying a tape is simply an authentication problem. Federal Evidence Rule 901 governs authentication. Rule 901(a) states that "[t]he requirement of authentication . . . is satisfied by evidence sufficient to support a finding that the matter in question is what its proponent claims." Given this lax test, many jurisdictions have opted for the view that it is sufficient if a person who heard the conversation vouches for the tape's accuracy. Hence, after Giles had testified to his conversation with Hillary, Giles himself could authenticate the tape:

Q Your honor, I request that this be marked plaintiff's exhibit number one for identification.

J It will be so marked.

Q Please let the record reflect that I am handing the exhibit to the opposing counsel.

J It will so reflect.

Q I request permission to approach the witness.

J Granted.

Q Mr. Giles, I now hand you plaintiff's exhibit number one for identification. What is it?

A   It's a tape of my conversation with the defendant — the conversation I just testified about.

Q   How do you know that?

A   We played this tape in the judge's chambers before the trial began.

Q   How accurate is the tape recording?

A   Perfect as far as I can remember.

Q   How can you identify this tape as the tape you heard in the judge's office?

A   After we played it, I held onto it. I had it on me until you called me to the stand.

Q   What did you do with it then?

A   As I walked to the stand, I put it on your counsel table. I've had it in view while I've been up here testifying.

A   Your honor, I now offer plaintiff's exhibit number one for identification into evidence as plaintiff's exhibit number one.

J   It will be received.

Q   I request permission to have the bailiff play the tape recording for the jury.

J   You have my permission. Bailiff, please set up the tape recorder.

Sec. 5-5.   Conventional Consideration

In addition to demonstrating mutual assent, the plaintiff must prove either conventional consideration or a substitute for consideration such as promissory estoppel. We shall examine conventional consideration in this section and turn to consideration substitutes in the next section.

The plaintiff is asking the court to enforce the defendant's promise, and the court will do so only if the plaintiff gave the defendant legally sufficient consideration. For practical and ideological reasons, the courts do not enforce every promise. The courts use the concept of conventional consideration as the rough dividing line between enforceable promises and the commitments a court will not enforce. The core of conventional consideration is bargained-for legal detriment. The core concept has two components: a bargain element and a legal value element.

LEGAL RESEARCH REFERENCE:
Murray §§72-73

a.   The Bargain Component of Conventional Consideration

The common denominator of mutual assent and consideration is the concept of bargain. We have already seen that through an offer and a matching acceptance, the parties must manifest mutual assent to the same bargain. Moreover, the thing the courts treat as consideration must be bargained over; the plaintiff must give the consideration in exchange for the defendant's promise, and the defendant must make the promise because the defendant is bargaining for the consideration.

Holmes expressed the doctrine in slightly different terms. Holmes wrote that the defendant's promise must induce the plaintiff's detriment (the consideration) and that the plaintiff's detriment must induce the defendant's promise. What did Holmes mean by that statement?

"The defendant's promise must induce the plaintiff's detriment" means that the plaintiff gives the consideration because the plaintiff wants or desires the defendant's promise. From the plaintiff's perspective, the plaintiff is bargaining for the defendant's promise. For example, the plaintiff wants the defendant's promise to pay $5,000.

"The plaintiff's detriment must induce the defendant's promise" focuses on the other side of the bargain; the expression means that the defendant makes the promise because the defendant wants or desires the consideration. From the defendant's perspective, the defendant is bargaining for the consideration. For instance, the defendant wants the plaintiff's car. In short, we have a two-sided, bargained-for exchange—an exchange of the plaintiff's car for the defendant's promise to pay $5,000.

Thus, to prove the bargain component of conventional consideration, the plaintiff must show on the record that

1. The plaintiff was bargaining for the defendant's promise; and,
2. The defendant was bargaining for the consideration.

BARGAINING BY THE PLAINTIFF

In concrete terms, how does the plaintiff prove that he or she was bargaining for the defendant's promise? The plaintiff should first testify to his or her subjective state of mind. The plaintiff has personal knowledge of his or her state of mind during the negotiations, and the plaintiff may testify directly to state of mind. The plaintiff should testify that he or she wanted and was bargaining for the defendant's $5,000:

Q   Why did you make this agreement with the defendant?   (1)
A   Because I wanted the money. I thought that $5,000 was a real good price for the car. The car was in good condition, but it was three years old. I didn't think that I could get a better offer from anyone else.

In addition, the plaintiff should show that the plaintiff objectively communicated this state of mind to the defendant:

Q   What, if anything, did you tell the defendant about the $5,000 figure? (1)
A   I told him that I was real pleased with it. I was happy to accept it.
Q   What, if anything, did you tell him about your finances at the time?   (1)
A   I told him frankly that I was a little short on cash and that the $5,000 was really coming at a good time.

If there is a written contract with a consideration recital or an "in consideration" clause, have the plaintiff authenticate the document and then quote the appropriate language:

Q   Please read recital #2 on page one to the jury.   (1)
A   It reads: "Whereas the party of the first part is desirous of obtaining $5,000 as a fair price for his car. . . ."

Q   Now read the first sentence in paragraph four to the jury.   (1)
A   Certainly. The paragraph says: "In consideration of the promise of the party of the second part to pay $5,000, the party of the first part promises to deliver his car to the party of the second part. . . ."

BARGAINING BY THE DEFENDANT

The plaintiff should also attempt to prove the second element, that is, that the defendant was bargaining for the consideration the plaintiff gave. To prove this, the plaintiff must ordinarily resort to evidence of the defendant's statements. These statements are not subject to a hearsay objection. In our hypothetical, the defendant's statements about the car would not be hearsay under Federal Evidence Rule 801(c). The statements are offered not for their truth but rather as circumstantial evidence of the defendant's state of mind. If the defendant explicitly states his desire for the car, the statement falls under the hearsay exception for statements of present state of mind, recognized in Evidence Rule 803(3). Finally, since the party-opponent, the defendant, made the statements, the statements are exempt from the hearsay rule as admissions under Evidence Rule 801(d)(2).

To prove that the defendant was also bargaining, the plaintiff's attorney should question the plaintiff in this fashion:

Q   What did the defendant say about your car?   (2)
A   He said he really liked it. He added that he'd been looking for a car of that model and year for a long time.
Q   What, if anything, did the defendant say about his reason for entering into the agreement?   (2)
A   He said he'd looked around and just couldn't find a car like mine. He said that he thought that he might not have this opportunity again.

As in the case of the first element, if a written contract contains passages tending to show the defendant's bargaining frame of mind quote those passages to the jury:

Q   Please read recital #3 on page one to the jury.   (2)
A   It states: "Whereas the party of the second part is desirous of obtaining the 1977 Chevrolet automobile now owned by the party of the first part. . . ."
Q   Finally, please read the first sentence in paragraph five to the jury.   (2)
A   The wording is: "In consideration of the promise of the party of the first part to sell or deliver his car, the party of the second part promises to pay $5,000. . . ."

LEGAL RESEARCH REFERENCE:
Murray §§79-81

b.   The Legal Value Component of Conventional Consideration

For conventional consideration, it is not enough that the consideration be bargained over; the second component of the conventional consideration doctrine demands that the consideration represent legal value. What is legal value? To answer that question, we must go back to fundamentals. Professor Hohfeld taught us that the most fundamental legal relationship is the correlative relationship of right and duty; the obligor has a duty, and the obligee has a correlative right. The plaintiff gives legal value when the plaintiff suffers legal detriment. More specifically, under Hohfeld's analysis, the plaintiff incurs legal detriment when the plaintiff loses a legal right or assumes a new legal duty. The plaintiff must persuade the court that in giving the consideration to the defendant, the plaintiff lost a legal right or undertook a legal duty.

The plaintiff can incur legal detriment absolutely or conditionally. The plaintiff would incur legal detriment absolutely if the plaintiff made an unconditional promise to deliver the car to the defendant. Before that promise, the plaintiff had a right to ownership of the car and no duty to deliver the car to the defendant. By making the promise, the plaintiff suffers absolute legal detriment; the plaintiff loses the right to ownership and assumes the new duty of delivering the car to the defendant.

The plaintiff can also satisfy the legal value requirement by incurring legal detriment conditionally so long as the condition is not within the plaintiff's complete, unfettered control. Suppose the plaintiff promises to deliver the car "on the condition that the party of the second part (the defendant) pay the party of the first part (the plaintiff) $5,000 ten days before the date scheduled for delivery of the car of the party of the first part." This promise is conditional, but the promise will qualify as legal value. It is not certain that the plaintiff will have to deliver the car to the defendant; but there is a possibility that the plaintiff will suffer that legal detriment. And that possibility is beyond the plaintiff's complete control.

Alternatively, assume that the plaintiff has promised to deliver the car for $5,000 "if the party of the first part desires to sell his car to the party of the second part." In form, this promise is similar to the first promise; both promises are expressly conditional. However, in substance, there is a radical difference between the two promises. In the case of the second promise, the plaintiff has complete control over the contingency; the plaintiff can merely change his or her mind and decide not to go through with the sale. The possibility of legal detriment is completely within the plaintiff's control, and consequently the promise does not satisfy the legal value requirement.

REQUIREMENTS AND OUTPUT CONTRACTS

With that general background in mind, consider some particular problems that can arise at trial. One frequent problem is proving consideration in requirements and output contracts. The early common-law view was that requirements and output agreements were not enforceable contracts; at least when the requirements buyer or the output seller did not have an established business, their promises were too illusory to qualify as consideration. Uniform Commercial Code 2-306(1) now generally validates requirements and output contracts. The consideration is the plaintiff's surrender of the legal right to deal with third parties. Before entering the requirements contract, the buyer had that right; and by promising to buy all requirements from the defendant seller, the requirements buyer lost the legal right to purchase from third parties. At trial, how do you prove that the plaintiff requirements buyer surrendered the right to buy from third parties?

Q   Under this agreement, whom were you going to buy all your requirements from?
A   The defendant.
Q   Under this agreement, how much could you buy from other suppliers?
A   Nothing. The agreement was that I'd have to buy everything from the defendant.

The analysis for the output seller is similar. The output seller surrenders the right to sell to third parties. Before entering the output contract, the seller had that right; and by promising to sell the entire output to the defendant buyer, the output seller lost the legal right to sell to third parties:

Q   Under this agreement, whom were you going to sell all your products to?
A   The defendant.
Q   Under this agreement, how much could you sell to the other buyers?
A   Nothing. The agreement was that I'd ship everything to the defendant.

ILLUSORY PROMISES

Another recurring problem is the so-called "illusory promise" issue. The "illusory promise" doctrine is another name for the rule that a conditional promise is insufficient consideration if the plaintiff has complete, unfettered control over the condition. In that circumstance, the courts characterize the plaintiff's promise as "illusory": The words create the illusion that the plaintiff has incurred legal detriment, but the plaintiff's complete control over the condition gives the plaintiff a free way out of the contract. Slight changes in the promise's wording can have a determinative effect on the question of whether the promise is illusory. Suppose that a wife gives her husband's creditor a promissory note; she does so to induce the creditor from delaying collecting the husband's note. She then defaults on her note, and the creditor sues as plaintiff.

What would be the result under the "illusory promise" doctrine if as consideration, the plaintiff creditor gave the wife his promise "not to collect the husband's note until I want your husband's money"? The promise is illusory; the creditor can change his mind and "want" the husband's money whenever he desires to. Since the plaintiff creditor's promise is illusory, the promise is insufficient consideration; and the creditor cannot collect from the wife.

What would be the result if the creditor had said that he promised "not to collect the husband's note until I have some good faith doubts about your husband's credit"? This promise is not illusory. It may be difficult for the court to determine the *bona fides* of any doubts the plaintiff entertains about the husband's credit rating; but the plaintiff does not have complete, subjective control over the contingency. Before trial, without encouraging your client's perjury, you must impress upon the client the importance of the precise wording of the promise your client made to the defendant. At trial, your questions should insistently elicit the precise wording of the promise:

Q What did you promise her in exchange for her note?
A I said I'd hold off on collecting her husband's note.
Q Now please think carefully before you answer this question. What were your precise words to her?
A As best I can remember, I told her that I would hold off on collecting her husband's note until I had real doubts about her husband's credit.

TERMINATION CLAUSES

Still another problem is the effect of a termination clause on the sufficiency of the consideration. Even if the plaintiff's promises satisfy the legal value requirement, a termination clause in the contract might render the promises illusory. If the plaintiff has the unfettered right to terminate the contract, the termination clause gives the plaintiff a free way out of the contract. In reality, a contract containing a termination clause creates alternative promises: The plaintiff must either perform the substantive promises or terminate according to the contract. If the termination clause is absolute, the second promise is illusory. However, most courts hold that the second promise is not illusory if the plaintiff must give advance notice to invoke the termination clause. Before the agreement, the plaintiff had no duty to give the defendant any notice; in promising to give the advance notice, the plaintiff assumes a new duty and thereby incurs legal detriment.

To illustrate the termination clause problem, assume that the plaintiff testified to his substantive promises on direct questioning. On cross-examination, the defense counsel forced the plaintiff to admit that the agreement contained a termination clause. On redirect, the plaintiff's attorney should ask these questions:

Q What did you have to do to terminate the agreement?
A Our agreement was that I would have to give advance, written notice to end the contract.
Q After you gave the notice, how soon would the agreement end?
A A month. The agreement was that I had to give a month's advance notice if I wanted to end the agreement.

CLAIMS SETTLEMENTS

A final problem is finding consideration in claims settlements. As consideration for a promise, the plaintiff may purport to release the defendant from a claim. For example, the plaintiff may have a tort claim against the defendant. The plaintiff then releases that claim in exchange for the defendant's promise (perhaps in the form of a promissory note) to pay $10,000. If the tort claim is valid, the plaintiff has unquestionably suffered legal detriment and given the defendant sufficient consideration; in releasing the valid claim, the plaintiff loses the legal right to title to the claim.

However, assume that the claim is invalid. If the claim had gone to trial and the jury had correctly found the facts and applied the law, there would have been a defense verdict. Can the release of an invalid claim ever qualify as legal value? At first, the common-law courts answered that question in the negative. However, many courts now treat the release of an invalid claim as sufficient consideration if the plaintiff's belief in the claim's validity is both subjectively honest and objectively reasonable. If the plaintiff has a good faith, reasonable belief, the plaintiff has the legal right to file suit on the claim; if the plaintiff has that state of mind, the plaintiff is not committing the tort of wrongful civil process by suing. On this assumption, the plaintiff incurs legal detriment by releasing the claim; the plaintiff loses the legal right to litigate the claim's validity. To invoke this doctrine, the plaintiff should show that

1. The plaintiff honestly believed that the claim was valid.
2. The plaintiff's belief was reasonable.
3. The plaintiff released the claim.
4. The plaintiff agreed not to sue on the claim.

Suppose that the prior claim was a contract claim. Mr. Dorsey was a seller of grain, and Mr. Skaggs was a grain buyer. They purported to enter into a contract for a sale of grain. In fact, the agreement was not a contract; there was a minor difference between Dorsey's offer and Skagg's acceptance, and consequently the attempted acceptance was ineffective. Neither party noticed the difference between the two documents. After signing the agreement, Skaggs told Dorsey that he would not accept the quantity of grain specified in the agreement. Dorsey consulted his attorney. The attorney erroneously advised Dorsey that he had a valid claim against Skaggs. When Dorsey threatened to sue, Skaggs reluctantly agreed to a settlement. In the new settlement agreement, Dorsey released his claim against Skaggs, and Skaggs promised to pay Dorsey $5,000. Skaggs now refuses to pay the $5,000, and Dorsey is suing to enforce the settlement agreement. The issue is whether Dorsey's release of the invalid claim was legally sufficient consideration for Skaggs' promise:

Q   What was your reaction when the defendant told you that he would not accept the grain?   (1)
A   I was angry.
Q   Why?   (1)
A   Because as far as I was concerned, we had a contract that he would take the grain.
Q   What do you mean by "contract"?   (1)
A   A legal obligation. The sort of duty that a court will enforce.
Q   What did you do after the defendant told you this?   (2)

A I went to see my attorney, Ms. Sachs.

Q Why did you go to see her? (2)

A I wanted to know whether I had legal grounds for suing the defendant.

Q What, if anything, did she tell you? (2)

A She said that I had a good, valid claim against the defendant.

> [*The attorney's statements are not subject to a hearsay objection. The plaintiff is offering the statements for a nonhearsay purpose: to show their effect on the state of mind of the hearer, the plaintiff. The fact that the attorney made these statements to the plaintiff tends to make the plaintiff's mistaken belief in the claim's validity more reasonable. Thus, the statements are exempt from the hearsay rule under Federal Evidence Rule 801(c)*].

Q What did you do after your attorney told you that? (3)

A I met with the defendant and confronted him.

Q What do you mean when you say you "confronted" him? (3)

A I told him that I thought that I had legal grounds for suing him and demanded that he pay me $5,000.

Q Why did you ask for that amount of money? (3)

A I figured that that was the loss he caused me—the money that a court would give me if I sued. At least that's what Ms. Sachs said.

Q How did the defendant respond to your demand for $5,000? (3)

A He said that he'd want to think it over. He promised to see me the next day.

Q What happened the next day? (3)

A He kept his promise and stopped by.

Q What, if anything, did he say? (3)

A He reluctantly agreed to pay the $5,000.

Q What did you promise him that you would do? (3)

A I told him that I'd drop my claim for his breach of the grain contract.

Q Under this new agreement, when would you be able to sue him on the grain contract? (4)

A That's the whole point; I wouldn't be able to do that. I assured him that I wouldn't haul him into court on that claim.

LEGAL RESEARCH REFERENCE:
Murray §§74-77, 84, 86, 90

Sec. 5-6.   Substitutes for Consideration

In some cases, the courts accept substitutes for conventional consideration. The courts will enforce a promise even though conventional consideration is lacking. The courts sometimes treat moral obligation and promissory estoppel as adequate substitutes for conventional consideration.

a.   Moral Obligation

The general rule is that moral obligation is not an adequate substitute for consideration. The courts fear that it will be too difficult to determine whether the defendant has a moral obligation to fulfill a promise; there are many schools of ethical thought, and it would have an unsettling effect on the stability of commercial transactions to enforce promises on the basis of the variable standard of "moral obligation." Other courts point out that a broad recognition of moral obligation as a consideration substitute could effectively abolish the consideration requirement. It is arguable that a person always has a moral obligation to perform his or her promises. If we begin with that premise and accept moral obligation as a consideration substitute, every promise becomes enforceable.

The courts have made a few limited inroads on the rule that moral obligation is not a consideration substitute. For example, many jurisdictions have embraced the material benefit doctrine. The thrust of the doctrine is that if the plaintiff performs an act materially benefiting the defendant and the defendant subsequently promises to pay the plaintiff for the act, the promise is enforceable. The antecedent conferral of material benefit substitutes for bargained-for consideration. Some courts apply this doctrine even when the plaintiff conferred the benefit without any expectation of compensation. In these jurisdictions, to trigger the material benefit rule, the plaintiff must show that

1. The plaintiff performed an act.
2. The act conferred a material benefit upon the defendant.
3. The act generated a sense of moral obligation to the plaintiff in the defendant's mind.
4. The sense of moral obligation prompted the defendant to make a promise to the plaintiff.

Take the typical situation in which the plaintiff acts as a Good Samaritan and saves the defendant's life. The plaintiff is boating and notices the defendant drowning near some jagged rocks by the ocean shore. The plaintiff courageously saves the defendant and, in the process, damages his boat. The defendant naturally feels a sense of moral obligation to the plaintiff and promises to pay for the repairs to the boat. Later, the defendant proves ingrate and reneges on his promise to the defendant. The plaintiff's attorney should question the plaintiff in this manner:

Q   Where were you on the morning of March 3rd?   (1)
A   I was boating in Mission Bay.
Q   What, if anything, unusual happened that morning?   (1)
A   As I rounded Reyes Point, I noticed someone in the water who seemed to be drowning.
Q   What is Reyes Point?   (1)
A   It's a very rocky area in the Bay where the waves crash in.
Q   Who was the person in the water?   (1)
A   The defendant.
Q   What is his name?   (1)
A   Neil Johnson.
Q   Where is he now?   (1)

A   In the courtroom.

Q   Where is he seated?   (1)

A   He's at that table just in front of the big picture over there.

Q   How is he dressed?   (1)

A   He's wearing a white shirt and blue slacks.

Q   Your honor, please let the record reflect that the witness has identified the defendant.

J   It will so reflect.

Q   Why did you think that the defendant was drowning?   (1)

A   To begin with, it was unusual for anyone to be swimming near the Point. It's just too dangerous. He was flailing with his hands. Most importantly, I thought I heard him crying for help.

Q   What did you do when you concluded that he was drowning?   (1)

A   I changed the direction of my boat and headed right for the Point to see if I could save him.

Q   What happened then?   (2)

A   I was lucky and was able to pull him out of the water.

Q   What, if anything, happened to your boat while you were helping the defendant?   (3)

A   I had to get real close to the rocks to grab the defendant, and the rocks banged up the boat very badly.

Q   What did you do after you had taken the defendant from the water?   (3)

A   I took him to the pier and got a doctor.

Q   What happened then?   (3)

A   A doctor arrived and checked him out before sending him home.

Q   What, if anything, did the defendant say to you before he went home? (3)

A   He thanked me for rescuing him. He said that he felt obligated and could never repay me.

Q   Where was your boat while you were talking with the defendant?   (4)

A   It was on the beach a few feet away.

Q   What, if anything, did the defendant say about the boat?   (4)

A   He noticed that it was badly damaged and asked whether that had happened when I rescued him.

Q   What did you say?   (4)

A   I said that it had.

Q   What did he say then?   (4)

A   He said that the very least he could do was pay for the repairs to the boat.

Q   As best you can recall, what were his precise words?   (4)

A   Something like, "That's the very least I can do for someone who saves my life. Whatever it costs, you get your boat fixed, and I'll pay everything."

LEGAL RESEARCH REFERENCE:
Murray §§94-102

b.   Promissory Estoppel

The modern doctrine of promissory estoppel has several historical antecedents. One is equitable estoppel *in pais*; if one party misrepresented facts to another party, in an equity suit between the two the equity court would preclude the first party from setting up the true facts. Another forerunner of modern promissory estoppel was the part performance doctrine; if the offeror made an offer for a unilateral contract and the offeree began part performance of the requested act, many courts then limited the offeror's power to revoke the offer. These two doctrines share a common theme: The innocent person's legitimate reliance is worthy of legal protection.

The courts next extended that theme to promissory estoppel in the donative context. To invoke equitable estoppel, the plaintiff had to show that the defendant misrepresented facts; equitable estoppel did not apply to promissory statements. However, like a factual statement, a promissory statement can induce reliance. The courts began enforcing promises on the basis of the innocent promisee's good faith reliance. At first, the courts enforced donative promises such as one family member's promise to convey property to another and a subscriber's promise to contribute to a charitable institution.

Then the courts made a dramatic breakthrough; they began applying the doctrine to promises made in a commercial context. The turning point in the doctrine's history was the promulgation of §90 in the first Restatement of Contracts. The draftsmen of the Restatement refused to limit the doctrine to the donative, family setting. Rather, they used sweeping language:

> A promise which the promisor should reasonably expect to induce action or forbearance of a definite and substantial character on the part of the promisee and which does induce such action or forbearance in binding if injustice can be avoided only by enforcement of the promise.

Progressive judges such as Justice Traynor of the California Supreme Court seized upon this broad language and extended the doctrine to commercial promises, including subcontractors' promises and promises to grant franchises. To invoke the promissory estoppel doctrine at trial, the plaintiff should lay the following foundation:

1. The defendant made a promise.
2. At the time the defendant made the promise, the defendant should have foreseen that the plaintiff would rely on the promise.
3. The plaintiff subsequently relied on the promise.
4. The plaintiff's reliance was objectively reasonable.
5. The plaintiff's change of position was substantial.

In our hypothetical fact situation, O'Neal is the general contractor, and Grady is the paving subcontractor. O'Neal used Grady's bid on the subcontract to compute the bid on the prime contract. O'Neal was awarded the prime contract; but before O'Neal could formally accept Grady's offer,

Grady discovered an error and attempted to revoke the offer. The plaintiff O'Neal is suing on a promissory estoppel theory. O'Neal is the witness:

Q   What is your occupation?
A   I am a general contractor in Missouri.
Q   How long have you been in that line of work?
A   For the past 20 years.
Q   Who is Charles Grady?
A   He's a paving contractor.
Q   Where is he now?
A   He's in the courtroom now.
Q   Where is he sitting?
A   He's seated at the counsel table to the left.
Q   How is he dressed?
A   He's wearing a gray tie and blue suit.
Q   Your honor, please let the record reflect that Mr. O'Neal has identified the defendant.
A   It will so reflect.
Q   How long have you known Mr. Grady?
A   For the past five years.
Q   How did you come to know him?
A   We've done a lot of business with each other during that time.
Q   What type of business?
A   He often was the low bidder for the paving work on the prime contracts I was awarded.
Q   Where were you on the morning of March 10th?
A   I was in my office.
Q   What were you doing?
A   I was phoning subcontractors to let them know about a prime contract I was bidding on—a new high school for Clayton, Missouri.
Q   Which subcontractors did you call?
A   Several, including the defendant.
Q   What did you tell the defendant?
A   I read him all the specifications and plans for the paving.
Q   What else, if anything, did you tell him?   (2)
A   I told him that if he was interested, I wanted his bid on the paving sub-contract by the close of business the next day.
Q   What did you tell him about what you were going to do with his bid?   (2)
A   I said if his was the lowest, I'd use it to compute my bid on the general contract.
Q   In your trade, how do general contractors customarily use the subcontractors' bids?   (2)
A   In exactly that fashion. The understanding is that you'll use their bid if it's low and that you'll let the subcontract to them if you use their bid.
Q   What happened the next day?   (1)
A   The various subs phoned back.
Q   Which subcontractors phoned?   (1)

A   Almost all of them that I had contacted, including the defendant.

Q   How did you know that it was the defendant calling?   (1)

A   We've known each other, as I said, for a good long time. I've become very familiar with his voice.

Q   What did the defendant say when he called?   (1)

A   He told me that he was definitely interested in the job and that his bid for the paving would be $75,000.

Q   What did you do then?   (3)

A   I reviewed all the bids on the various parts of the project and chose the lowest on each part.

Q   Which bid was the lowest on the paving part of the project?   (3)

A   The defendant's.

Q   What was the next lowest bid on the paving?   (4)

A $90,000.

Q   What were the other bids on the paving?   (4)

A   They were pretty well spread out all the way up to $115,000.

Q   How does that range of bids compare with the range of bids on most paving subcontracts?   (4)

A   About the same. You expect a bid spread.

Q   What is the normal range of bids on the paving subcontracts on your projects?   (4)

A   Sometimes the bids are closely bunched, but I'd say that in at least half the cases your high bid is 50% higher than your low bid.

Q   How would you characterize the defendant's bids over the years?   (4)

A   Consistently low. I don't think he's ever made the high bid; and we've done so much business together because he often comes in as the low bidder.

Q   What did you do after you identified the low bids on the various parts of the contracts?   (3)

A   I added them up, figured in our parts of the work, and put together my bid on the prime contract.

Q   What did you do then?   (3)

A   I submitted the bid to the school district.

Q   What did the school district do?   (3)

A   It opened the bids in about a week.

Q   How did your bid compare with the bids of the other general contractors?   (3)

A   My bid was low so that the school district awarded me the prime contract.

Q   What did you do after the school district awarded you the contract?

A   I notified all my subcontractors to gear up to get to work.

Q   Which subcontractors did you call?

A   All of them, including the defendant.

Q   What did the defendant say when you called him?

A   He said that he was real sorry, but he couldn't do the work for $75,000.

Q   Why?

A   He said they'd just made a mistake in putting their bid on the paving work together.

Q   What did you do then?   (5)

A   I had to go through with the work because I had already been awarded the prime contract. I had no way out.

Q   How did you do the paving part of the project?   (5)

A   I used the next lowest bid of $90,000.

Q   How much higher than the defendant's bid was that bid?   (5)

A $15,000 higher.

Q   When you first computed your bid, what was going to be your net profit on the prime contract?   (5)

A   I cut it pretty close. I figured a net profit of about $21,000.

Q   What effect did the defendant's refusal to do the paving have on your net profit?   (5)

A   It just about wiped it out. I was counting on a $21,000 profit; and when I had to ante up $15,000 more for paving, there went about 75% of the profit I had hoped for.

Q   When you made the bid on the high school project, what other projects, if any, were you considering?   (5)

A   There was a road work job for Webster Groves that I could have bid on, but I didn't.

Q   Why didn't you?   (5)

A   The net profit on that would have been only $15,000, and I thought that the high school was a better deal for me. Both projects were to be done in roughly the same time period, and I had only enough workers and equipment to do one of the jobs.

Q   If you had known that your net profit on the school would be only $6,000, which project would you have bid on?   (5)

A   Certainly the road work. I wouldn't have bid on the school at all if I had known that the defendant was going to try to back out of the $75,000 bid.

The promissory estoppel doctrine is now entering a new phase. Most courts still treat the promissory estoppel as a mere substitute for consideration; if the other requisites for a contract (such as a reasonably definite bargain) are present, it can subsitute for conventional consideration. However, some courts are now beginning to treat promissory estoppel as more than a substitute for consideration; these courts view it as a new, hybrid cause of action.[10] For example, they have used it as the theory of liability for awarding reliance damages even when the parties' bargain was too ambiguous to satisfy normal contract definiteness standards.[11] In this situation, the court may not award the plaintiff a full expectation measure of recovery (the profits the plaintiff would have realized if the defendant had fully performed); but it can grant reliance damages (the plaintiff's out-of-pocket expenditures).

LEGAL RESEARCH REFERENCE:
Murray §§91-93

CONTRACT FORMATION CHECKLIST

___ One party made a valid offer.

    ___ The proposal was a conditional promise.
        and
    ___ The proposal manifested intent to enter a binding agreement.
        and
    ___ The proposal manifested intent to enter a final agreement.
        and
    ___ The proposal had definite terms.

AND

___ The other party made an effective acceptance.

    ___ That party was a proper offeree.
        and
    ___ The second party knew of the offer.
        and
    ___ The second party intended to accept the offer.
        and
    ___ The second party gave the first party the requested return.
        and
    ___ The second party gave the requested return unconditionally.

AND

___ The plaintiff gave the defendant legally sufficient consideration.

    ___ The plaintiff bargained for the defendant's promise.
        and
    ___ The defendant bargained for the consideration.
        and
    ___ The plaintiff surrendered an old right or assumed a new duty.

OR

___ There is a promissory estoppel.

    ___ The defendant made a promise.
        and
    ___ At the time the defendant made the promise, the defendant should have foreseen that the plaintiff would rely on the promise.
        and
    ___ The plaintiff subsequently relied on the promise.
        and
    ___ The plaintiff's reliance was objectively reasonable.
        and
    ___ The plaintiff's change of position was substantial.

FOOTNOTES

[1] Uniform Commercial Code 1-201(3) uses the expression, "burden of establishing."

[2] Some jurisdictions treat different terms in the same manner as additional terms. If a provision in the purported acceptance addresses the same subject as a provision in the offer but prescribes other terms for that subject, the provision is a "different term." If the offer is silent on a subject and the purported acceptance contains an explicit provision addressing the subject, the provision is "an additional term."

[3] I have tried to begin most of the direct examination questions in this text in a non-leading fashion by using "who," "what," "where," "when," "how," "why," and "which." In the last chapter, we noted how important it is for the direct examiner to develop the habit of phrasing non-leading direct questions.

[4] "A" represents "answer" throughout this text.

[5] "J" represents "judge" throughout this text.

[6] The parenthetical statements indicate which element of the substantive Contract doctrine the question relates to.

[7] The number in parentheses indicates which foundational element the question relates to. Thus, this question relates to element #1, proof that the witness on the stand heard a person make a statement.

[8] This hypothetical is based on E. Imwinkelried, Evidentiary Foundations ch. 5, §B.3 (Michie/Bobbs-Merrill, 1980).

[9] *See* "Habit and Custom" Proof No. 2 in 5 American Jurisprudence Proof of Facts Proof 548 (1963).

[10] J. Calamari & J. Perillo, The Law of Contracts §§6-10 & 6-13 (2d ed. 1977).

[11] *See, e.g.*, Hoffman v. Red Owl Stores, 26 Wis.2d 683, 133 N.W.2d 267 (1965).

CHAPTER 6

How to Persuade the Court to Adopt Your Client's Interpretation of the Contract— The Second Element of the Plaintiff's Theory

Sec. 6-1.   Introduction—The Plaintiff's Hurdles

In Chapter 5, we discussed the various techniques the plaintiff may use to prove the first element of the plaintiff's theory, the formation of a contract between the plaintiff and the defendant. The next step in the plaintiff's case is to prove that the contract should be construed as creating certain conditions for the plaintiff to fulfill and a duty for the defendant to perform. To prove this second element, the plaintiff often must surmount three hurdles:

—The plaintiff must show that the provision plaintiff contends creates the condition or duty is part of the contract. The plaintiff may have to overcome a *parol evidence rule* objection to show that.
—The plaintiff must then convince the judge that the provision's language has a certain meaning. The plaintiff must use the *interpretation* rules to surmount this hurdle.
—Finally, the plaintiff must demonstrate that given the provision's meaning, the provision has the legal effect of creating a recital of fact, a condition, a duty, or a promissory condition. The *construction* rules govern this last step.

Sec. 6-2. The First Hurdle: Persuading the Judge to Include the Provision in the Contract

There are three doctrines that determine the scope and content of the contract: incorporation by reference, implication, and the parol evidence rule. These doctrines determine what is technically considered part of the contract. In effect, the doctrines determine the subject matter to be interpreted and construed. Even if one of the parties made an oral statement or sent a letter during the process of negotiation and contract formation, the letter or statement may not be considered part of the contract. The court will interpret and construe the language in the letter or oral statement only if under these three doctrines, the language is part of the contract.

a. Incorporation by Reference

The incorporation by reference doctrine can help the plaintiff expand the scope of the contract. The parties may have included most of the contract's terms in one document but stated the plans and specifications in a separate document. The judge will include the provisions of document #2 in the contract if the parties referred to document #2 and manifested their intention to incorporate the provisions of document #2 into their agreement.

Using the incorporation doctrine is a two-step process. First, the plaintiff must point the court to the language in the contract manifesting the intent to incorporate. For instance, assume that the plaintiff has already authenticated the basic contract document:

Q Mr. Mason, please read paragraph 23 on page 4 of the exhibit to the jurors.

A Right. It reads: "The parties hereby incorporate by reference the blueprints and specifications entitled 'Blueprints for Private Residence of Ronald H. Mason' and dated July 13, 1981."

The second step is authenticating the document to be incorporated. The plaintiff may authenticate that document by any of the techniques discussed in Chapter 5. It is possible to incorporate the terms of an oral agreement between the parties. In this circumstance, the plaintiff would authenticate the oral agreement by identifying the speakers and stating the tenor of the oral understanding. Chapter 5 also discusses the methods of authenticating oral statements.

b. Implication

Like incorporation by reference, the implication doctrine can help the plaintiff expand the scope of the contract. There are several different types of implied terms. Each type of implied term is governed by a different substantive test and presents the plaintiff with different evidentiary problems. The first type of term is an *implied-in-fact term based on the parties' ac-*

tual intent. The plaintiff must prove that the parties had the provision in mind when they contracted but they simply omitted the provision from the contract. It is not enough that the plaintiff prove that he or she wanted the provision; the plaintiff must show that both parties had the provision in mind at the time of contract formation. The courts routinely imply that the parties wanted well-settled trade usages to be part of the contract. If the provision in question does not qualify as a trade usage or custom under Uniform Commercial Code 1-205(2), the plaintiff must show that

1. The plaintiff had the provision in mind. The plaintiff has personal knowledge of his or her state of mind at the time of contracting, and the plaintiff may testify directly to his or her state of mind at that time.
2. The defendant also had that provision in mind. The plaintiff can show that the plaintiff placed the defendant on notice that the plaintiff considered the provision part of the contract. The plaintiff can prove that in the defendant's presence, the plaintiff made a statement indicating that the provision was part of the agreement. The plaintiff's statement is not subject to hearsay objection. The statement is admissible under Federal Evidence Rule 801(c); the statement is being offered for the nonhearsay purpose of showing its effect on the defendant's state of mind. Alternatively, the plaintiff can show the defendant's statements evidencing the defendant's desire that the provision be part of the agreement. These statements will qualify as nonhearsay under Rule 801(c), admissions under Rule 801(d)(2), or declarations of state of mind under Rule 803(3).

Suppose that the contract is an agreement for the delivery of lettuce. The written contract does not state explicitly that the defendant would pay upon delivery. The plaintiff is attempting to establish that payment at that time was an implied term of the contract. The plaintiff is testifying about the occasion on which the plaintiff and the defendant formed their agreement:

Q   When did you expect payment for the lettuce you delivered to the defendant?   (1)
A   I wanted the money as soon as we loaded it off the truck at his store.
Q   What, if anything, did you tell the defendant about the time of payment?   (2)
A   I made it clear to him that I wanted payment when we delivered the lettuce.
Q   How did you do that?   (2)
A   I told him that he could just hand the cash or check to my driver.
Q   How did the defendant respond to your statement?   (2)
A   He said O.K. That was all there was to it.

The second type of implied term is an *implied-in-fact term based on the parties' interpretative intent.* The contracting parties are human beings with limited foresight; they cannot anticipate all the developments that will occur during the performance phase of their contract. If an unforeseen development dramatically affects the contract, the court may have to rewrite the contract for the parties. The court asks itself: How would reasonable, fair contracting parties want me to revise their agreement in light of the unforeseen development?

Suppose that as in one case,[1] the plaintiff sold the defendant exclusive use of a secret formula for a vegetable cooking oil. In exchange, the defendant promised to pay the plaintiff royalties. After the parties entered into their contract, competitors penetrated the cooking oil market with cottonseed oils. The defendant countered with its own cottonseed oil, thereby reducing the sales of the vegetable cooking oil. The plaintiff argued that the defendant has an implied duty not to market the cottonseed so as to reduce the royalties. The plaintiff could hardly argue for an implied-in-fact term based on the parties' actual intent; the parties did not foresee the competitors' market invasion and did not have the implied duty in mind when they contracted. However, the plaintiff can argue for an implied-in-fact term based on interpretative intent; the plaintiff must show that

1. At the time of contracting, the plaintiff bargained for a particular benefit from the contract, for example, the royalty payments.
2. That benefit was a fundamental part of the original contract.
3. After contracting, a circumstance changed.
4. The changed circumstance was unforeseeable at the time of contracting.
5. The changed circumstance materially affects the benefit the plaintiff originally bargained for; if the judge does not make the implication, the plaintiff will not receive the basic benefit of the bargain the plaintiff initially entered into.

In our hypothetical, suppose that the plaintiff has already authenticated the original contract for the sale of the formula and the royalty payments:

Q   What basically did you want to get out of this agreement with the defendant?   (1)

A   I wanted the royalty payments.

Q   How important were those payments to you?   (2)

A   They were all-important. Really, they were the only thing the defendant was giving me in return for my formula.

Q   Aside from the royalties, what other payments did the defendant promise to make to you under the agreement?   (2)

A   None. There was nothing up front. The only way I could make any money on this deal was if I got royalties.

Q   What happened in 1976?   (3)

A   That's when X and Y entered the cooking oil market.

Q   What do you mean by "entered the market"?   (3)

A   They started selling a competitive product—a cooking oil that competed with the one made by my formula.

Q   When did those firms come into existence?   (4)

A   Not until the mid-1970's. I hadn't even heard of them until late 1975.

Q   What happened to your royalties when they started marketing their product in 1975?   (5)

A   At that time, the royalties dipped only about 5%.

Q   How did the defendant react to their marketing?   (5)

A   Throughout most of 1976, the defendant kept marketing the product made with my formula, but then the defendant developed its own cottonseed oil.

Q   When did the defendant do that?   (5)

A   I first saw the product on the market in February 1977.

Q   What happened to your royalties when the defendant started marketing its own cottonseed oil?   (5)

A   They showed a sharp dip, and they've gone down steadily since.

Q   What do you mean by a "sharp dip"?   (5)

A   By the end of 1977, they had declined 45% from their 1975 peak.

Q   How do your current royalties compare with the 1975 peak?   (5)

A   My royalties for this month are 8% of what they were in the same month in 1975.

Most judges will not permit either the plaintiff or a forensic economist to testify to the ultimate fact that reasonable, fair contracting parties would want the judge to imply a limitation on the defendant's right to market the competitive cottonseed oil. Almost all judges would exclude that testimony as improper opinion. Rather than offering that opinion, the plaintiff elicits the historical data; and then whether to make the implication based on interpretative intent becomes a question of law for the judge.

The final type of implied term is an *implied-in-law term*. This type of implication is not based on the parties' actual or interpretative intent. Rather, the court reads the term into the agreement to effect some public policy. Uniform Commercial Code 1-203 is illustrative. That section declares that regardless of the parties' intent, "[e]very contract or duty within this Act imposes an obligation of good faith in its performance or enforcement."

LEGAL RESEARCH REFERENCE:
Murray §§123, 143, 156, 196
White & Summers ch. 3

c.   The Parol Evidence Rule

Although incorporation and implication expand the scope of the contract, the parol evidence rule has the opposite effect; this rule narrows the contract's scope. By virtue of the rule's operation, a statement made during contract formation may be excluded from the contract. The parol evidence rule determines to what extent a writing *is* the contract; to that extent, the parties' other oral and written statements are excluded from the contract's scope. Figure 6-1 depicts the operation of the rule.

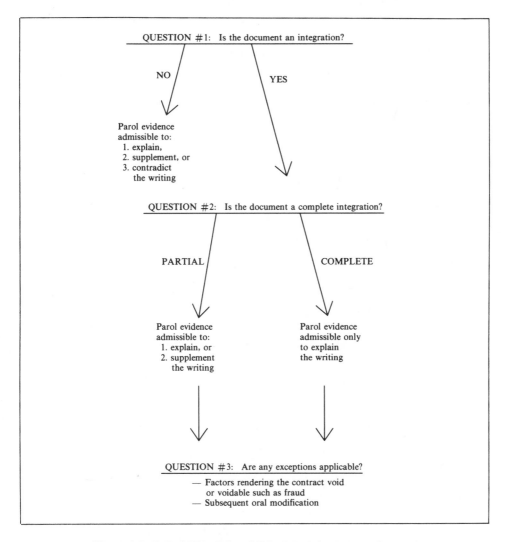

Figure 6-1: THE OPERATION OF THE PAROL EVIDENCE RULE

1. Is the document an integration?

The threshold question is always whether the parties' writing is an *integration*. If the parties intended the document to be a final expression of any part of their agreement, the document is an integration. The trial judge decides the question whether the document is an integration. The judge may consider any logically relevant evidence in making this decision. If the document is not an integration, plaintiff may introduce parol evidence (other oral and written statements of the parties) for three different purposes: to interpret, supplement, and even contradict the document. The plaintiff may attempt to add a provision to the agreement on the theory that the writing the parties used was not an integration at all:

Q   Why did you and the defendant write out exhibit four?

A   We wanted a preliminary draft of our deal.

Q   When you handed the defendant the exhibit, how did you describe it to him?

A   I called it "a rough draft."

Q   What, if anything, did you tell the defendant about a later meeting between the two of you?

A   I told him we'd have to meet later, in about a week.

Q   What reason did you give him for that meeting?

A   I said that since this was just a rough draft, we'd both have to think it over before making anything final.

On the other hand, if the document is an integration, the plaintiff may not contradict it. Whether the plaintiff may supplement it depends on whether the integration is partial or complete.

2. Is the integration partial or complete?

As Figure 6-1 shows, if the integration is *partial,* the plaintiff may use parol evidence for two purposes: to interpret the contract and to supplement the contract with consistent, additional terms. In contrast, if the integration is *complete,* the only permissible purpose for introducing the parol evidence is to interpret the contract.

How does the judge decide whether the integration is complete? There is a great deal of disagreement over this question. The courts and commentators have developed four different tests; and you must research to determine which test your jurisdiction subscribes to.

DEAN WIGMORE'S TEST

Some jurisdictions use Dean Wigmore's test. Dean Wigmore asked whether the document "at all deals with" the subject matter of the extrinsic, parol evidence. The judge looks to the writing; then considers the parol evidence; and finally compares the subject matter of the two. If the document mentions the subject matter of the parol evidence, the integration is complete. The parol evidence is inadmissible, and the jury will never hear it.

PROFESSOR WILLISTON'S TEST

One of the most popular modern tests is Professor Williston's. Professor Williston attached great importance to the face of the document. If on its face the document is obviously incomplete—there are blanks or omissions of major terms such as price or delivery—the integration is partial. However, if on its face the document is seemingly complete, there is a rebuttable presumption that the integration is complete. The plaintiff can overcome the presumption only by proving that reasonable contracting parties would naturally and normally have excluded the term from the writing. To overcome the presumption, the plaintiff could show that there was a special reason for excluding the provision from the writing:

Q   What did this oral agreement relate to?

A   The terms of financing.

Q   What was the agreement?

A   That I would receive a down payment of 25% of the total purchase price.

Q   Why didn't you include that agreement in the writing?

A   The normal down payment is only 20%. I was worried that if people knew I had insisted on such a big down payment, they'd think I really needed cash to keep my business going. There already had been some rumors about my credit rating, and I didn't want a report about my insisting on a big down payment to get around.

Q   What, if anything, did you tell the defendant about your reason for omitting the down payment from exhibit two (the written contract)?

A   I gave her the same reason I just mentioned.

Or the plaintiff can show that it is a trade custom to omit this type of term from the writing. One Texas case[2] involved a contract to buy steers to be delivered three months after the signing of the contract. The parties entered into an oral agreement on the food rations to be fed the steers during the three months. The court permitted the jury to hear the evidence of the oral agreement because it was the trade custom to leave the ration term oral. A plaintiff could question along these lines:

Q   Where do you live?

A   Austin, Texas.

Q   How long have you lived there?

A   All my life—55 years.

Q   What is your occupation?

A   I'm a steer buyer for a meat packing firm in Austin.

Q   How long have you had that job?

A   Over 31 years now.

Q   What are your duties as a steer buyer?

A   I'm the one who contacts the ranchers and actually signs the contracts for the meat packing house.

Q   Under these contracts, when does the rancher ordinarily deliver the steers?

A   Sometimes right away. But usually it's a couple of months down the road.

Q   Who feeds the steers between the signing of the contract and the time of delivery?

A   The rancher. They're still on his range before delivery.

Q   What does he feed them?

A   That all depends on the agreement.

Q   What agreement?

A   At the time you sign the contract, the custom is that you have an oral agreement over what they'll be fed before delivery.

Q   How do you make that agreement—orally or in writing?

A   It's always oral.

Q   How widespread is the practice to keep that agreement oral?

A   All the buyers do it that way in this part of Texas.

Q   Why do you do it that way?

A   New feeds are coming on the market all the time, and you want to be able to change—you want to be flexible. It's easier to leave it oral.

PROFESSOR CORBIN'S TEST

The third test is Professor Corbin's test. Professor Corbin wanted to give effect to the parties' actual intention. Even if the document appears complete, Professor Corbin would permit the judge to rely on the parol evidence and find the document to be a partial integration. Under this view, the only question for the judge is whether the parties actually intended the oral provision to be part of the contract. The plaintiff may introduce his own statements during contracting as nonhearsay under Evidence Rule 801(c) or declarations of state of mind under 803(3). The plaintiff may admit the defendant's statements as nonhearsay, admissions under Rule 801(d)(2), or declarations of state of mind.

THE U.C.C. TEST

The final test is the test embodied in Uniform Commercial Code 2-202. Comment 3 to 2-202 states that the test is whether reasonable contracting parties "would certainly have . . . included (the additional term) in the document. . . ." In one respect, this test is similar to Williston's; it uses an objective standard of reference, the conduct of reasonable contracting parties. However, in a critical respect, the test differs from Williston's; while Williston excludes the parol evidence unless reasonable parties would *normally* exclude the parol agreement, the U.C.C. includes the parol evidence unless the parties would *certainly* have included the parol agreement in the writing. In intent, the test is much more similar to Corbin's view. The examples we previously gave (the special reason for excluding the financing term and the trade custom of omitting the agreement on the steers' ration) would certainly lead to the conclusion that the writing was a partial integration under the Code.

3.   *Are any special exceptions to the parol evidence rule applicable?*

We have seen two arguments that the plaintiff can use to add a term to the writing and overcome the hurdle of the parol evidence rule. The first is that the writing is not an integration at all. The second is that the integration is partial and that the parol evidence is a consistent, supplementary term. The plaintiff's final argument would be that even if the integration is complete, a special exception to the rule is applicable. There are several exceptions.[3] In a text this short, we can make only passing mention of the most important exceptions. The most important exception for our present purposes is the subsequent oral modification doctrine: Even if the writing was a complete integration when the contract was formed, the parties may subsequently modify it orally. At common law, the modification requires both mutual assent and consideration. Everything that we said in Chapter 5 would apply here as well. Under the Code, mutual assent is necessary for the modification, but there is no need for additional consideration. Uniform Commercial Code 2-209(1) provides that "[a]n agreement modifying a contract within this Article needs no consideration to be binding."

> **LEGAL RESEARCH REFERENCE:**
> Murray §§103-08
> White & Summers §§2-9-12

Sec. 6-3.   The Second Hurdle: The Interpretation of the Contract Provision

By applying the incorporation, implication, and parol evidence rules, the judge determines the subject matter to be interpreted. Sometimes the plaintiff can prevail only if the provision has a particular meaning. By way of illustration, assume that the contract requires the defendant seller to deliver meat scraps that are "50% protein." The defendant tendered scraps that were 49.5% protein. The plaintiff will succeed on a breach of warranty claim if the language, "50% protein," means that 49.5% protein scraps do not conform to the contract. There are two bases the court can use to decide whether "50% protein" means that.

a.   The Primary Basis for Selecting an Interpretation of Contract Language: An Order of Preference Among the Types of Usages

1.   *The first step: proving that the meaning qualifies as a type of usage*

To establish the meaning of the language, the plaintiff first faces a problem of proof: proving that the meaning the plaintiff favors qualifies as a particular type of usage. There are four types of usage: popular or general, limited or trade, mutual, and individual.

The general or popular usage of a word is the meaning that the hypothetical, average lay person on the street would ascribe to the word. The plaintiff cannot simply assert that the meaning the plaintiff favors is the general usage; the plaintiff must prove that. In many jurisdictions, the plaintiff can request judicial notice of the popular meaning of words. The language of Federal Evidence Rule 201 is certainly broad enough to permit judicial notice of general usage. To support the request for judicial notice, the plaintiff should make copies of the dictionary pages listing that meaning as the first usage and insert the copies in the record of trial. If possible, dispose of your requests for judicial notice at the chambers conference before trial begins. The proponent (P), the party seeking judicial notice, could make the request in this fashion:

J   Are there any other matters you'd like to handle at this conference before the trial begins?

P   Yes, your honor.

J   And what would that be?

P   We would like you to judicially notice the fact that the general usage of "50%" is exactly one half rather than 49.5%.

J   Do you have support for that request?

P   Yes. Your honor, here are xerox copies of pages from the leading English language dictionaries in the United States. We would like to include them in the record of trial as appellate exhibits one through five.

J   Very well. Have you shown these to the opposing counsel.

P   Yes.

J   Then, if there is no objection, I'll notice the fact.

P   Your honor, will you please inform the jury that you've done that immediately after my client testifies and again during the final jury charge?

J   Yes.

In other jurisdictions, dictionaries are self-authenticating, and the plaintiff may read the definition in a purported English language dictionary into the record. In an important case, the plaintiff should consider calling an English language expert such as an English professor from a respected university. After qualifying as an expert under Federal Evidence Rule 702, the witness could testify that a particular meaning is the most generally accepted usage of the word in the United States. You could even call as a witness a pollster who had tested public opinion of the term's meaning.

The second type of usage is *limited or trade*. This is the usage that the hypothetical, average member of the relevant trade or resident of the relevant community would choose. In a given geographic area, a word may have acquired a meaning differing from the general usage in the rest of the United States. More commonly, a word may acquire a special meaning within a trade or industry. Uniform Commercial Code 1-205(2) states:

> [A] usage of trade is any practice or method of dealing having such regularity of observance in a . . . vocation or trade as to justify an exception that it will be observed with respect to the transaction in question. The existence and scope of such usage are to be proved as facts.

There may be a custom within the meat scrap industry that under a contract calling for "50% protein" meat scrap, the buyer must accept scrap that is 49.5% protein. The plaintiff would first qualify the witness as an expert on terms used in the meat scrap industry:

Q   What is your occupation?

A   I am a purchasing agent for the Striker Company.

Q   What line of business is the Striker Company in?

A   We process horse meat scraps.

Q   How long have you worked in the horse meat scrap industry?

A   I've been in the field a good long time. I'd say a little more than 22 years.

Q   How well do you know the terms used in the horse meat scrap industry?

A   Very well. I've had to use them on a daily basis for over two decades now. I ought to know them by now.

Then elicit the witness' testimony that the expression, "50% protein," has acquired a special meaning within the industry:

Q   In the meat scrap industry, what does the expression, "50% protein," mean?
A   It's a term we use to describe a certain grade of horse meat scrap. If you buy scrap of that description, you've got to accept scrap that tests out as 49.5% or higher protein. We round off to the higher number, 50%.
Q   How long has that been the meaning of "50% protein" in your industry?
A   As long as I can remember. That was the established meaning when I first started work in the late 1950's.
Q   Geographically, how widespread is the custom that 50% means 49.5% or better?
A   Gee. I can't tell you about the East Coast, but I know that all the way up and down the West Coast that's the accepted meaning of the term.

The third usage is *mutual usage*, the meaning that both contracting parties had in mind and shared at the time of contracting. The plaintiff can testify directly to the meaning he or she had in mind at the time of contracting; the plaintiff has personal knowledge of his or her own state of mind. The plaintiff may also introduce his or her own statements during contracting which evidenced that belief; statements to the defendant can be offered for a nonhearsay purpose (putting the defendant on notice that the plaintiff had a particular meaning in mind) under Federal Evidence Rule 801(c), and the plaintiff's other statements may qualify as declarations of state of mind under Rule 803(3). If the defendant made statements indicating that the defendant had the same meaning in mind, the plaintiff can introduce those statements on numerous theories; statements made during contracting may be nonhearsay (circumstantial proof of the defendant's state of mind) under Rule 801(c) or direct declarations of state of mind under 803(3), and subsequent statements can be introduced as admissions under 801(d)(2).

The plaintiff could give the following testimony to establish the existence of a mutual usage:

Q   When you used the expression, "50% protein," what did you mean?
A   I meant exactly 50% protein—no more and no less.
Q   What, if anything, did you say to the defendant about the meaning of the term?
A   I made it clear to him that that's what I meant.
Q   How did you do that?
A   I told him that I ran a first-rate processing plant and that I wouldn't accept anything that tested out even a bit under 50%. I told him that I didn't mess around with that fraction junk.
Q   What did the defendant say then?
A   He said something like, "O.K. I understand."
Q   What objection, if any, did he make?
A   None at all.

Finally, an *individual usage* is the meaning that one party, here the plaintiff, had in mind. The plaintiff can testify directly to the meaning he or she was thinking of. The courts opt for individual usage only when there is some policy basis for preferring the plaintiff over the defendant. Thus, in some jurisdictions, the courts use individual usage when as a reasonable person, the defendant should have known that the plaintiff ascribed a particular meaning to a contract term. The plaintiff may prove that he or she made statements, evidencing the meaning, in the defendant's presence. As previously stated, those statements are admissible under Evidence Rule 801(c) for the nonhearsay purpose of showing their effect on the hearer's state of mind: They would have placed a reasonable listener on notice that the plaintiff meant 50% or greater when the plaintiff said "50% protein."

2. The second step: establishing an order of preference among the usages

The first step is a question of fact: Has the plaintiff proved that the meaning, "50% or greater," is the general, trade, or mutual usage? The next step is a question of law and policy: In what order should we prefer the usages? As in the case of the test for complete integration, there is a sharp split of authority among the jurisdictions; and you must research your local law to determine whether your jurisdiction follows the Williston or Corbin view.

Professor Williston was interested primarily in protecting the stability of commercial transactions. He thought that the stability would be endangered if the courts were receptive to the argument that the parties meant a usage at variance with the popular meaning. For that reason, he fashioned the following order of preference: mutual usage only if the parties went to the trouble of including that usage in a glossary in the contract; limited or trade usage; general usage; mutual usage; and finally individual usage.

Professor Corbin's view is fundamentally different. His primary concern was carrying out the parties' actual, subjective intentions. Given that concern, he established a different order of preference: mutual usage; limited or trade usage; general usage; and individual usage.

The most important thing for the plaintiff to bear in mind is that step #1 is a question of fact and step #2 a question of law. In step #1, you must prove that the meaning favor qualifies as a particular type of usage. In step #2, you must do your legal research, know the order of preference in your jurisdiction, and be prepared to argue that your meaning is a usage higher in the order of preference than the defendant's meaning.

b.   The Secondary Basis for Selecting an Interpretation of Contract Language: The Maxims of Interpretation

In most cases, the court will be able to select an interpretation on the basis of its order of preference among the usages. In some cases, however, the order of preference will not dictate a result. For example, both parties may succeed in proving only individual usages, and the individual usages may be equally appealing. In this case, the court will resort to the secondary basis for choosing an interpretation, the so-called maxims of interpretation.

The maxims include such pithy expressions as these: We must give the language a reasonable interpretation; consider all the surrounding circumstances; interpret the contract to make all of its provisions effective; consider the parties' subsequent conduct (a "practical" interpretation); and—the law professor's favorite—*expressio unius est exclusio alterius* (the inclusion of one is the exclusion of the other).

The trial attorney uses these maxims during oral argument rather than in the presentation of evidence. In the final analysis, the maxims help us to circumstantially determine the parties' mutual usage; if a particular interpretation is more reasonable or the meaning the parties seemingly acted on during the contract's performance, that meaning is probably the mutual usage. In Chapter 17, we shall analyze closing argument at length. The techniques discussed in that chapter apply to the oral argument on interpretation; indeed, if the judge submits that issue to the jury, the argument on interpretation will be part of the closing argument. During that argument, the attorney should use the maxims as the basis for arguing that it is more plausible to believe that the parties' mutual usage was the meaning the attorney is now arguing for.

LEGAL RESEARCH REFERENCE:
Murray §§109-23
White & Summers §3-3

Sec. 6-4.   The Third Hurdle: The Construction of the Contract Provision

At this juncture, the plaintiff has surmounted the initial two hurdles. First, defeating a parol evidence rule objection, the plaintiff persuaded the judge that the parties' oral agreement that the scraps the defendant delivered would be "50% protein" was part of the contract. The plaintiff secondly established that "50% protein" should be interpreted as meaning 50% or greater protein. The last problem is determining the legal effect or construction of the provision.

The court can construe a particular provision in four different ways.

a.   A Stipulation or Recital of Fact

Some contract provisions merely recite the facts that are the background of the contract. You commonly find recitals in the WHEREAS clauses in lengthy contracts. The draftsman includes recitals to aid the court in later interpretation of the contract.

b.   A Duty or Covenant

The court may construe a particular provision as a duty or covenant. A duty is a promise or commitment. The legal consequence of a breach of duty is that the innocent party has a cause of action for at least nominal damages. Words such as "promises" and "covenants" are peculiarly appropriate for duty provisions. The plaintiff must persuade the court to construe the provision the defendant allegedly violated as a duty.

c. Condition

In addition to identifying the defendant's duty, the plaintiff must identify the conditions the plaintiff has to fulfill to activate the defendant's duty. A condition is a fact or event other than the mere lapse of time that creates or destroys a duty of immediate performance. If a condition to the defendant's duty fails, the legal effect is that the defendant's duty never becomes a duty of immediate performance; and the defendant then cannot be guilty of a breach. The courts weigh five factors in deciding whether to construe a given provision as a condition.

First, the courts look to the provision's language. Expressions such as "if," "subject to," "contingent upon," "unless," and "on the condition that" are strong indicators that the provision is a condition. The plaintiff should highlight that language. Suppose that the plaintiff contends that the only condition precedent to the defendant's delivery of the meat scraps was furnishing a suitable delivery dock. The plaintiff's attorney might question the plaintiff in this fashion:

Q   What part of the contract deals with the delivery of the scraps?
A   Let's see. I think that's paragraph 17.
Q   What is the first sentence in that paragraph?
A   That paragraph in the exhibits reads, "Subject only to the condition that the Buyer makes a suitable delivery dock available to the Seller, the Seller must deliver 350 tons of 50% protein horse meat scraps to the Buyer."

If that language is pivotal, the plaintiff should consider using an enlarged audio-visual aid such as an overhead projector or a chart quoting the language.

Second, the courts consider the purpose of the provision. Suppose that a provision in a construction subcontract states that the general contract will pay the subcontractor when the landowner pays the general. The landowner then goes bankrupt. The general wants to establish that the owner's payment was a condition to the general's duty to pay the sub; since the condition failed, the general has no duty to pay the sub. The general's attorney could attempt to show that

1. The general's purpose for including the provision in the contract was to shift the risk of the landowner's bankruptcy to the sub.
2. The general communicated that purpose to the sub:

Q   Why did you insist that the contract include Section 11?   (1)
A   Quite frankly, I wanted to protect my own hide. I had heard that Mr. Grimes (the landowner) was having some financial problems, and I didn't

> want to end up holding the bag. I didn't want to have to pay Schneider (the sub) unless I got the money from Grimes.
>
> Q   What, if anything, did you tell Mr. Schneider about the provision?   (2)
> A   I explained why I wanted it.
> Q   What did he say in response?   (2)
> A   He told me that he understood. I guess he had heard some of the same rumors about Grimes.

The court must construe this provision as a condition to carry out the parties' purpose; the only way to shift the risk to the sub is to construe the provision as a condition to the general's duty to pay the sub.

Third, the courts consider the materiality of the fact or event. The more important the fact or event the provision refers to, the more likely it is that the court will construe the provision as a condition. The court assumes that it is unlikely that the parties would condition a contractual duty on an unimportant or immaterial event. To continue our hypothetical, the general contractor's attorney can elicit testimony showing how important it was that the general receive the progress payments from the landowner:

> Q   How did you intend to finance your payments to the subcontractors?
> A   I intended to use the progress payments from the landowner.
> Q   Why did you intend to do it that way?
> A   This was a big project. I planned on paying the subs more than $100,000 a month, and I just couldn't finance those payments out of my own checking account.
> Q   How much money do you usually keep in your firm's checking account?
> A   I'd say that the account averages about $15,000 to $20,000 during the month.
> Q   What, if anything, did you tell the subcontractors about the way in which you were going to pay them?
> A   Just before we signed all the subcontracts, I held a meeting with all my subs. I explained to them that I was going to be using Grimes' progress payments to pay them.

The courts consider two other factors in deciding whether to treat a provision as a condition. Fourth, they consider the source of the language. Section 260 of the First Restatement of Contracts states:

> If . . . words that state that an act is to be performed purport to be the words of the person who is to do the act, the words are (generally) interpreted . . . as a promise by that person to perform the act. If the words purport to be those of a party who is not to do the act, they are (generally) interpreted . . . as . . . a condition.

The courts frequently apply this factor to insurance contracts. The insurer is the draftsman, and the words in the insurance policy are the insurance company's words. If the policy refers to an act the insurance company is to perform (such as paying benefits), the courts begin with the assumption that the reference creates a duty on the insurer's part. If the policy mentions an act the insured is to perform (such as paying premiums), the courts tentatively presume that the mention creates a condition to the insurer's duty.

Last, if all else fails, the courts fall back on the presumption that a provision should be construed as a duty rather than a condition. The courts employ this presumption only as a last resort.

d.   A Promissory Condition

Most important provisions in modern commercial contracts are promissory conditions; the provision is both a condition and a duty. Consider the provision that the general contractor pay the sub as work progresses. In one aspect, the provision is a duty; if the sub performs its own duty satisfactorily, the general has a duty to pay for the work. If the general fails to pay, the sub has a cause of action for breach. In another aspect, though, the provision is a condition; the general's payment is a condition to the sub's duty to continue work, and if the general does not pay, the sub has no duty to perform the next stage of the subcontract. The possibility that a provision is a promissory condition in turn creates the possibility of a countersuit by the defendant; the defendant can argue both that the plaintiff failed to fulfill the condition aspect of the provision and that the plaintiff breached the duty aspect of the provision. However, for purposes of constructing the plaintiff's prima facie case, simply remember that the plaintiff should identify both the defendant's duty and the plaintiff's conditions to that duty.

LEGAL RESEARCH REFERENCE:
Murray §§131-36, 144-50, 206

CHECKLIST FOR THE INTERPRETATION AND CONSTRUCTION OF THE CONTRACT

____ The provision is part of the contract.

____ The parties incorporated the provision by reference.

OR

____ The provision is an implied term of the contract.

   ____ an implied-in-fact provision based on actual intent.
              or
   ____ an implied-in-fact provision based on interpretative intent.
              or
   ____ an implied-in-law provision.

OR

____ The provision is provable under the parol evidence rule.

   ____ The document is not an integration.
              or
   ____ The document is a partial integration, and the provision is a consistent supplementary term.
              or
   ____ The document is a complete integration, but a special exception applies.

AND

___ The provision should be interpreted as having a certain meaning.

    ___ That meaning is the general or popular usage.
         or
    ___ That meaning is the limited or trade usage.
         or
    ___ That meaning is the mutual usage.
         or
    ___ That meaning was the plaintiff's individual usage.

AND

___ The provision should be construed as having a certain legal effect.

    ___ The provision is a stipulation or recital of fact.
         or
    ___ The provision is a duty or covenant for the defendant to perform.
         or
    ___ The provision is a condition for the plaintiff to fulfill.
         or
    ___ The provision is a promissory condition.

FOOTNOTES

[1] Parev Products Co. v. I. Rokeach & Sons, 124 F.2d 147 (2d Cir. 1941).

[2] Conner v. May, 444 S.W. 2d 948 (Tex.Civ.Apps. 1969).

[3] One notable exception is that the rule does not preclude proof of an oral statement relevant to render the contract void or voidable for fraud or mistake. Chapter 13 discusses the fraud and mistake doctrines.

CHAPTER 7

The Techniques of Proving the Satisfaction of the Conditions to the Defendant's Duty—The Third Element of the Plaintiff's Theory

Sec. 7-1.   Introduction

In Chapters 5 and 6, we discussed the first two basic elements of the plaintiff's theory in a Contract lawsuit. The plaintiff first shows that the plaintiff and defendant formed a contract (Chapter 5). The plaintiff then identifies the defendant's duty and the plaintiff's conditions to that duty (Chapter 6). The third step in the plaintiff's case is establishing that the plaintiff satisfied all the conditions to the defendant's duty. The duty never becomes a duty of immediate performance and the defendant cannot be guilty of an actionable breach until all the conditions to the defendant's duty are either fulfilled or excused.

A condition is fulfilled when the very event constituting the condition occurs. Sections 7-2 and 7-3 of this chapter review the methods the plaintiff may use to prove that the condition was fulfilled. In some cases, for reasons of policy, the law will activate the defendant's duty even when the conditions were not technically fulfilled. In these cases, the court is said to recognize an *excuse* for the technical failure of condition. Section 7-4 of this chapter analyzes the more common excuses for failure of condition.

LEGAL RESEARCH REFERENCE:
Murray §§131-35, 186, 195

Sec. 7-2. Fulfillment of the Condition—Proving the Occurrence of an Event

In many cases, the condition is an event such as the delivery of merchandise to the defendant. In some contracts, the plaintiff seller does not need to physically deliver the goods to the buyer. The contract may call for an "F.O.B." (free on board) shipment. Under Uniform Commercial Code 2-319(1)(a), in an F.O.B. place-of-shipment contract, the condition to the buyer's duty is the seller's delivery to the carrier. Under 2-319(2), in an "F.A.S." (free alongside) vessel contract, the condition is the seller's delivery of the goods alongside the vessel at the named port. Under 2-320, in a "C.I.F." contract, the conditions are the seller's delivery to the carrier, payment of the freight, and purchase of an insurance policy.

The simplest method of proving the occurrence of the event is the testimony of a witness having personal or firsthand knowledge of the event. For example, one condition to the buyer's duty to pay for goods is the seller's delivery of the goods ordered. The delivery of goods is an historical event, and proof of the event necessitates the following foundation:

1. Where the event occurred.
2. When the event occurred.
3. Who was present.
4. The nature of the event.

The plaintiff seller might call one of the plaintiff's delivery personnel to the stand:

Q   Where were you on the morning of July 17th?
A   I was at our warehouse just south of town.
Q   What were you doing?
A   The dispatcher was giving us the delivery orders for that morning.
Q   Which delivery orders did you receive?
A   Three, including one to the defendant's plant.
Q   What was the order for the defendant's plant?
A   The dispatcher said to deliver three crates of number nine size bolts to the defendant's plant.
Q   What did you do after the dispatcher gave you this order?
A   First I found three crates of the right-sized bolts.
Q   How did you know that they were the right size?
A   I checked the boxes' outside markings and partially opened each box just to make doubly certain.
Q   What did you do next?
A   We took them over to the defendant's plant.
Q   Where did you take the crates?   (1)
A   To the defendant's plant on South Broadway.

Q   How do you know that that is the defendant's plant?   (1)

A   I've been there lots of times before. Everybody in town in our line of business knows that that's the defendant's headquarters.

Q   When did you arrive there?   (2)

A   I think we pulled up at about 9:45 a.m. or so.

Q   Who was there when you pulled up?   (3)

A   It was just me, Jake our driver, Mike Evans who runs the defendant's delivery dock, and two or three other employees of the defendant.

Q   How do you know that this Evans is one of the defendant's employees? (3)

A   I've known him for years. He's headed up the dock for at least the last six years.

Q   What did you do when you met these people at the dock?   (4)

A   We unloaded the crates and left them there.

Q   How many crates did you unload?   (4)

A   All three of them.

If the plaintiff is a buyer rather than a seller, the condition might be the delivery of a check. Anyone who had observed the plaintiff drawer's delivery of the check to the defendant payee could testify to the condition's fulfillment.[1]

Unfortunately, the plaintiff sometimes cannot find a witness who personally observed and remembers the event. The event may have occurred several years before, or the plaintiff's business organization may be so large that it is impossible to determine which of hundreds of employees observed the event. In this situation, the plaintiff must resort to habit evidence under Federal Rule 406 or documentary proof of the event. For example, the plaintiff may attempt to introduce a bank's microfilm of a canceled check to prove the fact of payment.[2] The plaintiff intending to introduce documentary proof must be prepared to meet three primary objections: authentication, best evidence, and hearsay. If the plaintiff is going to use a document as substantive evidence of an event, the plaintiff must comply with all three evidentiary doctrines; and compliance will require laying foundations satisfying all three doctrines.

LEGAL RESEARCH REFERENCE:
Murray §§131-35, 138-43
White & Summers §§5-1-4

a.   Authentication

In Chapter 5, we discussed the evidentiary techniques of authenticating documents embodying the offer and acceptance. The same techniques are available for authenticating documents reflecting events during the performance of the contract. Thus, if a witness observed and remembers the document's execution, the witness can testify to the execution. After delivering the crates, the delivery person may return to the plaintiff's records department and execute a document reflecting the delivery of the crates. If a records department employee was present and observed the document's execution, the employee could testify to that effect. We also pointed out in Chapter 5 that business records can be authenticated by proof of proper custody. Assume that the records department employees did not observe or could not remember the document's execution. They are nevertheless familiar with the plaintiff's filing system. Consequently, a records department employee could authenticate the delivery document simply by testifying that he or she removed the document from the right file cabinet.

COMPUTERIZED BUSINESS RECORDS

The problem of authentication becomes more complex, however, if the plaintiff has computerized business records. When the plaintiff relies upon computerized records, there are in reality two authentication problems: the authentication of the document produced in the courtroom and the validation of the scientific computer process that generated the document. The techniques mentioned in Chapter 5 suffice to solve the first problem. The second problem necessitates an extensive foundation. To validate the computer process, the plaintiff should lay the following foundation:[3]

1. The plaintiff uses a certain make and model of computer.
2. The computer is trustworthy.
3. The plaintiff uses a particular input procedure for inserting factual data into the computer.
4. The procedure includes features designed to enhance the process' accuracy.
5. The plaintiff maintains the computer in good working order.
6. The witness instructed the computer to output certain data.
7. The witness employed correct procedures to obtain the readout.
8. The computer functioned properly when the witness obtained the readout.
9. The witness recognizes the exhibit as the readout generated by the computer.

In this variation of our hypothetical, the plaintiff calls as a witness one of the plaintiff's computer technicians:

Q   What is your occupation?
A   I am a computer technician for the plaintiff, Clark Corporation.
Q   How long have you worked for Clark Corporation?
A   Ever since I left the Air Force in 1973.
Q   How long have you worked for Clark Corporation as a computer technician?
A   I've held that job the whole time I've worked for Clark. I got my computer training while I was on active duty with the Air Force, and I stepped right into a computer job when I got my discharge.
Q   What are your duties as a computer technician?
A   I'm in charge of the processing of our delivery records.

Q   How do you keep your delivery records?   (1)

A   We do it with an **IBM** model 833 computer.

Q   How long has Clark Corporation owned the computer?   (1)

A   Four years.

Q   How long has that model computer been on the market?   (2)

A   Five years. We bought ours just a short time after the model came out.

Q   How widely used is that model computer?   (2)

A   It's used extensively by medium- and large-sized businesses not only in the United States but throughout the world. For example, I understand that it's really popular in Europe.

Q   What procedure do you use for preparing your computer delivery records?   (3)

A   Since we're only a moderate-sized firm, we use a pretty simple procedure. As soon as the delivery personnel return from their daily dropoffs, they check in at the computer center before leaving for the night.

Q   What do they do at the center?   (3)

A   They make out a new delivery form and leave the original delivery order the dispatcher gave them.

Q   What information is on the form?   (3)

A   All the details about the delivery—place, date, time, anything that relates to the delivery.

Q   What do you do with the forms?   (3)

A   One of the technicians uses a typewriter-like keyboard and makes the input directly into the computer memory.

Q   How do you know that this is the procedure?   (3)

A   I ought to know it—I've used it probably thousands of times myself while I've worked for Clark. It's been the SOP ever since I've been there.

Q   What do you mean by "SOP"?   (3)

A   The standing operating procedure—the way we always do it.

Q   What safeguards, if any, do you use to make certain that the records are accurate?   (4)

A   We have several checks. After the delivery person fills out the form, one of our technicians verbally reviews the form with the delivery person. Then another employee checks the form against the original delivery order. Then and only then do we hand it to a third employee working at the keyboard.

Q   Who does the maintenance on the computer?   (5)

A   I do a check each morning, and an **IBM** representative stops by every Monday morning at 8:00 a.m. for a weekly check before we crank up and get to work.

Q   Where were you this morning?   (6)

A   I was at my office as usual.

Q   What did you do while you were there?   (6)

A   I had the computer printout some information you told me we needed for this trial.

Q   What information?   (6)

A   You said that you wanted to know whether we had delivered anything to the defendant's plant on July 17th.

Q   How did you get the information?   (7)

A   The computer's program permits us to retrieve that sort of information from the memory. I asked the computer for the information, and it displayed the information on a cathode-ray tube display screen.

Q   How many times did you ask the computer for the information?   (7)

A   Twice. I wanted to make certain that I had the right data. It displayed the same information both times.

Q   What did you do then?   (7)

A   I then instructed the computer to use its printer to give me a human-read-able text.

Q   What did the computer do then?   (7)

A   It printed out the data I had seen on the screen.

Q   How well was the computer working when you did this?   (8)

A   It seemed to be just fine. There were no mechanical malfunctions that I could detect.

Q   Your honor, I request that this be marked plaintiff's exhibit number four for identification.

J   Yes.

Q   Please let the record reflect that I am showing the exhibit to the opposing counsel.

J   It will so reflect.

Q   I request permission to approach the witness.

J   Granted.

Q   I now hand you plaintiff's exhibit number four for identification. What is it?   (9)

A   It's the readout I just mentioned.

Q   How do you recognize it?   (9)

A   I can recognize it two ways. I generally recall the data printed out on the readout, and I also initialed the readout before I left to drive over here. I know my own initialing when I see it.

LEGAL RESEARCH REFERENCE:
McCormick ch. 22

b.   The Best Evidence Rule

The plaintiff's use of a document as substantive evidence of an event unquestionably triggers the best evidence rule under Federal Evidence Rules 1001-08. Whether the document is handwritten, typed, or computer-printed, the document is a "writing" for purposes of the rule; and the writing's terms are "in issue" when the plaintiff relies on the document as proof that the event stated in the document occurred. Nevertheless, it is relatively easy for the plaintiff to surmount a best evidence objection. The plaintiff's best arguments are these:

1.   *The exhibit offered in court is the original.*

When a writing's terms are in issue, the best evidence rule dictates that the proponent produce or account for the original. The "original" is the document that is legally significant—the document the offeror mailed to the offeree or the letter in which the defendant repudiated the contract. In most cases, the original is the first document prepared in point of time. Thus, the records department employee could authenticate the delivery form by identifying it in this fashion:

Q I now hand you plaintiff's exhibit number five for identification. What is it?

A It's the delivery form that Max, the delivery man, filled out when he returned from the defendant's plant.

Q How do you recognize it?

A I remember Max's handwriting style and generally the information he wrote down.

Q How many copies of the form did Max make?

A Under our procedure, you make an original and two carbons.

Q Which one is this exhibit—the original or one of the copies?

A It's the original one.

Q How can you tell that?

A Well, this obviously has an ink signature rather than a carbon impression. The original on top will be the only one with a real ink signature.

2. The exhibit offered in court is a duplicate original.

At common law, a "duplicate original" is as admissible as the original; the plaintiff may introduce a duplicate without accounting for either the original or other duplicates. However, the common law adopted a narrow definition of "duplicate original." To qualify a document as a duplicate at common law, the plaintiff must show that

1. The person made the copy at the same time as the original.
2. The person intended it to have the same legal effect as the original.
3. The person executed the duplicate with roughly the same formalities as the original. Most courts accept a carbon impression of a signature as the rough equivalent of an ink signature and treat carbon copies as duplicate originals.

Suppose that in the previous hypothetical, the plaintiff was offering a copy of the delivery form:

Q Which one is this exhibit—the original or one of the copies?

A It's one of the copies.

Q Who makes the copy?   (3)

A The same delivery person who fills out the original.

Q When do delivery persons make the copy?   (1)

A They do it at the very same time they make out the original in our office.

Q Why do they make the copy?   (2)

A We use it for roughly the same purposes as the original but stick them in different drawers in the file cabinet. We just want to be on the safe side and keep several copies around. It's protection against loss of the original.

Q How does the delivery person make the copy?   (3)

A It's lying under the original and attached to the original. There are carbons between the various sheets. So when the delivery person signs the original on top, it's pressed through to mark the copies.

The Federal Evidence Rules have opted for a broader definition of "duplicate." Federal Rule 1001(4) defines the term as including "a counterpart produced by the same impression as the original, or from the same matrix, or by means of photography, including enlargements and miniatures, by mechanical or electronic re-recording, or by chemical reproduction, or by other equivalent techniques which accurately reproduce the original." Under this definition, a document can qualify as a duplicate even if it was made after the execution of the original. The key to establishing the document's status as a duplicate is proving that the document was prepared by a reliable, mechanical means of reproduction. The following line of questioning invokes the broader definition of duplicate:

Q What is this exhibit?
A It's a copy of the original delivery form that Max filled out in our office.
Q How was this copy prepared?
A I personally ran it off on our Xerox machine.
Q What condition was the machine in when you made this copy?
A It seemed to be in good working order.
Q How do you know that?
A There were no evident mechanical problems when I used it. In addition, I know that I compared the original and the copy after the copy was run off.
Q How did the two documents compare?
A As far as I could tell, the Xerox seemed to be a perfect copy of the original form.
Q Why did you run off the copy?
A I was going through our files, and I noticed that we had mislaid one of the carbons. I figured I'd better run off another copy just to make sure that all our files were complete and had the proper documentation.

3. There is an adequate excuse for the non-production of the original.

If the exhibit does not qualify as an original or duplicate, you must classify the exhibit as secondary evidence. Before introducing secondary evidence, the plaintiff must establish an adequate excuse for the non-production of the original and any duplicates. Federal Evidence Rules 1004-06 list several of the excuses. We shall illustrate some of the most commonly used excuses.

One excuse is proof that the plaintiff innocently destroyed the original. Federal Rule 1004(1) states that secondary evidence is acceptable if "(a)ll originals . . . have been destroyed, unless the proponent . . . destroyed them in bad faith." Intentional, good faith destruction is a common business practice. Most businesses now have a records retention and destruction policy. The business may keep invoices in the current file cabinets for three years, then retire them to the warehouse for another five years, and finally destroy them. The business retains only a computer or microfilm copy of the original. The foundational questioning should establish that the destruction was in good faith:

Q   Where is the original invoice?
A   I'm afraid I can't locate that any more.
Q   Why not?
A   In all probability, we simply destroyed it a year ago.
Q   Why would you destroy it?
A   In our firm, we have a policy on the retention of documents. We hold them for only so long. Then we destroy them and keep only our microfilm copy.
Q   When would this document have been destroyed?
A   My best estimate is that we have done it in May of this year.
Q   Why would you have done it then?
A   As I said, we hold onto the originals for only so long, namely, three years. This invoice relates to a transaction that occurred over three years ago last May. The odds are that when May of this year rolled around, we simply burned it.
Q   Who is in charge of the destruction of original records?
A   I am.
Q   In May of this year, what, if anything, did you know about this lawsuit?
A   Nothing. That's the job of the guys in legal, but I didn't even know we had been sued. I'm sorry, but I just didn't realize that anyone would want the original invoice.

Another frequently invoked excuse is proof that the plaintiff lost the original. Federal Evidence Rule 1004(1) sanctions this excuse. In rare cases, the plaintiff will have direct evidence of the loss. However, in most cases, the plaintiff must present circumstantial evidence of the loss. The circumstantial proof usually consists of the following elements:

1. The witness realized that the document was lost.
2. The witness looked for the document.
3. By an objective standard, the search for the document was reasonably diligent.
4. Notwithstanding the diligent search, the witness could not locate the original.

The plaintiff might question the records department employee in this fashion:

Q   Where is the original invoice?   (1)
A   I don't know.
Q   Where should it be?   (1)
A   It should be in the file marked for invoices in that month. But when I looked for it in that file, it just wasn't there.
Q   When did you discover that the original invoice was missing?   (2)
A   Only about two weeks ago. I was going through the files to get ready for

this trial, and that's when I realized it was gone.

Q What did you do when you discovered it was gone? (3)

A First I went through that whole drawer in the file cabinet. I thought maybe that somebody had misfiled it.

Q What was the result of your search through the rest of the drawer? (3)

A I'm afraid that it just wasn't there.

Q What did you do next? (3)

A I questioned all the other employees in records and asked them if they had the original on their desk. I thought that somebody might be using it.

Q What did they say when you asked them about the invoice? (3)

A They didn't know where it was either.

Q What did you do then? (3)

A I went through my desk in the faint hope that it might turn up, but it didn't.

Q What happened then? (3)

A I ended my search. There was just nothing else I could do.

Q To the best of your knowledge, where is the original invoice right now? (4)

A I wish I could answer. It's missing. That's all I can tell you. I looked everywhere I thought it might be, but I came up empty.

The final excuse we shall mention is proof that the originals are too voluminous or bulky to conveniently introduce at trial. Federal Rule 1006 allows the excuse. To trigger this excuse, the plaintiff must first show that the originals would be admissible. The plaintiff must establish the originals' existence and that the originals would be admissible, that is, that they would fall within the business entry exception to the hearsay rule under Evidence Rule 803(6). The plaintiff then shows that the originals are too numerous or large to use conveniently in court:

Q How many pages of journals and ledgers did you review?

A I'd say conservatively that I browsed through 600 pages.

Q How many days did it take you to review these pages?

A I was working at the head office for a whole week.

Q How many hours did you spend on this project?

A I estimate that I spent 55 hours doing it. I had to work late and overtime every night that week.

With this foundation in the record, the plaintiff can now elicit a summary of the originals' contents. Suppose, for instance, that the plaintiff wanted to show the plaintiff's total sales during the three-month period covered by the 600 pages of records:

Q What was the total amount of sales shown by these records?

A The figure I arrived at was $673,450.00.

LEGAL RESEARCH REFERENCE:
McCormick ch. 23

c. **The Hearsay Rule**

The third objection the plaintiff must be prepared to face is hearsay. The plaintiff will counter by contending that the documents fall within the business entry exception to the hearsay rule. Federal Evidence Rule 803(6) states this exception. In most jurisdictions, the foundation for this exception requires proof that

1. An employee of the plaintiff executed the record.
2. The employee who was the ultimate source of the information had a business duty to make the report.
3. That person had personal knowledge of the event recorded.
4. The record was made at or near the time of the event.
5. It was the regular, routine practice of the plaintiff's business to make such records.
6. The report was made in writing.
7. The report was made in the regular course of business.

Assume that the plaintiff's business follows this practice. When the delivery personnel return after the delivery, they immediately visit the dispatcher's office and report the delivery. The dispatcher then records delivery data in the logbook of the delivery department. The witness is the assistant dispatcher.

Q   What is your occupation?
A   I am the assistant dispatcher for Clark Corporation.
Q   What are your duties?
A   I help the dispatcher make certain that the right merchandise gets delivered to the right place.
Q   What records, if any, do you keep as assistant dispatcher?
A   Well, we maintain a logbook of all deliveries.
Q   Your honor, I request that this be marked plaintiff's exhibit number six for identification.
J   It will be so marked.
Q   Please let the record reflect that I am showing this exhibit to the opposing counsel.
J   The record will show that.
Q   I request permission to approach the witness.
J   Permission granted.
Q   I now hand you plaintiff's exhibit six for identification. What is it?   (1)
A   It's our logbook for 1980.
Q   Who maintains this logbook?   (1)
A   The chief dispatcher and I.
Q   How do you recognize this exhibit as the logbook?   (1)
A   I know my handwriting and George's handwriting style. I can tell easily that it's the book.
Q   Where do you get the information to record in the logbook?   (2)
A   We get most of the info from the delivery personnel whom we dispatch to make the actual deliveries.
Q   What are their duties?   (2)

A   They pick the stuff up at the warehouse, make delivery, and then return and report to us.

Q   Who makes the report directly to you?   (3)

A   One of the guys who actually make the delivery.

Q   When do they make the report?   (4)

A   They're supposed to do it as soon as they get back from the delivery. In fact, we dock their pay if they are late and don't get their report in before the close of business on the delivery day.

Q   How often do the delivery people make these reports?   (5)

A   At least once every business day. We send every delivery crew out at least once a day—sometimes more often. Every time they come back to the warehouse, they're supposed to make the report.

Q   How many reports do you receive each week?   (5)

A   We've got six delivery crews, so we get a minimum of 30 reports a week. Most of the time we average about 50 or so reports. We keep the crews pretty busy.

Q   What form does the report take?   (6)

A   They come in and report to us.

Q   What do you do when they make the report?   (6)

A   We write it down immediately.

Q   Where do you write it down?   (6)

A   In our logbook, this exhibit.

Q   Why do you keep this logbook?   (7)

A   It's an important doublecheck. The delivery people also check with records when they get back, but records is all the way across the building. It's a big building, and its inconvenient if we have to run over to records whenever we need some info. The boss thought it would be a good idea if we had our own delivery logbook.

Q   Your honor, I now offer plaintiff's exhibit number six for identification into evidence as plaintiff's exhibit number six.

J   It is received.

Q   Your honor, I request permission to have the witness read the entry on the top of page 49 of the exhibit to the jurors.

J   Permission granted.

LEGAL RESEARCH REFERENCE:
McCormick ch. 31

Sec. 7-3.   The Fulfillment of the Condition—Proving a Quality or Condition

Sometimes, to activate the defendant's duty, the plaintiff will have to prove a condition rather than an event. For example, it may not suffice to prove that the plaintiff delivered a certain quantity of merchandise to the defendant; the event of delivery may be only one of the conditions to the defendant's duty. It may be an additional condition that the merchandise be of a particular quality, such as "first-rate condition." What evidentiary techniques may the plaintiff employ to prove the condition?

a.   A Jury View

One of the most neglected techniques is a jury view. In most jurisdictions, in both civil and criminal cases, the trial judge has discretion to order a jury view. In the presence of a shower such as the court bailiff, the jurors visit a site outside the courtroom and view a relevant scene or object. If the issue is the physical condition of a house, why not take the jurors on a tour of the house? If the issue is the physical condition of a piece of earth-moving machinery too large or cumbersome to bring into the courtroom, why not take the jurors to the site where the machinery is located? In an appropriate case, a view will have much more impact upon the jury than the highest quality photograph or the clearest verbal description.

When the plaintiff moves for the jury view, the plaintiff should argue that the subject matter is complex and that a witness' courtroom description of it would be inadequate. The most common objection to the view is that the object has changed since the date relevant to the lawsuit. Thus, the issue may be whether the house was sound structurally on the date scheduled for closing, July 1, 1980; but the case may not come to trial until July 1, 1981. The house's condition may have changed in the interim. The plaintiff should anticipate this objection. When the plaintiff moves for the jury view, the plaintiff should attach an affidavit, based on the affiant's personal knowledge, that the present condition of the object to be viewed is in substantially the same as its condition at the time involved in the suit.

LEGAL RESEARCH REFERENCE:
McCormick §216

b.   The Identification of Physical Evidence

A jury view is necessary only when the object is too large to be brought into the courtroom. In most cases, the object will be small enough to bring into the courtroom. When it is possible to do so, introduce the object and permit the jurors to personally inspect it to determine its condition. Some psychological studies show that we gather 83% of our data about the outside world through the sense of sight and only 11% through hearing. Moreover, the long-term retention rate for information gained through sight is more than twice as high as the rate for information gained through hearing. If you want the jurors to understand and remember the object's condition, by all means show them the object. There are two basic methods of identifying or authenticating a physical object.

The first method is the ready identifiability theory. This theory applies when the object has a unique, one-of-a-kind trait. A weapon's serial number makes the weapon a unique article. A witness may identify a readily identifiable article by testifying that he or she observed the unique trait at the time relevant in the lawsuit and recalls the trait at the time of trial. Suppose that the issue is the condition of an antique firearm. The plaintiff can quickly elicit the witness' identification of the firearm:

Q   What is this exhibit?
A   It's the antique pistol I mentioned, the one I sold to the defendant at the auction.
Q   How do you recognize it?
A   The serial number. I've got a great memory for numbers.
Q   When did you first see the number?
A   I noticed it just before I stepped up to the auction block. I inspected all the items for sale before I began the auction.

The second method of identifying physical evidence is chain of custody. The plaintiff will have to prove a chain of custody when the article does not have a unique trait or if the witness did not observe or cannot remember the trait. To lay a chain of custody foundation, the plaintiff must first identify the links in the chain. A person qualifies as a link in the chain if that person physically handled the article; a person is not a link if the person merely had access to the article, for example, by having a key to the safety deposit box the object was kept in. With respect to each link, the plaintiff should show that

1. At a certain place and time, the witness originally received the object.
2. The witness took steps to safeguard the object. The case law does not require that the witness constantly keep the object under lock and key. It is sufficient if the surrounding circumstances make it improbable that substitution or tampering occurred:

Q   What did you do with the antique after the defendant gave it to you?
A   I immediately put it in my safe.
Q   What do you mean by "immediately"?
A   I put it in the safe about five minutes after I got it. It was in the room the whole time.
Q   Where is the safe?
A   It's right behind the desk in my office.
Q   How secure is this safe?
A   There's a combination lock on it.
Q   Who knows the combination?
A   Only two people. I know it, and so does my confidential secretary.
Q   What happened to the antique after you put it in the safe?
A   With one exception, it's been in the safe until the trial today.
Q   What was that exception?
A   You and an appraiser came over to my office to examine it. I took it out so that the two of you could inspect it.
Q   Where did this inspection take place?
A   In my office.
Q   Where were you during this inspection?
A   I was there the whole time.
Q   What happened when the inspection was complete?
A   I stuck it right back in the safe.
Q   When was the next time you took the antique out of the safe?
A   I didn't remove it again until a couple of hours ago before coming over here to the courtroom.

3. The witness should explain how he or she finally disposed of the object. The witness might have retained, destroyed, or transferred the object.
4. The witness should conclude the direct testimony by adding that as best he or she can tell, the object is now in substantially the same condition it was in when he or she first received it.

LEGAL RESEARCH REFERENCE:
McCormick §212

c. Photographs

If the plaintiff cannot locate the article or it is inconvenient to bring the article to trial, the plaintiff should still not be content with a witness' verbal description of the object. Help the jury visualize the object's condition by introducing a photograph of the article. The foundation for a photograph is simple in the extreme; the foundation requires that the plaintiff show that

1. The plaintiff's witness is familiar with the article or scene shown in the photo.
2. The witness describes how he or she acquired his or her familiarity.
3. The witness states that the photograph depicts the article or scene.
4. The witness vouches that the photograph is an "accurate," "fair," or "true" depiction of the article or scene.

Assume that the plaintiff sold the defendant an automobile and the defendant refused to accept delivery. The contract states that it is a condition to the defendant's duty to accept that the automobile be in "first-rate, clean" condition. The defendant contends that the plaintiff did not fulfill that condition. The plaintiff was supposed to deliver the auto on August 9th. The plaintiff calls a local auto mechanic as a witness:

Q   What is your occupation?
A   I'm an auto mechanic at the Dalton Garage in downtown Denver.
Q   Where were you on August 8th?
A   I was at work as usual.
Q   What happened that day at work?   (1)
A   Nothing much. I do remember that the plaintiff, Ms. Schwartz, brought her car in for maintenance. She said she was going to sell it the next day and wanted it in tip-top shape.
Q   How much time did you have to observe the car's condition that day? (2)
A   I worked on the car for at least three hours that day.
Q   How familiar did you become with the car's appearance?   (2)
A   Very familiar. In my line of business, you tend to remember things about the cars you work on.
Q   Your honor, I request that these be marked plaintiff's exhibit numbers eight through eleven.

J   They will be so marked.

Q   Please let the record reflect that I am showing the exhibits to the opposing counsel.

J   Yes.

Q   I request permission to approach the witness.

J   Please proceed. Go right ahead.

Q   I now hand you plaintiff's exhibits numbers eight through eleven. What are they?   (3)

A   They're photographs of the plaintiff's car.

Q   Which view does each exhibit show?   (3)

A   The one marked eight is the front. Nine is the rear. Ten is the driver's side, and eleven is the passenger's side.

Q   How accurate are the exhibits?   (4)

A   They seem to me to be good photographs.

Q   How well do they show the car's condition as it was on August 8th?   (4)

A   Very well.

Q   How does the car's condition in the photographs differ from the car's condition on that day?   (4)

A   To be honest, I don't notice any differences.

Q   Your honor, I now offer plaintiff's exhibits eight through eleven for identification into evidence as plaintiff's exhibits eight through eleven.

J   They will be accepted.

Q   Your honor, I request permission to distribute the exhibits to the jurors.

J   Permission granted.

LEGAL RESEARCH REFERENCE:
McCormick §214

d.   Lay Opinion Testimony

There is a general prohibition against opinion testimony, but there are numerous exceptions to the norm. Even lay witnesses may express opinions on certain subjects. The collective fact or shorthand rendition doctrine admits lay opinions on subjects such as height, color, distance, identity, and sanity. Federal Evidence Rule 701 codifies a liberal version of the collective fact doctrine.

The plaintiff may have occasion to use lay opinion testimony to prove the article's condition. Suppose that the contract is for the sale of wallpaper. A wallpaper company sold a large quantity of wallpaper to a contractor. The contractor's representative picked out a pink wallpaper. The plaintiff wallpaper company delivered a pink wallpaper, but the defendant rejected the shipment on the ground that the color of the paper delivered was not the color the defendant's representative picked out. The plaintiff calls its salesperson as a witness. The plaintiff has already introduced a sample of the paper delivered; the sample was admitted as plaintiff's exhibit number three:

Q   When the defendant's foreman picked out the wallpaper, what color paper
    did he choose?
A   It was a shade we call Rose Petal Pink.
Q   How do you know that?
A   I've shown Wallmart products for nine years, and that's one of the stan-
    dard colors in the Wallmart line of products. They've got four pink
    shades in their line, and Rose Petal Pink is the deepest.
Q   I now hand you the plaintiff's exhibit number three. What is it?
A   It's a sample of wallpaper.
Q   What color is the exhibit?
A   Rose Petal Pink.
Q   How certain are you that this color is Rose Petal Pink?
A   I'm 100% positive.

LEGAL RESEARCH REFERENCE:
McCormick §11

e.   Scientific Expert Opinion About the Object's Physical Properties

Just as the plaintiff may use lay opinion testimony to prove the condition's fulfillment, the plaintiff may have occasion to resort to expert opinion
testimony. The expert testimony may be scientific in nature. Suppose, for example, that the plaintiff chemical manufacturer contracted to deliver twenty
barrels of phosphoric acid to the defendant. The defendant rejected the delivery on the ground that the barrels delivered did not contain phosphoric
acid. The plaintiff calls a technician from a testing laboratory as a witness.
The plaintiff has already traced a chain of custody for one of the barrels
from the time of attempted delivery to the time of the technician's analysis.
The foundation for the expert's opinion would require that the plaintiff
prove that

1. The technician was qualified to conduct and interpret the test.
2. The technician used a certain technique to test the material.
3. The test used is reliable.
4. The test used is generally accepted.
5. At the time of the test, any instrumentation used was in good operating condition.
6. The technician used proper test procedures.
7. The technician states the test result.
8. The technician interprets the test result.

In our hypothetical, the foundation would proceed in this fashion:

Q   What is your occupation?   (1)
A   I am a chemist with Merton Testing Laboratories here in Des Moines.
Q   What is your educational background?   (1)
A   I have a B.S. in Chemistry from Iowa State University. I also have a Mas-
    ter's degree in Chemistry from Washington University in St. Louis.
Q   How long have you worked for Merton Laboratories?   (1)

A   I've been employed there for seven years.

Q   What are your duties at the laboratory?   (1)

A   I specialize in chemical analysis.

[*Here the plaintiff should prove the witness' receipt of a sample from the barrel the plaintiff delivered to the defendant.*]

Q   What did you do with the sample after it arrived?   (2)

A   I tested it.

Q   How did you do that?   (2)

A   I used a thin layer chromatography test.

Q   What is a thin layer chromatography test?

A   It's a qualitative test. It enables you to determine the chemical composition of an unknown. You spot some of the unknown on the bottom of a small testing plate. Then you immerse the plate in a solution such as a gel. You then permit a certain period of time to elapse; during that time, the unknown moves or migrates up the plate. At the end of the period of time, you take the plate out and spray it with a coloring agent. When you have applied the coloring agent, a streak of a given length and color will appear. The length and color indicate the chemical identity of the unknown.

Q   How reliable is the test?   (3)

A   It's an excellent analytic technique in my opinion.

Q   How widely accepted is the test?   (4)

A   It's used almost universally. Police laboratories and civilian testing laboratories use the test extensively as a tool for qualitative analysis.

Q   How long has this been an accepted test?   (4)

A   For decades. The test is described in some of the oldest of the modern chemistry texts.

Q   What equipment did you use to conduct this test?   (5)

A   You use the plate, the container for the solution, the solution, and the coloring agent.

Q   What condition was the equipment in?   (5)

A   The plate and container were in good, clean condition. I personally cleaned the glass plate and container before using them. The solution and coloring agent were relatively fresh; we had just received a new delivery from our chemical supplier. We had tested the delivery, and both the solution and the coloring agent had tested out properly.

Q   How did you conduct the test?   (6)

A   I used the procedure I previously outlined for you.

Q   How did you deviate from the procedure you outlined for us?   (6)

A   I didn't. I conducted the test by the book. As best I remember, I followed the prescribed procedure exactly.

Q   What was the result of the test?   (7)

A   After I applied the coloring agent, I could see a streak on the plate.

Q   What was the appearance of the streak?   (7)

A   Its color was light green, and it was three-fifths of the plate in length.

Q   What does that indicate?   (8)

A   That indicates that the unknown was phosphoric acid.

Q   How do you know that?   (8)
A   In the first place, that's the set of results that all the chemistry texts on
    TLC say you should get for phosphoric acid. Secondly, I've tested phos-
    phoric acid several times in the past. I know that that's the color and
    length a TLC test of phosphoric acid is supposed to produce.

Some jurisdictions still require that the expert vouch that the opinion is
a reasonable scientific certainty or probability. In these jurisdictions, before
eliciting the ultimate opinion, the plaintiff's attorney should ask:

Q   Do you have an opinion whether the liquid in the barrell was phosphoric
    acid?
A   Yes.
Q   How certain are you of this opinion?
A   I think it's reasonably certain.
Q   In your opinion, to a reasonable scientific certainty, what was the liquid?
A   Phosphoric acid.

LEGAL RESEARCH REFERENCE:
McCormick ch. 20

f.   An Expert on Trade Usage or Custom

Like scientific analysis, trade usage is a proper subject for expert testimony under Federal Evidence Rule 702. Sometimes the object's physical
properties are not in dispute. The only question is whether, given its physical properties, the object is in the condition required by the contract. Suppose that the plaintiff seller has contracted to deliver a quantity of lumber
to the defendant retailer. The contract specifies that the lumber must be "of
good, merchantable quality." Uniform Commercial Code 2-314(2)(a) defines
merchantable goods as merchandise that will "pass without objection in the
trade under the contract description. . . ." It is undisputed that much of the
lumber has water stains. The defendant claims that the stains render the
lumber unmerchantable and, for that reason, the plaintiff has not fulfilled
the condition to the defendant's duty to accept and pay for the lumber. The
plaintiff calls an expert in the lumber industry:

Q   What is your occupation?
A   I'm a buyer for a wood dealer here in Portland.
Q   How long have you held that position?
A   I've been in the lumber industry for 20 years, and I've had this job with
    Big Bear Lumber for the past 11 years.
Q   How familiar are you with the special terms in the lumber industry in
    Portland?
A   I know them backwards and forwards. I use them just about every day in
    my trade.
Q   What does it mean when a contract says that lumber must be "merchant-
    able"?
A   Just as the word implies, it's got to be in a condition that would let you
    sell it to the general public under the contract description.

Q   More specifically, what does it mean if a contract says that some pine
    lumber must be "merchantable"?
A   You've got to be able to merchandise it as pine to the retail buyers. It's
    got to be fit for their purposes.
Q   How would water stains affect the merchantability of pine lumber?
A   They wouldn't. The stains don't affect the strength of the wood. You've
    got to understand that you're almost always going to paint or stain over
    pine when you use it. Even if there are water stains on it, the retailer is
    going to be able to sell it as good, fit pine lumber.

LEGAL RESEARCH REFERENCE:
McCormick §§13-16

Sec. 7-4.   Excuses for Failure of Condition—Excuses Based Upon the Nature of a Bargain

As we previously noted, the law sometimes activates the defendant's
duty even though the plaintiff has not literally fulfilled the conditions to the
defendant's duty. In these cases, the courts are said to recognize an *excuse*
for the failure of condition. There are three excuse doctrines based upon the
very nature of a contract bargain: substantial performance, impossibility,
and prevention of forfeiture.

a.   Substantial Performance

Even if the plaintiff did not strictly fulfill the condition to the defendant's duty, the plaintiff may have "substantially" fulfilled the condition. In
most jurisdictions, the courts treat substantial performance as an excuse for
failure of condition. Suppose that in a construction contract, the plaintiff
contractor fulfills most contract requirements with a few minor omissions.
The likely result is that the court will excuse the technical failure of condition and activate the defendant landowner's duty to pay. However, the court
will deduct from the plaintiff's recovery the damage caused by the plaintiff's
omissions (measured in most cases by the cost of repairing or correcting the
omissions). To utilize the substantial performance excuse, the plaintiff must
show that

1. The plaintiff's deviations from the contract were innocent. The early
   common law precluded the plaintiff from resorting to this excuse
   whenever the deviation was intentional. In most jurisdictions, the current test is whether the deviation was willful and in bad faith. If the
   plaintiff deviated from the contract specifications to cut costs, the
   plaintiff cannot invoke substantial performance.
2. The plaintiff's deviations from the contract were trivial. In its present
   condition, the building will still serve the basic purposes the parties
   had in mind at the time of contracting. Some jurisdictions have developed more specific criteria to determine whether the plaintiff's performance is sufficient. For example, some courts deny the plaintiff

recovery if there are any structural defects in the building or if the cost of repairs exceeds 10% of the total price named in the contract.

Assume that the plaintiff's only deviation from the contract specifications was that the plaintiff installed Cohoes pipe rather than Reading pipe in the plumbing. The contract specified Reading pipe, but the plaintiff contractor innocently installed the wrong brand of pipe. To invoke the substantial performance excuse, the plaintiff would first present his or her own testimony, showing the mistake's innocence:

Q   What brand of pipe were you supposed to install?   (1)
A   Reading pipe.
Q   What brand of pipe did you in fact install in the defendant's new house? (1)
A   I'm afraid that we accidentally installed Cohoes pipe.
Q   How did that happen?   (1)
A   The day I was going to buy the pipe was real busy. I had been rushed all morning, and I was lucky to find time that afternoon to get to the plumbing supplies store. I told the dealer the specifications for the pipe for the defendant's house, and I guess he showed me Cohoes pipe that otherwise met the specifications and I just approved it.
Q   Which brand of pipe did you tell the dealer you needed?   (1)
A   I thought I had mentioned Reading, but I guess I was mistaken. I was so rushed that day that I may not have mentioned a brand at all.
Q   When did you discover that you had the wrong brand of pipe?   (1)
A   Not until September 18th.
Q   How much of the pipe had been installed by then?   (1)
A   Every bit of it. We had put it all in place. It was already part of the building.

To show the second element of substantial performance, the plaintiff might call both a plumbing contractor and a real estate appraiser. After qualifying the plumbing contractor as an expert, the plaintiff could ask:

Q   How does Cohoes pipe differ from Reading pipe?   (2)
A   Really the only difference is the name.
Q   How similar are the two types of pipe?   (2)
A   They're almost identical. They have the same compositions and the same size specifications.
Q   How do their uses differ?   (2)
A   There's no difference at all. In my opinion, one brand of pipe is just as good as another. The Cohoes pipe will do everything that the Reading pipe will.

Then the plaintiff calls the real estate appraiser. After qualifying the appraiser as an expert, the plaintiff could pose these questions:

Q   What is the current value of the house Mr. Giles (the plaintiff) built for the defendant?   (2)

A In my professional judgment, the current market value is $125,000.
Q What would the market value be if the house had Reading pipe rather than Cohoes pipe?   (2)
A $125,000.
Q How does the installation of the Cohoes pipe affect the property's market value?   (2)
A I honestly don't think that it affects it at all. Whether you've got Cohoes or Reading pipe, it serves the same purposes and has the same market value.

LEGAL RESEARCH REFERENCE:
Murray §§166-69

b. Impossibility

The courts treat substantial performance as an excuse because if the plaintiff has substantially performed, the defendant is assured of receiving the basic benefit of the bargain. The same theme underlies the second excuse doctrine, impossibility. To establish this excuse, the plaintiff should show that

1. A supervening event (an event occurring after contract formation) made it actually or virtually impossible for the plaintiff to fulfill a particular condition to the defendant's duty.
2. At the time of contract formation, it was not reasonably foreseeable that the supervening event would occur.
3. The condition itself is not a material part of the contract; the condition played only a minor or relatively unimportant role in the bargain.
4. Unless the court excuses the failure of condition, the plaintiff will suffer a severe forfeiture.

The best example of the impossibility excuse arises in the construction contract context. Suppose that the contract provides that the contractor must furnish a certificate of completion from a particular architect, Ms. Jensen. Furnishing the certificate becomes an implied or constructive condition precedent to the defendant's landowner's duty to pay. The contractor completes on schedule, but the architect dies unexpectedly before signing the certificate. Assume that the plaintiff contractor has already presented the expert testimony of an architect, contractor, or civil engineer that the plaintiff complied with the substantive plans and specifications for the building. The court will probably excuse the failure to furnish the decedent architect's certificate if the plaintiff testifies along these lines:

Q When did you complete construction?
A As I recall, the crew wrapped up the project on August 8th.
Q What, if anything, unusual happened on August 9th?   (1)
A I had planned on phoning Ms. Jensen, the architect, that day.
Q What happened?   (1)

A   I phoned and learned that she had suffered a heart attack that day.

Q   What happened to Ms. Jensen?   (1)

A   She died about a week later.

Q   How do you know that?   (1)

A   I attended the funeral. She was a friend of the family for years.

Q   When you signed the contract with the defendant, what did you know about Ms. Jensen's state of health?   (2)

A   I thought she was in excellent condition.

Q   What did you know about her heart problem?   (2)

A   I didn't have the faintest idea that she had a heart problem. The first I heard was when her secretary told me that she had suffered the seizure.

Q   Why did you name Ms. Jensen as the architect in the contract?   (3)

A   The contract is a standard form we use for construction projects in the Memphis area. It has a blank for the name of the architect to give final approval.

Q   Why did you fill Ms. Jensen's name in the blank?   (3)

A   The defendant and I were filling out the form, and we just came to that blank. He didn't know any architects and asked me for a name. I named Ms. Jensen because I knew her so well.

Q   What special qualifications did she have?   (3)

A   She was a good architect, but I wouldn't say that she had any special qualifications to sign off on the certificate. It was a simple project, and any experienced architect could readily determine whether I had complied with the blueprints. I just pulled her name out of the air.

Q   How much money have you received on this construction project?   (4)

A   Not one red cent. The deal was that he would pay when the work was done, and now he's saying that he won't pay anything because I can't give him Ms. Jensen's certificate.

LEGAL RESEARCH REFERENCE:
Murray §§173, 192

c.   Prevention of Forfeiture

The third excuse doctrine is closely akin to the second. The third excuse, prevention of forfeiture, is a distinct minority view in the United States. The jurisdictions adhering to this view excuse the plaintiff's failure of condition if the plaintiff proves that

1. The condition being excused was an immaterial part of the bargain.
2. The plaintiff's failure to satisfy the condition was not willful.
3. Unless the court excuses the condition, the plaintiff will suffer an extreme forfeiture.

The courts have applied this doctrine to the renewal of option contracts. Suppose that the defendant landowner gives the plaintiff a renewable option to buy a parcel of land the plaintiff leases from the defendant. The parties enter into the contract on January 10, 1977. The option is to run for ten years. The contract provides that to renew the option, the plaintiff must mail the defendant a $6,000 check no later than January 10th of each year. The plaintiff makes the first through fourth payments in 1977–80. Then in 1981, the plaintiff accidentally mails the payment late. When the plaintiff relies upon this excuse doctrine, it is helpful to establish that the plaintiff's failure of condition caused the defendant little or no damage. Assume that the plaintiff has already called the defendant as an adverse witness and forced the defendant to admit that the plaintiff's tardiness in mailing the check did not cause the defendant any actual damage. The plaintiff's attorney now calls the plaintiff as a witness:

Q   When you signed the option contract, why did you and the defendant choose January 10th as the payment date?   (1)
A   We didn't have any particular reason. We had to name some date, and January 10th was as good as any.
Q   What, if anything, did the defendant say about the necessity for mailing the check on time?   (1)
A   I don't recall him saying anything. We basically discussed the amount of the payment, picked the January 10th date out of the air, and then signed the thing. We didn't have time to discuss every term of the deal.
Q   When did you mail the payment in 1981?   (2)
A   I didn't get it into the mail until January 12th.
Q   Why did you mail the check in late?   (2)
A   It was really stupid. I went to my office the morning of January 9th and first thing made out the check. I intended to mail it that afternoon. I went to lunch, and I guess I ate something that didn't agree with my stomach. To make a long story short, my stomach acted up; and I felt so bad when I got back to the office, I went straight home to bed. I just entirely forgot about the check. I didn't come across the check sitting on the top of my desk until I returned to work on January 12th.
Q   What did you do then?   (2)
A   I dropped the letter containing the check in the mail right away.
Q   What did you do next?   (2)
A   I phoned the defendant immediately and told him what had happened. I apologized and told him not to worry because the check was on its way.
Q   What did the defendant say?   (2)
A   He said it was tough, but the whole deal was off because I was late.
Q   What did you say then?   (2)
A   I asked if he'd been harmed by my delay.
Q   What did he say?   (2)
A   He said that he hadn't lost any money, but a deal's a deal and I hadn't met the January 10th deadline.
Q   To this date, how much money have you paid the defendant for the option?   (3)
A   Excluding the last $6,000 I mailed late, I've already given him $24,000.
Q   What improvements, if any, have you made on the land?   (3)
A   I've put in a paved parking lot, had the front landscaped, and purchased an access easement from the south.
Q   How much money have you spent on these improvements?   (3)

A   Over $32,000.

Q   Why did you make these improvements?   (3)

A   They were of immediate benefit to me in my lease, but I also thought it was a long-term investment in the likelihood that I eventually exercised the option.

Q   Which improvements can you remove from the land?   (3)

A   I can't remove any. They're all improvements to the land itself. I think they're called fixtures, and the option paper says expressly that I can't take the fixtures. If I lose the option, I've lost everything.

LEGAL RESEARCH REFERENCE:
Murray §168

Sec. 7-5.   Excuses for Failure of Condition—Excuses Based Upon the Defendant's Conduct

There is another set of excuse doctrines with an entirely different policy basis. The first group of excuse doctrines rests upon the nature of a bargain; the courts excuse the plaintiff's failure of condition because the defendant will get most of what he or she bargained for and the plaintiff stands to suffer an intolerable forfeiture. The second set of excuse doctrines focuses on the defendant's conduct.

a.   Prevention or Hindrance by the Defendant

Common fairness demands that the court excuse the plaintiff's failure of condition if the defendant wrongfully prevents the plaintiff from fulfilling the condition. The modern consensus is that the plaintiff's failure of condition is excused if the defendant's wrongful conduct completely prevents or substantially hinders the plaintiff's fulfillment of the condition. The complete foundation requires the plaintiff to prove that

1.   The defendant's conduct was wrongful. However, the real question is whether the plaintiff assumed the risk of the defendant's conduct.

     Suppose that the plaintiff contracted to sell the defendant a commodity that was in short supply and that at the time of contracting, the defendant made it clear that the defendant would continue making other purchases of the commodity from any available source. The defendant's other purchases might drive the price of the commodity so high that the plaintiff finds it difficult to buy the quantity of the commodity to deliver to the defendant. The defendant's other purchases are intentional acts; but since the plaintiff knew that the defendant contemplated continuing such purchases, the plaintiff assumes the risk.

     Foreseeability is a key factor in deciding the allocation of the risk. Suppose that the plaintiff entered into a life care contract with an elderly person. The elderly person's eccentric acts might drive the plaintiff out the door. However, since the plaintiff should anticipate such conduct by an elderly person, there is no prevention. On the other hand, if the defendant's acts amounted to criminal assaults, the plain-

tiff could invoke prevention. Criminal assaults are not reasonably foreseeable, and the plaintiff does not assume the risk of their occurrence.
2. The defendant's act was intentional or negligent.
3. The defendant's act caused the plaintiff's failure of condition.

Our fact situation is a construction contract. The plaintiff general contractor did not complete the construction project, but the reason for the plaintiff's failure was that the landowner's employees barred the plaintiff's crew for the work site. The plaintiff must show that the defendant's act was wrongful. The defendant would not have the right to bar the plaintiff from the site (and thereby terminate the contract) unless the plaintiff had already committed a material breach of duty. The plaintiff should negate a material breach in the plaintiff's case-in-chief; the plaintiff should present testimony that the plaintiff had strictly or substantially complied with the contract specifications. The plaintiff would give the following testimony to trigger the prevention excuse:

Q   What, if anything, unusual happened on September 2d?   (1)
A   The defendant's employees barred my crew from the work site.
Q   How do you know that?   (1)
A   I always ride to the project with the crew in the morning. When we got there, the gate was down and locked. The defendant's employees were standing by the gate.
Q   What happened when you saw the gate closed and locked?   (1)
A   I asked the defendant's employees what was going on. They said they had strict orders not to let me or my crew on the site.
Q   What did you do then?   (2)
A   I phoned the defendant immediately.
Q   Whom did you speak with?   (2)
A   The defendant himself.
Q   How do you know it was the defendant?   (2)
A   I've known him for easily seven years. I'm very familiar with his voice, and I recognized it at the other end of the line.
Q   What did you tell the defendant?   (2)
A   Pardon my French, but I told him that I wanted to know what in the hell was going on.
Q   What did he say?   (2)
A   He was real insulting. He said that any idiot would realize what was going on: he was firing me.
Q   What did you say?   (2)
A   I demanded to know why.
Q   How did he answer you?   (2)
A   He said he had legal grounds for doing it.
Q   What did you say then?   (2)
A   Again, excuse me. I told him to cut out the legal bullshit and tell me what the so-called legal grounds were.
Q   How did he answer you?   (2)

A   He said that his attorney said there were legal grounds and that that was
    all I was entitled to know.
Q   Until this day, how far had you progressed in the construction project?
    (1)
A   We were about half-way done.
Q   How far behind schedule were you?   (1)
A   That's the crazy thing. We weren't behind schedule at all. As far as I
    knew, we were bringing it in right on time.
Q   How had you deviated from the specifications in the contract?   (1)
A   We hadn't. I can only tell you what I knew, but I thought that we had
    done everything according to the specs. That's why I phoned the defen-
    dant. I wanted to know where we had fouled up, and he wouldn't tell me.
Q   Why didn't you complete the construction project?   (3)
A   The only reason was the defendant's interference.
Q   What capability did you have to complete the project?   (3)
A   I had everything I needed. I was ready, willing, and able to do it; and I
    would have done it if the defendant and his goons hadn't kept us off the
    work site.

LEGAL RESEARCH REFERENCE:
Murray §187

b.   Prospective Failure of Conditioned Duty

The law does not favor the waste of economic resources. It is a futile
waste of resources for the plaintiff to fulfill a condition to the defendant's
duty when the defendant has already indicated that the defendant will not
perform his or her duty. The policy of avoiding economic waste has
prompted the courts to formulate another excuse—prospective failure of the
conditioned duty. The *duty* the doctrine refers to is the defendant's duty.
The *prospective failure* mentioned in the doctrine's title is a certainty or
probability that the defendant will not perform the duty. If that certainty or
probability arises, the excuse doctrine comes into play. The legal consequences of the doctrine depend upon whether the prospective failure is certain or merely probable.

In some cases, it will be certain that the defendant cannot perform.
Suppose that on September 1st, the plaintiff contracts to buy the defendant's
automobile for $5,000. The contract provides that the plaintiff must put $500
down and pay the balance on the day set for delivery, September 20th. On
September 10th, through the defendant's negligence, the car is destroyed.[4]
The plaintiff would ordinarily have to tender the $4,500 on September 20th
to activate the defendant's duty to deliver. However, since it is certain that
the defendant cannot perform, the condition of tendering $4,500 is perma-
nently excused; the plaintiff can sue the defendant for breach without tendering the balance. The foundation is proof that

1. It became certain that the defendant could not perform his or her
   duty under the contract.

2. The plaintiff could and would have fulfilled the condition to the defendant's duty.
3. Because of the certainty that the defendant would not perform the duty, the plaintiff refrained from fulfilling the condition.

The plaintiff could testify:

Q What, if anything, unusual happened on the evening of September 10th? (1)
A That night, while I was at home, the defendant phoned.
Q What did the defendant say? (1)
A He said that he was sorry but his car had just been totally destroyed by fire.
Q What did you do then? (1)
A I drove right over to the defendant's car lot to inspect the car.
Q What did you see when you arrived? (1)
A The car was just a heap. It was burned to a cinder.
Q How do you know that it was the car you had contracted to buy? (1)
A The license number was the same, and the car had some special features like spoke wheels that helped me identify it.
Q How much money were you supposed to pay the defendant on September 20th? (2)
A I was supposed to give him the balance of $4,500.
Q How much did you give him that day? (2)
A Nothing.
Q What was your financial position on September 20th? (2)
A It was good. I could have paid him the money.
Q Why didn't you? (3)
A It was just a waste. I knew he couldn't deliver the car, so I didn't hand over any more money. In fact, he was refusing to return my down payment. I couldn't believe him!

In other cases, it is merely probable that the defendant will not perform. If the failure is probable rather than certain, the excuse is temporary at first; as soon as the 51% probability of failure arises, the plaintiff may suspend fulfillment of the condition. Uniform Commercial Code 2-609(1) recognizes the plaintiff's right in this situation "to suspend any performance for which he has not already received the agreed return." If the defendant removes the uncertainty in time to permit the plaintiff to fulfill the condition, the condition is reinstated. If the defendant does not remove the uncertainty in time, the excuse becomes permanent. The foundation for this variation of the doctrine is the following:

1. It became probable that the defendant could not perform his or her duty under the contract.
2. The plaintiff then suspended fulfillment of the conditions to the defendant's duty.
3. In the interim before the due date before the defendant's performance, the defendant did not remove the uncertainty about his or her performance.

4. In reliance, the plaintiff failed to fulfill the condition.
5. The plaintiff had the ability to fulfill the condition.

Suppose that on October 1st, the plaintiff contracted to sell a generator to the defendant. Under the contract, the plaintiff was to put the generator in place on October 10th and complete installation on October 20th. On October 5th, the defendant called the plaintiff to inform the plaintiff that the defendant would not accept delivery. The plaintiff's testimony attempts to invoke the prospective failure excuse:

Q   What, if anything, unusual happened on October 5th?   (1)
A   I had a phone call from the defendant.
Q   How do you know that it was the defendant?   (1)
A   I can recognize his voice.
Q   How did you become familiar with his voice?   (1)
A   We've been acquaintances for the past eight years. We've spoken on numerous occasions.
Q   What did the defendant say when he called?   (1)
A   He said he was calling the deal off. I guess someone had offered to sell him another generator for about $15,000 less.
Q   What did you say to the defendant?   (1)
A   I said that a contract's a contract and I expected him to live up to his word.
Q   What were you supposed to do on October 10th?   (2)
A   The contract called for us to deliver the generator then and set it in place in the defendant's factory.
Q   What did you do that day?   (2)
A   I phoned the defendant. When he repeated that he wouldn't accept delivery, I told the delivery crew that it was no use driving out there with the generator.
Q   What contact did you have with the defendant between October 10th and October 20th?   (3)
A   I called him a couple of times and asked whether he had seen the light and was gonna take the generator.
Q   What did he say?   (3)
A   In no uncertain terms, he said he wouldn't take it. He told me that I could take a leap.
Q   What were you supposed to do on October 20th?   (4)
A   We were supposed to complete installation of the generator at the defendant's plant.
Q   What did you do?   (4)
A   Nothing.
Q   Why didn't you try to complete installation that day?   (4)
A   He had made it crystal clear to me that he wouldn't accept or pay for the generator.
Q   What capability did you have to deliver and install the generator that day?   (5)
A   We could have done it easily. I had the generator, the delivery trucks, and

the installation crew. The only reason we didn't do it was that the defendant kept insisting that the deal was off.

LEGAL RESEARCH REFERENCE:
Murray §178-82, 188

c. Waiver

The defendant's conduct may have the effect of waiving the plaintiff's condition to the defendant's duty. There are three types of waiver.

1. *Estoppel waiver*

To prove an estoppel waiver, the plaintiff must show that

1. The defendant engaged in certain voluntary conduct.
2. The defendant's conduct created a reasonable belief in the plaintiff's mind that the defendant would not insist on the fulfillment of the condition.
3. Given that belief, the plaintiff failed to fulfill the condition.
4. The plaintiff had the ability to fulfill the condition.

Suppose that the plaintiff contracts to build a warehouse for the defendant landowner. The contract provides that the plaintiff must complete the work in four stages. At the end of each stage, when the plaintiff furnishes the defendant with an architect's certificate of completion, the defendant will pay plaintiff 25% of the total price. When the plaintiff completed the first three parts of the project, the defendant paid the plaintiff without insisting upon the architect's certificate. The contract specified that the plaintiff would complete the work by July 30th and furnish the architect's certificate by August 10th. The plaintiff requested payment on August 10th, but the defendant notified the plaintiff on August 11th that the defendant would not pay because of the lack of the architect's certificate. To establish the estoppel excuse, the plaintiff would give the following testimony:

Q   Under the agreement, what were you supposed to do to obtain the progress payments?   (1)
A   I was supposed to complete the work and submit the architect's certificate of completion.
Q   When you completed the first stage and requested the defendant's progress payment, what did you submit to the defendant?   (1)
A   Just my letter asking for payment.
Q   When, if ever, did you give the defendant the architect's certificate?   (1)
A   I didn't. He paid without the certificate.
Q   What, if anything, did the defendant say about the certificate?   (1)
A   He said not to worry about getting one. He'd take my word, since we'd known each other for so long.
Q   What happened when you asked for the second payment?   (1)
A   The same thing. I asked for it, and he paid without a certificate.
Q   What about the third payment?   (1)

A   Again, he paid without insisting that I go to the trouble of obtaining a completion certificate from the architect.

Q   After the defendant paid three times without a certificate, what did you think you had to do to get the last payment?   (2)

A   I assumed that he'd take my word again. He never gave me any indication that he would demand a certificate.

Q   When you asked for the fourth and last payment, what did you submit to the defendant?   (3)

A   Just my letter—as I did three previous times.

Q   Why didn't you submit an architect's certificate?   (3)

A   As I just said, I honestly believed that the defendant wouldn't insist on one. The defendant's action has led me to believe that.

Q   When were you supposed to give the defendant the certificate according to the agreement?   (3)

A   On August 10th.

Q   When did you give the defendant your letter asking for the last payment?   (3)

A   On the 10th.

Q   How did the defendant answer your letter?   (3)

A   He said he wouldn't pay.

Q   When did he tell you that?   (3)

A   Not until August 11th.

Q   When you requested the last payment, how much of the project had you completed?   (4)

A   My crew had wrapped it up. We had finished the project.

Q   To the best of your knowledge, how did you deviate from the specifications in the contract?   (4)

A   We didn't. As far as I could tell, we had done everything according to the contract.

To corroborate his own testimony on element (4), the plaintiff should call the architect named in the contract or another expert to testify that the work conformed to the contract specifications.

2. Election waiver

To establish an election waiver, the plaintiff should show that

1. At a certain point in the performance of the contract, the plaintiff failed to fulfill a condition.
2. The plaintiff's failure put the defendant to an election between inconsistent rights.
3. The defendant elected to exercise the right that entailed waiving the plaintiff's failure of condition.

Our fact situation is another construction contract. The contract contains a "time of the essence" clause, and the clause applies to the landowner's progress payments. The general contractor completed the first stage of work. The contractor then requested payment from the landowner and submitted a proper architect's certificate. The landowner delayed paying for two days.

Since time was of the essence, the landowner's delay was not only a failure of the landowner's condition to the contractor's duty to continue work; the delay was also a material breach of the landowner's duty to pay. Because the delay was a material breach, it put the contractor to an election between inconsistent rights: (1) treat the delay as a material breach and terminate the contract immediately; or (2) treat the delay as a minor breach and continue the contract. The contractor accepted the late payment and continued work for two days. Then the contractor changed his mind and decided to abandon the project. The landowner is the plaintiff. The defendant contractor argues that he is not guilty of a breach because the condition of payment on time failed. The plaintiff counters with the argument that there was an election waiver of the failure of condition. The plaintiff testifies:

Q   Please read paragraph four of exhibit one (the contract) to the jury.   (2)
A   Yes. It says: "Time is of the essence of this agreement. The builder's work and the landowner's payments must both be strictly on time."
Q   Under the agreement, when were you supposed to pay the defendant for the first phase of the work?   (1)
A   On the tenth of the month.
Q   When did you pay the defendant?   (1)
A   On the 12th of the month.
Q   What did the defendant do when you offered the late payment to him? (3)
A   He accepted it.
Q   How did the work at the site progress between the 10th and the 12th? (3)
A   The defendant kept his crew working even though my payment was late.

3.   Intentional waiver

The intentional waiver doctrine decrees that even absent an estoppel or election, the defendant may intentionally waive the right to insist upon the plaintiff's fulfillment of a condition. Some jurisdictions do not recognize this doctrine at all; they insist that there be consideration or a consideration substitute for a waiver. Other courts apply the doctrine only to minor conditions in the contract. A minority of courts purports to apply the doctrine across the board. Most of the cases announcing this broad excuse doctrine are insurance cases; the court finds that the insurance company representative waived a condition to the company's duty to pay benefits. To lay a solid factual foundation for this doctrine, the plaintiff should show that

1. The defendant knew that the defendant had the right to insist upon the plaintiff's fulfillment of the condition.
2. Nevertheless, the defendant voluntarily waived the condition.

Our fact situation is an insurance contract case. The contract provided that the insured had to submit proof of loss within 30 days after the incident. In this case, the plaintiff insured suffered a fire loss but did not submit proof until June 20th, 35 days after the loss. The plaintiff had just testified that she entered the office of the insurance company representative, Mr. Francis, on the 20th:

Q   Under exhibit one (the insurance policy), when were you supposed to give Mr. Francis the proof of loss?
A   I was supposed to do that within 30 days after the loss.
Q   When did the fire occur?
A   It happened on May 15th.
Q   When did you go to Mr. Francis' office to give him the proof of loss?
A   I'm afraid that I was late. I didn't get there until the 20th of June.
Q   What did you tell Mr. Francis when you went to his office?   (1)
A   I told him that I was sorry I was late with the proof.
Q   What did you tell him about the date when you should have submitted the proof?   (1)
A   I told him I knew that it should have been in by the 15th.

[*The plaintiff's statements put Francis on notice that the condition had already failed.*]

Q   What did Mr. Francis do when you handed him your proof?   (2)
A   He accepted it.
Q   What force, if any, did you use to get him to accept the proof?   (2)
A   None.
Q   What threats, if any, did you make to get him to accept your proof?   (2)
A   None.
Q   What, if anything, did he say about the lateness of your proof?   (2)
A   He told me not to worry about it because the date was just a technical part of the policy.

By proving the conditions' fulfillment or excuse, the plaintiff thus establishes the third element of his or her theory. The conditions' fulfillment or excuse activates the defendant's duty of immediate performance. The plaintiff should now proceed to prove the defendant's breach of duty.

LEGAL RESEARCH REFERENCE:
Murray §§189-91, 193

CHECKLIST FOR PROVING THE SATISFACTION OF THE CONDITIONS TO THE DEFENDANT'S DUTY

____ The plaintiff fulfilled the condition.

    ____ The event constituting the condition occurred.

        or

    ____ The condition was that the plaintiff's goods or services have a certain quality, and they possessed that quality.

OR

____ The technical failure of condition was excused.

    ____ The plaintiff substantially performed the condition.

        or

    ____ The fulfillment of the condition became impossible.

        or

    ____ An excuse is necessary to prevent the plaintiff from suffering a severe forfeiture.

        or

    ____ The defendant's wrongful conduct prevented or hindered the fulfillment of the condition.

        or

    ____ It became probable that the defendant would not perform the conditioned duty.

        or

    ____ The defendant waived the condition.

        ____ Estoppel waiver

            or

        ____ Election waiver

            or

        ____ Intentional waiver

FOOTNOTES

[1] T. Mauet, Fundamentals of Trial Techniques 207 (1980).

[2] *Id.*

[3] This section is based on E. Imwinkelried, Evidentiary Foundations 63 (Michie/Bobbs-Merrill, 1980).

[4] We are assuming the defendant's negligence to make this hypothetical more realistic. If the car were destroyed without the defendant's negligence, the defendant could probably invoke impossibility to discharge his duty. In this situation, the plaintiff probably would not sue at all. Suit is a realistic possibility only when there is some evidence of the defendant's negligence.

CHAPTER 8

How to Establish the Defendant's Breach of Duty—The Fourth Element of the Plaintiff's Theory

Sec. 8-1.   Introduction

In the last chapter, we discussed the methods of proving that all the conditions to the defendant's duty have been fulfilled or excused—the third element of the plaintiff's theory. If all the conditions are fulfilled or excused, the defendant's duty is activated; that is, the duty becomes a duty of immediate performance. The next part of the plaintiff's theory is proof that the duty was not performed. If the plaintiff proves that the duty was not performed and the defendant does not establish a discharge for the duty (Chapter 14, *infra*), the defendant is guilty of an actionable breach of contract.

This chapter first analyzes the methods of establishing that the defendant's duty was breached. The last two sections of this chapter deal with characterizing the breach as material or minor. The legal consequences of a breach depend largely upon whether the breach is material or minor. For example, the remedies available for the breach vary, depending upon whether the breach is material or minor.

LEGAL RESEARCH REFERENCE:
Murray §§135, 168, 206, 215

Sec. 8-2. Establishing the Defendant's Breach of Duty

There are two types of breach: present and anticipatory.

a. Present Breach of Duty

1. *An affirmative act*

Proving a present breach of duty is a relatively simple matter. In some cases, the breach is an affirmative act by the defendant. Suppose that the defendant is the plaintiff's former employee. As part of the original employment contract, the defendant had made a non-competitive promise; the defendant promised that if he left the plaintiff's employ, the defendant would not engage in a competitive business in the same metropolitan area for a two-year period. After quitting the plaintiff's firm, the defendant immediately opened a competitive business. The breach is the affirmative act of starting the competitive business.

When the defendant's breach is an affirmative act, the plaintiff may use basically the same evidentiary techniques outlined in Section 7-2 of the previous chapter. One difference is that if the plaintiff uses documentary proof at trial, it is likely that the plaintiff will be resorting to the defendant's records rather than to the plaintiff's own records. The defendant's records can be introduced as admissions under Federal Evidence Rule 801(d)(2). The plaintiff will have to authenticate the records as documents obtained during pretrial discovery, but the plaintiff will not have to lay the complex business entry foundation under Evidence Rule 803(6). A second difference is that if the defendant retains the original record, the plaintiff can rely on Federal Evidence Rule 1004(3) (original in opponent's possession) to satisfy the best evidence rule.

2. *Negative evidence*

PROOF OF THE FAILURE TO PERFORM AN ACT

In other cases, the breach is negative in nature: The defendant breached because *the defendant did not perform an act* or because the merchandise the defendant delivered lacked a quality required by the contract.

In Uniform Commercial Code litigation, the plaintiff must often prove two negative failures on the part of the defendant. Uniform Commercial Code 2-508(1) provides that "[w]here any tender or delivery by the seller is rejected because non-conforming and the time for performance has not yet expired, the seller may seasonably notify the buyer of his intention to cure and may then, within the contract time, make a conforming delivery." To prove a breach and defeat the defendant's right to cure under U.C.C. 2-508(1), the plaintiff must prove not only the defendant's initial failure to perform; the plaintiff must also show a failure to cure:

Q   What happened when the defendant delivered the goods to you on July 5th?   [INITIAL FAILURE]

A   I rejected them.

Q   Why did you reject them?   [INITIAL FAILURE]

A   They didn't conform to the contract. They were the wrong color and size.

Q   Under the agreement, what was the latest date on which the defendant could deliver?   [FAILURE TO CURE]

A   July 10th.

Q   Why did you choose that date in the contract?

A   I had to have them ready to ship to my buyer by the 11th. If I didn't receive the goods by the 10th, there was just no way I could meet my deadline.

Q   Before the 10th, what efforts, if any, did the defendant make to correct the defects in the shipment the defendant sent you?   [FAILURE TO CURE]

A   None.

Q   What new goods, if any, arrived from the defendant by the 10th? [FAILURE TO CURE]

A   None.

Q   What assurance, if any, did the defendant give you that he would correct the color and size problem?   [FAILURE TO CURE]

A   None.

The plaintiff can often use the plaintiff's own records to show that the defendant did not perform a required act. For instance, assume that the defendant breached by not paying for goods the plaintiff delivered. The plaintiff may prove that the plaintiff's records do not reflect the receipt of any payment from the defendant. Federal Evidence Rule 803(7) authorizes the admission of "evidence that a matter is not included in the memoranda, reports, records, or data compilations, in any form, kept in accordance with the provisions of paragraph (6), to prove the nonoccurrence or nonexistence of the matter, if the matter was of a kind of which a memorandum, report, record, or data compilation was regularly made and preserved. . . ." The plaintiff argues that the lack of a record of payment proves that payment never occurred.

The probative value of this negative evidence depends upon the plaintiff's proof that the plaintiff's employees maintain accurate, complete records. The plaintiff could put one of the plaintiff's bookkeepers or accountants on the witness stand:

Q   What information do you record in the ledgers for the individual clients?

A   All the debits and credits—all the debits representing goods delivered to that client, and all the credits representing payments by the client on the account.

Q   What percentage of the payments is supposed to be recorded in the ledger?

A   100%. Our records people are supposed to make certain that all payments are properly credited to the customers' accounts.

Q   How long have you worked in records?

A   As I previously testified, I've worked there about 11 years. I've been employed there ever since I graduated from the University of Pennsylvania.

Q   During those 11 years, to the best of your knowledge, how many times have the bookkeeping personnel failed to properly credit a customer's account with a payment?

A   It happens but only very rarely. I'd say I've discovered only about an error a year.

Q   During the average year, how many payments credit entries does the bookkeeping department make in all the customers' ledgers?

A   I can't give you a specific number, but I know that the number has to be in the several thousands.

This foundation gives the plaintiff the ammunition for arguing during summation that if the plaintiff's records do not reflect the defendant's payment, the only reasonable inference is that the defendant did not make the payment.

PROOF OF LACK OF A QUALITY

The negative breach of duty may be that *the goods the defendant delivered lacked a quality required by the contract.* The merchandise may lack physical properties specified in the contract; or given their physical properties, the goods may not satisfy a contract description such as "merchantable" or "first-rate quality." Proving the lack of quality may necessitate the type of expert testimony analyzed in Section 7-3 in the last chapter.

The predicate for the expert testimony will often include proof of the goods' chain of custody between the time of defendant's delivery and the time of the expert analysis. The defendant may argue that the merchandise lacked the required quality at the time of analysis because of rough handling by the plaintiff's employees after the defendant's delivery. The plaintiff's proof of chain of custody should negate mishandling. The plaintiff could first call the employee in charge of the warehouse:

Q   Where was the barrel kept?

A   We kept it in the acids part of our supply warehouse.

Q   Who has access to that part of the warehouse?

A   Access is limited to authorized personnel. When you've got acid sitting around, you don't let anybody and his uncle come into contact with it.

Q   How do you limit the access to that part of the warehouse?

A   We keep it under lock and key.

Q   Who has the key?

A   I have one, my assistant has one, and there's a third key at headquarters.

Q   What happened to the barrels after you placed them in the acids part of the warehouse?

A   They just sat there for several days. As far as I know, nothing unusual happened.

Q   What happened then?

A   Then the boss had one of the barrels sent over to the lab for testing.

Q   How was the barrel sent to the laboratory?

A   One of the guys from delivery, Jake, picked it up and took it over there.

The plaintiff can then call Jake, the delivery person:

Q   Where were you on the morning of March 13th of this year?

A   I was at work.

Q   What did you do that morning?

A   I had orders to pick up a barrel of the phosphoric acid from the warehouse and take it over to the lab.

Q   How did you do that?

A   First I checked in at the warehouse, and the guy in charge showed me the barrel I was supposed to get to the lab.

Q   How did you get it to the laboratory?

A   I loaded it on one of our vans and drove it over.

Q   How did you load the barrel into the van?

A   I personally carried it.

Q   What accidents, if any, did you have while you were loading it into the van?

A   I didn't have any accident. Everything went fine.

Q   How long a trip is to the laboratory?

A   It's only about five minutes from the warehouse. I drove straight over there.

Q   What, if anything, unusual happened during the trip?

A   Nothing. I wasn't involved in any collisions or anything like that.

Q   What happened when you arrived at the laboratory?

A   I gave them the barrel for analysis.

LEGAL RESEARCH REFERENCE:
Murray §§135, 206

b.   Anticipatory Breach of Duty

In addition to recognizing present breaches, Anglo-American law posits the possibility that the defendant can breach before the due date for performance. A contract gives the plaintiff a legally protected expectation of future performance by the defendant, and the defendant's words and acts before the due date for performance may impair that expectation. This doctrine is called *anticipatory breach*.

1.   At common law

In order to prove an anticipatory breach at common law, the plaintiff must lay the following foundation:

1. The defendant repudiated the defendant's duty under the contract.
2. The defendant did not retract the repudiation.
3. The plaintiff elected to treat the repudiation as a present breach of duty.

REPUDIATION

The first step is proving that the defendant expressly or impliedly repudiated a duty under the contract. The plaintiff must prove that the defendant positively stated that he or she would or could not perform the duty: "I shall not perform" or "I cannot perform." The plaintiff could testify:

Q Where were you on the afternoon of July 12th of this year?   (1)
A I was sitting in my office in Albuquerque.
Q What happened that morning?   (1)
A I received a phone call from the defendant.
Q How do you know that the caller was the defendant?   (1)
A I recognized her voice.
Q How did you become familiar with her voice?   (1)
A I've had business dealings with her for the past couple of years, and we've spoken many times.
Q What was she calling about?   (1)
A She wanted to talk about the delivery she was supposed to make in September.
Q What did she say about the delivery?   (1)
A She said that she was not going to be able to do it.
Q To the best of your recollection, what were her precise words?   (1)
A I think she said, "I just am not going to be able to make that deadline."

The plaintiff may also prove an implied repudiation. The courts often refer to an implied repudiation as a *voluntary disablement.* The defendant impliedly manifests an intent to repudiate by voluntarily performing an act that disables the defendant from performing. For example, the defendant may sell the subject matter of the contract to a third party without reserving a right to repurchase. That act gives rise to a strong inference that the defendant intends to repudiate the contract with the plaintiff. Assume that on August 4th, the plaintiff contracted to buy a particular car from an auto dealer and that the dealer was supposed to deliver the car to the plaintiff on August 30th. The plaintiff could testify:

Q What happened on the afternoon of August 10th?   (1)
A I was driving by the dealership, and I thought I'd just stop and take a look at the car. They were supposed to be putting a luggage rack on top and installing an FM radio, so I thought I'd check to see how the work on the accessories was coming.
Q What happened when you stopped by the dealership?   (1)
A First I noticed that the car was not on the showroom floor any more.
Q What did you do then?   (1)
A I went into the workshop to see if they were doing the installation.

Q   What did you see in the workshop?   (1)
A   The real question is what I didn't see. I didn't see my car anywhere.
Q   What did you do then?   (1)
A   I went to see the manager.
Q   What happened then?   (1)
A   I found him and asked him where my car was. He said that that car had been sold to somebody on the 6th and that they had picked it up the next day.
Q   What did you say then?   (1)
A   I asked him how they were going to get the car back for me.
Q   How did the manager answer your question?   (1)
A   He said flatly that they couldn't get the car back. He told me that they had sold it unconditionally to this other guy.

RETRACTION

The second step is proving that the defendant did not retract the repudiation before the plaintiff's election. Assume that the plaintiff's election occurs on August 20th. The plaintiff has just testified that the defendant repudiated on August 10th:

Q   What contact, if any, did you have with the defendant between August 10th and August 20th?   (2)
A   I phoned the dealership's manager twice.
Q   How did you know that it was the manager you spoke with?   (2)
A   As I said, I'd talked to him at the showroom; and so I could recognize his voice.
Q   Why did you phone the manager?   (2)
A   I wanted to know whether they'd made arrangements to get my car back.
Q   What response did the manager give you the first time you called?   (2)
A   He said that nothing had changed. They'd sold the car and that was that.
Q   What response did the manager give you the second time you called? (2)
A   After I identified myself, he hung up on me.
Q   What other contact did you have with the defendant before August 20th? (2)
A   None. I didn't call them, and they didn't call me.

ELECTION

The final step is establishing that the plaintiff elected to treat the defendant's repudiation as a present breach of duty. An anticipatory breach is a peculiar type of breach; it does not become a material breach until the plaintiff elects to treat it as a present breach. There are several methods of election. In every jurisdiction, the plaintiff can make an effective election by materially changing position in reliance on the defendant's repudiation. The plaintiff's acts must amount to a change of position, the change must be in reliance on the defendant's repudiation, and the change must be both material and reasonable. After testifying about the auto dealership's implied repudiation, the plaintiff could add:

Q   What, if anything, did you do on August 20th?   (3) [CHANGE OF PO-
SITION]

A   I bought a car from another dealer, Delta Cars, on Potomac Street.

Q   What type of car did you buy from Delta Cars?   (3)

A   The same make, model, and year car the defendant had promised to sell
me.

Q   When you say you "bought" the car, what do you mean?   (3)

A   We signed all the papers, and I even took possession that day.

Q   Why did you buy the car on August 20th?   (3) [REASONABLE]

A   I needed a car badly before the end of the month, and it was apparent at
that point that the defendant didn't intend to honor its promise.

Q   Why did you need the car before the end of the month?   (3)

A   I had a new job as a traveling salesman for a pharmaceutical company,
and I was supposed to hit the road for my new employer on September
1st. I just couldn't wait any longer to get another car.

Q   How many auto dealerships other than Delta Cars did you contact?   (3)

A   Four others.

Q   Why did you buy the car from Delta Cars?   (3)

A   Next to the defendant, they offered me the lowest price and the best deal.

Q   What was the purchase price of the new car?   (3) [MATERIAL]

A   It was $7,600, a couple of hundred more than the defendant was going to
charge me.

Q   How large was your down payment?   (3)

A   Because I wanted the car on such short notice, Delta demanded a big
down—almost $2,000. That was more than twice what I was supposed to
pay up front on the car from the defendant.

Q   How did that down payment affect the balance of your savings accounts?
(3)

A   It just about wiped them out. After making the down, I had a little under
$300 left in savings.

The plaintiff may also elect by filing suit. The plaintiff could describe
filing suit:

Q   What, if anything, did you do on August 19th?   (3)

A   I visited you at your office.

Q   Why did you do that?   (3)

A   I wanted to see what my legal rights were against the defendant.

Q   What did I advise you to do?   (3)

A   You recommended that I file suit against the defendant.

Q   What, if anything, happened on August 20th?   (3)

A   We filed the suit.

Q   When you say "filed suit," what do you mean?   (3)

A   You had me sign the complaint, and we went down to court to give it to
the clerk.

Q   What amount, if any, did you have to pay to get the clerk to accept your
complaint?   (3)

A   I guess you're referring to the filing fee.

Q   Yes. What was the filing fee?   (3)
A   I think it was $30.
Q   What fee did I charge you for filing suit?   (3)
A   Right off the bat, even before we walked over to the clerk's office, I paid you $115.

Finally, in a growing number of jurisdictions, the plaintiff may elect by simply informing the defendant that the plaintiff has decided to treat the repudiation as a present breach of contract:

Q   What, if anything, did you do on August 20th?   (3)
A   I was fed up with the defendant, so I marched down to their dealership to confront them.
Q   What happened when you arrived there?   (3)
A   I met the manager and had a conversation with him.
Q   What was the conversation about?   (3)
A   We had a heated discussion about their refusal to deliver the car to me.
Q   What did you say to the manager?   (3)
A   I told him that I was giving them one last chance to make good on their promise to deliver the car.
Q   What did the manager say?   (3)
A   He said that if he'd told me once, he'd told me ten times that they couldn't deliver the car.
Q   What did you say then?   (3)
A   I told him that as far as I was concerned, they'd broken their contract with me.
Q   What, if anything, did you say you were going to do?   (3)
A   I told him that I would hold them responsible for my loss and that they'd probably see me in court pretty soon.

LEGAL RESEARCH REFERENCE
Murray §§207-14

2. *Under the Uniform Commercial Code*

The Code makes it easier for the plaintiff to resort to the anticipatory breach doctrine. At common law, to trigger the doctrine, the defendant's repudiation must be positive and unequivocal. Uniform Commercial Code 2-609(1) relaxes that standard; it states:

> A contract for sale imposes an obligation on each party that the other's expectation of receiving due performance will not be impaired. When *reasonable grounds for insecurity* arise with respect to the performance of either party, the other may in writing demand adequate assurance of due performance. . . .

Even if the defendant's statement falls short of a positive, unequivocal repudiation, the statement may create reasonable grounds for insecurity. Thus, the plaintiff could invoke 2-609(1) by testifying:

Q   Where were you on the afternoon of July 12th of this year?
A   I was sitting in my office in Albuquerque.
Q   What happened that morning?
A   I received a phone call from the defendant.
Q   How do you know that the caller was the defendant?
A   I recognized her voice.
Q   How did you become familiar with her voice?
A   I've had business dealings with her for the past couple of years, and we've spoken many times.
Q   What was she calling about?
A   She wanted to talk about the delivery she was supposed to make in September.
Q   What did she say about the delivery?
A   She said that there had been a work stoppage at her mine in Montana and that there was a good chance that she could not deliver on time.
Q   To the best of your recollection, what were her precise words?
A   I think she said, "It's probable that we may not be able to get that ore shipment to you to make that deadline."

The report giving rise to the reasonable ground for security need not emanate from the defendant; the plaintiff might receive a credit report indicating that the defendant is fast approaching insolvency. So long as there is an objectively "reasonable" ground for the plaintiff to believe that the defendant will not perform, the plaintiff can resort to 2-609(1).

The plaintiff resorts to 2-609(1) by making a demand "in writing" for "adequate assurance of due performance." After testifying to the grounds for insecurity, the plaintiff should establish that the plaintiff made the demand. The plaintiff should authenticate a copy of the written demand sent to the defendant and quote the key passages:

Q   Please read paragraph four of the exhibit to the jurors.
A   Yes. It reads: "During our recent telephone conversation, you told me that the work stoppage at your Montana mine threatens to interfere with the delivery schedule for the ore shipments. My attorney has advised me that your statements give us 'reasonable grounds for insecurity' about your performance. Consequently, under the provisions of Uniform Commercial Code 2-609(1), I hereby demand an adequate assurance of due, future performance."

The original demand is the letter sent to the defendant. The plaintiff's copy may qualify as an original under Federal Evidence Rule 1001(3) or a duplicate under 1001(4). Alternatively, the plaintiff may satisfy the best evidence rule under Rule 1004(3) (original in opponent's possession).

The defendant must respond to the plaintiff's demand. Uniform Commercial Code 2-609(4) prescribes the effect of the defendant's failure to respond:

After receipt of a justified demand, failure to provide within a reasonable time not exceeding thirty days such assurance of due performance as is adequate under the circumstances of the particular case is a repudiation of the contract.

The plaintiff may show either that the defendant did not respond at all or that the defendant's response was inadequate. Hence, the plaintiff could testify:

Q   When did you mail this demand to the defendant?
A   I did so on March 1st of this year.
Q   How long does it usually take mail to reach Minneapolis?
A   Three days.
Q   How do you know that?
A   I've corresponded with the defendant on numerous occasions, and she'll sometimes phone to acknowledge receipt of my letter.
Q   What response, if any, did you receive from the defendant before April 5th?
A   I didn't receive any response to my letter. Not a word.

Or the plaintiff could testify:

Q   Where were you on the morning of March 10th of this year?
A   I was sitting in my office.
Q   What happened that morning?
A   The defendant called from Minneapolis.
Q   What did the defendant say?
A   First she said that she had my letter demanding assurance of performance.
Q   What assurance did she give you?
A   She didn't.
Q   What were her precise words?
A   As best I remember, she said that she'd been working to end the strike but to no avail. The miners just seemed adamant in their wage demands.
Q   What did you say then?
A   I told her that that was no improvement. I said I wanted some indication that she was going to be able to deliver.
Q   How did she respond?
A   She said she was sorry, but her negotiators hadn't made any headway in resolving the work stoppage.

If the defendant does not give adequate assurance of due performance, the plaintiff may then elect under Uniform Commercial Code 2-611(1). Section 2-611(1) permits the plaintiff to elect by materially changing position or indicating to the defendant "that he (the plaintiff) considers the repudiation final."

LEGAL RESEARCH REFERENCE:
White & Summers §6-7

Sec. 8-3. Establishing the Materiality of the Defendant's Breach of Duty—The General Factors Determining Materiality

As previously stated, the legal consequences of the defendant's breach of duty depend upon whether the breach is material (major, total) or minor (immaterial, partial, collateral). If the breach is minor, the contract continues in existence; the innocent plaintiff may suspend his own performance until the guilty defendant cures; the plaintiff has a cause of action for the actual damage caused by defendant's breach;[1] and in some jurisdictions, as under Uniform Commercial Code 2-717, the innocent plaintiff may deduct the amount of actual damage from any sum the plaintiff must pay under the contract.

The effect of a material breach is markedly different. In most cases,[2] the defendant's material breach puts the plaintiff to an election. On the one hand, the plaintiff may treat the breach as a minor breach and continue the contract. On the other hand, the plaintiff may elect to terminate the contract and sue for total damages for material breach.[3]

The question next arises as to what factors the courts look to in determining whether to characterize a breach as material or minor. Section 275 of the first Restatement of Contracts contains a helpful list of factors.

LEGAL RESEARCH REFERENCE:
Murray §§168-69

a. The Extent to Which the Plaintiff Has Already Received Substantially What He Bargained For

Section 275(a) states that in deciding whether a breach is material, the court should weigh "the extent to which the injured party will obtain the substantial benefit which he could have reasonably anticipated." If the court characterizes the defendant's breach as material, the defendant cannot recover on the contract and may suffer a severe forfeiture. The general feeling is that a harsh forfeiture is unwarranted if at the point of breach, the plaintiff has already received basically what he or she bargained for. The task facing the plaintiff's attorney is to demonstrate that at the point of breach, the plaintiff had not received any substantial benefit.

Suppose that the plaintiff runs a brokerage house. The plaintiff hired the defendant as a stock broker. Under the contract, the defendant would attend a three-month training course and then work as a broker for plaintiff for two years. The defendant quit before completing the training program. The plaintiff testifies:

Q Why did you hire the defendant?
A Her business background and personality led me to believe that she would be an excellent broker.
Q When did you hire her?

A   She joined our brokerage house in February of this year.

Q   What sort of work was she supposed to do at first?

A   I guess you really shouldn't call it work at all. We have a three-month training program that all new employees go through before we turn them loose to begin working with clients.

Q   During this training program, what income does a new employee create for your business?

A   None. The months the employee spends in the training program are not money makers for us. Rather, they cost us; we're paying both the employee and the trainers, and the employee isn't generating any income for us. They only begin bringing in money after the training program when they're dealing with clients.

Q   When did the defendant tell you she was quitting?

A   In early March.

Q   At that time, how much of the training program had she completed?

A   She hadn't even reached the halfway point yet.

Q   As a trainee, how much income had she generated for your business?

A   None. She hadn't persuaded a single client to buy or sell a single share of stock yet.

b.   The Extent to Which the Plaintiff Can Be Adequately Compensated for the Defendant's Breach

If the court holds that the defendant's breach was minor, the plaintiff must be content with the defendant's performance to the time of breach and money for the actual damages caused by the minor breach. That result is just when the court can calculate the damages caused by the breach with reasonable certainty. However, the more difficult it is to compute damages, the less certain we can be that the plaintiff is receiving fair compensation. Hence, the more difficult it is to compute damages, the more likely the court is to characterize the breach as material. In the words of §275(b), the court must consider "the extent to which the injured party may be adequately compensated in damages for lack of complete performance." The plaintiff's attorney attempts to establish the difficulty of computing damages.

Suppose that the defendant contracted to sell the plaintiff some antique furniture including a loveseat. The defendant delivered all the furniture except the loveseat. The plaintiff herself is an antique dealer and can give expert testimony. She is testifying to show the difficulty of computing the damages caused by the defendant's failure to deliver the loveseat:

Q   At the time of the scheduled delivery, what was the fair market value of the loveseat?

A   That's really difficult to say.

Q   Why?

A   Just stop to think about the expression you used, "fair market value." The expression suggests that there is a market and a market price that is easy to determine. You can't determine a price for an antique in the same way that you determine the price for a share of stock.

Q   What trade journals, if any, list market prices for antiques?

A   There really are none that do that. In the antique industry, there are journals that report prices paid for particular pieces recently purchased.

Q   How does the information in that journal differ from the information in a daily stock exchange listing?

A   The stock exchange listing gives you a price for a category of items, for example, a certain class of stock from a particular company. When you look at the journals in the antique industry, you'll find reports of prices for specific items sold; but the journal is not going to say that all French provincial loveseats from a particular year command $2,650. Designs differ, wood differs, the condition of the piece differs, and the buyer's style preferences differ. It's a very individualized thing.

c.   The Extent to Which the Defendant Has Already Performed

If the court holds the breach to be material, the defendant in effect forfeits the amount the defendant has spent in performance prior to breach; the defendant cannot sue on the contract to recover that amount. Consequently, the court is interested in the extent to which the defendant has already performed; that factor is important evidence of the forfeiture the defendant may suffer. Section 275(c) instructs the judge to consider "[t]he extent to which the party failing to perform has already partly performed or made preparations for performance." The earlier the breach, the more likely the court is to characterize the breach as material. Indeed, in a minority of jurisdictions, any breach *in limine* (at the outset of the contract) is considered material.

The plaintiff's attorney should attempt to show that in both an absolute and a relative sense, the defendant had rendered little performance prior to breach. In our hypothetical, the defendant is a contractor, and the plaintiff is a landowner. The defendant contractor walked off the job. The plaintiff testifies:

Q   When did the defendant begin work at the site?

A   It was April 1st of this year.

Q   How many days did the defendant's crew spend at the site? [ABSOLUTE NUMBERS]

A   Actually, it was less than five complete days.

Q   When you signed the contract, how long did the defendant estimate he would need to complete the project?   [RELATIVE NUMBERS]

A   He told me that they would need at least 100 complete workdays at the site.

The plaintiff may also show how little the defendant had accomplished before the breach:

Q   When the defendant walked off the site, how much work had the defendant completed?

A   His crew was still laying the foundation.

Q   How many floors had the defendant completed?

A   None. The foundation was going to be the floor of the basement.

Q   Under the agreement, how many stories was this building supposed to be?

A   Twenty-seven stories.

A chart, to scale and depicting both the work contemplated and the work completed, can graphically dramatize how little the defendant did.

Finally, the plaintiff may show how little the defendant spent in performance before the breach. During pretrial discovery, the plaintiff should obtain both the defendant's cost estimates and the documents reflecting the defendant's expenditures before breach. These documents may be introduced as admissions under Federal Evidence Rule 801(d)(2) and business entries under Rule 803(6).

LEGAL RESEARCH REFERENCE:
Murray §170

d. The Extent of the Hardship the Defendant Will Suffer If the Judge Characterizes the Breach as Material

If the court characterizes the breach as material, the defendant cannot sue on the contract. However, in many jurisdictions the defendant may recover in quasi-contract, especially if the contract was a personal services agreement. Uniform Commercial Code 2-718(2) grants a breaching buyer a limited right to restitution. If your case arises in a jurisdiction allowing a breaching defendant quasi-contract recovery, that remedy's availability mitigates the defendant's loss and cuts in favor of treating the breach as material. Even if the court characterizes the breach as material, the defendant will not suffer a complete forfeiture. The availability of the quasi-contract remedy should be pointed out during oral argument. Its availability is a question of law rather than one of fact, and the plaintiff usually does not have to prove any facts as a predicate for the argument.

e. The Character of the Breach as Willful, Negligent, or Accidental

Section 275(e) directs the judge to consider "the willful, negligent, or innocent behavior of the party failing to perform." As a practical matter, this is the most important factor in the materiality balance; if the plaintiff can show that the breach was in bad faith, the trier of fact will probably find the breach material. A few jurisdictions even subscribe to the view that any bad faith breach is automatically a material breach. Moreover, proof of a bad faith breach often has a spillover effect; angered by the defendant's bad faith, a jury may disregard factual weaknesses in the plaintiff's case or return a much higher verdict. How does the plaintiff prove bad faith?

The plaintiff should first show that the defendant had the ability to perform. Suppose that the defendant breached a contract to deliver 100 aluminum file cabinets. Use the defendant's own business records to show that on the date of the breach, 600 aluminum file cabinets were sitting idly in the defendant's warehouse. During pretrial discovery, search the defendant's records to prove that the defendant did not have any previous orders that the defendant needed the 600 cabinets to fill. This proof preempts the defendant's argument that he or she could not perform.

Next prove the motive for a bad faith breach. Assume that on December 4th, the defendant promised to sell the cabinets to the plaintiff for $55 each. The defendant was to deliver the cabinets on December 24th. The plaintiff can establish a motive for a bad faith breach by proving that the wholesale price increased between December 4th and 24th. In some jurisdictions, even without a live, sponsoring witness, the plaintiff can introduce the contents of a trade journal; a periodical is self-authenticating under Federal Evidence Rule 902(6), and Evidence Rule 803(17) recognizes a special hearsay exception for market reports. After introducing market reports for December 11th and 20th, ask the judge's permission to read to the jury the statements in the reports that the wholesale price first advanced to $60 and then to $62. If the jurisdiction does not treat trade journals as self-authenticating, have your client or another member of the industry authenticate the magazine as a specialized magazine for the trade, containing trustworthy market information.

The plaintiff should also prove that at the time of breach, the defendant's statements evidenced bad faith:

Q How many file cabinets did the defendant deliver on December 24th?
A None.
Q What did you do then?
A As soon as it became apparent that the shipment wasn't going to arrive before 2:00 p.m. as he had promised, I phoned the defendant.
Q What did you say to the defendant?
A I demanded to know where the file cabinets were.
Q What did the defendant say?
A He said to forget about the file cabinets. He had reconsidered and was not going to deliver.
Q What did you say?
A I reminded him that he had a contract, a legal obligation, to me.
Q How did the defendant respond?
A He said that that was tough and that I'd better wise up and learn how things are done in the real world.

The defendant's statements can qualify as nonhearsay under Evidence Rule 801(c) (circumstantial evidence of state of mind), admissions under Rule 801(d)(2), or declarations of state of mind under Rule 803(3).

Next, show that shortly after the breach, the defendant disposed of the goods at a higher price. It is best if there are goods that were identified to the contract.[4] You can use the defendant's own business records to trace them to the new buyer. Elicit the testimony showing (1) the short time lapse between the breach and the resale; and (2) the higher resale price. Often the new buyer acted innocently without realizing he or she was buying goods destined for the plaintiff. The new buyer will sometimes agree to appear as a plaintiff's witness. The new buyer can testify to the historical data about purchase price and date, and the new buyer can establish that the defendant did not disclose the prior transaction with the plaintiff.

Finally, consider introducing proof that the defendant committed other breaches of this contract or of similar contracts with the plaintiff and third parties. In the past, many judges have been reluctant to admit such proof. However, the Federal Evidence Rules provide a powerful argument for the admissibility of the proof. The plaintiff is not offering the proof as general character evidence forbidden by Rule 404(a) in all cases; the plaintiff is not arguing that the defendant is by character a contract breaker. Rather the plaintiff has a much more specific theory of logical relevance; the defendant's other breaches are logically relevant to show intent and bad faith in the instant case. Federal Evidence Rule 404(b) liberally authorizes the admission of "other . . . wrongs or acts" to establish elements of the cause of action such as "intent." Rule 404(b) is used more frequently in criminal cases; but on its face, the Rule also applies in civil actions, and the other breaches indisputably have logical relevance to prove the intentional character of the defendant's breach. To prove the other breach, you might call as a witness the victim of the other breach. The testimony should stress how strikingly similar the two situations are. Assume that your client had agreed to buy 100 aluminum file cabinets from the defendant on December 4th for $55 each. After identifying himself and stating that he had contracted with the defendant, the witness could testify:

Q   What type of agreement did you have with the defendant?
A   I was going to buy 100 file cabinets from him.
Q   What type of cabinets?
A   Just aluminum file cabinets.
Q   What price were you going to pay him?
A   As I recall, we agreed on $55 per cabinet.
Q   When did you make this agreement with the defendant?
A   In early December.
Q   When did the defendant deliver the file cabinets?
A   He never did.
Q   What happened?
A   When the cabinets never arrived, I phoned him to ask what was going on.
Q   What did he say?
A   He said he'd changed his mind. He said he had a better deal with another buyer.
Q   What did you say?
A   I reminded him we had a deal.
Q   How did he answer you?
A   He said, "So sue me, jerk."

LEGAL RESEARCH REFERENCE:
Murray §172

f. The Degree of Certainty That the Defendant Will Perform the Balance of the Contract

If the court holds the breach to be minor, the contract continues in existence; and the plaintiff must live with the defendant for the balance of the contract. It is fair to do so only if there is a reasonable assurance that the defendant will perform his or her remaining contract duties. Section 275(f) recognizes this reasoning by directing the judge to factor into materiality analysis "[t]he greater or less uncertainty that the party failing to perform will perform the remainder of the contract."

To prove the diminished certainty of future performance, the plaintiff can use much of the same evidence relevant to intent. If the breach was intentional and in bad faith, the breach's character decreases the likelihood that the defendant will perform the rest of the contract in good faith; an intentional, bad faith breach makes the defendant less trustworthy. Here again the defendant's other breaches of this contract and similar contracts are logically relevant under Evidence Rule 404(b); the defendant's repeated, past breaches decrease the probability of future performance.

The plaintiff should also attempt to show that the defendant's conduct after breach diminished the likelihood of future performance. Revisit the hypothetical involving the file cabinets. The defendant's resale of the file cabinets to a third party not only is relevant to show bad faith; the defendant's resale is also relevant to this factor. If the defendant sold goods identified to the contract (that is, if the plaintiff and defendant agreed upon 100 particular file cabinets), the resale makes it virtually certain that the defendant cannot perform unless the defendant reserved a right to repurchase. Even if any 100 file cabinets meeting the contract description will satisfy the defendant's duty, the resale will make it more difficult for the defendant to perform in the future. The plaintiff should use the defendant's records to show that after the resale, the defendant's inventory was inadequate to fill the plaintiff's needs. For example, the plaintiff could introduce the defendant's own inventory records to establish that immediately after the resale, the defendant's inventory stock included only 45 file cabinets; even if the defendant shipped the entire remaining inventory to the plaintiff, the defendant could not have performed the defendant's duty to the plaintiff.

LEGAL RESEARCH REFERENCE:
Murray §171

Sec. 8-4. Establishing the Materiality of the Defendant's Breach of Duty—Specific Applications of the Materiality Rules

There are two breach problems for which the common-law courts developed special rules: time of the essence and perfect tender.

a.   Time of the Essence

In most contracts, time is not of the essence. Suppose that a realty contract specifies that the seller will deliver the deed on September 1st. If the seller delays delivering the deed, the seller breaches; but at least at first the breach is minor. The breach can become material after the lapse of a substantial period of time.

However, in some contracts, time is expressly or impliedly of the essence. If time is of the essence of the defendant's performance of a duty, any delay is a material breach. Assume that the parties included a "time of the essence" clause in the realty contract and that the court construed the clause as applying to the seller's duty to deliver the deed. Then the seller's delay of even one day in delivering the deed would be a material breach.

If the contract contains a recital or clause suggesting that time was of the essence, the plaintiff should have that language read to the jury. After authenticating the contract, the plaintiff could testify:

Q   Please read the third recital on page one of the exhibit to the jurors.
A   Yes. The third recital reads: "WHEREAS the parties both realize that the market for pork fluctuates rapidly and frequently."
Q   Now please read the 12th clause on page three of the exhibit to the jurors.
A   "The parties expressly agree that time shall be of the essence of this contract. Time shall be of the essence of the performance of both parties' obligations under this contract."

Absent express language, the plaintiff can attempt to show that time was impliedly of the essence of the contract. Our fact situation is a contract for the sale of pork. The plaintiff was buying the pork from the defendant farmer, and the plaintiff had already contracted to sell the pork to the United States Army. The plaintiff's contract with the Army provided for a stiff, *per diem* penalty; the plaintiff had to pay the Army $2,000 for every day he delayed making delivery. The plaintiff could first describe the volatile market for pork:

Q   What is your occupation?
A   I've been a wholesale pork buyer for about ten years now.
Q   What is the defendant's occupation?
A   He's a hog farmer.
Q   To the best of your knowledge, how long has he been a hog farmer?
A   I know that I've done business with him for over eight years now.
Q   How stable is the pork market?
A   It's not very stable at all. The prices for pork vary greatly from day to day.
Q   How much does the price vary on a daily basis?
A   It's not unusual for the price on day #2 to be 30% higher or lower than the price on day #1.
Q   How often does the price change?

> A Almost daily. There are lots of things that affect the price: import quotas, feed prices, production in other countries. All sorts of things can cause the price to change, and the price in fact changes all the time.

The plaintiff should also establish that the defendant knew that the plaintiff had a special need for prompt performance. The plaintiff authenticates his contract with the Army and then testifies:

> Q Under your agreement with the defendant, when was he supposed to deliver the pork?
>
> A On July 12th.
>
> Q Why did you want the pork on that date?
>
> A I definitely needed it no later than that time because of my contract with the Army. I had to specially process the pork for overseas shipment under my Army contract; and if I didn't get the pork by the 12th, I'd never meet my deadline.
>
> Q What was your deadline?
>
> A I had to have the pork processed and prepared for shipment no later than the 20th.
>
> Q What, if anything, did you tell the defendant about this deadline?
>
> A I told him specifically that I needed to have the pork ready for shipment by that date.
>
> Q When did you tell the defendant that?
>
> A Before we signed our agreement.
>
> Q Under your agreement with the Army, what would happen if you did not meet your deadline?
>
> A I had to pay them $2,000 for every day of delay.
>
> Q What, if anything, did you tell the defendant about this $2,000 penalty?
>
> A I mentioned to him that every day he was late would cost me $2,000.
>
> Q When did you mention this to him?
>
> A Before I signed my contract with him.

LEGAL RESEARCH REFERENCE:
Murray §175

b. Perfect Tender

At early common law, the courts tended to hold that the commercial seller had to strictly perform his or her duties. Some courts even suggested that any deficiency in the seller's tender was a material breach; any defect in the quantity or quality of the tendered goods entitled the buyer to collect total damages for a material breach.

A superficial review of the Uniform Commercial Code might lead the reader to believe that the Code has enshrined the perfect tender rule. Uniform Commercial Code 2-601(a) provides that if the seller's tender "fail[s] in any respect to conform to the contract, the buyer may . . . reject the whole. . . ." Section 2-711(1) adds that if the buyer "rightfully rejects" all the goods under 2-601, the buyer may recover total damages for a material breach.

However, 2-601(a) and 2-711(1) should not be read literally. Section 2-508 often overrides and permits the seller to cure a quantitative defect in the tender. Further, the courts have begun to apply the substantial performance excuse doctrine to the condition of the seller's tender. Finally, U.C.C. 2-612 explicitly abolishes the application of the perfect tender rule to installment contracts. Under 2-612(2), the buyer may reject a particular installment only "if the non-conformity substantially impairs the value of that installment and cannot be cured. . . ." Under 2-612(3), the buyer may terminate the contract for a deficiency in one installment only if the "non-conformity or default with respect to (the installment) substantially impairs the value of the whole contract. . . ." There is a substantial impairment when, under the normal materiality test, the seller commits a major breach of duty.

In short, to recover damages for a major breach, the plaintiff buyer will ordinarily have to demonstrate that the defendant's breach satisfies the normal materiality test. If the seller's breach is seemingly minor, the plaintiff may need expert testimony to prove the breach's materiality. Suppose, for instance, that the plaintiff aerospace firm ordered miniature transistors from the defendant electronics manufacturing firm. The contract specified that the transistors were to be 0.27 centimeters in length but the defendant delivered transistors 0.275 centimeters in length. If the court balks at applying the perfect tender rule, the plaintiff will have to prove the breach's materiality. The plaintiff may have entered into a contract with the National Aeronautics and Space Administration to manufacture a component for a space capsule. After authenticating his contract with NASA, the plaintiff could testify:

Q Under your agreement with the defendant, what was the length of the transistors the defendant was supposed to deliver?

A The contract specified 27 hundredths of a centimeter.

Q Why did you specify that precise length?

A As I just indicated, we were manufacturing a monitor for a NASA space capsule. Our NASA contract imposes very severe length and weight constraints on the size of the monitor. We couldn't afford to waste any space or weight at all, and our best engineering judgment was that the transistors could be no longer than 27 hundredths.

Q What, if anything, did you tell the defendant about the length of the transistors?

A I told the defendant that he had to meet our specifications on the nose.

Q What words did you use when you told the defendant that?

A I said something like, "You can't just be close, George. This time you guys have to be right on."

Q When did you tell the defendant that?

A The first time I mentioned the proposal to him, about a month before we finalized the deal and signed the contract documents.

Q How well will the transistors the defendant delivered fit into the monitor you are building?

A That's the whole point. Those transistors don't do us any good. Five thousandths of a centimeter may not seem much to you, but there's just no room to spare on this project. Those transistors don't fit in at all.

It would be ideal if the plaintiff could testify that the plaintiff gave the defendant a copy of the NASA contract. When a prime contractor subcontracts work, it is common practice to attach the prime contract as an appendix to the subcontract. If a copy of the NASA contract was incorporated in the plaintiff's contract with the defendant or the plaintiff at least gave the defendant a copy, the plaintiff should testify to that effect.

LEGAL RESEARCH REFERENCE:
Murray §176

BREACH CHECKLIST

____ The defendant breached a duty.

    ____ The defendant committed a present breach of duty.
          or
    ____ The defendant committed an anticipatory breach of duty.
        ____ The defendant expressly or impliedly repudiated the duty.
            and
        ____ The defendant did not retract the repudiation.
            and
        ____ The plaintiff elected to treat the repudiation as a present breach of duty.

AND ____

____ The breach was material under the general test.

    ____ The defendant did not give the plaintiff substantially what the plaintiff bargained for.
            and
    ____ The plaintiff cannot be adequately compensated for the defendant's breach.
            and
    ____ At the point of breach, the defendant had not performed much of his or her duty.
            and
    ____ The defendant may be able to recover in quasi-contract.
            and
    ____ The defendant's breach was willful.
            and
    ____ It was uncertain that the defendant would perform the balance of the duty.

OR

____ The breach was a delay, and time was of the essence.

FOOTNOTES

[1] *See* Section 9-4, *infra.*

[2] One exception to this norm is the case of divisible contracts. A contract is divisible if the contract has three characteristics: The performance on each side is divided into parts; the parts on each side are paired, for example, a certain price for every unit of production the seller delivers; and each pair represents a proportionate exchange of benefit or "mini-contract." Installment contracts and contracts quoting unit prices are often divisible. If the defendant breaches a divisible contract, the defendant may collect at the contract rate on the parts of the contract the defendant completed; but the defendant is liable for damages for a material breach of the remainder of the contract.

[3] *See* Section 9-5, *infra.*

[4] Uniform Commercial Code 2-501(1) sets forth the rules governing when the goods become identified to a particular contract.

CHAPTER 9

How to Prove the Plaintiff's Entitlement to Remedies for the Defendant's Breach— The Last Element of the Plaintiff's Theory

Sec. 9-1.   Introduction

In Chapters 5 through 8, we analyzed the first four elements of the plaintiff's theory: The plaintiff and the defendant formed a contract; the contract should be construed as creating certain conditions and duties; all the conditions to the defendant's duty were fulfilled or excused; and the defendant breached the duty. If the plaintiff establishes these four elements, the plaintiff has shown an actionable breach, entitling the plaintiff to some remedy.

This chapter highlights the major remedies peculiar to Contract litigation. The Uniform Commercial Code contains two "index" sections, listing remedies; 2-703 catalogues the principal remedies for the seller, and 2-711 lists the buyer's remedies.

The plaintiff should remember that in addition to the peculiar Contract remedies, general remedies may also be useful in Contract litigation. At the outset of a Contract lawsuit, the plaintiff should consider seeking a temporary restraining order and preliminary injunction. In the past decade, the courts have been granting such relief more liberally in commercial suits. The plaintiff should likewise bear in mind the availability of a declaratory judgment authorized by legislation such as 28 U.S.C. §2201. A dispute may arise over the proper interpretation of a long-term supply contract; and rather than desiring damages and the contract's termination, the buyer might well prefer a declaration of the parties' respective rights and a continuation of the contract. We mention these other remedies in passing, but our primary focus in this chapter is on remedies ordinarily available only in Contract lawsuits.

LEGAL RESEARCH REFERENCE:
Murray §§219-21
White & Summers §§6-1, 7-1

Sec. 9-2.   Stipulated Damages

The parties may simplify the court's task by specifying a remedy in their contract. It is quite common for the parties to include a stipulated or agreed damages provision in commercial agreements. The courts refuse to enforce stipulated damages provisions when the stipulated damages are so high that the provision is in reality a penalty clause. However, the courts will enforce a reasonable liquidated damages provision. To show the enforceability of a stipulated damages clause, the plaintiff should prove that

1. At the time of contracting, it was foreseeable that in the event of a breach it would be difficult or impossible to compute damages. There are several methods of proving foreseeable difficulty in computation. The courts often find the requisite difficulty when the agreement is a public contract such as a contract for highway construction. In this situation, the courts reason that if the private contractor breaches by delaying, one element of damage is the injury each member of the public suffers in the form of inconvenience and that it is virtually impossible to attach a monetary value to that injury. Or the plaintiff can have an expert testify that there is no established market for the product and, hence, it will be troublesome to ascertain a market value to apply the damages formulae:

Q   What is your occupation?   (1)
A   I am an antique dealer.
Q   How long have you been in that line of business?
A   For the past 25 years.
Q   What is the market value of a 17th century French colonial dresser?   (1)
A   It's hard to answer that question. You don't have a market for antiques in the same sense that you have a market for stocks.

Q   What do you mean that you do not have a market for antiques?   (1)

A   Prices for antiques are really individualized. A lot depends on the condition of the article and the stylistic preferences of the buyer.

Q   How does that contrast with the stock market?   (1)

A   When I want to know how much I should pay for ITT stock, I can turn to the *Wall Street Journal* and find out the prices paid for the stock the day before. You just can't do that with antiques.

Or the plaintiff can show that at the time of breach, it would be foreseeably difficult to ascertain the quantity to multiply the market value by. The courts routinely sustain stipulated damages provisions in requirement and output contracts for this very reason. Rather than specifying a number as the quantity term, a requirements or output contract defines the quantity as the buyer's needs or the seller's production. If one party breaches during the performance of a requirements or output contract, to compute damages the court will have to make a speculative projection of future need or output. The parties may eliminate the necessity for a conjectural prediction by inserting a stipulated damages provision.

2.   The amount stipulated must be a reasonable forecast of just compensation. This requirement initially seems inconsistent with the first requirement: If it will be difficult to compute damages, how can the court judge whether the amount specified is "reasonable"? The inconsistency is apparent rather than real. To begin with, the courts are very lax in enforcing the second requirement; they are much more concerned about the first requirement. Further, even when the parties cannot foresee the precise amount of a loss resulting from a breach, they can often foresee a probable range of loss. Assume that a requirements contract specified a contract price of $1.00 above the prevailing market price at the time of delivery. The contract contains a stipulated damages clause for $10,000:

Q   Why did you choose the figure $10,000?   (2)

A   It was really sort of an average.

Q   What do you mean by that?   (2)

A   It fell between our maximum and minimum volume. Our minimum volume of business, our minimum output, has been 5,000 units in a year.

Q   What would your damages have been if the defendant had breached in a year in which you had a minimum output?   (2)

A   If the defendant didn't buy anything in that sort of year, our loss would be $5,000.

Q   How do you arrive at that figure?   (2)

A   Since the contract sets the price at one dollar above market, we lose a dollar per unit. Five thousand units—five thousand dollars.

Q   What has been your maximum output?   (2)

A   For this line of product, the maximum has been 15,000 units.

Q   If the defendant breached in a year in which you matched your previous maximum output, what would be your damage?   (2)

A $15,000.

Q   Again. How did you happen to choose $10,000 as the figure for clause ten?   (2)

A   It should be obvious. We figured our loss would be somewhere between the maximum and minimum possible—that is, somewhere between $15,000 and $5,000. We chose $10,000 because that figure was right smack in the middle.

It is also helpful if the plaintiff shows that the stipulated damages clause is graduated. For instance, in a construction contract, there may be a *per diem* stipulated damages clause; the contractor pays so much for every day of delay. It makes eminent good sense to vary the size of the stipulated damages with the length of the delay. More sophisticated construction contracts vary the size of the daily payment with the part of the project the contractor delays completing. The more graduated the clause, the more precisely the amount will approximate the actual damage; and the more likely the court is to uphold the clause.

Lastly, the plaintiff should remember that Uniform Commercial Code 2-718(1) takes a very liberal stance on the second requirement for liquidated damages clauses. That subsection provides that the second requirement is satisfied if the amount of stipulated damage is "reasonable in the light of the anticipated or *actual* harm. . . ." If by happenstance the plaintiff can compute actual damage and the amount of stipulated damage is in the same ballpark as the actual damage, the coincidence satisfies the second requirement.

LEGAL RESEARCH REFERENCE:
Murray §234

Sec. 9-3.   Incidental Damages for Minor Breach

If the defendant's breach was minor or a material one the plaintiff elected to treat as minor, the plaintiff may recover the actual economic damage caused by the breach. The Uniform Commercial Code uses the expression "incidental" to label these damages. Thus, U.C.C. 2-710 permits a plaintiff seller to recover

> any commercially reasonable charges, expenses or commissions incurred in stopping delivery, in the transportation, care and custody of goods after the buyer's breach, in connection with return or resale of the goods or otherwise resulting from the breach.

Section 2-715(1) similarly allows a plaintiff buyer to collect

> expenses reasonably incurred in inspection, receipt, transportation and care and custody of goods rightfully rejected, any commercially reasonable charges, expenses or commissions in connection with effecting cover and any other reasonable expense incident to the delay or other breach.

a. General Requirements

To recover incidental damages, the plaintiff should lay this foundation:

1. The defendant's breach caused the incidental damage. The plaintiff should show that the breach directly caused the damage and that the plaintiff could not have *mitigated* or avoided the damage.

   Suppose that the plaintiff seller was shipping goods to the defendant. The contract required the plaintiff to bear the expense of railroad transportation until actual delivery to the defendant. Since the defendant's delivery dock was overloaded, the plaintiff had to delay unloading the railroad cars. Consequently, the plaintiff had to pay the railroad an additional $800 rental fee. The plaintiff testifies:

   Q   What additional cost, if any, did you incur because of the defendant's delay?   (1)

   A   It cost me another $800.

   Q   Why did you incur that cost?   (1)

   A   It was right in my contract with the railroad. It's the standard term. You in effect rent the cars; and understandably if you use the cars beyond the rental period the railroad originally agreed to, you've got to pay them additional rent. In this case, the additional rent was $800.

   Q   How could you have avoided paying this additional $800?   (1)

   A   I don't think I could have avoided it. The railroad dropped the cars off at the defendant's siding, and I couldn't get another locomotive in there to divert the goods to another buyer. I didn't expect the delay, and the defendant's delay gave me no choice but to let the railroad cars sit there until the defendant got around to unloading them.

2. At the time of contract formation, it was *foreseeable* that if the defendant breached, the plaintiff would incur this type of damage. Many judges classify incidental damages as specials. As specials, incidental damages must comply with the rule of forseeability in the landmark case of *Hadley v. Baxendale.* The plaintiff must show that the defendant could reasonably have foreseen this type of loss. In our hypothetical, the plaintiff must prove that the defendant had notice that during any delay, the plaintiff would incur additional rental expense for the railroad cars.

   Under Uniform Commercial Code 1-205(2), the plaintiff could prove that there is a trade usage that the seller in another city ships by rented railroad car and pays a rental based on the length of the rental period. Under 1-205(3), the plaintiff could prove a prior course of dealing between the plaintiff and defendant to that effect. Ideally, the plaintiff could call the court's attention to specific contract language, putting the defendant on notice:

   Q   Please read paragraph 14 on page three of the exhibit (the contract).   (2)

   A   The paragraph reads: "It is understood that the Seller will ship the above-described goods to the buyer by rented railroad cars and that the Seller will pay a rental for the said cars, based on the number of days in the rental period. It is agreed that the Seller shall bill the Buyer for reimbursement of the necessary and customary rental cost of the railroad cars."

3. The amount of the damages is reasonably *certain*. There is a split of authority on the question of how certain the amount of the damage must be. Some jurisdictions still adhere to the view that the amount must be "reasonably certain." Even these jurisdictions do not demand mathematical certainty. A growing number of jurisdictions takes a more liberal view; these jurisdictions demand that the fact of damage be reasonably certain but tolerate relative uncertainty about the amount of damage. These courts reason that if there is uncertainty, the uncertainty is the fault of the defendant who committed the breach.

The shift toward the more liberal view is especially evident in the courts' attitude toward the recovery of lost profits. Suppose that the defendant contracted to build a drive-in theatre for the plaintiff. The defendant delays completing the project, and the plaintiff then seeks the actual damage caused by the delay. The damage is the operating profit lost during the period of delay. However, until recently, many jurisdictions felt that new businesses' profits are too speculative and uncertain. More and more jurisdictions are allowing new businesses to recover lost profits as actual damages. There are two keys to presenting expert testimony to persuade a court to allow lost profits as actual damages.

The first key is showing the qualifications of the plaintiff's expert. The plaintiff could call any experienced member of the industry, even the plaintiff. However, perhaps the best witness is an economist who has done market and profitability research in that industry.[1] In qualifying the witness, the plaintiff should create the impression that the witness is a specialist in estimating profits for businesses in this particular industry.

Q   What is your occupation?   (3)
A   I am an economist.
Q   Where do you work?   (3)
A   I teach at Stanford University.
Q   How long have you taught there?   (3)
A   For the past ten years.
Q   What is your title?   (3)
A   I am a full professor in the Economics Department.
Q   What is your educational background?   (3)
A   I obtained my master's degree in economics and statistics from the University of Chicago.
Q   What were the requirements for the master's degree?   (3)
A   I did some course work and wrote a thesis.
Q   What was the topic of your thesis?   (3)

A My subject was profitability trends in the American entertainment industry in the 1960's.

Q What other degrees, if any, do you have? (3)

A I acquired a Ph.D. in economics from Harvard University, and I have done other graduate study at the London School of Economics.

Q How many articles, if any, have you published? (3)

A A total of 34 articles.

Q What is the topic of these articles? (3)

A Most of them deal with the economics of the entertainment industry. That is my specialized research interest.

The second key is convincing the court that the basis for the witness' opinion include extensive profitability data for very comparable firms:

Q Before coming to court today, what research have you done on the profitability of drive-in theatres? (3)

A First I gathered as much profitability data as I could from the National Association of Theatre Owners. They have profitability data for all types of theatres, including drive-ins, dating back to the 1930's. I exhausted all their data.

Q What other research have you done? (3)

A I personally conducted a study of the first year of operation of 20 comparable drive-in theatres.

Q Why do you say that these other drive-in theatres are "comparable" to the plaintiff's? (3)

A I chose the 20 theatres because in several important respects, they were similarly situated to the plaintiff's.

Q What respects did you consider? (3)

A For example, one factor was the number of competing, established theatres in a ten-mile radius. Another was the size of the nearest center city. A third factor was the capacity of the theatre. I also considered the quality of the motion picture projection equipment. I tried my best to identify the factors most likely to affect profitability in the first year of operation and then find theatres that were similar to the plaintiff's in terms of these factors.

Q How similar were some of the theatres you found? (3)

A In some cases, the similarities were remarkable. For example, I found one theatre in the Phoenix area that was strikingly similar to the plaintiff's— only one established competitor in the ten-mile radius, in a suburb with a population of 55,000, capacity of approximately 300 cars, and first-rate projection equipment and screen.

If the plaintiff's expert specializes in market studies in this industry and has gathered profitability data on truly comparable businesses, the plaintiff has not only maximized the likelihood that the judge will admit the expert's testimony, but more importantly, the plaintiff has maximized the probability that the jurors will believe the testimony.

LEGAL RESEARCH REFERENCE
Murray §§224-28, 237, 249
White & Summers §6-5

b.   Damages Caused by Subcontractors' Delays

The problem of proving the actual damages caused by a subcontractor's delay on a construction project warrants special mention. It is often difficult to show all the damages caused by one subcontractor's delay. The work of other subcontractors may depend on the defendant subcontractor's work, and the defendant's delay in excavating or pouring the foundation may put other parts of the construction project behind schedule.

When the breach is one subcontractor's delay, the plaintiff should consider using Critical Path Method (CPM) diagrams.[2] A CPM diagram helps the jury visualize the precedence and dependence of the various parts of the construction project. The chart shows which work must be completed first and which parts of the project depend on other parts. Figure 9-1[3] is a CPM chart. The chart can be time scaled and calendar dated like Figure 9-2.[4]

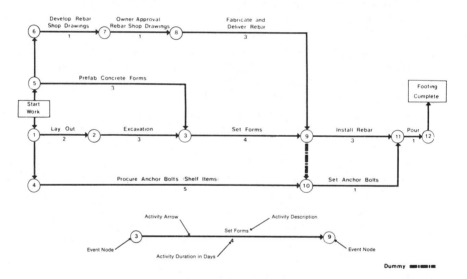

Figure 9-1: CPM SCHEDULE FOR A TYPICAL CONCRETE FOOTING (Typical Arrow Diagram)
Courtesy of John M. Wickwire and Richard F. Smith, *Public Contracts Law Journal,* October 1974.

To depict the effect of one subcontractor's delay on the other parts of a construction project, the plaintiff's attorney can use two CPM diagrams— an "as planned" chart and an "as built" chart. Call an experienced contractor as an expert witness. First give the contractor the plans and specifications for the project, and have the expert vouch for the "as planned" chart: Given the plans and specifications, the work on the project should have proceeded in the sequence depicted on the chart. The "as planned" chart can be done all in black lettering and lines.

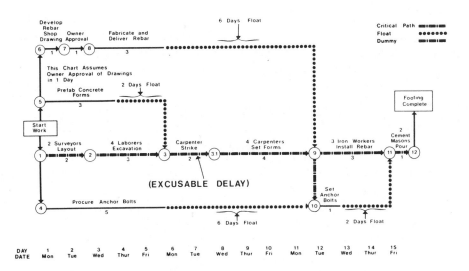

"ADJUSTED" SCHEDULE
(ESTABLISHING PROJECT COMPLETION DATE ABSENT OWNER DELAYS)

Figure 9-2: "AS PLANNED" SCHEDULE (Time Scaled, Calendar Dated, Critical Sequence (Path) and Float Highlighted). Courtesy of John M. Wickwire and Richard F. Smith, *Public Contracts Law Journal,* October 1974.

Then give the expert the project records and have the expert vouch for the "as built" chart. The "as built" chart shows both the defendant's delay and the delays caused by the defendant's delay. Change the colors to highlight the delays. For example, show the defendant's delay in red lettering and lines, and use green lettering and lines to show the delays in other parts of the project caused by the defendant's delay. This chart greatly assists the jury in visualizing and understanding the causation.

Finally, have the expert cost out all the delays. If the defendant's delay affected several parts of the project, you may want to use another chart to summarize the expert's testimony about increased costs. On the left-hand margin list all the affected parts of the project. The top columnar headings would be "as planned" and "as built." The "as planned" column lists the expert's estimates of the time and expense each part of the project would have required if the project had been completed as planned. The "as built" column lists the time and expense actually required due to the defendant's breach.

Sec. 9-4.   Damages for Breach of Warranty

As Chapter 8 points out, the defendant's breach is sometimes the fact that the goods the defendant delivers lack a particular quality, such as a physical property or merchantability. The defendant may have expressly or impliedly warranted that the goods would have that quality. If the plaintiff has accepted the goods but the goods lack the warranted quality, the plaintiff's remedy is recovering damages for breach of warranty. The remedy includes damages for two types of injury.

a.   Economic Loss

The most obvious damage caused by a breach of warranty is economic loss; the lack of the warranted quality usually reduces the economic value of the goods on the market. To recover economic loss, the plaintiff must establish that

1. The plaintiff accepted the goods. "Acceptance" is a term of art defined in Uniform Commercial Code 2-606. A plaintiff seller must make a strong showing of acceptance when the seller is suing for the price of the goods, but a plaintiff buyer suing for breach of warranty need not go into detail. It usually suffices for the plaintiff to prove physical acceptance and retention of the goods.

2. Within a reasonable time after acceptance, the plaintiff buyer notified the seller that the warranty had been breached. Uniform Commercial Code 2-607(3)(a) imposes the notification requirement. The notice can be very general. A Comment to 2-607 states:

    > The content of the notification need merely be sufficient to let the seller know that the transaction is still troublesome and must be watched. There is no reason to require that the notification which saves the buyer's rights under this section must include a clear statement of all the objections that will be relied on by the buyer. . . .

    The plaintiff could introduce a letter the plaintiff had sent to the defendant seller. After authenticating the letter, the plaintiff testifies:

    Q   What did you do with exhibit three after you finished typing it?   (2)
    A   I sent it to the defendant.
    Q   How did you send it to the defendant?   (2)
    A   I mailed it to him. I placed it in an envelope addressed to him and sent it off.
    Q   Where did you get the defendant's address?   (2)
    A   From the Dallas telephone directory.
    Q   Please read the salutation and first paragraph of the letter to the jury. (2)
    A   It says: "Dear Mr. Grimes: Your shipment arrived yesterday, and my people stacked it in the refrigerated storage area. However, there's a problem. You represented that the scraps would be at least 50% protein. My inspector checked out the shipment this morning, and she tells me that most of your shipment is only 48 or 49% protein. I consider this to be a serious violation of your warranty."

3. The plaintiff proves the difference between the fair market value of the goods in their actual condition and the value the goods would have had if the goods had complied with the warranty. Uniform Commercial Code 2-714(2) declares:

    > The measure of damages for breach of warranty is the difference at the time and place of acceptance between the value of the goods accepted and the value they would have had if they had been as warranted. . . .

Sometimes the plaintiff can use documentary evidence of both values. There may be a trade journal or newspaper reporting market prices for scrap, depending upon its protein content; and the newspaper might cite the price for 48% protein scrap and 50% protein scrap. In the next section of this chapter, we shall discuss in detail the evidentiary problems posed by documentary proof of market value. The plaintiff would use the evidentiary techniques discussed in the next section to prove the two market values, and the court would then compute damages by taking the difference between the two values.

However, in many cases, the plaintiff will need live expert testimony. There may be a reported market price for the goods as warranted; but the breach of warranty may render the goods unmerchantable, and there is often no reported market price for the goods in that condition. The plaintiff will have to present the testimony of an experienced member of the industry. The witness can (1) opine on the extent to which the breach of warranty reduces the market value, (2) describe the goods' scrap or salvage value, or (3) testify flatly that the breach of warranty renders the goods worthless.

LEGAL RESEARCH REFERENCE:
Murray §238
White & Summers ch. 10

b.   Personal Injury

A breach of warranty can cause personal injury as well as economic loss. A breach of warranty for a car or saw may even cause death. Uniform Commercial Code 2-719(3) classifies personal injury as consequential damage, and 2-714(3) adds that the buyer may recover consequential damage caused by a breach of warranty. The techniques for proving consequential personal injury in Contract actions are roughly the same as the techniques for establishing personal injury in tort actions. You should consult texts on proof of damages in tort actions when you claim personal injury as consequential damage in a commercial lawsuit. The reader will find I. Duke Avnet, *How to Prove Damages in Wrongful Personal Injury and Death Cases* (2d ed. 1978), to be a helpful reference.

Sec. 9-5.   General Damages for Material Breach—The Traditional Rules

The formulae for computing general damages vary with the type of contract breached. The following is a discussion of the formulae for the types of contracts most frequently encountered in commercial litigation:

a.   Contracts for the Sale of Goods

In the last section, we assumed that the buyer accepted the goods. This section makes the contrary assumption; the buyer has rejected or revoked acceptance, and one of the parties to the contract is suing for total breach.

The plaintiff buyer and seller use essentially the same formula. The formula is based on a hypothetical transaction. The court assumes that the innocent party arranged a substitute transaction on the open market and that the innocent party's damages are then the difference between the contract price and the market price. Uniform Commercial Code 2-708(1) provides that the plaintiff seller may recover "the difference between the market price at the time and place for tender and the unpaid contract price. . . ." Section 2-713(1) prescribes a similar formula for the plaintiff buyer: "the difference between the market price at the time when the buyer learned of the breach and the contract price. . . ." To apply this formula, the plaintiff must prove:

1. The contract price. The plaintiff can testify directly to the agreed-upon price, or the plaintiff can read the controlling contract language to the jury.
2. The market price at the appropriate time and in the appropriate market. At common law, the time and place were the time and place of tender. As you can see from the language of U.C.C. 2-708 and 2-713, the Code has modified the common-law rule. The Code has both modified and confused the rule for anticipatory breach. Section 2-723(1) states that in the case of anticipatory breach, the market price is "the price of such goods prevailing at the time when the aggrieved party learned of the repudiation." To this date, it is unsettled whether the plaintiff "learns" of the repudiation when the defendant makes the statement or when the plaintiff elects to treat the statement as a breach.[5] In any event, you should research local Contract law to determine the controlling time and place in your jurisdiction; and whatever the time and place are, the evidentiary problems are the same.

If there is no established market for the subject matter of the contract, the plaintiff will want to call an experienced dealer in the goods to express an opinion on market value. However, there usually is a market, and the market's fluctuations are often reported in trade publications. Uniform Commercial Code 2-724 permits the plaintiff to resort to "official publications or trade journals or . . . newspapers of general circulation published as the reports of such market. . . ." Under the Federal Evidence Rules, the plaintiff could introduce documentary proof without live, sponsoring testimony.

Suppose that the defendant contracted to buy stock in a certain corporation from the plaintiff. The defendant promised to accept and pay for the stock on October 4th of this year. To prove the market value of the stock, the plaintiff is attempting to introduce the October 5th issue of the *Wall Street Journal*:

Q Your honor, I request that this be marked plaintiff's exhibit number four for identification.   (3)
J It will be so marked.
Q Please let the record reflect that I am showing the exhibit to the opposing counsel.   (3)
J The record will so reflect.

Q   Your honor, I now offer plaintiff's exhibit number four for identification into evidence as plaintiff's exhibit four.   (3)

O[6] I object to the introduction of this exhibit on several grounds.

J   Namely?

O   Well, your honor, my first objection is that it hasn't been properly authenticated.

Q   This exhibit is self-authenticating. Evidence Rule 902(6) explicitly states that "printed materials purporting to be newspapers or periodicals" are self-authenticating. I don't need a live, sponsoring witness.   (3)

J   Objection overruled. Do you have any other objections.

O   I certainly do, your honor. My next objection is that this document isn't the best evidence. The best evidence would be the original made at the *Wall Street Journal*'s printing offices.

Q   Your honor, it would certainly be inconvenient to have to produce that whenever you wanted to use a newspaper in the courtroom. For that reason, Federal Evidence Rule 1001(4) defines "duplicate" as including any "counterpart produced by the same impression as the original, or on the same matrix. . . ." Under Evidence Rule 1003, this duplicate should be admitted just as an original.

J   I concur. The second objection will likewise be overruled. Are there any further objections?

O   Yes, your honor. My final objection is that using this exhibit as substantive evidence of the market price violates the hearsay rule.

Q   Your honor, like the first two objections, this objection is unsound. In no uncertain terms, Evidence Rule 803(17) carves out a hearsay exception for "market quotations." [*If the contract were a contract for the sale of goods, the plaintiff would add the next sentence.*] Moreover, Commercial Code 2-724 states that market reports in trade journals and newspapers are admissible as evidence of the market price.

J   Objection overruled. The exhibit will be admitted into evidence.

Q   Your honor, I request permission to read the market quotation for Cyclatron stock on page 17 to the jury.

J   Permission granted.

LEGAL RESEARCH REFERENCE:
Murray §§238-39, 242, 246
White & Summers §§6-2, 6-4, 7-7

b.   Contracts for Real Property

1.   Damages for a plaintiff seller

The formula for computing the seller's damages is similar to the formula for computing damages for breach of a contract for the sale of personal property. The seller is entitled to recover the difference between the contract price and market price at the time for delivery of the deed. Thus, the seller should prove:

1. The contract price. If the contract is oral, the plaintiff may testify directly to the price. If the contract is written, the plaintiff should au-

thenticate the contract; and after the court admits the exhibit, the plaintiff should read the passage stating the price to the jurors.

2. Market value. The plaintiff will ordinarily need live, expert testimony to establish the market value of the land. The plaintiff may content himself or herself with a secondary expert such as a real estate broker or experienced land speculator. However, in an important case, the plaintiff should present the best possible testimony, that is, testimony by a professional real estate appraiser such as a member of the American Institute of Real Estate Appraisers.[7] The appraiser can take one or more of three approaches to the valuation of the property: cost (the acquisition cost of the vacant land plus the depreciated reproduction cost of all improvements), market (prices voluntarily paid for similar properties sold within a reasonable distance and reasonable time of the property in question), and income (based on the reasonably foreseeable rent and operating expenses of the property for its productive life).[8] The market approach is the most direct and usually the most persuasive for lay jurors. The keys to presenting market testimony effectively are similar to the keys for presenting testimony about the lost profits of a new business.

First, the plaintiff must persuade the jury that the witness is an expert on local property:

Q   How long have you lived in this county?   (2)
A   All my life.
Q   How many years is that?   (2)
A   Forty-three years.
Q   What is your occupation?   (2)
A   I am a real estate appraiser.
Q   How long have you worked as a real estate appraiser?   (2)
A   For 17 years.
Q   Where is the property you appraise usually located?   (2)
A   Sometimes a local bank will be making a loan on property outside the county, and I'll have to travel away from home to appraise. However, most of the time I appraise property within a 30-mile radius of the city— you know, property somewhere in this county.

Second, the plaintiff must convince the jury that the basis for the witness' opinion is extensive data about very comparable parcels. The witness should be asked to describe in detail the proximity of the other property in time and place and the extent of the improvements on the other property. The plaintiff should concentrate on this part of the foundation. The more comparable the other properties are, the more weight the jury will attach to the witness' opinion.

2. *Damages for a plaintiff buyer*

The majority, American view is that the innocent buyer is entitled to the same measure of recovery as an innocent seller: the difference between contract price and market price at the time for delivery of the deed. However, there is a minority view that unless the seller breaches in bad faith, the buyer is entitled to recover only the down payment and expenses of title examination; the minority rule is sometimes called the English view. When the court decides to follow the English view, the plaintiff can testify directly to the amount of the down payment and the title examination expenses. The plaintiff may do so even if receipts for the payments exist; payment is an event that occurs independently of the receipt, and the payor may testify to the event of payment without violating the best evidence rule. However, it is usually best to corroborate the testimony by authenticating and introducing the receipts.

Alternatively, the plaintiff may attempt to overcome the English view and recover full damages by showing that the defendant's breach was in bad faith. To do so, the plaintiff should use the evidentiary techniques discussed in Section 8-3e. That subsection analyzes the defendant's bad faith as a factor in deciding whether the defendant's breach was material. Here too, to show the seller's bad faith, the plaintiff may show the seller's ability to perform, motive to breach (an advancing market price), statements evidencing bad faith, subsequent resale at a higher price, and similar acts logically relevant to show intent and bad faith.

c. Employment Contracts

1. Damages for a plaintiff employer

If the employee breaches the contract, the employer may recover as damages the additional cost of substitute help. For example, suppose that the defendant employee had promised to work for $1,000. The defendant breaches, and the employer hires a substitute employee for $1,500. The employer's damages are $500. To recover these damages, the plaintiff employer should lay a foundation, including these elements:

1. The compensation specified in the contract the defendant breached. The plaintiff may testify directly to the compensation agreed to in an oral agreement, or authenticate and introduce a written agreement with the defendant.
2. The plaintiff hired a new employee as a substitute for the defendant. The plaintiff should show that the new employee assumed the defendant's duties and contracted to complete the time remaining on the defendant's contract. Assume that the defendant had promised to do the gardening for the plaintiff for a calendar year. The defendant abandoned the contract at the end of March. The plaintiff testifies:

Q   What did you do when the defendant quit?   (2)
A   I looked around for someone to take his place.
Q   What success, if any, did you have?   (2)
A   I hired a new gardener, James Wilkinson.
Q   Under your agreement with the defendant, what were his gardening duties?   (2)
A   He was responsible for all the outside gardening. He promised to keep the grounds, both front and back, in first-rate shape.

Q   Under your agreement with Mr. Wilkinson, what were his duties?   (2)

A   He took over for the defendant. He was responsible for the same parts of the premises. I made him promise, just like the defendant, to keep the grounds in first-rate shape.

Q   How long did you hire Mr. Wilkinson for?   (2)

A   I had him finish out the term of the defendant's contract. That is, I hired him until the end of the year.

3. The compensation paid the substitute employee. The plaintiff should prove that figure in the same fashion as the plaintiff proves element #1.

4. The plaintiff attempted to mitigate the damages by paying a reasonably low salary. The defendant has the burden of proving that the plaintiff did not mitigate. However, many experienced plaintiffs' attorneys prefer to anticipate the issue on direct and pre-empt any cross-examination:

Q   How did you find Mr. Wilkinson?   (4)

A   I checked the yellow pages here in Center City for other gardeners.

Q   How many gardeners did the yellow pages list?   (4)

A   I think there were seven.

Q   How many did you contact?   (4)

A   I contacted all but one. One always had a busy line.

Q   Why did you ultimately choose Mr. Wilkinson?   (4)

A   He quoted me the lowest price for the work.

Q   How long did you discuss the price with Mr. Wilkinson before hiring him?   (4)

A   I talked to him about half an hour before hiring him.

Q   What did you discuss with him before hiring him?   (4)

A   At first, he quoted me a figure that I thought was a little high, so I dickered with him a bit to get the figure as low as I could.

2. *Damages for a plaintiff employee*

The rules for the employee's recovery are even simpler. The employee is presumptively entitled to the contract price. The defendant employer has the burden of proving that the plaintiff could have mitigated damages by obtaining other employment. The plaintiff's foundation can include the following:

1. The contract price specified in the original contract with the defendant.

2. Despite the exercise of reasonable diligence, the plaintiff could not find similar employment or employment that paid as well as the contract with the defendant. The plaintiff need not present any evidence on this issue during the case-in-chief, but many seasoned commercial litigators like to cover the issue to defuse any cross-examination. Suppose that the plaintiff had specialized training in the use of the scanning electron microscope (SEM)[9] and the defendant manufacturer hired the plaintiff for a year to use the SEM in the defendant's quality control program. The defendant then breached by firing the plaintiff:

Q   What employment did you obtain after the defendant fired you?   (2)

A   I was unemployed for almost six months.

Q   Why were you unemployed?   (2)

A   Nobody in the whole state seemed to need anyone with my experience.

Q   To your knowledge, how many private firms in Minnesota use a scanning electron microscope in their quality control program?   (2)

A   I know of only one other firm that does so, and they already have someone to do that for them.

Q   What opportunities for teaching did you have when the defendant fired you?

A   Virtually none.

Q   Why?

A   The defendant fired me in November. All the university science departments had hired their instructors during the previous summer. I wrote to them all, but there were no openings.

Q   To your knowledge, what was the closest city where there was a business firm with an opening for an SEM technician?   (2)

A   I had heard of one in Boston.

Q   Why didn't you move there?   (2)

A   I didn't have the money to make the move, and my understanding was that the job offer didn't include moving expenses.

d.   Construction Contracts

1.   *Damages for a plaintiff contractor*

The courts use two basic formulae for computing the contractor's damages. The formulae involve the following variables:

D = damages
P = profits
C = contract price
Z = total cost of performance
X = cost of part performance to the date of breach
Y = cost of remainder of performance

The formulae are:

$$D = X + P$$

and

$$D = C - Y.[10]$$

$$D = X + P$$

To use the first formula, the plaintiff contractor initially must prove X, the amount the plaintiff spent in part performance before the landowner's breach. If the plaintiff personally made the payments and can remember the amounts, the plaintiff can testify directly to the amounts spent; as an historical event, the payment occurs independently of any receipt, and the plaintiff can testify to payment without triggering the best evidence rule. If there are numerous expenditures, the plaintiff will probably want to introduce the plaintiff's business records reflecting the payments. Section 7-2 explains the application of the authentication, best evidence, and hearsay doctrines to the plaintiff's own business records. Remember that if the expenditures were numerous, the plaintiff may be able to invoke Federal Evidence Rule 1006 as an excuse for introducing a convenient summary rather than the cumbersome records themselves.

The only other variable in the first formula is P, the profit the plaintiff expected to realize on this construction project. The original estimate of P requires subtracting the probable Z (total cost of performance) from C (the contract price the landowner agreed to pay the contractor). There is obviously a strong element of conjecture in any estimate of Z, but the plaintiff can use the following technique to make the estimate of Z as persuasive as possible. Initially, ask the contractor or the expert who made the calculation to list the costs that are included in Z: "What items of cost do you have to consider in estimating the total cost of performance?"

Then take the items one by one: "How much did you estimate for the shingles for the roof?" As the witness cites the figure for each individual cost item, force the witness to explain how he or she arrived at that figure. It is best if the witness can use a unit price to derive the figure: "I estimated that the roof surface was 1,500 square feet. We usually use four shingles per square foot. The local roofing supply company sells the shingles to us at 80¢ a single or $4,800. . . ." The next best evidence is the witness' testimony to an actual expenditure on a similar project: "The house we were building for the defendant had roughly the same size and shape roof that we built for a fellow in Echo Canyon seven months ago. When I ran the estimate on the shingles for the defendant's roof, I used the figure, $4,800, that we spent on the roof in Echo Canyon." As the witness testifies to each figure, write the figure on a chalkboard or easel; if the jurors can see the numbers being written on the board and finally added, the aggregate Z has much more credibility in their eyes. If the plaintiff follows this technique, the estimate of Z will be much less vulnerable to the defense argument that the plaintiff pulled the figure out of the air.

$$D = C - Y$$

The second formula, $D = C - Y$, will yield the same number as D; but use of the second formula requires different evidence. The variable C is easy to prove, since C is the price specified in the contract. If the contract is oral, the plaintiff may testify directly to C. If the contract is written, the plaintiff introduces the contract and quotes the language specifying C to the jury.

Under the second formula, the plaintiff can prove Y (the cost of the remainder of performance) in much the same fashion as the plaintiff proves Z under the first formula. Begin the line of questioning by asking, "What parts of the project were still incomplete when the defendant ordered you off the worksite?" Then, taking the cost items one by one, elicit a figure for each item. Post each item on a chalkboard or easel; and at the end of the list of items, total the figure to arrive at Y.

2. Damages for plaintiff landowner

COST OF COMPLETION

Most jurisdictions begin with the assumption that the landowner is entitled to recover as damages the full cost of completing the project the defendant contractor undertook. In essence, the landowner recovers the amount that it will cost the landowner to hire another contractor to complete the project. The plaintiff ordinarily proves that figure by calling one or more contractors to elicit what they would charge the plaintiff to complete the work. The contractors may testify in either of two manners. One manner is to directly assert their opinion of what it will cost the landowner in the current market to hire another contractor to finish the work. As the basis for the opinion, the contractor may cite the rate charged for similar projects the contractor is familiar with. This manner of testimony is ordinarily satisfactory.

However, if the defendant has indicated that the defendant is going to seriously dispute the amount of damage, the plaintiff may want to elicit more detailed testimony from the contractor appearing for the plaintiff. The first part of this detailed testimony would be proof of Z in the same fashion we previously described. Z now represents what the new contractor will have to spend to complete the original project. The second part of the testimony would be proof of P for a new contractor. The contractor could testify to the average profit margin of similarly situated contractors in the vicinity and then use that average to estimate P:

Q   In this country, what is the average profit margin for contracting firms of the defendant's size?
A   I'd say it's about 5% profit on each project.
Q   How do you know that?
A   Most of the contractors belong to a county-wide association. We exchange figures; and as I recall, a 5% profit on each project was the figure we came up with for last year.
Q   What would be a reasonable profit on the remaining work to be done on Mr. Freeman's (the plaintiff's) building?
A   As I said, I think the out-of-pocket cost for the remainder of the work would be about $95,000. To get a net 5% profit, you'd have to have a $5,000 profit on this job.

You then add the estimates of the cost of and profit on the work remaining to be done.

DIMINISHED VALUE

In some cases, the cost of completion will be disproportionate to the increase in the property's market value; the cost of completion may be

$100,000 although completing the work would increase the property's fair market value by only $10,000. In a growing minority of jurisdictions, the courts have asserted the power to balance the cost of completion against the increased market value and award only diminished market value when the cost of completion is disproportionate. In the last hypothetical, the court might well award only $10,000 rather than the $100,000 cost of completion.

The plaintiff can defeat the defendant's attempts to limit the plaintiff's recovery to diminished value in several ways. One way is to offer the plaintiff's own expert's estimate of diminished market value. The defendant's expert may be understating the diminished market value.

A second way is to prove that the defendant's breach was in bad faith. Some jurisdictions never use diminished market value as the measure of recovery when the defendant's breach was in bad faith. Again, the plaintiff can show the defendant's ability, motive, statements proving bad faith, and other acts evidencing intent.

A third way is to prove that completing the project will not require the destruction of any existing structure. Some courts award diminished value only when completion would necessitate destroying an otherwise usable structure. For example, if the defendant's breach was the installation of the wrong pipe and the defendant has already enclosed the pipe in wall, completing the project would require tearing down the wall and tearing out the old pipe. If the pipe the defendant installed is just as serviceable as the pipe the contract called for, the court might deny cost of completion recovery. It is quite another matter if the defendant merely left work undone. The plaintiff's contractor could testify:

Q   What would you as a contractor have to do to complete this project according to the specifications in Mr. Freeman's contract with the defendant?

A   I would have to finish the roof, paint the second floor, put in the drain pipes, and erect the detached garage.

Q   What parts of the existing structure, if any, would you have to destroy or demolish to complete the work?

A   You wouldn't have to do any demolition. It's just that the previous contractor didn't finish what he started. You don't have to rip anything out or do anything destructive like that.

Sec. 9-6.   General Damages for Material Breach—The Uniform Commercial Code

In most cases, the common-law remedies for material breach are based upon hypothetical transactions. We assume hypothetically that the plaintiff buyer re-entered the market and purchased a substitute good at the prevailing rate. We then compute the buyer's damages on the basis of the prevailing market rate rather than the actual price the buyer paid for a substitute good. At common law, we compute the seller's damages on the same basis.

The draftsmen of the Uniform Commercial Code wanted to simplify proof of damages by permitting both the seller and buyer to compute their damages on actual prices rather than on the hypothetical market prices. The Code authorizes the seller to compute damages on the basis of the actual resale price and similarly enables the buyer to compute damages on the basis of the actual repurchase or "cover" price.

a. Resale by the Plaintiff Seller

Uniform Commercial Code 2-706(1) sanctions the use of the actual resale price in computing the seller's damages:

> Where the resale is made in good faith and in a commercially reasonable manner, the seller may recover the difference between the resale price and the contract price. . . .

Section 2-706(2) generally requires that "every aspect of the sale including the method, manner, time, place, and terms must be commercially reasonable." Subsections (3) and (4) specifically require that the seller give the buyer certain notice, depending on whether the resale is private or public. However, the key to understanding 2-706 is that if the resale is in good faith and commercially reasonable, the actual resale price is used to compute the seller's damages—even when the price is lower than the hypothetical market price. By analogy, the courts have applied the rule explicitly stated in Section 9-507(2):

> The fact that a better price could have been obtained by a sale at a different time or in a different method from that selected by the (seller) is not of itself sufficient to establish that the sale was not made in a commercially reasonable manner.

To invoke 2-706, the plaintiff seller must prove the following elements:

1. The merchandise the plaintiff sold to the third party was the merchandise originally intended for the defendant. Subsection 2-706(2) states:

   > The resale must be reasonably identified as referring to the broken contract, but it is not necessary that the goods be in existence or that any or all of them have been identified to the contract before the breach.

2. The plaintiff gave the defendant buyer the requisite notice. If the resale is by private sale, subsection (3) dictates that "the seller . . . gives the buyer reasonable notification of his intention to resell." If the resale is at public sale, the seller must ordinarily notify the buyer of the time and place of the resale and the location of the goods for inspection.

3. The plaintiff resold in a commercially reasonable manner. The plaintiff's foundation should show that

   —the plaintiff's choice between a public and private resale was reasonable,

—the plaintiff conducted the sale in a reasonable manner, and
—the price the plaintiff realized was reasonable.

Suppose that the plaintiff built a private airplane for the defendant. The defendant breached by refusing to accept the plane. The plaintiff resold the plane and wants to use the actual resale price to compute damages. The plaintiff should testify along these lines:

Q   How did you dispose of the plane when the defendant told you that he would not take delivery?   (1)
A   I decided to resell it. I had invested a lot of time and money in building it, and I couldn't let it just sit on the lot.
Q   Which plane are we talking about now?   (1)
A   The one that I built for the defendant. It has ID TN 7796.
Q   How did you resell it?   (3)
A   I decided to hold a public auction.
Q   Why did you choose a public auction rather than a private sale?   (3)
A   There would be some interested buyers locally here in Anaheim, but I figured that I'd have a much wider market and hopefully get a better price if I went public.
Q   What do you mean by going public?   (3)
A   I advertised the auction to the general public by ads in magazines and on posters.
Q   Which magazine did you advertise in?   (3)
A   I ran ads in *Flight* and *Private Pilot*.
Q   Why did you choose those magazines?   (3)
A   They're the most widely read magazines for private pilots. I figured that they were the best media for reaching prospective buyers.
Q   When did you run the ads in these magazines?   (3)
A   I ran them in the January and February issues.
Q   What did you do with the posters?   (3)
A   I had about 200 of them placed at private airports throughout the western United States. I mailed them to various friends who agreed to put them up.
Q   When did you hold the auction itself?   (3)
A   On March 15th of this year.
Q   What day of the week was March 15th?   (3)
A   It was a Saturday.
Q   Why did you choose a Saturday?   (3)
A   A lot of private plane owners have full-time businesses, and it's usually easier for them to get around on weekends.
Q   Why did you advertise for only two months before holding the auction? (3)
A   First, I figured that two months would be long enough. Secondly, the market trend in the private aircraft industry was downward; and I feared that the longer I waited, the lower the final selling price would be.
Q   Where did you hold the auction?   (3)
A   At the clubroom at the Anaheim Airport.

Q   Why did you choose that location?   (3)

A   Our airport is one of the largest in the US for private planes. And even on a typical day, there's lots of traffic in and out from other states. The traffic is especially heavy from out of state on weekends.

Q   What time of the day did you schedule the auction for?   (3)

A   Two in the afternoon.

Q   Why did you choose that time?   (3)

A   That would give even out-of-state buyers a chance to fly in that day and still make the auction with time to spare. I wanted as many prospective buyers as possible.

Q   What notice, if any, did you give the defendant before the auction?   (2)

A   I phoned him in January and gave him all the details.

Q   What did you tell him?   (2)

A   I gave him all the info about the time and place of the auction.

Q   What, if anything, did you tell him about the location of the plane?   (2)

A   I said that as the ads indicated, the plane would be at the Anaheim Airport for two full weeks before the auction to permit prospective buyers to inspect it. I told him exactly where the plane would be—parked near hangar C.

Q   How many people attended the auction?   (3)

A   When I started at two, I'd say that there were about 40 people in the room.

Q   How long did the auction take?   (3)

A   Only about ten minutes.

Q   What was the result of the auction?   (3)

A   I sold the plane to a buyer from Seattle for $175,000

Q   Your honor, I now request that this be marked plaintiff's exhibit number six for identification.   (3)

J   It will be so marked.

Q   Please let the record reflect that I am showing the exhibit to the opposing counsel.   (3)

J   The record will state that.

Q   (*To the witness*) I now hand you plaintiff's exhibit number six for identification. What is it?   (3)

A   It's the April issue of *Flight* magazine.

Q   What is that magazine?   (3)

A   It's the private aircraft industry magazine with the biggest circulation.

Q   What appears on page 14 of this issue?   (3)

A   It's the monthly auction report.

Q   What is that?   (3)

A   One of the features of *Flight* is a summary of prices paid at aircraft auctions throughout the United States for the previous month, in this case, March.

Q   Your honor, I now offer page 14 of this exhibit into evidence as plaintiff's exhibit number six.

J   It will be admitted.

Q   How is the information on this page arranged?   (3)

A   By type of aircraft. First you find the type of aircraft you're interested in, and then the category lists the prices paid for those craft during March.

Q   Which category would your plane fall into?   (3)

A   Category 5 for planes of its size and range. In fact, my auction price is reported here.

Q   How many other auction prices are reported for Category 5?   (3)

A   Five others.

Q   What are those prices?   (3a)

A   They range from $150,000 to $195,000.

Q   How many of those prices are under $175,000?   (3)

A   Three are below that figure, and only two are above.

LEGAL RESEARCH REFERENCE:
Murray §241
White & Summers §7-6

b.   Cover (Repurchase) by the Plaintiff Buyer

Cover by the buyer is the parallel to resale by the seller. Section 2-712 of the Code governs cover. Like 2-706, 2-712 requires that the buyer act "in good faith" and a commercially reasonable manner. The parallel is complete; if the buyer acts in that manner, the buyer may use the actual cover price rather than the hypothetical market price to compute damages. To utilize 2-712, the buyer must prove that

1. The goods the plaintiff bought from the third party replaced the goods the plaintiff intended buying from the defendant. The goods need not be identical. However, if the plaintiff buys a higher quality good for a higher price, some courts reduce the cover price to reflect the higher quality.
2. The plaintiff made the cover purchase "without unreasonable delay."
3. The plaintiff made a commercially reasonable cover. To show the repurchase's reasonableness, the plaintiff may show that

   —the plaintiff conducted a thorough search for substitute goods at a reasonable price, and
   —the price the plaintiff finally paid was reasonable.
   If the plaintiff acts reasonably, the plaintiff may base the damages computation on the cover price even if the cover price is higher than the hypothetical market price.

Reverse the roles in the private airplane hypothetical. In this variation of the hypothetical, the seller breaches; and the buyer is testifying:

Q   What did you do when the defendant told you he would not deliver the plane?   (1)

A   I bought another one.

Q   What type of plane did you buy?   (1)

A   It was another Mohawk four-seater.

Q   How does this plane compare to the plane the defendant was going to sell you?   (1)

A   It's almost exactly the same plane. The color of the interior was different, but all the mechanical features are exactly the same. It's a standard model you can get almost anywhere.

Q   When did you buy this new plane?   (2)

A   A month after the defendant informed me that he wouldn't deliver.

Q   Why did you wait a month?   (2)

A   The market was uncertain. For a couple of weeks, it looked as if prices were headed down. I figured the longer I waited, the less I'd have to pay. But then it became clear that prices were leveling out. As soon as that became evident, I bought a plane within a week.

Q   Where did you buy the plane?   (3)

A   From another dealer here in Stillwater.

Q   Why did you buy from that dealer?   (3)

A   I contacted roughly 15 dealers throughout the Midwest and got their quotations. This dealer was offering the best deal.

Q   What do you mean by the best deal?   (3)

A   To put it simply, the lowest price.

Q   What was that price?   (3)

A   I paid him $160,000.

> [*As in the resale illustration, the plaintiff should now introduce the trade journal.*]

Q   How many prices for Mohawk four-seaters are quoted in this exhibit?   (3)

A   Five.

Q   What are the prices?   (3)

A   They range from $140,000 to $180,000.

Q   How many prices are above $160,000?   (3)

A   Three are above $160,000, and two are below.

LEGAL RESEARCH REFERENCE:
Murray §245
White & Summers §6-3

Sec. 9-7.   The Recovery of Lost Profits

In most suits involving the breach of contracts for the sale of goods, the courts do not award the innocent party full net profits on the contract. The courts assume that the innocent party can re-enter the market place and form a substitute contract. When this assumption holds true, the innocent party's only loss is the benefit of the bargain, namely, the difference between the contract price and the market price. However, the assumption occasionally breaks down; and when it does, the courts award lost profits as damages.

a.   The Recovery of Lost Profits by the Buyer

In exceptional circumstances, the courts permit the buyer to recover lost profits as special, consequential damages. Since lost profit damages are special damages, to recover lost profit damages, the plaintiff must satisfy *Hadley v. Baxendale*'s foreseeability requirement. Thus, Uniform Commercial Code 2-715(2)(a) authorizes the buyer to recover lost profits by the following language:

> Consequential damages resulting from the seller's breach include . . . any loss resulting from general or particular requirements and needs of which the seller at the time of contracting had reason to know and which could not reasonably be prevented to cover or otherwise. . . .

The jurisdictions vary on how rigorously they enforce the foreseeability requirement, but the following foundation would be adequate in any jurisdiction:

1. The plaintiff buyer had already contracted or was contemplating contracting to resell the goods to a third party. The plaintiff could testify:

   Q   Why did you want to buy this brand of seed from the defendant?   (1)
   A   I wanted the defendant to act as my supplier. I had already contracted with farmers in Michigan to resell the seed to them. I knew that you could get this type of seed only in Oregon, and the defendant had much better West Coast contacts than I did.

2. At the time of contracting, the defendant knew or had reason to know that the plaintiff intended to resell the subject matter of the contract:

   Q   What, if anything, did you tell the defendant about what you intended to do with the seed?   (2)
   A   I told him point blank that I was already under a contract with some Michigan dealers. In fact, when we were writing up our own contract, I think I took out one of my Michigan contracts and copied the description of the seed from the Michigan contract onto this contract.

3. At the time of contracting, the defendant should have foreseen that if the defendant breached, it would be difficult for the plaintiff to find an alternative supply and perform the resale contract:

   Q   How many suppliers of this type of seed are there in the United States?   (3)
   A   Only about three. This seed was imported from Argentina only a couple of years ago, and there are just a handful of American suppliers, including the defendant.
   Q   Why did you buy the seed from the defendant rather than any of the other suppliers?   (3)
   A   I went to them first, and they said that they had more orders than they could handle.
   Q   Before you signed the contract with the defendant, what, if anything, did you tell him about your contact with the other suppliers?   (3)
   A   I told him that he was my last resort. I mentioned that I had contacted the other suppliers but they couldn't help me.

4. When the defendant breached, the plaintiff was unable to obtain an alternative supply and, consequently, lost the resale.

Q   What did you do when the defendant told you that he could not deliver the seed?   (4)

A   I immediately contacted the other suppliers of the seed.

Q   How many of them did you contact? (4)

A   I think it was four. I know I contacted all of them, but I'm not sure of the specific number.

Q   How did they respond to your offer to buy seed?   (4)

A   It was the same story as before. They turned me down flat because they had already booked more orders than they could handle for months. I was just plain out of luck.

5. The plaintiff shows the profit the plaintiff would have realized on the resale, that is, the difference between the price the plaintiff was going to pay the defendant and the price the plaintiff was going to charge the third party. If the contract with the third party was oral, the plaintiff can testify directly to the resale price. If the contract was written, the plaintiff should introduce the contract and quote the language setting the resale price. If the resale was contemplated but the plaintiff had not yet signed a contract, the plaintiff could prove the market price prevailing at the time when the plaintiff probably would have made the resale.

LEGAL RESEARCH AND REFERENCE:
Murray §249

b.   The Recovery of Lost Profits by the Seller

Uniform Commercial Code 2-708(2) announces that if the normal measure of damages for the seller is "inadequate to put the seller in as good a position as performance would have done, then the measure of damages is the profit . . . which the seller would have made from full performance by the buyer. . . ." When will the normal measure be inadequate? The answer is that the normal measure is inadequate when the plaintiff is an "expansible" seller.[11] An expansible seller is usually a middleman or jobber. A middleman such as an auto dealer does not have to invest capital in manufacturing equipment; consequently, the middleman can increase volume without increasing capital investment. Assuming sufficient customer demand and adequate supply from the manufacturer, the expansible seller can handle two auto sales as easily as one. For the expansible seller, the defendant's breach results in a loss of profits and warrants the recovery of full profits as the measure of recovery. To justify the award of net profits, the plaintiff should lay this foundation:

1. The plaintiff is an expansible seller. The plaintiff describes his or her own business to show on the record that the plaintiff could expand volume without increasing capital investment in equipment:

Q   What additional equipment, if any, would you need to buy to increase the volume of your business?   (1)

A   Really none. We just sell the cars; we don't make them. Maybe you'd buy another desk or chair, but that's about it.

Q   How do you handle an increase in your volume?   (1)

A   We just ship the orders off to Detroit, receive the deliveries, and then release the cars to the buyers. It's really no problem whether we're selling ten cars a month or 100.

2. At the time of the defendant's breach, the plaintiff's supplier could have filled the plaintiff's order for an additional auto. If the plaintiff's supplier could not have filled the order, the plaintiff would not have been able to make two sales rather than one. It is ideal to call a representative from the manufacturer to testify to the supplier's capacity, but the judge usually accepts circumstantial evidence of the supplier's capacity. The plaintiff could supply such circumstantial evidence:

Q   How quickly does your supplier usually fill your orders?   (2)

A   They usually turn them around and get us the car three weeks after we send in the order.

Q   How quickly was your supplier filling orders when the defendant refused to accept his car?   (2)

A   The same as usual—two and a half or three weeks. The supply of cars was coming in as smoothly as usual.

Q   At that time, what difficulty, if any, did you have getting the supplier to fill orders?   (2)

A   We didn't have any difficulty. We'd send the order in, and Detroit would fill it as promptly as usual.

3. At the time of the defendant's breach, there was demand for the type of car the defendant ordered. Like the supplier's inability to fill an order, the lack of demand can break the chain of causation the plaintiff must prove; if there is no demand, the plaintiff could not have made a second sale. The plaintiff should describe the demand for the product:

Q   What happened to the car you ordered for the defendant?   (3)

A   We sold it to somebody else in about a week.

Q   At the time the defendant refused to accept the pickup truck, what was the demand for that type of car?   (3)

A   I'd say that the demand was about normal.

Q   What is the normal demand?   (3)

A   We usually sell one or two every week; and as far as I can remember, the week the defendant refused delivery was a pretty regular week. The demand was about as steady as usual.

4. The plaintiff proves the amount of the lost profits. The plaintiff would prove lost profits here in roughly the same fashion as the plaintiff proves P in a construction contract. The plaintiff can establish P by subtracting Z from C. The contract with the defendant specifies the C, and the plaintiff will have to prove the various components of Z, most importantly the price the expansible seller must pay the supplier.

LEGAL RESEARCH REFERENCE:
Murray §243
White & Summers §§7-8-11

Sec. 9-8.   Account Stated

In credit transactions, the plaintiff seller has an alternative method of proving the amount of the defendant buyer's debt. This method is the account stated doctrine. To invoke the doctrine, the plaintiff lays the following foundation:

1. The plaintiff and the defendant engaged in several previous transactions of a monetary character:

Q   What is your occupation?   (1)
A   I run a building supply store. I sell building materials to contractors throughout the Salt Lake area.
Q   Who is Mr. Philo?   (1)
A   He's the defendant in this case, seated over there and wearing the gray tie.
Q   Your honor, please let the record reflect that Mr. Sanders has identified the defendant.   (1)
J   It shall so reflect.
Q   What dealings, if any, have you had with Mr. Philo?   (1)
A   I agreed to supply him materials at cost plus 10% on a school gym project that he was working on.
Q   How were you going to supply him these materials?   (1)
A   His crew would come in and pick up materials whenever they needed them during the course of the project.
Q   How was the defendant going to pay you for the materials?   (1)
A   I was selling them to him on credit. I told him I'd tally up the bill at the end of the project and send the bill to him then.
Q   How many times did the defendant's crew come in to pick up materials?   (1)
A   They came in on a daily basis during the seven weeks the defendant was working on that project.

2. After the transactions, the plaintiff added up the defendant's bill and prepared a statement of the account balance:

Q   What happened after these pickups?   (2)
A   They evidently finished the job in mid-June, and at the end of the month I tallied up the bill.
Q   What do you mean when you say you "tallied up the bill"?   (2)
A   I reviewed all the records of the defendant's credit purchases, added up the total, and prepared a written statement of the account.

3. The plaintiff submitted the account to the defendant:

Q   What did you do with the statement of the account?   (3)
A   I sent the original to the defendant.

4. The defendant received the statement of the account. In some cases, the plaintiff can testify to a subsequent conversation in which the defendant acknowledged receipt of the statement. The defendant's acknowledgment qualifies as an admission under Federal Evidence Rule 801(d)(2). In other cases, the plaintiff must rely on the presumption that an addressee receives the letter if the letter is properly stamped, addressed, and mailed:

Q How did you send the account to the defendant?   (4)
A I mailed it to him.
Q Specifically, what steps did you use in mailing it to the defendant?   (4)
A I put it in an envelope, addressed it to the defendant, and deposited it in the box on the sidewalk outside my store.
Q How did you find the defendant's address?   (4)
A The address was stated in the account ledger, and I think I doublechecked it by looking at the Salt Lake telephone directory.

When the plaintiff did not personally mail the letter or cannot recall doing so, the plaintiff can introduce evidence of the business' customary mailing procedures under Evidence Rule 406.

5. The defendant retained the statement of the account for a substantial period of time without voicing an objection:

Q When did you mail the statement of the account to the defendant?   (5)
A It was on July 1st.
Q How long does it usually take for mail to get across town?   (5)
A At most only two days.
Q How do you know that?   (5)
A I'm constantly sending the bills to my local customers. They sometimes phone in. They phone in usually a day or two after I drop the bill in the mail.
Q What contact did you have with the defendant during the month of July? (5)
A I didn't hear from him at all.
Q What contact did you have with him during the month of August?   (5)
A He didn't phone me, so I finally got a little nervous about the bill and phoned him.
Q How do you know that it was the defendant you spoke with on the phone?   (5)
A I recognized his voice.
Q How did you become familiar with the sound of his voice?   (5)
A During the work on the gym, he stopped by lots of times. We'd chat while his workmen were loading the supplies on the pickup truck.
Q What did you say to the defendant when you phoned him?   (5)
A I asked him when he intended to pay the bill.
Q What did he say?   (5)
A He said the school district was a little slow in paying him, but that he'd get around to it as soon as he could.

In essence, the defendant's silence is a tacit admission of the account's correctness under Evidence Rule 801(d)(2)(B).

6. The amount stated in the account. If, as is usually the case, the plaintiff retained a copy of the statement of account, the plaintiff should first authenticate the copy. The plaintiff can easily satisfy the best evidence rule. The copy may qualify as an original under Federal Evidence Rule 1001(3) or a duplicate under 1001(4). Even if the copy is deemed secondary evidence, there is usually an adequate excuse for non-production of the original under Rule 1004(3); the defendant has the original, and the pleadings should put the defendant on notice that the original will be needed at trial. In most jurisdictions, the plaintiff pleads account stated as a separate, common count in the complaint; the plaintiff may have even attached a copy of the statement of the account as an exhibit to the complaint. After satisfying the authentication and best evidence doctrines, the plaintiff introduces the account:

Q   Please read exhibit four (the statement of the account) to the jurors.   (6)

A   It lists all the various pickups. The list runs on for four and a half pages. At the very end of the fifth page, it reads: "Grand total—$12,577.92."

Q   Your honor, I request permission to distribute these copies of the exhibit to the jurors.

J   Permission granted.

LEGAL RESEARCH REFERENCE:
Murray §257

Sec. 9-9.   Specific Performance

Money damages are the normal legal remedy for breach of a contract duty. However, equity courts and courts exercising equity jurisdiction sometimes grant the extraordinary relief of decreeing specific performance of a contract duty. The buyer and seller both may seek specific performance.

a.   The Seller's Action for the Price

When the court awards the seller the full contract price, the court in effect is decreeing specific performance by the buyer. Uniform Commercial Code 2-709(1) lists the situations in which the seller may recover the full contract price.

1.   *The buyer's acceptance of the goods*

Under the Uniform Commercial Code, the buyer's acceptance of the goods is a critical event. As subsection 2-607(1) prescribes, "The buyer must pay at the contract rate for any goods accepted." The buyer may have a counterclaim for the seller's breach of warranty; but if the buyer accepts, the buyer is presumptively liable for the full contract price. To prove acceptance, the plaintiff seller should show that

1. When the plaintiff delivered the goods, the defendant physically accepted them.
2. The defendant had a "reasonable opportunity to inspect the goods." Subsection 2-606(1)(a) makes that opportunity a requirement for effective acceptance. The defendant's retention of the goods for any substantial time period gives the defendant that opportunity. The lapse of that period terminates the defendant buyer's right to reject under 2-602(1).
3. The defendant then "signifies to the seller that the goods are conforming or that he will take or retain them in spite of their nonconformity." This is another requirement of subsection 2-606(1)(a).
4. The defendant did not effectively revoke the acceptance. Subsection 2-608(1) controls whether the buyer initially has a right to revoke acceptance:

> The buyer may revoke his acceptance of a lot or commercial unit . . . if he has accepted it . . .
>
> (a) on the reasonable assumption that its non-conformity would be cured and it has not been seasonably cured; or
> (b) without discovery of such non-conformity if his acceptance was reasonably induced either by the difficulty of discovery before acceptance or by the seller's assurances.

Subsection 2-608(2) adds that the buyer must exercise the right to revoke "within a reasonable time after the buyer discovers or should have discovered the ground for it. . . ."

Our fact situation is a contract for the purchase of an automobile. The original contract specified that the car would be a manual shift rather than automatic. The plaintiff dealer tendered an automatic, and the defendant physically accepted and retained the car. The defendant now refuses to pay the purchase price on several grounds, including the ground that the automatic does not conform to the contract specifications. The plaintiff's sales manager is testifying:

Q   Where were you on the afternoon of July 1st of this year?   (1)
A   I was in my office at the dealership.
Q   What happened that afternoon?   (1)
A   The defendant came in to pick up his car. I had phoned him the day before to let him know that it was in from the Coast.
Q   What did you do when the defendant came in?   (1)
A   I gave him possession of the car.
Q   How did you do that?   (1)
A   I handed him the keys.
Q   What, if anything, did you tell him when you handed him the keys?   (1)
A   I said that he should take a quick drive around the lot before he headed out on the highway. You know, just to get the feel of the car before he pushed it up to freeway speeds.
Q   What did the defendant do then?   (1)
A   After I handed him the keys, he got into the car.

Q   What, if anything, did he say about the car when he got into it?   (2)

A   He noticed that it was an automatic.

Q   What did you say then?

A   I said that he was right. I said that I knew the contract called for a manual, but I didn't think he was all that concerned whether it was manual or automatic.

Q   How did he respond to your statement?   (3)

A   He said that that was O.K.

Q   To the best of your recollection, what were his precise words?   (3)

A   I can't recall his exact words, but I think he said something like, "I guess so. This should do just fine."

Q   What did he do then?   (3)

A   He just drove around the lot for a couple of minutes and then headed out on the highway.

Q   Before he left, what assurance, if any, did you give him that you would change the automatic to manual?   (4)

A   I didn't give him any assurance like that. I had pointed out that it was an automatic, he hadn't objected, and I thought that that was the end of it.

Q   When did you next hear from the defendant?   (2), (4)

A   It wasn't until about seven weeks later, in late August.

Q   What happened then?   (4)

A   He drove the car back and said that he wanted one with a manual. He said that he'd had some trouble with the automatic and that he was more used to a manual.

Q   What did you say then?   (4)

A   I told him I was sorry, but all the station wagons on the lot were automatic, and all our orders for the next two months had been placed. We didn't have a manual station wagon to give him.

Q   What did he say then?   (4)

A   He told me that he wanted us to take back the car.

Q   What did you say?   (4)

A   I flatly refused to do it.

Q   How did he respond to your refusal?   (4)

A   He said that that was O.K. He'd just keep the car without paying the balance. And that's exactly what he's tried to do.

2.   The loss or destruction of the goods after the risk of loss passed to the buyer

If the goods are lost or destroyed after the risk passes to buyer, the buyer must still pay the seller under subsection 2-709(1)(a). The buyer's only recourse is against the insurer. Uniform Commercial Code 2-509 sets out the rules governing when risk of loss passes. If the plaintiff relies on this theory for recovering the full contract price, the plaintiff must prove that

1.   An event, shifting the risk of loss, occurred. For example, under 2-509(1)(a), in an F.O.B. place of shipment contract, the risk passes to the buyer "when the goods are duly delivered to the carrier." The

plaintiff seller could prove delivery by the testimony of the seller's employees who delivered to the carrier or through the seller's business records stating the fact of delivery. The employee's testimony would have to be based on personal knowledge to satisfy Federal Evidence Rule 602, and the records would have to comply with Rule 803(6) governing business entries. The record must reflect the date of the event shifting the risk.

2. After that event occurred, the goods were lost or destroyed. There are numerous evidentiary techniques for proving the goods' loss or destruction. An employee of the carrier who witnessed the goods' destruction in a railroad derailment could testify to the destruction. Under 803(6), the plaintiff could introduce the carrier's business records reflecting the goods' destruction. If a public agency investigated the event such as the derailment causing the destruction, the plaintiff could introduce the report of the investigation under Rule 803(8) for official records. If the report were properly attested, the report would be self-authenticating under Evidence Rule 902(1). Whatever technique the plaintiff uses, the plaintiff must make certain that the record reflects the date on which the loss or destruction occurred—a date subsequent to the time at which risk of loss passed.

3. The seller's inability to resell

Finally, under 2-709(1)(b), the seller may recover the full price "if the seller is unable after reasonable effort to resell them at a reasonable price or the circumstances reasonably indicate that such effort will be unavailing." Under this subsection, the plaintiff will ordinarily have to prove that

1. The plaintiff made a diligent effort to resell the merchandise.
2. The effort was unsuccessful.
3. The plaintiff should specify the reason why the effort was unsuccessful. Most goods are resellable. The jury will usually think that it is suspicious if the merchandise cannot be resold. The plaintiff should explain the special circumstances making it difficult to resell this merchandise.

Suppose that the plaintiff manufactured a microwave stove for the defendant homeowner and the defendant refused to take delivery. The plaintiff testifies:

Q   What did you do with the stove when the defendant told you that she would not accept it?   (1)
A   I tried to resell it.
Q   What effort did you make to resell it?   (1)
A   First I left it on my showroom floor for two weeks.
Q   What result did that have?   (2)
A   A lot of people looked at it, but no one was interested enough to buy.
Q   What did you do then?   (1)
A   I advertised in the local papers for several weeks.

Q   Which papers?   (1)

A   The *Post-Dispatch* and the *Globe-Democrat.*

Q   How many times did you run the advertisement?   (1)

A   I ran it ten times in each paper.

Q   What result did the ads have?   (2)

A   Three people stopped by to look at the stove, but again no one offered to buy it.

Q   What did you do then?   (1)

A   I consigned it to another dealer for two months, but she couldn't sell it either.

Q   Where is the stove now?   (2)

A   It's back on my showroom floor because I can't seem to get rid of it.

Q   Why are you having difficulty reselling it?   (3)

A   It has a strange design. The defendant wanted to put in in an odd-shaped corner of the kitchen, and I had it specially modified to fit in there. It's not going to fit in a normal corner of a square or rectangular kitchen.

Q   What, if anything, did the prospective buyers tell you about the stove?   (3)

A   They said it was beautiful, but it physically wouldn't fit in any of their kitchens.

[*If the defendant objects to the last question as calling for hearsay, the plaintiff should invoke Evidence Rule 801(c). It is arguable that this testimony is nonhearsay. One issue is whether the plaintiff has exercised diligence in trying to resell the stove; and the fact that prospective buyers made these statements to the plaintiff is logically relevant in deciding whether the plaintiff should have made more extensive resale efforts.*]

LEGAL RESEARCH REFERENCE:
Murray §244
White & Summers §§7-3-5

b. Specific Performance for the Buyer

1. Under traditional equity rules

Equity traditionally demanded that the plaintiff show two things before equity would decree specific performance:

1. The buyer's remedy at law is inadequate. The remedy of money damages is usually adequate, but it fails when the contract's subject matter is a unique object. If the article is one of a kind, the plaintiff cannot make a substitute transaction; even if the court awards money damages, the plaintiff will not obtain what he or she bargained for. To prove this first element, the plaintiff should describe the object's physical properties and explain why those properties make the object unique. It is relatively easy for the plaintiff to make this factual showing in the case of objects such as antiques and original paintings. In his or her testimony, the plaintiff should describe the object's unique characteristics and assert that the object is one of a kind:

Q What did the defendant promise to sell you?

A She was going to sell me her Helmholz painting.

Q Why did you want that painting?

A For several reasons.

Q What were the reasons?

A He's my favorite 19th century American painter. I have quite a collection of his works. This painting, "The Scholar," was the only painting in which he worked extensively with browns.

Q How many copies of the painting are there?

A There's just the one original that the defendant had, and I don't even know whether there are any copies in existence. As far as I know, this is the only one.

Today, the courts are beginning to find the remedy inadequate whenever it is difficult to compute money damages. Computing damages for the seller's breach of a long-term requirements or output contract is highly speculative, and that difficulty has prompted some courts to order the seller to specifically perform such contracts.

2. It will be feasible for the court to supervise the performance of the contract. Equity courts enforce their decrees by contempt, and they are reluctant to issue decrees unless it will be fairly easy to determine whether the defendant has violated the contract and committed a contempt. To counter the courts' reluctance, the plaintiff should go into detail in describing the definiteness of the contract's terms. In Section 5-3, we considered the evidentiary techniques of proving the contract's definiteness. The same techniques apply here.

LEGAL RESEARCH REFERENCE:
Murray §247

2. Under the Uniform Commercial Code

The spirit and the letter of the Uniform Commercial Code have led to a liberalization of the standards for decreeing specific performance. Subsection 1-106(1) voices the Code's spirit by declaring that "(t)he remedies provided by this Act shall be liberally administered to the end that the aggrieved party may be put in as good a position as if the other party had fully performed. . . ."

Subsection 2-716(1) is the Code's letter governing specific performance by the buyer. That subsection states that specific performance is available not only when "the goods are unique" but also "in other proper circumstances." The Code Comments indicate that the buyer's inability to cover is a proper circumstance. That rule is at odds with the early equity practice. Under that practice, if there was an ascertainable market price for the goods, the court would not decree specific performance even if the buyer could not cover. Thus, during World War II, when there were acute short-ages of even mass-produced items such as automobiles, many courts refused to decree specific performance of contracts for the sale of mass-produced items. Under the Code, since the buyer cannot cover when there is a short supply, the courts routinely decree specific performance.

The key to obtaining a specific performance decree under the Code is demonstrating the infeasibility of covering. Suppose that the defendant contracted to sell the plaintiff a classic 1936 Rolls-Royce. The defendant refused to deliver the car, and the plaintiff is testifying to show the impracticality of covering:

Q   What did you do after the defendant told you that he would not deliver the car?
A   I looked around to see whether I could buy a '36 Rolls elsewhere.
Q   What success did you have?
A   I didn't have any success. I couldn't find one on the market.
Q   Whom did you contact?
A   I got hold of all the major classic car auctioneers to see if they knew of any '36 Rolls cars available for purchase.
Q   How many auctioneers did you contact?
A   I think it was 12.
Q   How did you learn where to contact these auctioneers?
A   I belong to the National Association of Classic Car Owners. Each year they put out an information booklet. Among other things, the booklet lists major dealers and auctioneers.
Q   How many auctioneers does the booklet list in the Midwest?
A   Twelve. I contacted all the auctioneers listed for my part of the country.
Q   What other efforts, if any, did you make to find another 1936 Rolls Royce?
A   I phoned several of my friends who are also classic car enthusiasts.
Q   How many friends did you phone?
A   Five or six.
Q   Where do they live?
A   They're pretty well spread out thoughout the country from one Coast to another.
Q   What did they tell you?
A   They said they didn't know of any car like that that was up for sale.

[*This testimony is nonhearsay under Evidence Rule 801(c). The issue is whether the plaintiff made a reasonably diligent attempt to find a substitute car. The mere fact that the plaintiff's friends made these statements is logically relevant. The statements tend to show that the plaintiff made a reasonably diligent attempt to find a substitute car. The statements tend to show that the plaintiff acted reasonably in deciding not to search further.*]

LEGAL RESEARCH REFERENCE:
White & Summers §6-6

Sec. 9-10.   Rescission and Restitution as a Remedy for Material Breach

If the defendant commits a material breach, the plaintiff usually has a choice of remedies. The plaintiff may sue on the contract for total damages (Sections 9-5 and 9-6), or the plaintiff may sue in restitution. Like total damages, the restitutionary remedy is available only when the defendant's breach is material. The rules stated in Section 8-2 governing materiality apply here. If the breach is material, the plaintiff can obtain restitution by proving the following:

1. After discovering the material breach, the plaintiff restored or offered to restore to the defendant the benefits the defendant conferred upon the plaintiff. Suppose that the defendant auto dealer materially breached a warranty of the car's quality. The plaintiff buyer testifies:

    Q   What did you do when you learned that the car's engine needed so much repair work?   (1)
    A   I phoned the defendant.
    Q   What, if anything, did you tell the defendant about the car?   (1)
    A   I told him that I was going to bring the car back to him.

    The early view was that the plaintiff had to make this offer prior to filing suit. Many states now permit the plaintiff to make the offer of restitution in the complaint filed against the defendant.
2. The plaintiff demanded that the defendant return to the plaintiff the benefits the plaintiff had conferred on the defendant:

    Q   During this conversation, what did you tell the defendant about the down payment you had given him?   (2)
    A   I told him I wanted it back. I said he could have the car back, and I expected the money.

    As in the case of element #1, many jurisdictions now permit the plaintiff to make this demand in the complaint.
3. The plaintiff must make the offer and demand promptly upon discovering the ground for rescission. The trend in the decided cases is to hold that the plaintiff's offer and demand are "reasonably prompt" so long as the plaintiff's delay has not prejudiced the defendant. Absent prejudice, in many states the plaintiff may make both the offer and the demand for the first time in the complaint. In these states, at most the plaintiff must read the appropriate passages of the complaint into the record:

    Q   Your honor, I request permission to read paragraphs 23 and 24 of the complaint on file in this case to the jury.

J   Granted. Ladies and gentlemen, the plaintiff's attorney will now read to you. The plaintiff's attorney is reading from the complaint the plaintiff filed against the defendant at the start of this lawsuit.

Q   Thank you, your honor. Paragraph 23 reads: "The plaintiff hereby offers to restore to the defendant all property and benefits the defendant has conferred on the plaintiff on condition that the defendant return all benefits the plaintiff has given the defendant." Paragraph 24 is: "The plaintiff hereby demands that the defendant return to the plaintiff the $1,100 the plaintiff paid defendent as a down payment toward the purchase of the car described in paragraph six of this complaint."

4. The plaintiff shows the fair market value of the affirmative benefit the plaintiff conferred on defendant. A restitutionary measure of recovery is an affirmative measure. The plaintiff should show what it would have cost the defendant to have obtained the same services or goods on the open market. In short, the plaintiff can use the same evidentiary techniques that a plaintiff landowner would use to prove the cost of completion in a construction contract suit. Section 9.5.d.2 describes the two basic techniques that the plaintiff may employ.

LEGAL RESEARCH REFERENCE:
Murray §236

Sec. 9-11.   Reliance Damages

There are three basic types of damages: expectation, restitution, and reliance. The money damages discussed in Sections 9-2 through 9-7 are expectation damages; they are calculated to fulfill the plaintiff's expectations by putting the plaintiff in the position the plaintiff would have been in if the defendant had performed. Restitutionary recovery has a different objective; restitution is calculated to return the plaintiff to the *status quo ante*, the position the plaintiff was in before contracting with the defendant. To do so, the restitution remedy uses an affirmative measure of recovery: the fair market value of the property or services the plaintiff rendered to the defendant. Like restitution, reliance damages attempt to place the plaintiff back in the *status quo ante*. However, reliance damages differ from restitutionary damages in one important respect: Reliance is a negative measure, the plaintiff's out-of-pocket expenditures.

a.   When Is Reliance an Appropriate Measure of Recovery?

There are several situations in which reliance damages are the most appropriate measure of recovery. First, sometimes the plaintiff's expectation interest is virtually non-existent. The classic example is a contract to ship goods for a display at a marketing convention. The plaintiff ships the goods by carrier, and the carrier delays the shipment past the date of the convention. Perhaps the plaintiff did not expect any sales at the convention itself.

It is virtually impossible to calculate expectation damages here. It would be best to reimburse the plaintiff for out-of-pocket expenditures such as travel expenses to and from the convention and hotel expenses at the convention site. Second, reliance damages may be a much more certain basis for measuring recovery. The trial judge may conclude that the plaintiff's evidence of expectation damages is too uncertain. Rather than denying an injured plaintiff any recovery, the court may shift to a firmer basis such as reliance damages. Third, when the plaintiff's theory of liability is promissory estoppel, a reliance measure of recovery is especially apt.

b. Proving the Amount of the Reliance Interest

When the court uses a reliance measure of recovery, the plaintiff's task is to prove the plaintiff's out-of-pocket expenditures. If the plaintiff can remember the amount of the expenditures, the plaintiff can testify directly to the payments without violating the best evidence rule. If the plaintiff has informal notes or records of the payments, under Evidence Rule 612 the plaintiff's attorney may use the documents to refresh the plaintiff's recollection on the witness stand:

Q   How much did you spend for roofing materials?
A   I'm afraid that I can't remember.
Q   What, if anything, might help you remember?
A   Well, there would be entries in my business journal.
Q   Your honor, I request that this be marked plaintiff's exhibit number three for identification.
J   Yes.
Q   Please let the record reflect that I am showing the exhibit to the opposing counsel.
J   The record will reflect that.
Q   I now hand you plaintiff's exhibit number three for indentification. What is it?
A   It's the journal.
Q   How can you recognize it?
A   I ought to know my own handwriting. I make all the entries myself. I have a pretty small business, and I can't afford a bookkeeper.
Q   Please read page 97 of the journal silently to yourself.
A   Yes.
Q   Please hand the journal to me.
A   Here it is.
Q   Your honor, please let the record reflect that I am holding the journal behind my back and out of the witness' sight.
J   Yes.
Q   You've had a chance to review your journal. Did reading the journal refresh your memory?
A   Yes.

Q   Let me repeat the question then. How much did you spend for roofing materials?

A   I can remember now that it was $3,500.

If the witness cannot recall, the plaintiff's attorney may attempt to introduce the document as past recollection recorded. Federal Evidence Rule 803(5) recognizes this hearsay exception. To lay this foundation, the plaintiff should show that

1. When the record was prepared, the witness had personal knowledge of the facts recorded.
2. The witness personally prepared the record, or someone else made the record and the witness approved the record. Many jurisdictions also admit cooperative records: *A* testifies that he gave *B* an accurate oral report, and *B* testifies that she accurately transcribed *B's* oral report.
3. The record was made while the fact or event was "fresh" in the witness' memory.
4. The witness vouches that when the record was made, the record correctly reflected the witness' knowledge.
5. Even after reading the record in the courtroom, the witness cannot "fully and accurately" recall the fact or event recorded.

In many jurisdictions, after laying this foundation the plaintiff may formally introduce the record. Federal Evidence Rule 803(5) adopts the contrasting view that "the memorandum may be read into evidence but may not itself be received as an exhibit unless offered by an adverse party."

On a major project, the plaintiff may have to introduce numerous, formal business records to prove all the reliance expenditures. The plaintiff should first qualify the documents as business entries under Evidence Rule 803(6). The plaintiff should then offer a convenient summary to the jury and cite Evidence Rule 1006 (voluminous writings) as the excuse satisfying the best evidence rule.

LEGAL RESEARCH REFERENCE:
Murray §§223, 236

REMEDIES CHECKLIST

____ The plaintiff is entitled to stipulated damages.

     ____ At the time of contracting, it was foreseeable that in the event of a breach, it would be difficult to compute damages.

         and

     ____ The amount stipulated must be a reasonable forecast of just compensation.

OR

____ <u>The plaintiff is entitled to incidental damages for a minor breach.</u>

    ___ The defendant's breach caused the damage.
             and
    ___ The plaintiff could not have mitigated the damage.
             and
    ___ At the time of contract formation, it was foreseeable that if the defendant breached, the plaintiff would suffer this type of damage.
             and
    ___ The amount of damages is reasonably certain.

OR

____ <u>The plaintiff is entitled to damages for breach of warranty.</u>

    ___ The plaintiff accepted the goods.
             and
    ___ Within a reasonable time after acceptance, the plaintiff buyer notified the seller that the warranty had been breached.
             and
    ___ The plaintiff proves the difference between the goods' fair market value in their actual condition and the value they would have had if the goods had complied with the warranty.

OR

____ <u>The plaintiff is entitled to total damages for material breach.</u>

    ___ *(See* Section 9-5 for a discussion of the computation of damages for material breach of the various types of contracts.)

OR

____ <u>The plaintiff is entitled to a decree of specific performance.</u>

    ___ The buyer's remedy at law is inadequate.
             and
    ___ It would be feasible for the court to supervise the performance of the contract.

OR

____ <u>The plaintiff has a cause of action for rescission and restitution.</u>

    ___ The plaintiff restored or offered to restore to the defendant the benefits the defendant conferred upon the plaintiff.
             and
    ___ The plaintiff demanded that the defendant return the benefits the plaintiff conferred upon the defendant.
             and
    ___ The plaintiff made the offer and demand promptly.
             and
    ___ The plaintiff proves the fair market value of the affirmative benefit the plaintiff conferred upon the defendant.

OR

___ The plaintiff is entitled to reliance damages.

FOOTNOTES

[1] Eden, *Forensic Economics* in 13 American Jurisprudence P.O.F.2d 45, 99-102 (1977).

[2] Wickwire & Smith, *The Use of Critical Path Method Techniques in Contract Claims*, 7 Public Contract Law Journal 1 (1974).

[3] *Id.* at 4.

[4] *Id.* at 6.

[5] A third possibility is that the innocent party "learns" of the breach when a commercially reasonable time after the defendant's repudiation passes. *See* Uniform Commercial Code 2-510(a).

[6] "O" refers to the opposing attorney throughout this text.

[7] Weinstein & Keating, *Real Estate, Including Eminent Domain,* in Using Experts in Civil Cases 159, 161 (Practicing Law Institute 1977).

[8] *Id.* at 170-75.

[9] The SEM produces magnifications ten to one hundred times greater than the most powerful optical microscopes. The SEM has great potential in the quality control programs of manufacturers producing extremely small end-products such as miniaturized transistors.

[10] A third formula is $D = x/z\,C + y/z\,P$.

[11] For a description of the "expansible" seller, *see* Harris, *A General Theory for Measuring Seller's Damages for Total Breach of Contract*, 60 Michigan Law Review 577, 599-605 (1962).

CHAPTER 10

Proving the Sufficiency of the Plaintiff's Evidence—How to Defeat Defendant's Motion for a Directed Verdict

Sec. 10-1.   Introduction

The last five chapters dealt with the admissibility of the evidence the plaintiff offers to prove his or her theory. This chapter focuses on the cumulative *sufficiency* of the plaintiff's evidence rather than the admissibility of individual items of the plaintiff's evidence. The defendant can challenge the sufficiency of the plaintiff's evidence as soon as the plaintiff rests at the end of the plaintiff's case-in-chief. The defendant mounts the challenge by a motion. The title of the motion varies from jurisdiction to jurisdiction—motion for a directed verdict, a motion for dismissal, demurrer to the evidence, nonsuit motion, or motion for judgment. Whatever the title of the motion in your jurisdiction, the motion asserts that the plaintiff's evidence is legally insufficient: Even if the jury believes all the evidence, as a matter of law the evidence lacks sufficient probative value to sustain a verdict for the plaintiff.

The judge's ruling on the motion depends on whether the plaintiff has sustained the initial burden of production or going forward with the evidence. The initial burden is a duty the plaintiff owes the trial judge. If the plaintiff fails to sustain the burden, the judge must make a peremptory ruling in the defendant's favor. Some jurisdictions still adhere to the view that the plaintiff can sustain the burden by presenting even a "scintilla" of evidence on all the elements of the theory. However, most jurisdictions now use the standard that the plaintiff must introduce sufficient evidence to permit a rational juror to conclude that all the facts on which the plaintiff has the burden exist.

Sec. 10-2. The Substantive Aspects of a Directed Verdict Motion

a. From the Plaintiff's Perspective

At the outset of the argument on a defense motion for a directed verdict, the plaintiff should remind the judge how lax the standard is for meeting the initial burden of going forward. The reminder is especially helpful in jurisdictions using the scintilla standard.

Turning to the body of the argument, the plaintiff should reiterate the plaintiff's theory of the case: "Your honor, as you know, our theory of recovery is that the defendant breached a contract formed by the defendant's April offer and our May acceptance."

The plaintiff should then list the essential elements of the plaintiff's theory. As we have emphasized in Chapters 5 through 9, the five basic elements of most plaintiffs' theories will be:

1. The plaintiff and defendant formed a contract (Ch. 5);
2. The contract should be construed as creating certain conditions for the plaintiff to fulfill and a certain duty for the defendant to perform (Ch. 6);
3. All the conditions to the defendant's duty were fulfilled or excused (Ch. 7);
4. The defendant materially breached the duty (Ch. 8); and
5. Any special facts the plaintiff must prove to obtain the remedy the plaintiff prays for (Ch. 9).

Using these five elements as a checklist, the plaintiff should then review the evidence. The plaintiff should remind the judge of the evidence presented on each element of the theory. At this point, it is neither necessary nor appropriate to argue the evidence's credibility. Simply show the judge that you have presented some substantial evidence on each element of the theory. Place particular emphasis on any documentary or physical evidence you have introduced: "To show mutual assent, your honor, we introduced exhibits one and two. As you will recall, exhibit one is the letter the defendant mailed us in April. On its face, the letter shows every element of an offer: definite terms, the intent to enter a binding bargain, and the intent to enter a final bargain. Exhibit two is the letter of acceptance we mailed the defendant in May. Our letter is a perfect match to the defendant's offer."

To defeat the motion, you must persuade the judge that you have created a permissive inference of the existence of all the facts requisite for your theory. Your position is even stronger if you can show that you can invoke a presumption of the existence of one or more of the facts.[1] Cite local legal precedent, and then show that you have introduced evidence of all the presumption's foundational facts. A presumption of a fact's existence automatically sustains the burden of going forward on that issue.

The plaintiff should conclude the argument by declaring that "we have presented ample evidence on every element of our case of action. For that reason, your honor, we respectfully request that you deny the defendant's motion."

LEGAL RESEARCH REFERENCE:
McCormick §§336-38, 342-45

b.   From the Defense Perspective

Rather than surveying the evidence on all the elements of the plaintiff's theory, the defendant should focus on the weakest element. As a practical matter, judges rarely grant these motions. The defense's only hope is to focus the judge's attention on the single weakest element of the plaintiff's case and to convince the judge that the record contains *no* evidence of that element.

The defendant should be particularly attentive to the following elements of the plaintiff's case; these are the elements the plaintiff is most likely to overlook:

—With respect to contract formation, the plaintiff's exhibits may disclose some difference between the terms of the offer and those of the acceptance. Point out the difference between the two documents; invoke the mirror image rule; and argue that as a matter of law, the difference is fatal to the formation of the contract.

—With respect to contract construction, the plaintiff may neglect to prove that the meaning favoring the plaintiff qualifies as a preferred type of usage. For example, suppose that under this jurisdiction's substantive law, the plaintiff's meaning will prevail only if it qualifies as a mutual usage. The plaintiff testified that she had that meaning in mind at the time of contract formation; but the plaintiff forgot to add that she communicated that meaning to the defendant. Without that additional testimony, as a matter of law the meaning cannot qualify as a mutual usage.

—With respect to the plaintiff's fulfillment of the conditions, it is quite easy for the plaintiff to overlook a condition. *All* the conditions must be fulfilled or excused. For instance, the defendant can point out that the plaintiff's own exhibits show that there was another condition to the defendant's duty; a clause buried on the reverse side of the contract the plaintiff introduced might have required the plaintiff to obtain an insurance policy covering the goods. The defense should argue that the plaintiff presented no evidence of the fulfillment or excuse of that condition.

—With respect to anticipatory breach, the defendant's statement the plaintiff testified to may not be sufficiently positive. To qualify as an anticipatory breach, the statement must be positive and unequivocal.

If the plaintiff hedged even a bit and quoted the defendant as using an adverb such as "probably," as a matter of law the proof of anticipatory breach is insufficient.

—Finally, with respect to contract remedies, the plaintiff sometimes neglects to prove special facts needed for a particular remedy. The plaintiff may not have shown the foreseeability necessary to recover specials or the malice requisite for exemplary punitive damages. If that remedy is the only remedy the plaintiff seeks, the plaintiff's inability to obtain that remedy may result in a nonsuit or a judgment for only nominal damages. If the plaintiff is seeking other remedies, the judge will deny the nonsuit motion; but the judge will not instruct the jury on the remedy the plaintiff failed to establish the factual predicate for.

Sec. 10-3. The Procedural Aspects of a Directed Verdict Motion

a. From the Defense Perspective

In criminal cases, many defense counsel make it a uniform practice to move for a directed verdict at the close of the prosecution's case. That practice is not as uniform in civil actions. It is true that some civil defense counsel follow the practice, but others make the motion only when they think it has a fair chance of success. It is probably unwise to move for a directed verdict in a bench trial where the motion has little prospect for success. The judge who rules on the motion will also decide the merits of the case; if your directed verdict motion strikes the judge as frivolous, you have lost credibility in the judge's eyes.

If the trial is by jury, make the motion out of the jury's hearing. At the close of the plaintiff's case, use this procedure:

P   Your honor, the plaintiff rests.
D   Your honor, may we approach the bench?
J   Yes.
D   At this time, your honor, we would like to move for a nonsuit. I anticipate that this argument may be lengthy, and I would therefore request that you excuse the jurors.

The odds are that the judge will either deny the motion or reserve ruling until the jury returns its verdict. If the lay jurors hear the judge deny your motion, they may misinterpret the judge's ruling as an endorsement of the plaintiff's evidence. On your request, the judge will later instruct them that they must evaluate the plaintiff's evidence by a different standard than that the judge used. However, it may be difficult for the jurors to understand the instruction. The one thing the jurors know is that you challenged the plaintiff's case and the judge ruled against you.

When you argue your motion, consider using two weapons. The first is legal precedent. Judges are reluctant to grant nonsuit motions. At least cite legal precedent establishing that the element the plaintiff neglected is an essential element of the cause of action. It is ideal if you can find a reported case holding that an evidentiary presentation like the plaintiff's does not sustain the burden of going forward, but you rarely have the good fortune of finding a case on all fours. If the cases you rely on are not readily available to the judge, hand the judge a memorandum of law. If you go to the trouble of preparing a memo, you in effect signal the judge that this is not a typical, frivolous nonsuit motion.

The second weapon you may resort to is a partial or interim transcript. If the stakes in the case are high enough, they may warrant the additional expense of having the court reporter prepare a transcript of part of the plaintiff's case before the argument on the motion. As previously stated, if the plaintiff relies on an anticipatory breach theory, the plaintiff must establish a positive, unequivocal repudiation by the defendant; if the plaintiff quotes the defendant as saying "probably," as a matter of law the plaintiff has not shown a common-law anticipatory breach. Before granting your nonsuit motion, the judge will want to be certain that the plaintiff's testimony used the fatal adverb. You maximize the likelihood of winning the nonsuit motion by presenting the judge with a partial transcript:

D   Your honor, I know that your ruling on my motion depends on precisely how the plaintiff described my client's alleged repudiation. So that there will be no disputes over the tenor of the plaintiff's testimony, two days ago I asked the court reporter to prepare a partial transcript of the plaintiff's direct examination. I now offer you that transcript and request that it be marked defense exhibit A for identification.

J   Yes.

D   I have already given a copy of this partial transcript to the plaintiff's attorney.

J   (*To the plaintiff's attorney*) Is that true?

P   Yes, your honor. Counsel gave me the copy yesterday.

D   Your honor, I call your attention to the bottom of page eleven of the transcript.

J   All right.

D   That passage clearly shows that the plaintiff did not testify to an unequivocal repudiation. The plaintiff testified that my client said he "probably" would not perform.   [SECOND WEAPON] The cases in this jurisdiction have uniformly held that this is not sufficient for an anticipatory breach. I've listed three such cases in my memorandum of law.   [FIRST WEAPON]

If the judge denies the motion but you are convinced that the motion is meritorious, remember that in many jurisdictions, you must renew the motion to preserve the issue of the legal sufficiency of the plaintiff's evidence for appeal. You may have to renew the motion at the close of all the evidence in the case, and you may even have to include the issue in a new trial motion after an adverse verdict or a motion for judgment notwithstanding the verdict.

b. From the Plaintiff's Perspective

If it becomes apparent that the judge is inclined to grant the nonsuit motion, all is not lost. Consider this illustration. Suppose that the judge indicates that he or she is leaning toward granting the motion because you overlooked a condition and failed to prove its fulfillment or excuse. Although you neglected to present the proof, the proof is available; the client sitting next to you may be able to supply the testimony, or documentary proof may be in your attaché case. In this situation, in addition to urging the denial of the motion, alternatively ask for permission to reopen your case and present the omitted proof.

The judge has discretion to permit you to reopen. It is best to frankly confess your oversight; tell the judge that you were wrong and that you will gladly supply the missing evidence. Add that as far as you can tell, reopening the case at this point will not prejudice the defendant. You can use the defendant's motion to your own advantage; the defendant's oral argument itself is evidence that the defendant anticipated the issue and could therefore prepare to meet the evidence that you now want to place in the record. If the defendant foresaw the issue, reopening should not prejudice the defendant.

CHECKLIST FOR PLAINTIFF'S ARGUMENT IN OPPOSITION TO DIRECTED VERDICT MOTION

____ Remind the judge how lax the standard is for meeting your initial burden of going forward.

____ Restate your theory of the case.

____ List the elements of your theory.

____ Take the elements one by one, and review the evidence you have presented on each element.

   ____ Stress any documentary or physical evidence you have presented.

____ Assert that you have created a permissive inference (or a presumption) of the existence of each element of your theory.

____ Request that the judge deny the motion.

____ If you think the judge is inclined to grant the motion, alternatively move to reopen your case.

   ____ Confess your error.

   ____ Explain why you innocently reached that erroneous conclusion.

   ____ State that the missing evidence is immediately available.

   ____ Point out that reopening will not prejudice the defendant; the defendant must have foreseen the issue because the defendant moved for a directed verdict on the ground of the absence of evidence on that issue.

FOOTNOTE

[1] Uniform Commercial Code 1-201(31) sets out a definition of "presumption."

PART III

The Defendant's Evidence

CHAPTER 11

How to Plan the Defense Theory and Theme

Sec. 11-1.   Introduction

In Chapter 4, we discussed the planning of the plaintiff's theory. Many of the remarks in that chapter apply equally to planning the defense. However, there are some notable differences between the plaintiff's and the defendant's cases, and the objective of this chapter is to identify and analyze those differences. We shall first consider formulating a theory and theme for the defense. We shall then discuss the development of the theory and theme through (1) cross during the plaintiff's case and (2) direct during the defendant's case-in-chief.

Sec. 11-2.   Developing a Theory and Theme for the Defense

a.   Going on the Offensive

The expression, "The best defense is a best offense," is trite, but there is a measure of truth in it. People tend to identify with the positive and affirmative; and to seize the psychological advantage in a trial, the attorney must set a positive, offensive tone for his or her case.

For the defense attorney, a positive, offensive tone translates into a counterclaim against the plaintiff. It will be difficult for the defense to maintain the psychological initiative if the defense's thrust is purely negative: "We did not breach." Adding a positive tone is preferable: "Not only didn't we breach; the plaintiff is the guilty party because the plaintiff breached."

In some cases, it will be impossible for the defendant to file a counterclaim. For example, the plaintiff buyer may be suing for breach of warranty, and the plaintiff has already paid the defendant seller the full purchase price. In this situation, the defendant cannot counterclaim. However, in most cases, a counterclaim is possible. If the plaintiff terminated the contract on the ground of material breach but guessed wrong (there was no breach or at least no material breach), the plaintiff probably later committed a present or anticipatory breach. When the due date for the plaintiff's performance arrived and the plaintiff did not perform, there was a present breach. Even if the due date had not yet arrived, the plaintiff's announced termination would constitute an anticipatory repudiation in most jurisdictions.

You certainly should pause before filing a counterclaim for nominal damages. The counterclaim will shift the equities in the defense's favor only if the defense shows that the plaintiff's breach caused the defendant real injury. But when there is substantial, provable injury, the defendant should file the counterclaim. Moreover, it makes a sort of *Catch 22* sense to understate the counterclaim—especially when you think that the plaintiff has overstated his or her damage. If you slightly understate your claim, you can easily convince the jurors during summation that your damages claim is more reasonable than the plaintiff's. By impeaching the amount of the plaintiff's damages, you may call into question the credibility of the plaintiff's entire case and prompt the jury to deny the plaintiff any recovery.

b. The Theory and the Theme

How does the defense develop a simple theory and theme—especially in light of the complicating factor of counterclaims? Theory and theme development is quite simple when the defense is relying only on a simple or affirmative defense, but the process of development becomes more complex when the defense goes on the offensive and files a counterclaim.

1. Simple defense theories

A simple defense is a defense which attempts to negate an essential element of the plaintiff's *theory*. By way of illustration, it would be a simple defense to argue that the defendant was not liable because the plaintiff gave insufficient consideration to form a contract. The plaintiff has the burdens of going forward and proof on the issue of consideration; and in this defense, the defendant is merely attempting to negate something the plaintiff is obliged to prove. When the defendant uses a simple defense, the defense case should be relatively short. The defense theory is a frontal assault on the plaintiff's theory; the defendant contends that an essential element of the plaintiff's theory is missing.

Like the plaintiff, the defendant should attempt to capsulize the theory and reduce it to a short, memorable expression. If you are attempting to negate formation and mutual assent, tell the jury that the plaintiff and your client had an "innocent misunderstanding." If your argument is that the plaintiff did not fulfill the conditions to your client's duty, ask: "How can the plaintiff expect Acme (the defendant) to perform when he won't perform his part of the bargain?" If you admit breach but deny its materiality, characterize the breach as "small and innocent." Couch your theory in simple terms; humanize your legal theory.

What about the *theme*? Again, the theme is the strongest argument for your theory. If you are attempting to negate mutual assent, the documents exchanged between the parties during negotiations may be your most potent ammunition; if the documents reflect numerous different terms, the jury will think it is quite plausible that at the end of this confused negotiating process, there was still disagreement. The argument is especially effective when the documents misquote each other: "Ladies and gentlemen, you've had a chance to see all the letters the plaintiff and my client sent each other. Those letters show how much confusion there was during the negotiations. You can see for yourselves that the plaintiff's May letter (exhibit four) misquotes Mr. Zillman's April letter. The plaintiff contends that at the end of the bargaining, there was complete agreement and a contract. Our position is that at the end of the bargaining, you had the same thing you had throughout the bargaining—the confusion and innocent misunderstanding written all over the face of these letters." "The misunderstanding written on the face of the letters" is a defendant's theme for formation just as "the case of the boxes labeled for shipment to the plaintiff" is a plaintiff's theme for contract formation.

2. Affirmative defense theories

An affirmative defense differs from a simple defense. A simple defense attacks an element of the plaintiff's theory. An affirmative defense concedes the elements of the plaintiff's theory but adds facts that have the legal effect of avoiding the defendant's liability. At early common law, the expression for this type of pleading was "confession and avoidance": the defendant confessed the facts the plaintiff pleaded, but alleged other facts that avoided the defendant's liability.

In Chapters 13 and 14, we shall consider affirmative defenses to formation and breach. Some of these defenses permit you to frame a theory based on the innocence of your client's conduct. For instance, one defense to formation is proof of a mutual, material mistake. A defense theory for the affirmative defense of mistake will sound very much like a defense theory for the simple defense of lack of mutual assent: "an innocent misunderstanding about an important part of the bargain." One defense to breach is proof that an unforeseeable event intervened and made it impossible for the defendant to perform the duty. You can capsulize an impossibility discharge theory by repeatedly telling the jury that your client "did everything humanly possible" to perform.

Other affirmative defenses lend themselves to even more appealing theories. If your affirmative defense is the plaintiff's fraud or economic duress, you can not only characterize your client's conduct as "innocent"; you can portray your client as "the innocent victim" and cast the plaintiff in the villain's role. When the plaintiff made the misrepresentation to your client, your client "innocently believed and trusted the plaintiff." When your client learned the truth, your client was "shocked and hurt." This type of affirmative defense enables you to go on the offensive without a counterclaim; when you discuss the facts showing the affirmative defense, in words and tone you can become accusatory and damn the plaintiff.

As in the case of a simple defense theory, you must use your judgment and select the most powerful *theme* argument for your affirmative defense theory. In the pretrial discovery stage, it may become clear that the plaintiff's attack on your fraud theory will be his testimony that he was unaware that the representation inducing the contract was false. You have evidence of other, similar frauds admissible under Federal Evidence Rule 404(b). Your theme should be the sheer number of misrepresentations: "Ladies and gentlemen, maybe once. Maybe even twice. But six times. Six times, ladies and gentlemen. Common sense tells us that you just don't slip up that often accidentally. The numbers tell the story, and it's not a story about a mistake —it's a story about an outright lie." "The numbers tell the story" becomes the theme for the affirmative defense fraud theory.

3. *Counterclaim theories*

The defendant selects the counterclaim theory and theme in the very same fashion as the plaintiff selects the plaintiff's theory and theme.

The question that may occur to you now is this: How can I keep my case simple if I clutter it up with both a simple or affirmative defense and a counterclaim? In the process of gaining the offensive arguing a counterclaim, don't I make my case too complex for the jurors to follow? There is certainly a danger of confusing the jury by adding the counterclaim, but a skilled defense attorney can meet that risk by *integrating* a simple or affirmative defense with a counterclaim. The integration should be accomplished both factually and legally.

Both the defense and the counterclaim will arise from the same set of *facts*, namely, the sequence of events constituting contract formation and performance. You can incorporate your counterclaim facts into the sequence by lengthening the sequence only slightly. If your theory was a simple defense ("We didn't breach"), your theory might end at the time your delivery personnel unloaded the air conditioners at the plaintiff's plant. Your counterclaim may be that the plaintiff erroneously believed you were guilty of material breach and committed an anticipatory breach by phoning you after delivery and terminating the installment contract. The only facts you have to add to your chronology are the facts about the plaintiff's telephone call. By adding one simple event to your chronology, you create the possibility of going on the offensive with a counterclaim.

Legally, your defense and counterclaim theories are not only consistent; they are two sides of the same coin. If you were not guilty of a breach, you are not liable to the plaintiff for damages; and on the very same assumption, the plaintiff's repudiation during the telephone call was an anticipatory breach. Show the jury that there is only one real legal issue: "Ladies and gentlemen, there's only one real question in this case: Did Mr. Nelson's delivery of the air conditioners amount to a breach?" Then show the jurors that the answer to that question dictates their verdict on both the plaintiff's claim and your counterclaim: "That's the key question in this case. And the answer to that question is really the answer to two questions. First, it answers the question whether Mr. Nelson owes the plaintiff the money he is asking for. As the judge will instruct you, if you find that the air conditioners were in good condition and that there was no breach, the plaintiff isn't entitled to any damages. Second, it answers the question whether Mr. Nelson is entitled to the $4,000 he is asking for. The judge will instruct you that if there was no breach by Mr. Nelson, the plaintiff's telephone call was a breach. Those two questions are simply sides of the same coin. If Mr. Nelson's delivery of the air conditioners satisfied his duties, Mr. Nelson doesn't owe the plaintiff anything but the plaintiff owes Mr. Nelson $4,000."

Sec. 11-3. Developing the Theory and Theme by Cross-Examination During the Plaintiff's Case-in-Chief

Your first opportunity to present the defense theory and theme comes during the plaintiff's case-in-chief; you can begin developing your theory and theme by cross-examination during the plaintiff's case-in-chief. If you are going to rely heavily on cross and the judge has consented to give an opening instruction on the plaintiff's substantive law theory, request that the judge include your substantive law theory in the opening instruction. If the judge does so, the jury will better understand the significance of the admissions you elicit during cross. What about the tactics and mechanics of cross-examination? Section 4-5 of this handbook contains a discussion of direct examination. This section is a parallel discussion of cross-examination. To prepare for cross-examination, ask yourself three questions:

a. Should I Cross-Examine This Witness?

One of the most difficult things for a young cross-examiner to learn is that often the wisest tactic is to say, "No questions, your honor." Trial attorneys seem to have a compulsion to cross-examine; they like to hear themselves talk. Many neophyte cross-examiners regurgitate the direct; they repeat the questions posed on direct in the hope that an inconsistency will develop. Inconsistencies do not develop that often. When they do, they are usually minor; and lay jurors both understand and forgive innocent misrecollections by the witness. If you seize upon miniscule inconsistencies, you will lose the jury; the jurors sympathize with the witness, and they will regard your attack on such inconsistencies as evidence of how desperate you are.

There is only one instance when the regurgitation technique is effective. Suppose that a witness has a memorized story. The pretrial statement, the deposition transcript, the direct, and cross may be almost identical—word for word. If you believe that the witness has a memorized story, by all means invite him or her to repeat the direct. When you point that out during closing—perhaps by quotations from the pretrial statement, deposition transcript, and partial trial transcript—the jurors will suspect fabrication.

In some cases, the opposing witness' testimony is so harmful that you must cross-examine or practically concede defeat. However, in most cases, start with a rebuttable presumption against cross-examining. In the typical case, cross-examine only if you think that you can probably attain one or more of the following objectives:

1. Elicit from the witness testimony favoring your theory of the case on the historical merits.
2. Elicit from the witness favorable testimony on credibility, for example, testimony impeaching one of the plaintiff's other witnesses.
3. Impeach the witness on the historical merits by techniques such as prior inconsistent statement.
4. Impeach the witness by *ad hominem* attacks on credibility such as prior convictions.

The first two objectives are the most important; you use the plaintiff's witnesses to support your case. It impresses the jury if you can state during closing argument that "even the plaintiff's witnesses conceded these facts." Whenever possible, use the plaintiff's witnesses as a source of favorable testimony.

b.   In What Sequence Should I Conduct the Cross-Examination?

After you attempt to attain the third or fourth purpose during cross-examination, the witness will probably turn hostile. The opposing witness will resent you after your attempted impeachment. For that reason, elicit favorable information from the witness *before* attacking the witness. First elicit the favorable testimony on the historical merits or credibility (purposes #1 and 2). Then attack the witness on the merits (purpose #3). Finally, launch the *ad hominem* attacks on the witness' credibility (purpose #4). Defer this type of impeachment to the very end of the cross.

Do not begin where the direct examiner left off or use the same sequence the plaintiff used. The topic the plaintiff left off on is fresh in the witness' mind; and if the plaintiff's counsel is competent, the last topic on direct is likely to be one of the strong points in the plaintiff's case. Beginning on that topic will only help the witness. Following the same general sequence as the direct will have the same effect. The witness is more likely to make a slip if you use a different sequence.

c. How Should I Draft the Cross-Examination Questions?

1. General considerations

Even on cross, you should ordinarily have a friendly, conversational demeanor. The friendlier you are, the more cooperative the witness will be, and the more favorable testimony you will elicit. Your tone should become accusatory only when you are pursuing impeachment purposes #3 and 4. No matter which purpose you are pursuing, you must maintain control over the plaintiff's witness. To maintain control, *the norm is that you should use short, plainly worded, narrowly phrased, leading non-argumentative questions to elicit the favorable facts you are morally certain the witness will concede.*

"The norm." This is not an absolute rule. Sometimes an attorney should ask an open-ended question on cross. The plaintiff's expert may use very vague, abstract diction; and the more the witness talks, the less likely the jury is to believe the witness. Or, as previously stated, the plaintiff's witness may have a memorized story, and an open-ended question gives the witness an opportunity to repeat the story verbatim.

"Short, plainly worded questions." The norms of brevity and simplicity apply with greater force on cross than they do on direct. The plaintiff's witness may be hostile and straining to misinterpret your question. The defense attorney must word questions that are so short and clear that they cannot be misinterpreted.

"Leading." Leading questions help the examiner maintain witness control.

"Non-argumentative questions." The most common objection to cross-examination questions is that they are "argumentative." What is an objectionable, argumentative question? The question does not call for new factual information; rather, the question challenges the witness about an inference from the facts. When you ask an argumentative question, in effect you are arguing with the witness about the conclusions to be drawn from the facts in the case.

Although leading questions are permissible on cross, argumentative questions are improper. Suppose that the plaintiff's witness testifies on direct that he mailed the plaintiff's acceptance to the defendant. The witness made a prior inconsistent statement that she could not remember mailing the acceptance. On cross, after laying a proper foundation, it would be leading but perfectly proper to ask, "Isn't it true that you told my client that you couldn't remember whether you mailed the acceptance"? The witness admits the inconsistent statement. You then ask, "How do you explain that inconsistency?" or "How can you expect us to believe your testimony on direct?" Those questions are argumentative and improper. Avoid asking argumentative questions; they are objectionable, they rarely yield the answer you want, and in the process of badgering the witness you may offend the jurors.

"*Favorable facts.*" As a general proposition, elicit facts rather than opinions. Again, this is a norm rather than an absolute rule. In the rare case, you may know the plaintiff's expert well, and you are certain that the expert is so honest that he or she will express an opinion favoring your case. In the typical case, though, do not seek inferences or opinions from the plaintiff's witnesses. Avoid questions loaded with opinion words such as "reasonable," "prompt," "merchantable," "substantial," "considerable," or "high quality." The witness will often argue with you before stating the opinion you want; and a clever witness may express an opinion that is even more harmful than the one the witness expressed on direct. When in doubt, limit your questions to queries eliciting facts. In the best cross-examination, you really are not asking questions. Rather, under the guise of asking questions, you are making factual statements and forcing the plaintiff's witness to express assent to those statements.

"*You are morally certain the witness will concede.*" In some situations, you do not care what answer the witness gives; sometimes any answer will be favorable. On other occasions, an unfavorable answer is expectable; but you have immediate access to very credible evidence to impeach the unfavorable answer if it is given.

However, in most situations, be on the safe side. Ask the question only if you are confident that the answer will be favorable. You can be especially confident if the witness has already made a statement to the same effect in a writing such as a deposition transcript. When you draft your cross questions, in the margin annotate a reference to the writing where the statement appears, e.g., "Hinds' deposition—pg. 14, lines 17–18." If the witness gives the favorable answer, go on to the next planned question. If the witness does not give the expected answer, you are ready to refresh the witness' recollection or confront the witness immediately with prior inconsistent statement impeachment.

LEGAL RESEARCH REFERENCE:
McCormick §§19-27, 29-31

2. *Specific impeachment techniques*

There are three impeachment techniques that attack the weight of the witness' testimony about the historical merits: The witness has a bias relevant to the case; the witness made a prior statement inconsistent with his or her testimony at trial; and the witness' ability to perceive, remember, or narrate the facts testified to is deficient.

PROOF OF A RELEVANT BIAS

The defendant may impeach a witness for the plaintiff by showing that the witness has a relevant bias or prejudice. The courts liberally admit proof of bias; the defendant may prove any fact, event, or relationship that is logically relevant to show a pertinent bias. If an expert is a professional witness who always testifies for contractors and against landowners, the expert is impeachable by the bias technique.

The defendant may use this technique during the cross-examination of the plaintiff's witness. Do not belabor the obvious; if the witness admits on direct an employment or family relationship with the plaintiff, you can argue the inference of bias during closing. If you cross-examine about obvious bias, you may insult the jurors' intelligence. Cross-examine in detail about bias when it is necessary to do so to reveal covert prejudice. On direct the witness admitted being the defendant's employee, and on cross the defense counsel asks:

Q[1] Isn't it also true that you own 2,000 shares of stock in the plaintiff corporation?

Q Isn't it a fact that the stock has a face value of over $15,000?

It is best to defer this questioning until the very end of the cross. Just before questioning about the bias, force the witness to repeat the most implausible part of his or her testimony. By juxtaposing that part of the testimony and the evidence of bias, you suggest to the jury that the witness is making that extreme, implausible statement precisely because the witness is biased.

The defense attorney may use extrinsic evidence[2] of bias in addition to cross-examining the witness to be impeached. However, most courts require that before introducing extrinsic evidence, the defense attorney lay a foundation on cross. In these jurisdictions, as a condition precedent to proffering extrinsic evidence, you must confront the witness to be impeached with the fact, event, or relationship on cross and give the witness an opportunity to explain or deny the fact. If the witness fully admits the biasing fact, the judge will probably exercise discretion and exclude further evidence of bias; extrinsic evidence would be cumulative and unnecessary. However, if the witness denies any or all of the impeaching facts, the defense attorney may offer the extrinsic evidence during the defense case-in-chief.

LEGAL RESEARCH REFERENCE:
McCormick §40

PROOF OF A PRIOR INCONSISTENT STATEMENT

As in the case of bias impeachment, the defense attorney may use both cross-examination and extrinsic evidence to prove the witness' prior inconsistent statement.

CROSS-EXAMINATION

On cross, a complete, traditional foundation for a prior inconsistent statement includes the following elements:[3]

1. The defense attorney should commit the witness to the inconsistent testimony on direct. If you do not lock the witness into that testimony, the witness may later explain away the inconsistency by claiming that the witness misspoke himself or herself. Some counsel attempt to commit the witness by asking point-blank, "Isn't it true that on direct examination you testified. . . ?" Other counsel use a more subtle ploy; at various points in the cross, they ask the same question, on each occasion coming closer to the precise language of the prior inconsistent statement. If the plaintiff objects that the questioning is repetitive ("asked and answered"), approach the bench and explain your tactic to the judge out of the witness' hearing.
2. The witness made the statement at a particular place. This element is usually omitted in the case of written prior inconsistent statements.
3. The witness made the statement at a particular time.
4. The defense attorney specifies the persons present when the statement was made. If the statement took the form of a letter, specify the addressee.
5. The defense attorney specifies the content of the statement.
6. The circumstances indicate that the prior statement is likely to be more reliable than the present testimony.

Suppose that the plaintiff's employee testifies on direct that he mailed the acceptance of the defendant's offer on June 15th. Before trial, the witness told one of the defendant's employees, Ms. Martinez, that he could not remember whether he mailed the letter of acceptance:

Q   Isn't it true that on direct, you testified that you mailed the letter of acceptance to my client?   (1)

A   Yes.

Q   Isn't it a fact that on July 6th of this year, you had a conversation with Ellen Martinez at your office in Manhattan?   (2), (3), (4)

A   Yes.

Q   At that time, didn't you tell her that you couldn't remember whether you had mailed the letter?   (5)

A   Yes.

Q   Isn't it correct that in point of time, your July conversation was closer to June 15th than your testimony today?   (6)

A   Yes.

The orthodox view is that if the prior inconsistent statement was written, you have to show the writing to the witness before asking about the prior inconsistent statement. Under this view, the foundation is even lengthier:

7. Display the exhibit to the witness.

8. Have the witness authenticate the exhibit.

> Q Isn't it true that on direct, you testified that you mailed the letter of acceptance to my client?
>
> A Yes.
>
> Q Your honor, I request that this be marked defense exhibit C for identification.
>
> J It will be so marked.
>
> Q Please let the record reflect that I am showing the exhibit to the opposing counsel.
>
> J It shall so reflect.
>
> Q (*To the witness*) I now hand you defense exhibit C for identification. What is it? (7)
>
> A It's a letter.
>
> Q Isn't it a fact that this is your handwriting style? (8)
>
> A Right.
>
> Q Isn't it true that you wrote this letter? (8)
>
> A Yes.
>
> Q And you sent this letter to a Ms. Ellen Martinez. Isn't that correct? (8)
>
> A Yes.
>
> Q Now let me direct your attention to the fourth paragraph of the letter. [*If the exhibit were a deposition, you should specify the page and lines of the transcript.*] Isn't it true that in that paragraph, you wrote Ms. Martinez that you couldn't remember whether you mailed the letter of acceptance? (5)
>
> A Yes.

The courts and legislatures are beginning to relax these strict, traditional requirements for cross. Some permit the defense attorney to ask general questions on cross:

> Q You testified on direct that you mailed the letter of acceptance to my client. Is that correct?
>
> A Yes.
>
> Q Have you ever told anyone that you couldn't remember whether you had mailed the letter?

EXTRINSIC EVIDENCE

The traditional view also decrees that a complete foundation on cross is a requirement for the presentation of extrinsic testimony. Thus, the defense counsel could elicit Ms. Martinez' testimony during the defense case-in-chief only if during cross the defense attorney gave the plaintiff's witness a chance to deny or explain the inconsistent statement. Here too the courts and legislatures are beginning to ease the traditional restrictions. Federal Evidence Rule 613(b) requires that the cross-examiner give the witness "an opportunity to explain or deny" the prior statement, but many judges construe this Rule as requiring only that the defense attorney excuse the plaintiff's witness subject to recall. If the witness is excused in that fashion, the plaintiff can recall the witness to deny or explain the defense's extrinsic evidence of the prior inconsistent statement.

LEGAL RESEARCH REFERENCE:
McCormick §§28, 34-39

PROOF OF THE WITNESS' DEFICIENT ABILITY TO PERCEIVE, REMEMBER, OR NARRATE EVENTS

The weight of a witness' testimony depends in part on the witness' ability to accurately observe, recall, and relate events. If the defense attorney can attack any of those abilities, the witness' testimony is impeached.

Often the best attack is to show that the witness had not focused his or her attention on the event. The event may have been unexpected. In that circumstance, elicit the witness' concession that the event was unexpected, and then argue during closing that the witness probably did not pay close attention at least at the beginning of the event. Or the event may have been of very short duration. Elicit that concession, and argue that the witness had an inadequate opportunity to perceive the event. Do *not* ask for witness' opinion that he or she did not have an "adequate opportunity" to perceive. If you elicit the admission that the event was "unexpected" or "lasted only ten seconds," you have all the ammunition you need for summation.

If the witness seems hesitant and forgetful on direct, on cross the defense attorney should press for answers about very specific details: the "precise" time of the telephone call or the "exact" number of boxes delivered. If the witness is honest, nervous, and forgetful, the witness' own hesitancy will impeach the witness' memory. Some defense attorneys try to make the witness seem forgetful by "testing" or "hop, skip, and jump" cross: During cross, they jump around from topic to topic out of chronological sequence to confuse the witness. You may confuse the witness, but you will probably confuse the jury as well. If the jury becomes confused, they will not hold the mistake against the witness.

Many jurisdictions permit the defense attorney to introduce extrinsic evidence that the witness was drunk at the time he or she supposedly observed the event; the witness is a drug abuser; or the witness has a mental disorder. Such evidence is much more common in criminal cases than in civil litigation. However, the attorney should be alert to the possibility of intoxication whenever the case involves a business meeting away from the office. Some business people are heavy drinkers, and you may be able to prove that during an evening business meeting at a restaurant, the plaintiff's witness consumed three to five drinks.

LEGAL RESEARCH REFERENCE:
McCormick §45

The final three impeachment techniques are legalized character assassination; they are *ad hominem* assaults on the opposing witness' credibility.

PROOF THAT THE WITNESS HAS COMMITTED A "BAD ACT"

Some jurisdictions limit "bad act" impeachment to acts that have already resulted in a conviction. However, most states and the federal courts permit the cross-examiner to inquire about acts that reflect adversely on the witness' truthfulness. In the words of Federal Evidence Rule 608(b)(1), the cross-examiner may ask about "(s)pecific instances of the conduct of a witness" if the acts are "probative of . . . untruthfulness. . . ." The defense attorney should elicit the details of the act and highlight that the nature of the act evidences the witness' untruthfulness. The defense attorney is cross-examining one of the plaintiff's employees:

Q   Isn't it true that you turn in a time sheet at the end of every month?
A   Yes.
Q   And on this time sheet you're supposed to list your overtime hours. Isn't that correct?
A   Right.
Q   You turned in a time sheet for last month, August. Didn't you?
A   I did.
Q   Isn't it correct that on that time sheet, you listed 20 hours of overtime for August?
A   Yes.
Q   Isn't it true that you personally prepared that time sheet?
A   Yes.
Q   Isn't the truth that you put in only two overtime hours in August?
A   Yes.

Note that the cross-examiner does not ask whether the employer fined or disciplined the witness for the bad act. Rather, you ask directly and bluntly whether the witness committed the act. If your question mentions a third party's action such as a fine or arrest for the bad act, the question is objectionable on hearsay and opinion grounds.

In jurisdictions permitting bad act impeachment, the courts usually apply the collateral fact rule; although the defense attorney may cross-examine about the bad act, the attorney must "take the answer." "Take the answer" does *not* mean that you may not vigorously press the witness for an admission of the act; rather, the expression means that you may not introduce extrinsic evidence of the act's commission. If the witness is willing to commit perjury, you cannot unmask the perjury later during the present trial. However, the witness may not be familiar with the collateral fact rule. In Perry Mason style, some cross-examiners have a witness to the bad act walk into the back of the courtroom just before the questioning about that act. When the plaintiff's witness sees the witness to the bad act in the courtroom, the plaintiff's witness may leap to the mistaken conclusion that the witness to the bad act can testify. Hence, the plaintiff's witness is much more likely to admit the commission of the untruthful act.

Many jurors resent this sort of character assassination. Resort to this impeachment technique only when the act is both recent and serious.

LEGAL RESEARCH REFERENCE:
McCormick §§41-42

PROOF THAT THE WITNESS HAS SUFFERED A CONVICTION

Like bad act impeachment, conviction impeachment is a form of mud-slinging. Most jurisdictions recognize this impeachment technique in civil actions, but they differ on the type of conviction the defense attorney may prove. The majority of courts permit the use of any felony. A few courts limit the attorney to crimes having an essential element of fraud or deceit. Federal Evidence Rule 609(a) adopts a compromise stance:

> For the purpose of attacking the credibility of a witness, evidence that he has been convicted of a crime shall be admitted if elicited from him or established by public record during cross-examination but only if the crime (1) was punishable by death or imprisonment in excess of one year under the law under which he was convicted, and the court determines that the probative value of admitting this evidence outweighs its prejudicial effect to the defendant; or (2) involved dishonesty or false statement, regardless of the punishment.

CROSS-EXAMINATION

On cross-examination, the defense attorney should elicit the following admissions as the foundation:[4]

1. The witness is the same person who suffered the previous conviction. In many jurisdictions, if the witness' name is the same as the name appearing on the judgment of conviction, there is a rebuttable presumption of identity.
2. The witness was convicted of one of the types of crimes the jurisdiction treats as impeaching.
3. The conviction was entered in a particular place.
4. The conviction was entered in a particular year. You should be reluctant to use this technique unless the conviction is relatively recent. Many jurors resent the use of convictions that are remote in point of time; they feel that the witness has already paid his or her debt to society.
5. The witness received a certain sentence. Some jurisdictions prohibit questioning about the sentence.
6. Other details maximizing the impeaching value of the conviction. Most jurisdictions severely restrict your ability to prove aggravating details. However, some jurisdictions permit you to prove that the witness had pleaded not guilty. You must research your jurisdiction's own evidence law to determine the extent to which you can probe the details surrounding the crime or conviction.

Suppose that the plaintiff's witness is Martin Gresham. On cross, the defense attorney might ask:

Q   Are you the same Martin Gresham who was once convicted of a felony?
    (1),   (2)
A   Yes.
Q   Isn't it true that the felony was embezzlement?   (2)
A   That's right.
Q   And you were convicted of that crime in 1980 in Florida. Isn't that correct?   (3),   (4)
A   Yes.
Q   You were sentenced to ten years' imprisonment. Weren't you?   (5)
A   Yeah.
Q   And isn't it a fact that you plead not guilty in that case?   (6)
A   Right.

EXTRINSIC EVIDENCE

Some jurisdictions either permit or require the defense attorney to forego cross-examination about the conviction and simply present extrinsic proof in the form of a properly attested copy of the judgment of conviction. In most jurisdictions, the defense attorney may offer extrinsic proof when the witness refuses to admit the conviction on cross. If the copy of the judgment bears a proper attesting certificate, the copy is readily admitted. The copy is self-authenticating under Federal Evidence Rule 902, there is an adequate excuse for the non-production of the original under Rule 1005, and the copy falls within the public records hearsay exception stated in Rule 803(8).

LEGAL RESEARCH REFERENCE:
McCormick §§41, 43

PROOF THAT THE WITNESS HAS A CHARACTER TRAIT OF UNTRUTHFULNESS

As soon as the witness testifies, the witness' credibility becomes a material fact of consequence in the case. The defense attorney may attack the witness' credibility by the extrinsic testimony of a character witness. The character witness testifies that the plaintiff's witness has a character trait of untruthfulness. Again, this type of impeachment may offend some jurors; you should ordinarily use this attack only if you have very powerful evidence, e.g., the testimony of a very respectable character witness who is intimately familiar with the plaintiff's witness. Character evidence can take one of two forms.

REPUTATION

The first form is reputation evidence. The reputation foundation includes proof that

1. The character witness is a member of the same community as the plaintiff's witness. The original meaning of "community" was residential community. The courts have now expanded the term's meaning to

include virtually any large social group, including business, financial, and academic groups.

2. The character witness has been a member of the community for a substantial period of time.
3. The plaintiff's witness has a reputation for untruthfulness in the community.

The plaintiff's witness is Mr. Morris, an employee of the carrier the plaintiff hired. To impeach Morris, the defense calls Ms. Farrel during the defense case-in-chief:

Q   Who is Mr. Morris?
A   He's just somebody I know.
Q   When did you last see him?
A   I saw him in the courtroom a few hours ago. He was up here on the witness stand.
Q   Where does he work?   (1)
A   He works for Foote Trucking Company.
Q   How do you know that?   (1)
A   I also work there.
Q   How many employees work for Foote Trucking Company?   (1)
A   We're the main headquarters, and we've got almost 250 people—truckers, bookkeepers, dispatchers, and support personnel—at our offices.
Q   How long has he worked there?   (2)
A   Approximately 11 years.
Q   How long have you worked there?   (2)
A   I joined the firm a few months before he did. I've been there now almost 12 years.
Q   Does Mr. Morris have a reputation for truthfulness or untruthfulness among the Foote employees?   (3)
A   Yes.
Q   What is that reputation?   (3)
A   He's known as an habitual liar. Very few people trust the guy.
Q   Given his reputation, would you believe him under oath?   (3)
A   In a word, no.

OPINION

The second form is opinion evidence. Federal Evidence Rule 405(a) sanctions opinion evidence as well as reputation evidence. Since 22 jurisdictions have already adopted the Federal Rules, it is now probably the majority view that either form is permissible. This foundation is slightly different than the reputation foundation:

1. The character witness personally knows the plaintiff's witness.
2. The character witness has known the plaintiff's witness for a lengthy period of time.
3. The character witness' opinion is that the plaintiff's witness is an untruthful person.

Q Who is Mr. Morris?

A He's just somebody I know.

Q When did you see him last?

A I saw him in the courtroom a few hours ago. He was up here on the witness stand.

Q How did you come to know him?   (1)

A We work at the same trucking plant.

Q How long have you known him?   (2)

A I'd say about 11 years. That's how long we've both worked at Foote Trucking.

Q How much contact do you have with him?   (2)

A We both work in dispatching, so we're always bumping into each other.

Q How often do you talk with him?   (2)

A Lots of times every day. His office is just next door.

Q Do you have an opinion of his truthfulness?   (3)

A I sure do.

Q What is your opinion?   (3)

A In my opinion, he's a liar. I've never felt comfortable around him.

Q Given that opinion, would you believe him under oath?   (3)

A I most certainly would not.

Whenever you use one of these *ad hominem* impeachment techniques, try to move close to the witness; ideally, stand right next to the witness. Impeachment is most dramatic and effective when the witness' demeanor suggests that the cross-examiner is hitting the mark—for example, the witness' facial expression registers guilt or the witness refuses to look the cross-examiner in the eye. Proxemics studies the effect of spatial relations on human behavior; and it tells us that as the cross-examiner approaches the witness, the witness' anxiety increases.[5] In the words of one author, "invade (the witness') territory, and that makes him uptight."[6] An anxious witness is much more likely to act as if you have damaged the witness' credibility.

LEGAL RESEARCH REFERENCE:
McCormick §§41, 44

Sec. 11-4. Developing the Theory and Theme by Direct Examination During the Defense Case-in-Chief

Everything said in Section 4-5 about direct examination during the plaintiff's case applies to direct examination during the defense case. Just as the plaintiff would like the judge to preface the direct examination with an instruction on the plaintiff's substantive law theory, the defendant should request a midtrial instruction of the defense's substantive law theory. After the judge's instruction, present your evidence by conducting direct. The only major difference between direct examination during the plaintiff's case and direct during the defense case is a difference in emphasis.

The defendant should de-emphasize the points of agreement with the plaintiff. Devote very little time during your direct to the factual issues on which you agree with the plaintiff. Regurgitating the plaintiff's *questions* on your cross is dangerous, and regurgitating the plaintiff's *answers* during your direct is wasteful. Elicit enough detail about the points of agreement so that (1) the jury will understand the context of your witness' testimony; and (2) you will be able to say during closing argument that your client "freely admitted" that the scraps were only 49% protein or that the market price on July 1 was $120.00 per bushel. Once you have elicited that minimal detail, move off the points of agreement.

Quickly move to and emphasize the points of disagreement. The defense has a major advantage. The plaintiff must spend much of the plaintiff's case-in-chief acquainting the jury with the historical setting of the legal dispute: the places, times, names, and amounts. The plaintiff has done that for the defendant; and more so than the plaintiff, the defendant can concentrate squarely on the theory and theme. The defense should spend little time on the background details of the historical setting; the defense should go straight for the jugular—the theory and theme.

It is most dramatic if the defense concludes the direct examination by showing the flat, stark contrast with the plaintiff's theory. Suppose, for example, that the plaintiff testified that in an October 4th telephone conversation, the defendant unconditionally repudiated the contract. The defendant is just concluding her own direct testimony:

Q   During the October 4th conversation, what did you tell the plaintiff about your ability to perform the agreement?
A   I told him that there was an outside chance we wouldn't be able to meet the scheduled delivery.
Q   If you can recall, what were your precise words?
A   I can't remember exactly, but I said something like "there's a possibility I think you ought to know about."
Q   During this conversation, when did you make the flat statement that you would not perform?
A   I didn't. I didn't say that.
Q   When, if ever, did you make that flat statement?
A   I never did. All I said was that there was an outside chance.

The direct examination should highlight the point of disagreement between the plaintiff's and defendant's theories; the direct examination should end by peaking with a convincing unequivocal contradiction of the plaintiff's version of the facts.

Sec. 11-5.   A Preview of Chapters 12 Through 15

When you rely primarily on an affirmative counterclaim theory, you should follow the guidelines outlined in Chapters 5 through 9. With respect to the counterclaim, you are functionally a plaintiff; and you have to prove all the basic elements of the plaintiff's theory: contract formation, construction, satisfaction of conditions, the opposing party's breach of duty, and the facts your remedies depend upon. However, as we pointed out in Section 11-2 of this Chapter, you may be unable to use a counterclaim theory. If you cannot, you will have to rely on a simple or affirmative defense. The simple and affirmative defenses can be grouped into four basic theories or lines of defense. Chapter 12 discusses the first theory, namely, the parties never formed a valid contract. Chapter 13 shifts to the second line of defense, the argument that the parties' agreement is unenforceable. Chapter 14 analyzes the third basic theory that the defendant did not breach. Finally, Chapter 15 addresses lines of defense to the particular remedies the plaintiff seeks.

CHECKLIST FOR PLANNING THE DEFENSE CASE

____ Choose your defense theory.

> ____ Ideally, select a counterclaim theory that permits you to go on the offense.
>> or
> ____ Select an affirmative defense theory such as fraud that enables you to portray your client as the innocent victim of the plaintiff's bad faith wrongdoing.
>> or
> ____ Select a simple defense theory such as lack of mutual assent that permits you to emphasize the innocent nature of your client's conduct.

____ Decide whether to cross-examine the opposing witness.

> ____ Cross-examine if the witness' testimony is so damning and powerful that the jury would probably interpret your failure to cross as a concession of defeat.
> ____ Otherwise, cross-examine only if you believe that your cross will probably achieve one of the following objectives:
>> ____ Elicit testimony favoring your theory of the historical merits (purpose #1),
>> ____ Elicit favorable testimony on credibility (purpose #2),
>> ____ Impeach the witness on the historical merits (purpose #3),
>> ____ Impeach the witness by *ad hominem* attacks (purpose #4).

____ Determine the sequence of the cross-examination.

> ____ Do not begin on the same topic the direct examiner ended on.
> ____ Do not use the same sequence as the direct examiner.
> ____ Generally pursue purposes #1 and #2 before attempting to impeach the witness (purposes #3 and #4). Pursue purpose #4 last.

___ Draft the cross-examination questions.

Use:

___ short questions (15 or fewer words)
___ plainly worded questions
___ leading questions
___ non-argumentative questions
___ questions that call for factual data rather than opinions.

FOOTNOTES

[1] To help the reader develop the mind set for cross-examination, most of the cross-examination questions in this text begin in blatantly leading fashion with prefatory language such as "Isn't it true. . . ?" "Wouldn't you admit. . . ?" or "Didn't you. . . ?" In the courtroom, you should not begin every cross question in this fashion; doing so would bore and irritate both the judge and the jurors. You want "elegant variation," a mix of non-leading, gently leading, and brutally leading questions. However, many young trial attorneys do not realize the importance of maintaining witness control by using leading questions, and it is hoped that the phrasing of the cross questions in this text will make them more conscious of the phrasing of their questions.

[2] "Extrinsic evidence" refers to evidence other than testimony adduced during the cross-examination of the witness to be impeached. Consider that witness as witness #1. To impeach witness #1 by proof of a character trait of untruthfulness, the defense would have to call a character witness. The character witness' testimony is extrinsic evidence. To impeach witness #1 by proof of a conviction, the defense could introduce a properly attested copy of the judgment of conviction. The copy would also be extrinsic evidence.

[3] E. Imwinkelried, Evidentiary Foundations 44-45 (Michie/Bobbs-Merrill, 1980).

[4] *Id.* at 40.

[5] Peskin, *Proxemics,* Trial Diplomacy Journal 8 (Spring 1980).

[6] Burgess, *Principles and Techniques of Cross Examination,* Trial Diplomacy Journal 19, 23 (Winter 1979).

CHAPTER 12

The First Line of Defense—The Mechanics of Proving Theories Attacking the Contract's Validity

Sec. 12-1. Introduction.

In Chapter 11, we discussed the four basic theories the defendant may use. The first basic defensive theory is that the parties never formed a valid contract. An attack on the contract's validity is the first line of defense.

In some cases, the defense can mount this attack simply by contradicting the plaintiff's testimony. For example, if the defense attempts to negate mutual assent or consideration, defendant usually presents evidence directly contradicting the plaintiff's evidence. The plaintiff testifies that he said, "I'll buy twenty;" but the defendant testifies that the plaintiff said, "I'll buy thirty."

In other cases, the defense must do more than contradict the plaintiff's testimony. Specifically, the defendant will have to prove new, additional facts to attack the contract's validity by showing that

—the offer terminated before it was accepted and formed a contract, or
—the plaintiff did not give the defendant legally sufficient consideration because the plaintiff had a pre-existing duty.

The sections in this chapter discuss the foundations for defense theories based on termination of offer and pre-existing legal duty.

Sec. 12-2.   Termination of Offer

Even if the plaintiff proves that there was a valid offer and a matching acceptance, the defendant can disprove contract formation. The defendant can do so by persuading the trier of fact that the offer terminated before it was accepted. There are six methods of terminating an offer.

LEGAL RESEARCH REFERENCE:
Murray §§31, 35

a. The Supervening Death of an Essential Person Such as the Offeror

It is still the majority view in the United States that the death of the offeror or offeree after the making of the offer automatically terminates the offer. Most courts apply this view even when the other negotiating party had no notice of the death. Thus, in these jurisdictions, the offeror's death ends the offer even if the offeree later attempts to accept in good faith.

To trigger this termination doctrine, the defendant must show that

1. A person died. The attending physician who witnessed the death can testify to the death from personal knowledge. A properly attested death certificate is also competent evidence of the death; the attestation authenticates the certificate under Federal Evidence Rule 902, there is an excuse for the nonproduction of the original under Rule 1005, and there is an applicable hearsay exception under Rule 803(9).

   If no direct proof of death is available, the defendant can sometimes invoke the rebuttable presumption that a person is dead if he or she has disappeared and has not been heard from in seven years. The defendant will rarely have occasion to use this presumption because very few offers will stand open for that substantial a time period; most will terminate by lapse of time well before the expiration of the seven years. In the exceptional cases when the defendant must resort to this presumption, the defendant should prove such facts as (1) the witness and the offeror were so closely related that the offeror would naturally stay in contact with the witness; (2) the offeror disappeared under suspicious circumstances; (3) the witness unsuccessfully attempted to locate the offeror; and (4) the requisite time period (in most jurisdictions, seven years) lapsed:

   Q   What is your relation to Mr. Clinton (the offeror)?   (1)
   A   He is my father.
   Q   How close were you to your father?   (1)
   A   We have a very close family relationship. Mom died when I was quite young, so dad had to raise me. He's the only parent I've really even known.
   Q   When did you last see your father?   (2), (4)
   A   It was in June 1973.
   Q   What were the circumstances?   (2)

A   Dad was going on a fishing trip up to the Lake Tahoe area. I stopped by just before he left.

Q   Who went with him?   (2)

A   No one. He often went on these fishing trips alone. He was quite an outdoorsman.

Q   When did you see him next?   (2)

A   I didn't. He never contacted me. As far as I know, he never returned from the trip.

Q   What did you do when you realized he had not returned?   (3)

A   I made an effort to locate him.

Q   Specifically, what efforts did you make to find him?   (3)

A   I contacted all the police and sheriff departments in the Lake Tahoe region, and I spent some time up there myself looking.

Q   How much time did you spend at Lake Tahoe searching for your father?   (3)

A   I spent over a month up there.

Q   Where did you go in the Lake Tahoe region?   (3)

A   I went to every fishing or camping spot he had ever mentioned to me.

Q   Who else did you contact in your attempt to find your father?   (3)

A   I got in touch with all our relatives and as many of dad's old friends as I could think of.

Q   How many people did you contact?   (3)

A   I'd say easily 50. I can't give you a specific number.

Q   What was the result of your efforts?   (3)

A   I couldn't find him anywhere. I have no idea what happened to dad.

It would be permissible to elicit the local law enforcement agents' statements to the witness that they could not locate the witness' father. These statements are logically relevant to the question whether the witness' search for the offeror was diligent, and the statements are thus admissible for a nonhearsay purpose under Federal Evidence Rule 801(c).

2. The person who died was the offeror. The death certificate will state the decedent's name and often lists other identifying personal information such as address and physical characteristics. In some jurisdictions, the identity of name creates a presumption of identity of person. Whenever possible, show that the other information (address, height, etc.) also matches the offeror's background.

3. The date of the death. Make certain that the record clearly reflects the date of death—a date before the attempted acceptance. If you are relying on the presumption of death arising from absence and silence for seven years, the presumption is that the death occurs on the last day of the seven-year period.

LEGAL RESEARCH REFERENCE:
Murray §41

b.   The Destruction or Serious Deterioration of an Essential Object

The destruction of an essential object has the same legal effect as the death of an essential person: The offer terminates automatically—even without notice to the contracting parties. If an auto dealer offers to sell a consumer a particular car and the car is destroyed before the consumer effectively accepts the offer, the offer is at the end. The consumer cannot create a contract by accepting later even if the acceptance is in good faith and in complete ignorance of the car's destruction.

The foundation for this termination technique is similar to the foundation for the first method of termination:

1. An object was destroyed. A witness to the event causing the destruction may testify from personal knowledge. Alternatively, the defendant can present documentary proof of destruction such as the defendant's own business records (Federal Evidence Rule 803(6)) and official reports of the incident (Rule 803(8)). There may even be a newspaper report of the incident if it is of widespread interest such as a tornado or cyclone that swept through the town. The defendant may have offered to sell the plaintiff an ocean freighter which subsequently sank. The sinking is a newsworthy item. The newspaper article would be self-authenticating under Rule 902(6), and the judge may accept the argument that the news article is sufficiently trustworthy to fall within the Federal Evidence Rules' residual hearsay exception (Rules 803(24) and 804(b) (5)).

2. The object destroyed was "essential" to the contract. This issue is a question of the construction of the offer: Did the offeror promise to deliver a car meeting the contract description, or did the offeror promise to deliver the particular car that was destroyed in the tornado? To show that the object destroyed was essential, the defendant should establish such circumstances as the offeree's inspection of a particular object:

Q   What did the plaintiff do while he was on your lot?
A   He checked out some cars.
Q   Which cars did he inspect?
A   A couple, but he really seemed interested in the blue Corvette.
Q   Why do you say that?
A   He took a test drive in it and spent at least an hour examining the car.

the offeree's expression of the object's special suitability for the offeree's needs:

Q   What, if anything, did the plaintiff say about the car?
A   He said that it was ideal for him.
Q   In what respects did he say it was ideal?
A   He said that he'd been frustrated looking for a Corvette with just the right set of accessories, and this car he test drove was the only one he'd found so far.

and, finally, language in the offer indicating that the parties had an identified object in mind:

Q What changes, if any, did the plaintiff want you to make in the car?

A There was only one. It had an AM radio. He wanted an AM-FM radio.

Q Please read the handwritten notation on the left-hand margin of exhibit one (the offer) to the jurors.

A Yes, I will. It says, "Dealer shall remove AM radio now in car and have AM-FM radio installed."

3. The date of the destruction. As in the case of the date of the offeror's death, the defendant must make certain that the record reflects the specific date of destruction.

c. Outright Rejection, Outright Counteroffer, or Qualified Acceptance by the Offeree

If the offeree makes an outright rejection, an outright counteroffer, or a qualified acceptance, the original offer usually terminates. The offeree can prevent termination by telling the offeror that the offeree is still keeping the original offer "under advisement;" but absent that, the offer automatically terminates. In most jurisdictions, a rejection is legally effective only when it reaches the offeror; although acceptances are generally effective upon dispatch, rejections are usually effective only upon receipt.

To prove termination in this fashion, the defendant should lay a foundation including these elements:

1. The defendant received a communication. The defendant must testify to receipt of the phone call or letter.

2. The defendant received the communication at a particular date and time. Many businesses maintain a logbook of mail received or date stamp letters upon receipt. The logbook notation or date stamp may be admissible as a business entry under Federal Evidence Rule 803(6). Another theory of admissibility is past recollection recorded under Rule 803(5).

3. The communication came from the plaintiff offeree. The defendant must authenticate the communication as originating with the plaintiff. Chapter 5 discusses some of the major authentication techniques. If the communication is in the form of a letter and the defendant knows the plaintiff's handwriting style, the defendant may give lay opinion testimony identifying the handwriting. Or the plaintiff may use the reply letter or questioned document examiner techniques. If the communication is in the form of a telephone call and the defendant is familiar with the plaintiff's voice, the defendant can identify the voice or invoke the telephone directory doctrine.

4. The tenor of the communication was an outright rejection, outright counteroffer, or qualified acceptance. If the communication was oral, the defendant's attorney must carefully elicit the precise language the defendant used. The defendant may testify:

Q What, if anything, did the plaintiff say about your proposal? (4)

A He said that he wasn't interested.

Q   Now this is quite important. Please think carefully before you answer. To the best of your recollection, what were the plaintiff's precise words?   (4)

A   Our conversation was pretty short, since he seemed to be in a big rush. To the best of my recollection, his words were, "I can't accept. That price is too high to be appealing, and my warehouse is already packed to the rafters."

If the communication was written, the defendant should authenticate it, introduce it as an exhibit, and then read aloud the key passage to the jurors:

Q   Would you please read the second paragraph to the jurors?   (4)

A   Sure. That paragraph begins: "Your offer isn't very appealing. I purchased comparable fuel only two weeks ago from Memphis, and the price was $1.50 a barrel less than what you're asking. Besides, my warehouse is already full; the Memphis shipment just arrived, and there's just no place to put any more inventory. I'm afraid that I can't accept your offer."

LEGAL RESEARCH REFERENCE:
Murray §§42-43, 53-54

d.   Revocation by the Offeror

The courts and legislatures have progressively limited the offeror's power to revoke. The courts at first used the part performance doctrine under Restatement of Contracts §45 to limit the offeror's power to revoke when the offeror has begun to accept the offer for a unilateral contract. Later the courts used the promissory estoppel doctrine under Restatement of Contracts §90 to limit the power to revoke offers looking to bilateral and unilateral contracts. Most recently, the legislatures elected to include a "firm offer" provision in the Uniform Commercial Code. Section 2-205 of the Code enables a merchant to make a signed, written offer irrevocable by the simple device of giving "assurance that it (the offer) will be held open. . . ."

Notwithstanding the growing number of limitations on the offeror's power to revoke, the offeror usually retains that power. Given that power, the offeror may defend a Contract suit on the theory that the offeror effectively revoked before the plaintiff's attempted acceptance. Although some jurisdictions hold that a revocation is effective upon dispatch, most are of the view that a revocation takes effect only when the offeree receives it. The revocation may be direct or indirect.

LEGAL RESEARCH REFERENCE:
Murray §§36-38
White & Summers §1-3

1.   Direct revocation

OFFERS MADE TO AN INDIVIDUAL OFFEREE

To prove a direct revocation of an offer made to an individual offeree, the defendant should show that

1. The defendant drafted a document.
2. The defendant mailed the letter to the plaintiff offeree. If the defendant recalls mailing the letter, the defendant can testify to the mailing from personal knowledge. If not, under Federal Evidence Rule 406, the defendant can introduce habit evidence of the defendant's practice of mailing envelopes deposited in outboxes.
3. The plaintiff received the letter. If the defendant attached a return receipt form, the defendant may introduce the completed form as evidence of receipt. The defendant can authenticate the return receipt form as evidence of receipt; the defendant can authenticate the return receipt form by the reply letter doctrine. Absent direct proof of receipt, the defendant usually relies on the presumption that the addressee receives a letter that has been properly stamped, addressed, and mailed. As in the case of element #2, the defendant may introduce habit evidence to establish the foundation for the presumption. The head of the defendant's mailroom could testify:

Q   How familiar are you with May Company's (the defendant's) customary mailing procedures?
A   I know them backwards and forwards.
Q   How did you become familiar with those procedures?
A   I've worked in the mailroom for years.
Q   How many years?
A   I've been there over 23 years now.
Q   In May Company's procedure, what does an officer's secretary do with a letter after the officer signs it?
A   The secretary places it in an envelope, addresses it, and deposits it in a mail outbox.
Q   What happens then?
A   Three times a day someone from the mailroom makes a complete tour of the building and picks up the outgoing mail.
Q   What do they do with the mail?
A   They take it down to the basement where the mailroom is located.
Q   What happens when the mail reaches the mailroom?
A   I weigh each piece, examine the envelope to determine destination, and attach the appropriate postage.
Q   What happens to the mail after you attach the postage?
A   Twice a day—once at noon and again at four p.m.—we take it right down to the main post office on Lincoln Boulevard and get it on its way.

This testimony is both admissible and sufficient to support a finding that the defendant followed the procedure on the occasion in question. In turn, that finding gives rise to the presumption that the plaintiff received the letter.

If the communication was telephonic, the defendant must show that the person spoken to was the plaintiff or one of the plaintiff's agents. If the defendant is familiar with the plaintiff's voice, the defendant's voice indentification is admissible under Evidence Rule 901(5). Or the defendant can resort to the telephone directory doctrine under 901(6).

4. The date on which the plaintiff received the letter. If the return receipt form states the date and is purportedly signed by one of the plaintiff's agents, many judges will admit the date on the form as a vicarious admission by the plaintiff under Federal Evidence Rule 801(d) (2) (C) or (D). Other judges accept the argument that the date entry is a business entry by the post office and admissible under Rule 803(6). If there is no return receipt form, the defendant will have to introduce evidence of the course of mail between the two locations. The defendant can call a postal employee or one of the defendant's employees who has corresponded with persons in the other city on numerous occasions:

Q   How long does it take a letter to get from St. Louis to San Francisco?
A   It usually takes three full business days.
Q   How do you know that?
A   In addition to working on the plaintiff's account, I have responsibility for all our San Francisco's accounts. I have about 20 customers in San Francisco.
Q   How many letters do you send to San Francisco in the typical week?
A   I'd say easily ten or so each week.
Q   How do you know that it takes three business days for the letter to get there?
A   Many times the customer calls as soon as my letter arrives. In most cases, they ring me on the fourth business day when they've thought about my letter overnight.

5. The tenor of the communication was a revocation. If the communication was oral, the defendant can recite what he or she told the plaintiff. If the communication was written, the defendant should authenticate the retained copy, introduce it, and read aloud the language revoking the prior offer. Since the plaintiff presumably has the original letter, the defendant can invoke Evidence Rule 1004(3) to satisfy the best evidence rule.

OFFERS MADE TO THE GENERAL PUBLIC

The defendant may also directly revoke an offer made to the general public. Most advertisements do not constitute offers; but if an advertisement does qualify as an offer, the offeror can still revoke it. To revoke an advertisement offer, the courts usually require that the defendant offeror advertise the revocation in the same media and to the same extent. With respect to both the offer and the revocation, the defendant's attorney should ask:

Q   How did you advertise this?
Q   In what papers did you run this advertisement?
Q   How often did this advertisement appear?
Q   What was the period of time between the first day you ran the ad and the last day?

LEGAL RESEARCH REFERENCE:
Murray §§39-40

2. *Indirect revocation*

A revocation can result even if the offeror does not communicate directly with the plaintiff offeree. Some third party may inform the plaintiff of facts that clearly put the plaintiff on notice that the defendant offeror no longer intends to deal with the plaintiff. The foundation for indirect revocation includes proof that

1. A third party made a report to the plaintiff offeree.
2. The plaintiff should have regarded the third party as a reliable source of information.
3. The report made it clear to the plaintiff that the defendant no longer intended to contract with the plaintiff. All jurisdictions hold that the report works an indirect revocation if the report is that the defendant has already delivered or contracted to deliver the property to someone else. In some jurisdictions, the report effects a revocation even if the report's tenor is merely that the defendant has "offered" to sell the property to someone else.
4. The third party gave the plaintiff the report before the attempted acceptance.
5. The report is true.

Proof of an indirect revocation usually requires two witnesses. The third party describes the report he or she made to the plaintiff. Suppose that the defendant had offered to sell a parcel of land to the plaintiff. The plaintiff and defendant have the same stock broker. The stock broker is the defendant's witness:

Q   Where were you on the afternoon of August 10th?   (4)
A   I was at my brokerage house.
Q   What happened that afternoon?   (1)
A   Nothing much. A few customers came in.
Q   Which customers?   (1)
A   I can't remember them all. I do know that the plaintiff was one of them.
Q   How long have you known the plaintiff?   (2)
A   I've been his broker for the past 12 years.
Q   How much business do you do with him?   (2)
A   He's one of my best customers. I'd say that in any given year, he'll buy and sell over $50,000 worth of stock through me.
Q   How well do you know him?   (2)
A   We're not only business associates; we're friends. We belong to the same country club and sometimes go out together.
Q   What happened on August 10th when the plaintiff came in to your office? (3)
A   We talked for awhile.

Q   What did you talk about?   (3)

A   Well, for one thing, I knew he was interested in buying the defendant's property, and I'd just heard the defendant had sold out to a developer.

Q   What, if anything, did you tell the plaintiff about the defendant's property?   (3)

A   I told him that I had heard from a friend on the developer's staff that the defendant sold the property to the developer.

Q   Which property?   (3)

A   The property on Ghost Canyon Road.

The defendant would supply the last element of the foundation by showing that the report was true; the defendant would testify that the defendant had sold the property, as the plaintiff had been told.

LEGAL RESEARCH REFERENCE:
Murray §39

e.   Lapse of Time

An offer may terminate by lapse of time. If the offeror specified the period of time the offer would be open, the passage of that time period ends the offer. To establish termination in this fashion, the defendant must show that the original offer specified the time period. If the offer was oral, the defendant may testify directly to what the defendant told the plaintiff; the specification of the time period is an operative fact, a term of the contract, and the defendant's testimony about the time period is therefore exempt from a hearsay objection under Evidence Rule 801(c).

If the defendant's offer did not expressly state a time period, the courts will imply that the offer was to remain open for a reasonable time period. If the parties negotiate face to face, the courts usually say that the duration of the conversation is the reasonable time period; unless the offeror manifests a contrary intent, the offer terminates at the end of the conversation. If the parties are corresponding, it is much more difficult to determine what is a reasonable time period. Uniform Commercial Code 1-204(2) purports to define a "reasonable" time, but the only guidance that subsection gives the court is that the court must consider all the circumstances.

To persuade the court to make the period as short as possible, the defendant should prove such circumstances as the volatility of the market:

Q   How stable is the market for soy beans?

Q   How often does the market fluctuate?

Q   How much does the market change from day to day?

The defendant must first prove that the witness is an experienced trader in this commodity and then elicit the witness' description of the market's instability.

Another relevant factor is the method of communication the defendant used to convey the offer to the plaintiff:

Q How did you send the offer to the plaintiff?
A I sent it by telegram.

The defendant's use of an extraordinarily swift means of communication such as telegram signals the plaintiff that the defendant is in a rush to know whether the plaintiff wants to contract.

Finally, the defendant can testify to the defendant's statements to the plaintiff:

Q What, if anything, did you tell the plaintiff about replying to your offer?
A I told him that I was in a pinch and needed to know right away whether he was going to buy.
Q How did you describe this "pinch" to him?
A I told him that my warehouse was so full it was ready to burst. I said that I had to move the stuff out as quickly as possible.

The defendant's statements are logically relevant to show their effect on the plaintiff's state of mind; they put the plaintiff on notice that the defendant expected a prompt reply. Hence, the statements are admissible as nonhearsay under Evidence Rule 801(c).

LEGAL RESEARCH REFERENCE:
Murray §§32-34

f. Supervening Illegality

If a material term of the offer becomes illegal after the offer is made but before acceptance, the supervening illegality terminates the offer. The defendant must show that

1. The law changed, and the new law made a material part of the bargain proposed in the offer illegal. For example, the offer proposed a loan at 10% interest when a 10% interest rate was lawful. A new usury law lowers the maximum lawful rate to 9%.

   The defendant may prove the new law in several ways. In most jurisdictions, the defendant could request that the judge judicially notice the law.[1] The defendant should give the plaintiff advance notice of the request and supply the judge with copies of the law to be noted. Material submitted as the basis for judicial notice request need not be independently admissible. As we previously stated, it is best to make your judicial notice requests at the chambers conference before trial begins. The party requesting judicial notice, the proponent (P), should make the request in this fashion:

   J Is there anything else you'd like to take care of before we go into open court?
   P Yes, your honor. I would request that you judicially notice the new Oregon usury law, lowering the maximum lawful rate to 9%.
   J Where is the support for that?
   P Your honor, here is a Xerox copy from the latest pocket part supplement

to the official Oregon code. If you'd like, we can insert this into the record as an appellate exhibit.

J I would prefer to do it that way to make a complete record. (*To the opposing counsel*) Have you had an opportunity to review this?

O Yes, sir.

P I gave him a copy three days ago, your honor.

J (*To the opposing counsel*) Is that true?

O Yes.

J All right. Everything seems in order. I'll grant the request.

P Your honor, since this is a jury trial, I assume you'll be submitting the
termination issue to the jury.

J That's correct.

P Then I would ask that you inform the jury of this new law during the final jury charge.

Second, the defendant could introduce an attested copy of the statute,
ordinance, or administrative regulation. A certified copy would be self-
authenticating under Evidence Rule 902(4). Third, a statute or code
book containing the law would be admissible if the text purported to
be issued by public authority. Evidence 902(5) states that "[b]ooks,
pamphlets, or other publications purporting to be issued by public authority" are self-authenticating.

2. The change became effective before the plaintiff attempted to accept.
   The defendant must establish the effective date of the new law. The
   material submitted to the judge must not only quote the new law but
   also state the new law's effective date.

Sec. 12-3. The Pre-existing Duty Rule

Proof that the offer terminated before acceptance is a complete defense
to the plaintiff's argument that there was mutual assent. Similarly, proof of
the plaintiff's pre-existing legal duty is a complete defense to the plaintiff's
contention that the plaintiff gave legally sufficient consideration to make the
defendant's promise enforceable.

At common law, the plaintiff must give the defendant consideration not
only to initially form a contract but also to support any modification of the
contract's terms. Uniform Commercial Code 2-209(1) changes the rule for
contracts for the sale of goods by pronouncing that "(a)n agreement modifying a contract within this Article needs no (new) consideration." However,
for most types of contracts including realty, construction, and employment
agreements, the defendant can invoke the pre-existing duty rule to escape liability from the original contract or a subsequent modification of the original contract.

To successfully invoke the rule, the defendant must establish that

1. The plaintiff had a previous legal duty to the defendant. The previous
   duty need not arise from contract law; the duty can be founded on
   property or tort law. However, in most litigated cases, the duty is

based on a prior contract between the plaintiff and the defendant. If the evidence during the plaintiff's case-in-chief does not prove the existence of the prior contract, the defendant will have to prove the contract during the defense case-in-chief. The defendant will have to use the techniques outlined in Chapter 5 to prove the formation of the prior contract.

2. The consideration the plaintiff gave the defendant for contract #2 or the contract modification was the promise to perform the plaintiff's pre-existing duty. Suppose that the defendant landowner and the plaintiff contractor entered into a construction contract. The cost of materials increased during the course of performance. The contractor then threatened to abandon the contract unless the defendant agreed to increase the compensation from $120,000 to $170,000. The defendant should first establish the plaintiff's consideration under the original contract:

Q   What did the plaintiff promise to do in exchange for the $120,000?   (2)
A   He'd build our summer cottage according to the blueprints my architect, Ms. Graves, had drawn up.

You can then have the witness read aloud the contract language in which the plaintiff made that promise. Next, have the defendant testify that the plaintiff repeated the same promise at the time of the modification of the contract:

Q   When you said you would pay the additional $50,000, what did the plaintiff promise to do?   (2)
A   He repeated that he would build the cottage according to Ms. Graves' blueprints.
Q   How did these blueprints differ from the plans attached to exhibit two (the original contract)?   (2)
A   They didn't differ at all. They were the same plans.
Q   How did the schedule for completing the cottage change?   (2)
A   That didn't change either. The only thing that changed was that I was going to pay more.

3. The plaintiff did not give the defendant any additional consideration other than repeating the plaintiff's prior promise:

Q   What else did the plaintiff promise to do in exchange for the additional $50,000?   (3)
A   He didn't promise anything else.

4. The circumstances smacked of economic extortion. There is no logical necessity for applying the pre-existing duty rule to contract modifications. The rule has been extended to modifications for the policy reason of preventing economic extortion. We shall discuss the economic duress doctrine at length in Chapter 13, but many of the same policy considerations underpinning that doctrine support the pre-existing duty rule. It is therefore relevant to show that the defendant accepted the plaintiff's proposed contract modification because of the plaintiff's threats:

Q   If the plaintiff did not promise anything else, why did you agree to pay the additional $50,000?   (4)

A   Because of his threats. He demanded the $50,000 and threatened me if I didn't give in.

Q   What threats did he make?   (4)

A   He threatened to walk off the work site and bring the project to a halt.

Q   What reason did he give for demanding the additional $50,000?   (4)

A   He said that the cost of the material he was using on the project had increased. That's all he told me.

Q   Why did you give in to his threats?   (4)

A   The roof wasn't finished yet, and the snows come early up in the mountains where the cottage was being built. If he'd walked off the job, there was a good chance the cottage wouldn't have been completed before the snows; and if the snow got inside the house, the place would have been just ruined.

It is not only relevant to prove the plaintiff's economic duress; it is good trial strategy. The proof of the plaintiff's threats will make the jurors positively dislike the plaintiff. The jurors will then be inclined to resolve any doubt in the defendant's favor.

LEGAL RESEARCH REFERENCE:
Murray §§85-89
White & Summers §1-5

CHECKLIST FOR THE FIRST LINE OF DEFENSE

____ There was no valid offer.

    ____ The proposal did not manifest intent to enter a binding agreement.
        or
    ____ The proposal did not manifest intent to enter a final agreement.
        or
    ____ The proposal's terms were indefinite.

OR

____ The offer terminated before an effective acceptance.

    ____ The supervening death of an essential person such as the offeror.
        or
    ____ The destruction or serious deterioration of an essential object.
        or
    ____ Outright rejection, outright counteroffer, or qualified acceptance by the offeree.
        or
    ____ Revocation by the offeror.
        or
    ____ Lapse of time.
        or
    ____ Supervening illegality.

OR

___ <u>The attempted acceptance was ineffective.</u>

    ___ The person attempting to accept was not a proper offeree.
        or
    ___ At the time, the person did not know of the offer's existence.
        or
    ___ The person did not intend to accept.
        or
    ___ The person did not give the requested return.
        or
    ___ The person did not give the requested return unconditionally.

OR

___ <u>The plaintiff did not give the defendant legally sufficient consideration.</u>

    ___ One party was obviously acting out of a sense of moral obligation rather than bargaining.
        or
    ___ The plaintiff had a pre-existing legal duty.

FOOTNOTE

[1] On its face, Federal Evidence Rule 201(a) "governs only judicial notice of adjudicative facts."

CHAPTER 13

The Second Line of Defense—How to Prove Theories Attacking the Contract's Enforceability

Sec. 13-1. Introduction

In the last chapter, the defendant attacked the contract's formation by showing that the parties never formed a valid contract. This chapter deals with the second line of defense: the argument that even though the parties formed a contract, the contract is unenforceable or voidable on a ground such as the plaintiff's fraud or economic duress. When the defense relies on this argument, the defendant can concede both mutual assent and consideration; the defenses discussed in this chapter deprive the plaintiff of a remedy even when both mutual assent and consideration are present.

Many of these defenses are codified in the Uniform Commercial Code. However, the Code is silent on other defenses. The draftsmen of the Code did not intend their silence to be construed as an implied abolition of those other defenses. Rather, U.C.C. 1-103 provides that "(u)nless otherwise displaced by the particular provisions of this Act, the principles of law and equity, including . . . the law relative to capacity to contract, . . . , fraud, misrepresentation, duress, coercion, mistake, . . . or other . . . invalidating cause shall supplement its provisions." Thus, when the Code is silent on a defense, the defense attorney may resort to the common law.

Sec. 13-2. The Statute of Frauds

The English Parliament enacted the Statute of Frauds to reduce the incidence of perjury. To achieve this end, the Parliament decreed that certain contracts would be unenforceable unless the parties reduced the agreement to writing. It was hoped that the writing requirement would simplify the process of proof at trial and make it more difficult to fabricate a claim of an oral contract. Although there has been substantial criticism of the Statute, all American jurisdictions have adopted one form or another of the Statute.

In some cases, the plaintiff's own case-in-chief shows that the agreement sued upon is within the Statute and that the parties did not comply. For example, in his or her own testimony, the plaintiff might describe the contract as "an oral agreement to buy land." At the close of the plaintiff's case-in-chief, the defense should move for a directed verdict.

However, in other cases, the defendant will have to establish the factual predicate for invoking the Statute of Frauds during the defense case-in-chief. To establish that predicate, the defendant should show that

—The contract sued upon falls within the purview of the Statute.
—The parties did not satisfy the Statute.
—During the defense case-in-chief, many defense counsel also like to attack and preempt any mitigating doctrine they anticipate the plaintiff will raise during rebuttal.

> **LEGAL RESEARCH REFERENCE:**
> Murray §312
> White & Summers §2-1

a. The Contract Sued Upon Falls Within the Purview of the Statute of Frauds

The coverage of the Statute varies from jurisdiction to jurisdiction. We shall discuss the types of contracts covered by the Statute which are of greatest interest to commercial litigators.

1. *Contracts for the sale of personal property*

In most American jurisdictions, executory contracts for the sale of personal property in excess of a specified amount fall within the Statute. To trigger this provision of the Statute, the defendant must show the following:

1. The agreement was an executory sale contract. If the jurisdiction limits the Statute to executory contracts and excludes present sales from the Statute, the defendant must show that even after forming the contract, the parties had executory duties to perform in the future:

Q When did you shake hands on your agreement with the plaintiff? (1)
A We finished up the dickering on August 12th.
Q Under the agreement, when were you supposed to deliver the crane? (1)
A The understanding was that I'd get it to his foundry in Detroit by the end of the month.

Q   Under the agreement, when was the plaintiff supposed to pay you?   (1)
A   20 days after delivery.

The Uniform Commercial Code contains an expansive definition of "contract for sale." U.C.C. 2-106(1) defines that expression as including:

> . . . both a present sale of goods and a contract to sell goods at [a] future time. A "sale" consists in the passing of title from the seller to the buyer for a price. . . . A "present sale" means a sale which is accomplished by the making of a contract.

A present sale would fall under the U.C.C.'s Statute of Frauds even though it would be excluded under many state statutes.

2. The subject matter of the contract was personal property. It is sometimes difficult to distinguish a personalty contract from a personal services or realty contract. When a contractor completes a project for a landowner, one effect of the project's completion is to transfer title to the items of personal property the contractor includes in the building; title to the personalty transfers to the landowner, since the personalty becomes a fixture to the land. Nevertheless, the prevailing sentiment is that construction contracts *per se* are not within the Statute. The courts reason that the personal services element of a construction contract is the dominant component; the transfer of title to the personalty is viewed as an incidental effect of the performance of the personal services.

The line between personalty and realty contracts is sometimes difficult to draw. Suppose that the subject matter of the contract is a tree or growing crop in the ground at the time of contracting. Is the contract's subject matter personalty or realty? At common law, the courts struggled to determine when the parties intended title to pass. If the parties intended title to pass while the property was still in the ground, the buyer was purchasing realty. But if the parties intended title to pass after severance, the buyer was purchasing personalty. The contract rarely contained an express provision stating when title was to pass, and the courts often fictitiously manufactured the parties' "intent."

The Uniform Commercial Code gives the attorney clearer guidance. Subsection 2-105(1) sets out the Code's general definition of "goods," and 2-107 states some specific rules. U.C.C. 2-107(1) provides that

> . . . [a] contract for the sale of timber, minerals or the like or a structure of its materials to be removed from realty is a contract for the sale of goods within this Article if they are to be severed by the seller. . . .

Suppose that the defendant is the seller. The defendant could testify:

Q   Under your agreement with the plaintiff, who was going to remove the timber from your ranch?   (2)
A   I was. I had the logging equipment. The plaintiff agreed that I would be

responsible for that, and then he would send his trucks to pick up the timber.

Subsection 2-107(2) states another specific rule:

> [a] contract for the sale apart from the land of growing crops or other things attached to realty and capable of severance without material harm thereto but not described in subsection (1) is a contract for the sale of goods within this Article. . . .

Hence, even if the buyer is to sever, the agreement is a personalty contract if the severance can be done "without material harm" to the land. Assume that the defendant seller sold the plaintiff a lettuce crop and the understanding was that the buyer's pickers would sever the lettuce. The defendant could still invoke the statute by testifying:

Q   What is your occupation?   (2)
A   As I said, I'm a produce grower.
Q   Which crops do you grow?   (2)
A   I rotate about four crops during the year, including the lettuce.
Q   How long have you been a lettuce grower?   (2)
A   I've been in business as a lettuce grower for 25 years; and before I took over the business, as a child I worked on my dad's produce farm.
Q   How familiar are you with the procedures for picking lettuce?   (2)
A   I've stooped over many a lettuce plant in my time, and I've had pickers doing it for me for 25 years.
Q   How is the lettuce removed from the ground?   (2)
A   The root isn't very deep. One firm pull, and the lettuce pops out of the soil.
Q   How much damage does the removal of the lettuce do to the ground? (2)
A   None. You don't have to pour in any chemicals to loosen it up to remove it. It just pops out. It doesn't harm the soil in any way.

3. The amount of the agreement exceeded the amount specified in the Statute. The Code's Statute, U.C.C. 2-201, specifies $500 for contracts for the sale of goods. Other personal property transactions fall under the residual U.C.C. statute, U.C.C. 1-206(1), specifying $5,000 as the dividing line. The defendant may testify to the purchase price the parties agreed upon. If the agreement was a personal property exchange, the defendant should present expert testimony about the fair market value of the property being exchanged. Under U.C.C. 2-304(1), "the price can be payable in money or otherwise." Some jurisdictions would apply the Statute if the personal property on either side of the contract exceeded $500 in fair market value at the time of contracting.

LEGAL RESEARCH REFERENCE:
Murray §320
White & Summers §2-2

2. *Contracts for the sale of realty*

To invoke this clause of the Statute, the defendant must show that

1. The agreement was an executory contract. As in the case of the last clause, the defendant should testify that the parties' understanding was that there were duties to be performed after the time of contracting.
2. The subject matter of the contract was realty. The courts use the same tests to distinguish between realty and personalty under this clause that they use to draw the line under the prior clause. The realty clause differs from the personalty clause in that there is no dollar limitation. The Statute applies to a realty contract regardless of the fair market value or purchase price of the land.

LEGAL RESEARCH REFERENCE:
Murray §318

3. Contracts incapable of performance within a year from the making of the contract

The Statute requires certain long-term contracts to be reduced to writing. The requirement applies only if the contract is incapable of being fully performed within a year from the date the contract is formed. Most courts are hostile to this requirement, and they refuse to apply the requirement so long as there is any possibility that the contract can be performed within a year. It is not enough for the defendant to testify that the parties contemplated that performance would span more than a year. The defendant must show (1) the formation date and (2) that the contract required performance more than a year after the date the contract arose:

Q   What type of agreement did you reach with the plaintiff?
A   It was an employment contract.
Q   When did you make this agreement?   (1)
A   We shook hands on it on December 31, 1980.
Q   What was the length of the agreement?
A   She was supposed to work for me for 15 months at my Mobile office.
Q   Please think carefully before you answer this question. As best you can recall, what were the precise words you used to describe the length of the agreement to the plaintiff?   (2)
A   I think I said I wanted her promise to work "until the very end of March 1982."

LEGAL RESEARCH REFERENCE:
Murray §319

4. Surety or guaranty contracts

In most jurisdictions, the Statute applies to the "special," "secondary," or "collateral" promise of a surety or guarantor. U.C.C. 1-201(40) defines "surety" as including guaranty. Surety and guaranty agreements are quite common in commercial transactions—especially loan, private construction, and public works contracts. However, the courts will not bind a third party as a surety unless there is persuasive evidence that that person assumed secondary liability.

The plaintiff may have attempted to create the impression that the defendant was a joint obligor with another debtor. If the defendant was a joint obligor rather than a surety, the statute does not apply to the defendant's promise; even if the promise is oral, the promise is enforceable. To trigger the surety clause of the Statute, the defendant must establish that the defendant agreed to be a secondarily liable surety rather than a primarily liable joint debtor. Figure 13-1 depicts a surety relation. The defendant must show that

1. The principal debtor had at least a voidable duty to the creditor, the plaintiff. The principal debtor may have that duty at the time the surety and creditor contract. However, the critical time is the due date for the surety's performance; the principal debtor must at least come under a duty to the creditor before the time the surety is to perform. This element is rarely in dispute. The plaintiff and defendant usually agree that the other party (PD) was indebted to the plaintiff. The point of disagreement is that the plaintiff contends that the defendant was jointly liable with the other person. As previously stated, if the defendant was a joint obligor, the Statute is inapplicable; and the defendant's promise is enforceable even if it was never reduced to writing.

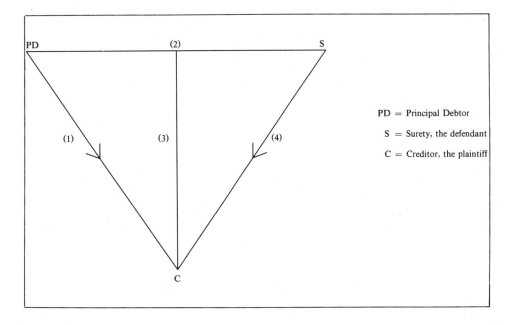

Figure 13-1: A SURETY OR GUARANTY CONTRACT

2. The relationship between the principal debtor and surety is a surety relation; the understanding between the two of them was that the surety was only secondarily liable for the debt:

Q Who was present in the loan department? (2)
A It was just the loan officer, my brother, and I.
Q Why were you there? (2)
A I was going to help my brother get a loan.
Q How would you do that? (2)
A I was going to be backup on the loan.
Q What, if anything, did you tell your brother about the way you would help him? (2)
A I said I'd back him up. The deal was that it would be his debt but that if he couldn't pay, then I would.
Q Under your agreement with your brother, when would you have to pay the bank? (2)
A Only if he defaulted and couldn't make the payment.

The defendant's statements to his brother are not subject to a hearsay objection. The statements are operative facts; they are part of the defendant's agreement with his brother and, hence, exempt from the hearsay rule under Federal Evidence Rule 801(c).

3. The creditor must know that the surety is only secondarily liable for the debt. It is not enough that the principal debtor understands that the defendant's role was the limited role of a surety; the role must be made clear to the creditor:

Q While you were talking to the loan officer, what, if anything, did you tell him about the way you were going to help your brother? (3)
A I explained to him the arrangement I'd made with Jeff.
Q What did you tell him about when you would pay on the loan? (3)
A I said I'd pay only if Jeff didn't.

Again, the defendant's statements are not objectionable as hearsay. These statements are operative facts in the contract with the plaintiff loan company or bank.

4. The surety must make the promise directly to the plaintiff creditor. If the surety makes this promise to the principal debtor, the court will construe the agreement as an exoneration or indemnity agreement; the surety pays the principal debtor before (exoneration) or after (indemnity) the debtor pays the creditor. The Statute does not apply to exoneration and indemnity agreements. The Statute applies to only surety contracts, and the agreement is a surety contract only if the surety makes the promise directly to the creditor:

Q When you said you'd pay if Jeff didn't, whom were you speaking to? (4)
A Mr. Nelson, the loan officer.
Q Whom did you make this promise to? (4)
A To Nelson. I had to make this promise to them so that Jeff could get the loan.

LEGAL RESEARCH REFERENCE:
Murray §§313-16

b. The Parties Did Not Comply with the Statute of Frauds by Preparing a Sufficient Note or Memorandum

In addition to showing that the Statute applies to his or her contract with the plaintiff, the defendant should show that the parties did not satisfy the Statute by preparing a note or memorandum.

1. Common-law requirements for the note or memorandum

The common law required a complete, correct memorandum of the contract. The memorandum had to correctly state the parties' agreement and list such essential terms as the parties' identity, the nature of the subject matter, quantity, quality, price, terms of payment, and delivery. The note must ordinarily be signed by the defendant. Under the common law, the defendant could show the parties' non-compliance in four ways.

First, the defendant could show that there was no note or memorandum:

Q When you reached this agreement, what writing, if any, did you prepare as evidence of the agreement?
A None.
Q When, if ever, did you prepare a writing setting out this agreement?
A We never did. It was a completely oral deal.

Second, the defendant could show that the seemingly complying memorandum incorrectly stated one or more material terms:

Q I now hand you plaintiff's exhibit number three (the note the plaintiff introduced). What is it?
A It's the note we roughed out as a draft of our deal.
Q According to exhibit three, what was the purchase price?
A $13,000.
Q What purchase price did you and the plaintiff agree upon?
A $13,500.
Q Why does the exhibit state $13,000?
A It was just a rough draft we dashed off. We didn't pay all that much attention for errors.

Third, the defendant can show that the memorandum is incomplete:

Q I now hand you plaintiff's exhibit number three. What is it?
A It's the note we roughed out on May 25th.
Q What, if anything, does the note say about the delivery of the refrigerators?
A It doesn't say anything about that.
Q What agreement, if any, did you and the plaintiff reach about the delivery date?
A We agreed that he would deliver by June 1st.

It is best to elicit testimony showing that the term omitted was a material part of the bargain:

Q   Why did you specify June 1st as the delivery date?
A   I was in a rush because I had to repaint the refrigerators and ship them on to West Germany before June 5th.
Q   What, if anything, did you tell the plaintiff about your reason for wanting the delivery by June 1st?
A   I explained my own delivery schedule and that I had this commitment for overseas shipment.

Finally, the defendant can show that the memorandum does not bear his or her signature:

Q   Whose signature appears on the bottom of exhibit three?
A   It purports to be mine.
Q   Whose is it?
A   It's not mine.
Q   How do you know that?
A   To begin with, I don't recall signing any such note. Secondly, it's very different from my handwriting style.

If the memorandum is purportedly signed by an agent, the defendant can deny the agency:

Q   What is written on the bottom of exhibit three?
A   The name of my firm is written first and then "by Grant Navin."
Q   Who is Grant Navin?
A   He's a guy who used to work for me.
Q   When did he work for you?
A   I had him on my payroll from early 1966 through 1979.
Q   When did he leave your employ?
A   I think it was December 1979.
Q   What is the date on the bottom of exhibit three?
A   February 5th 1980.
Q   What authority did you give Mr. Navin to sign this document for you?
A   None.   [NO ANTECEDENT AUTHORITY]
Q   When did you first learn he had signed it?
A   In mid-March 1980.
Q   How did you learn that?
A   The plaintiff called it to my attention.
Q   What, if anything, did you say when the plaintiff called this to your attention?
A   I repudiated the deal. I said I'd never given him authority to do it, and I had no intention of fulfilling Navin's agreement.   [NO SUBSEQUENT RATIFICATION]

LEGAL RESEARCH REFERENCE:
Murray §§321-24

2. *The Uniform Commercial Code requirements for the note or memorandum*

The Code dramatically relaxes the common-law requirements for the note. The basic requirements are set out in subsection 2-201(1). The only requirements are that

—The parties prepared a "writing." U.C.C. 1-201(46) broadly defines "writing" as including "printing, typewriting, or any other intentional reduction to tangible form."
—The writing "indicate[s] that a contract for sale has been made between the parties." Notice that this sentence is phrased in the past tense, "has been made." Some judges refuse to treat preliminary documents such as the offer as sufficient memoranda; preliminary documents reflecting the negotiating process do not reflect that a contract "has (already) been made."
—The writing must be "signed by the party against whom enforcement is sought or by his authorized agent or broker." U.C.C. 1-201(39) states that "signed" includes any "symbol executed or adopted by a party with present intention to authenticate a writing."
—The writing must state a quantity term.

Subsection 2-201(2) is even more revolutionary and heretical. Under that subsection, the plaintiff can satisfy the Statute even if the defendant never signed a note. The Statute is satisfied if

—The plaintiff and defendant were merchants as defined by U.C.C. 2-104(1).
—The plaintiff and defendant reached an agreement.
—"[W]ithin a reasonable time" after reaching the agreement, the plaintiff prepared a note.
—The note was "in confirmation" of the agreement. That is, the note refers to the agreement as an accomplished fact.
—The note is "sufficient against the sender." If the defendant were suing the plaintiff, the defendant could enforce the agreement because the note satisfies subsection 2-201(1).
—The plaintiff sent the note to the defendant.
—The defendant received the note.
—The defendant had "reason to know its contents."
—The defendant did not give the plaintiff "written notice of objection to its contents . . . within ten days after it is received."

Under this subsection, the defendant can invoke the Statute in at least three ways. The defendant can deny receiving the plaintiff's note within a reasonable time after the oral agreement:

Q   When did you make this agreement with the plaintiff?

A   I think it was on January 9th.

Q   When did you first see the plaintiff's exhibit three?

A   It wasn't until months later. I think it was sometime in October. I had forgotten about the whole thing when he finally sent this note.

Or the defendant can deny receiving the note at all:

Q   When did you receive this note at your office?

A   I never did.

Q   When did you first see exhibit three?

A   We went to some conference at the office of the plaintiff's attorney, and the attorney showed me a copy of this. He claimed his client had sent it to me.

Q   When did you receive the note?

A   Never.

Finally, the defendant can testify that he or she objected in writing within ten days of receipt of the plaintiff's memorandum:

Q   When did you receive exhibit three in the mail?

A   It arrived on January 12th, to the best of my recollection.

Q   What did you do then?

A   I wrote to him to tell him that the deal was off.

[*Here authenticate the writing and quote the key language to the jurors. You may authenticate the writing by the evidentiary techniques discussed in Chapter 5.*]

Q   When did you send defense exhibit B to the plaintiff?

A   On January 15th.

Q   How did you send it?

A   By regular mail. I mailed it to his business address.

LEGAL RESEARCH REFERENCE:
White & Summers §2-4

c.   Anticipating and Rebutting Mitigating Doctrines

Even if the parties did not comply with the Statute by preparing a satisfactory note, the court may enforce the contract by virtue of a mitigating doctrine. When they anticipate that the plaintiff will invoke a mitigating doctrine, many defense counsel prefer to preempt and rebut the doctrine during the defense case-in-chief.

Most of the mitigating doctrines do not pose any serious evidentiary problems for the defendant. For example, U.C.C. 2-201(3) (a) recognizes special manufacture as an exception to the Statute. The exception applies only when the goods to be manufactured "are not suitable for sale to others in the ordinary course of the seller's business" and the seller makes "either a substantial beginning of their manufacture or commitments for their procurement before notice of repudiation is received." The defendant buyer could present expert testimony that goods manufactured according to the contract specifications would be marketable to other buyers, or the defendant could introduce the plaintiff's own business records showing how small the plaintiff's manufacturing expenditures were before the defendant repudiated the contract.

The other mitigating doctrines include acceptance and receipt (U.C.C. 2-201(3) (c)), part payment (U.C.C. 2-201(3) (c)), part performance of a realty contract, equitable estoppel, and promissory estoppel. In the case of all these mitigating doctrines, the defendant can develop the defense rebuttal by cross-examination of the plaintiff's witnesses and direct examination during the defense case-in-chief, perhaps including calling one of the plaintiff's employees as an adverse witness under Federal Evidence Rule 611(c).

There is one mitigating doctrine that poses special evidentiary problems. Subsection 2-201(3) (b) provides that a contract is enforceable if "the party against whom enforcement is sought admits in his . . . testimony or otherwise that a contract for sale was made. . . ." This is a controversial provision that some states have refused to enact. If your jurisdiction does not recognize this exception, the evidentiary problem evaporates. However, most jurisdictions have enacted 2-201(3) (b); and in those jurisdictions, the defense attorney faces a difficult problem. If your client takes the stand and admits the contract's formation, you may lose your Statute of Frauds defense. If your client does not testify, the jury will suspect that your client has something to hide. Worse still, the prohibition against comment on silence does not apply in civil cases; during closing, the plaintiff's attorney could state, "The defendant never took the stand to deny that he and my client formed a contract. Ladies and gentlemen, ask yourselves why he didn't take the stand. The answer's clear: He didn't want to have to look you in the eye and admit that my client is telling the truth."

Before reaching the despairing conclusion that you must advise your client against testifying, consider these factors. First, the Statute of Frauds may be only a minor defense. Your principal theory may be that the acceptance did not match or that impossibility discharged your client's contract duty. In this situation, you should put your client on the stand even though you risk the loss of the Statute defense. Second, consider limiting the scope of your client's direct examination. Federal Evidence Rule 611(b) adopts the traditional view that the scope of cross is "limited to the subject matter of the direct examination. . . ." If you carefully restrict your client's direct examination to performance or damages, you may have a good scope objection when the plaintiff begins cross-examining about contract formation. Make the scope of your direct examination as clear as possible; whenever you come to a new topic in the direct, use declarative sentences as topic sentences before you begin questioning about the new topic:

Q Now, Ms. Powell, I've been asking you some questions about the meeting when you signed the contract. Now let's talk about the meeting a month later. Where did that meeting take place?

The more obvious you make it that you restricted the direct to specific topics, the more likely the judge is to sustain a scope objection to cross-examination about other topics. To be on the safe side, ask the trial judge for an advance indication of how he or she would rule on your scope objection. Finally, some authorities have argued that during cross-examination by the plaintiff, the defendant must be accorded an evidentiary privilege to refuse to answer questions about the Statute of Frauds issue. Research the local law to determine whether your jurisdiction recognizes this privilege. If the state of the law is unclear in your jurisdiction, again seek an advance ruling from your trial judge.

LEGAL RESEARCH REFERENCE:
Murray §§325-28, 332-33
White & Summers §§2-5-7

Sec. 13-3. Mistake

As we previously stated, one common defensive theory is that there has been an "innocent misunderstanding" between the plaintiff and defendant. The defense can use the "innocent misunderstanding" label for a mistake argument.

a. General Rules

The rules for unilateral and mutual mistake govern most types of errors, including mistakes in the choice of words, the meaning of words, the content of a document, and the nature of the subject matter.

1. Unilateral mistakes

The general norm is that the defendant's unilateral mistake does not affect the enforceability of the contract. Even if the defendant was mistaken about some circumstance relating to the contract, the plaintiff may enforce the contract.

MISTAKE CAUSED BY THE OTHER PARTY

However, there are two exceptional situations in which the defendant can avoid the contract on the ground of the defendant's unilateral mistake. The first situation is the case in which the plaintiff's conduct induced or caused the defendant's mistake. The defendant must show that

1. The defendant was laboring under a mistake.
2. The plaintiff's conduct before the formation of the contract caused the mistake.
3. The mistake was material.

Suppose, for example, that the defendant mistakenly assumed that the written contract included the oral warranty the plaintiff gave the defendant:

Q   What happened after you reached this agreement with the plaintiff?
A   He had his secretary type it up for our signature.
Q   What happened then?   (1)
A   We signed it.
Q   What did you think the writing said about the condition of the generator? (1)
A   I thought it was in good, working condition.
Q   What did the contract actually say about the condition of the generator? (1)
A   It said that I was taking the generator as is.

[Have the defendant quote the pertinent language in the writing. If the plaintiff has already introduced the writing, you can hand the exhibit to the defendant and have the defendant read the language aloud. If the plaintiff has not introduced the writing, the defendant should authenticate the writing by one of the techniques discussed in Chapter 5 and then quote the language to the jurors.]

Q   Why did you think that the writing included the representation that the generator was in working condition?   (2)
A   The plaintiff told me so. That's why.
Q   Specifically, what did the plaintiff say?   (2)
A   First I asked him whether the writing contained the whole deal, including the warranty. Then he said in no uncertain terms that it did. He said he'd given his secretary complete instructions on what to type in.

The defendant should then call a repairman experienced in working on this type of machinery to establish its disrepair and the cost of repairing the machinery. The repairman's testimony shows the third element, the materiality of the mistake.

MISTAKE KNOWN TO THE OTHER PARTY

The second exceptional situation is the case in which the plaintiff realizes that the defendant is mistaken. The foundation includes proof that

1. The defendant was laboring under a mistake.
2. Before the contract was formed, the plaintiff realized that the defendant was mistaken.
3. The mistake was material.

The defendant lays the foundation for a known unilateral mistake in roughly the same fashion as the foundation for an induced unilateral mistake. The defendant testifies to elements #1 and 2:

Q   What did you do then?
A   We drove from the realtor's office over to the plaintiff's house to sign the papers.

Q   What did you do when you arrived at the house?

A   We took one last inspection tour of the premises before we signed the papers.

Q   What were you looking for during this inspection?   (1)

A   The usual thing—evidence of wood rot or termite infestation.

Q   What, if anything, did you tell the plaintiff about the purpose of the inspection tour?   (2)

A   I mentioned to him that I was looking for any evidence of problems like termites.

Q   What evidence did you find?   (1)

A   None.

Q   What, if anything, did you say to the plaintiff when you completed this tour?   (2)

A   I told him that I was real pleased with the condition of the premises. I mentioned to him that I had had horrendous termite problems in my house in Kansas City, and I was happy that his house was free of termite damage.

Q   Whom were you speaking to when you said this?   (2)

A   The plaintiff.

Q   How close were you to the plaintiff when you said this?   (2)

A   Only a foot or so away.

Q   How did the plaintiff react when you said this?   (2)

A   He smiled and said that he was glad that I was so happy with the house. He said he'd worked real hard over the years to keep the house in good repair.

As in the last foundation, the defendant can call an expert to lay the third element. An expert member of the National Pest Control Association could testify to the difficulty of discovering termite infestation, the extent of infestation in the house in question, and the cost of eradicating the termites and repairing the house.

2. Mutual mistakes

A mutual, material mistake gives either party the right to avoid the contract. When the defendant relies on this ground for avoiding the contract, the defendant should prove:

1. The defendant was mistaken.
2. The plaintiff was mistaken. The plaintiff's and defendant's mistakes need not be identical, but they must relate to the same aspect of the contract. To show that the plaintiff was mistaken, the defendant may testify to the defendant's own statements evidencing the mistake if the statements were made in the plaintiff's hearing. These statements are nonhearsay under Evidence Rule 801(c) because they are offered for showing their effect on the plaintiff's state of mind. The plaintiff's statements evidencing the mistake are admissible as admissions under Rule 801(d) (2) and state of mind declarations under Rule 803(3).
3. The mistake was material.

Suppose that the defendant is attempting to avoid a release contract on the ground of mutual mistake. The defendant was injured in a traffic accident, and the plaintiff insurer obtained a settlement agreement while the defendant was in the hospital. The plaintiff has sued for a declaratory judgment that the release contract is valid and enforceable. The defendant testifies:

Q   What happened on the morning of September 19th?
A   Mr. Seymour, the plaintiff's claims adjuster, came to my hospital room.
Q   What happened then?
A   We talked about settling my claim against their insured.
Q   During this conversation, what, if anything, did you tell Mr. Seymour about the extent of your injuries?   (2)
A   I said that it appeared that my only injuries were the fractured finger and arm.
Q   Why did you say that?   (2)
A   Those were the only parts of me that hurt at the time, and besides that's what the doctor said.
Q   Which doctor?   (1)
A   Doctor Kiley, the physician who treated me at St. Luke's.
Q   What did Doctor Kiley tell you?   (1)
A   He said that he'd reviewed the file and that the only injuries he could find were the injuries to the finger and arm.

[*The doctor's statements are admissible as nonhearsay under Federal Evidence Rule 801(c). The statements are logically relevant to show their effect on the defendant's state of mind, namely, the creation of the mistaken belief that the finger and arm fractures were the only personal injuries.*]

Q   What did Mr. Seymour say after you described the extent of your injuries?   (2)
A   He said that that was what he had heard as well. He said he'd checked with Dr. Kiley before coming in to visit me.

The defendant could then call a back specialist to show that the defendant's belief was mistaken and that the mistake was material. The specialist could first testify that at the time the defendant signed the settlement contract, there were latent back problems and that the problems were caused by the accident. To show the mistake's materiality, the specialist should describe the extent of the back injuries, state their permanency, and estimate the long-term costs of treatment.

LEGAL RESEARCH REFERENCE:
Murray §§124-30

b.   Exceptional Situations

There are two types of mistakes that are not governed by the general rules.

1. Mistakes in economic value

The courts are stricter when the mistake relates to the economic value of the subject matter of the contract. Even if there is an ascertainable market value and both parties are materially mistaken about the economic value of the contract's subject matter, the courts ordinarily do not grant relief. The courts take the attitude that economic values are so variable and subjective that the contracting parties assume the risk of erring in valuation.

The courts usually grant relief on the ground of mistake in economic value only when there was a fiduciary relationship between the contracting parties at the time of contracting. Suppose that in February, the plaintiff attorney purchased some land from the defendant client. The client agreed to sell the attorney the land for $100,000, but the property's fair market value was $200,000. The client now refuses to deliver a deed to the plaintiff attorney. To avoid the contract on the ground of mistake in economic value, the defendant should testify to the first two foundational elements:

1. At the time of contracting, the plaintiff and defendant stood in a fiduciary relation:

   Q   How else were you acquainted with the plaintiff?   (1)
   A   He was my attorney.
   Q   How had he served you as an attorney?   (1)
   A   He was my defense counsel in a couple of suits brought against me.
   Q   What arrangements did you have to pay the plaintiff for his services as an attorney?   (1)
   A   I paid him $4,000 a year as a retainer. That way he was always available to handle my personal and business problems.
   Q   What payment, if any, did you give the plaintiff in January?   (1)
   A   I gave him the normal retainer for the entire year.

2. The contract between the plaintiff and defendant somehow related to the fiduciary relationship:

   Q   What property did you promise to sell the plaintiff?   (2)
   A   My land in Bonita.
   Q   How did you acquire that property?   (2)
   A   I bought it from a farmer three years ago.
   Q   Who represented you in your negotiations with the farmer?   (2)
   A   The plaintiff.
   Q   What other work, if any, had the plaintiff done in connection with the land in Bonita?   (2)
   A   About a year before this all happened, I wanted a zoning change; and the plaintiff represented me before the zoning commission.
   Q   How did your negotiations with the plaintiff for the sale of this land begin?   (2)
   A   He brought the subject up about six months ago.
   Q   Where were you when the plaintiff first mentioned the possibility of buying your Bonita land?   (2)

A   In his office on Front Street.

Q   Why were you there?   (2)

A   The plaintiff conducts sort of an annual review of my legal problems with me—a legal checkup, you might say. We were reviewing my land holdings, and he mentioned that he was interested in the property.

The defendant should then call a real estate appraiser to establish the third and last element of the foundation:

3. The defendant grossly underestimated the fair market value of the property. The defendant should qualify the witness as an appraiser, show that the witness' basis is a study of comparable properties, and elicit the ultimate opinion that at the time of contracting, the property's fair market value was $200,000.

LEGAL RESEARCH REFERENCE:
Murray §128

2. Mistakes in collateral assumptions of fact

A substantial minority of courts liberally allow a defendant to avoid a contract on the ground of mistake in a collateral assumption of fact. To invoke this ground, the defendant must show that

1. The defendant made a mistake in a collateral assumption of fact. The typical case is a subcontractor's arithmetic error in computing a bid. The subcontractor omits a cost item or misadds and, consequently, submits an unduly low bid.
2. The mistake was relatively innocent. There is almost always some element of negligence in committing the mistake. However, in many jurisdictions recognizing this defense, negligence must be gross to bar the defense. The defendant should testify to the mitigating circumstances surrounding the preparation of the bid:

Q   When did the plaintiff phone and ask you to submit the bid to him?   (2)

A   It was late the afternoon of November 4th.

Q   When did the plaintiff want the bid submitted?   (2)

A   He said that since he had a short deadline to make the bid on the prime contract, he needed the bid by 9:00 a.m. on November 7th.

Q   How long would it ordinarily take you to prepare a bid on a project of this size?   (2)

A   We would ordinarily take a full week to work it up.

Q   How did you manage to prepare your bid by nine on the 7th?   (2)

A   We worked overtime.

Q   How late did you work on the 6th?   (2)

A   We worked through the night.

Q   Who did the final addition of the items included in your bid?   (2)

A   I did that personally.

Q   When did you do the final addition?   (2)

A   I probably started about 6:00 a.m. on the ninth.

Q   How much sleep had you had on the evening of the eighth and the morning of the ninth?   (2)

A   None.
Q   How long had you gone without sleep?   (2)
A   About thirty hours.
Q   When was the last time you had eaten?   (2)
A   We had a pizza for dinner the evening of the ninth, but we were working so hard that we didn't have time for anything that morning.

 The defendant should also consider calling an expert. An experienced expert in the same industry may testify that such mistakes are common in the industry. Some judges will permit the expert to answer a hypothetical question asking whether the defendant's conduct violated the customary standards of care within the industry.

3. The mistake was material. Again, the defendant can explain the misaddition. If the mistake was an omission rather than misaddition, the defendant will have to assign a dollar value to the item omitted from the computation. If the defendant is an experienced member of the industry, the defendant himself or herself can express an opinion on the dollar value of the item omitted.

4. After discovering the mistake, the defendant promptly notified the plaintiff:

Q   When did you learn of the mistake?   (4)
A   The morning of the 12th.
Q   How did you discover it?   (4)
A   I was just doublechecking my figures when I realized for the first time I had misadded.
Q   What did you do then?   (4)
A   I immediately phoned the plaintiff to let him know about the mistake.
Q   How much time elapsed between your discovery of the mistake and your telephone call to the plaintiff?   (4)
A   No more than five minutes. I knew I had to get hold of him pronto.

5. The defendant notified the plaintiff in time to return the plaintiff to the *status quo ante*. If the defendant notifies the plaintiff in time to return the plaintiff to that position, the plaintiff's only loss is the benefit of the bargain with the defendant. There is no detriment to the plaintiff so long as the plaintiff can now enter into a substitute contract with another sub on the same terms that the plaintiff could have obtained from the new sub when the plaintiff entered into the contract with the defendant; that is possible so long as the prevailing market rate for the work has not changed in the interim. The defendant could present expert testimony that the going market rate remained stable between the time the plaintiff contracted with the defendant and the time the defendant notified the plaintiff of the error.

LEGAL RESEARCH REFERENCE:
Murray §129

Sec. 13-4. Misrepresentation

A misrepresentation defense is more powerful—and more dangerous—than a mistake defense. A misrepresentation defense is more powerful because it has greater potential for causing the jury to dislike the plaintiff; if the jurors are convinced that the plaintiff made a misrepresentation to the defendant, they will have great sympathy for the defendant. On the other hand, a misrepresentation is dangerous because it can backfire and cause the jury to dislike the defendant. An allegation of misrepresentation maligns the plaintiff's character. If the defendant fails to convince the jurors that the plaintiff made the misrepresentation, the jurors may turn against the defendant for slinging dirt at the plaintiff's good name. There are four basic variations of the misrepresentation defense.

a. Fraud in the Factum

The plaintiff commits fraud in the factum when the plaintiff knowingly misrepresents the nature of the document to the defendant. To prove fraud in the factum, the defendant must lay this foundation:

1. The plaintiff made a representation to the defendant about the nature of the instrument the defendant signed. The misrepresentation is usually verbal, but it can take the form of the plaintiff physically interfering with the defendant's reading of the document.
2. The representation was false.
3. The plaintiff knew that the representation was false.
4. The plaintiff made the representation with the intent to deceive the defendant.
5. The defendant subjectively relied on the plaintiff's misrepresentation and signed the document.
6. The defendant's reliance was objectively reasonable. More and more courts are eliminating this element of the doctrine; these courts reason that when the plaintiff is guilty of intentional wrongdoing, it should be sufficient if the defendant subjectively relied on the misrepresentation (element #5).

Even when the jurisdiction has dispensed with element #6, the defendant should testify to the mitigating circumstances explaining why he or she did not read the document more carefully. Some of the jurors may take a relatively hard-nosed attitude towards persons who foolishly sign documents without reading them, and the defendant should attempt to meet that attitude in his or her testimony. Suppose that a plaintiff finance company is attempting to hold the defendant liable as a surety on his sister's loan:

Q   Where were you on the morning of August 28th?
A   I went down to Preston Finance Company with my sister, Evonne.
Q   Why did you go there?
A   Evonne was going down to sign a loan, and she said that the finance company manager said she needed a witness to the loan.
Q   What happened when you arrived at the plaintiff's offices?

A   First Evonne introduced me to Mr. Butler, the manager. Then she signed for the loan.

Q   What, if anything, did Mr. Butler ask you to do?   (5)

A   He told me to sign on the line below Evonne as a witness to her signature.

Q   How, if at all, did Mr. Butler describe the legal effect of your signature?   (5)

A   He said it was just a formality. I was merely a witness to the signature.

Q   What did you say then?   (5)

A   I asked him whether I might get stuck on the loan by signing.

Q   How did he answer your question?   (6)

A   He said that there was no way that could happen. All I was was a witness.

Q   How carefully did you read the document before you signed it?   (6)

A   I didn't.

Q   Why not?   (6)

A   First I figured that Evonne knew what was going on, and then Butler had said flatly that I couldn't be held to pay any money.

Q   How much legal training have you had?   (6)

A   None.

Q   How much business experience have you had?   (6)

A   Not much.

Q   What is your occupation?   (6)

A   I'm a technician at a government testing laboratory.

Q   Why didn't you take the time to read the document before you signed it?   (6)

A   There was sort of a rush.

Q   What do you mean by that?   (6)

A   Mr. Butler said that he had to be at a bank across town in a couple of minutes, and he sort of rushed us through the signing.

To humanize your client, elicit your client's reaction upon discovering the plaintiff's misrepresentations:

Q   How did you react when the plaintiff told you that you had signed as surety and not a mere witness?

A   I guess that I was both shocked and angry.

b.   Fraud in the Inducement

The foundation for fraud in the inducement is very similar to the foundation for fraud in the factum:

1. The plaintiff made a representation about the subject matter of the contract.
2. The representation was false.
3. The plaintiff knew that the representation was false. Federal Evidence Rule 404(b) provides that a party may introduce uncharged misconduct to prove knowledge or plan. If the plaintiff has made similar misrepresentations in the past, introduce proof of those misrepre-

sentations to establish knowledge. As in the case of breaches of similar contracts, the trial judges have been reluctant to admit proof of other misrepresentations; but if the misrepresentation is strikingly similar, 404(b) certainly sanctions admission of the proof and the striking similarity should give the evidence sufficient probative value to overcome any objection based on Federal Evidence Rule 403.

4. The plaintiff made the representation with the intent to deceive the defendant. 404(b) applies here as well. Like knowledge, intent is provable by other acts of misconduct.

5. The plaintiff's misrepresentation induced the defendant to enter the contract. The defendant subjectively relied on the plaintiff's representation in entering the contract. Many judges permit defendants to directly testify that they would not have entered the contract if they had known the truth.

6. The defendant's reliance was objectively reasonable. Here again the trend is away from this requirement—a trend toward what Professors White and Summers have dubbed the "pure heart, empty head" rule.

7. The misrepresentation related to a material part of the contract.

Suppose that the defendant contracted to buy the plaintiff's house with a view to converting it into rental property. When the defendant learned that the zoning forbade rental property in this area, the defendant attempted to avoid the contract. The defendant is testifying about the plaintiff's fraud in the inducement:

Q   After you flew into town, what did you do?
A   I met the plaintiff at his house on Bleeker Street.
Q   What happened then?
A   We discussed my purchase of his property.
Q   What, if anything, did you tell the plaintiff about the reason you wanted to buy his house?
A   I told him that for tax reasons, I needed rental property and that I wanted to convert his house into three apartments.
Q   What did he say then?
A   He said that the house had six bedrooms and was certainly large enough to be converted.
Q   What, if anything, did you ask him about the zoning?   (1)
A   I asked him whether the zoning permitted commercial uses such as rental property.
Q   What did he say?   (1)
A   He said that it did. He said that at his realtor's suggestion, he had checked on the zoning. He said that the zoning permitted rental property.
Q   What happened then?   (1)
A   We closed the deal later that day.
Q   How willing would you have been to buy the plaintiff's house if you had known that you couldn't convert it into rental property?   (5)
A   I wouldn't have bought it at all. I already had a perfectly fine house in Bridgeport, and I didn't need another residence in Camden.

Q   When the plaintiff told you about the zoning, how familiar were you with zoning in Camden?   (6)

A   Not at all. This was only my second visit to Camden.

Q   Why did you believe the plaintiff's statement about the zoning?   (6)

A   I had no reason to disbelieve him. Moreover, I had seen some commercial property—a corner grocery—close by, and I thought that that was a good indication that the zoning in that area permitted mixed uses.

As in the case of your client's testimony about fraud in the factum, elicit your client's statement that he or she was surprised and angered when he or she learned the truth about the zoning.

In many cases, your client cannot supply competent proof of either the misrepresentation's falsity or the plaintiff's knowledge of its falsity. In our hypothetical, the defendant might have to present official records from the local planning department. The judge may be able to judicially notice the zoning in the community to prove the representation's falsity. As proof of the plaintiff's scienter, it would be ideal if you could introduce zoning commission records showing that a year earlier, the plaintiff had tried—and failed—to get a zoning variance to convert the same property to commercial uses. The plaintiff's participation in the variance proceeding would put the plaintiff on notice that the local zoning prohibited commercial usage.

c.   Negligent Misrepresentation

The traditional view is that the defendant must prove a knowing misrepresentation by the plaintiff to avoid the contract. However, a growing number of courts will grant the defendant relief for a material, negligent misrepresentation. The foundational proof includes these elements:

1. The plaintiff made a representation to the defendant about the subject matter of the contract.
2. The representation was false.
3. The plaintiff was negligent in making the representation. The first step in proving this element of the foundation is cross-examining the plaintiff; the cross-examination should elicit admissions showing that the plaintiff is an experienced, long-term member of the industry. As the second step, during the defense case-in-chief, the defendant should present an expert's testimony that a competent, experienced member of the industry should have realized the representation's falsity. The defense can present this expert testimony in the form of a hypothetical question. The hypothesis should include all the facts evidencing the plaintiff's experience in the industry. The question should ask, "Should a reasonable businessperson with that experience have known that the price quotation was wrong?"
4. The plaintiff's misrepresentation induced the defendant to enter the contract.
5. The defendant's reliance was objectively reasonable. The courts recognizing the negligent misrepresentation doctrine still rigorously insist

that the defendant's conduct be reasonable. In his or her direct testimony, the defendant should establish that the defendant was not a member of the industry or was a novice.

Conduct a parallel examination of the plaintiff and defendant to highlight the defendant's relative inexperience. On cross, ask the plaintiff:

Q   Is it true that you have owned your chemical manufacturing plant for over 25 years?   (5)
A   Yes.
Q   Isn't it a fact that you have both a bachelor's and a master's degree in chemistry?   (5)
A   That's right.

On direct, ask the defendant:

Q   When did you open your plant?   (5)
A   A year ago.
Q   How long had you been in operation when you entered into this contract with the plaintiff?   (5)
A   Two months.
Q   What educational background do you have in chemistry?   (5)
A   None. I have a business degree. I took one chemistry course in high school, but that's the extent of my chemistry background.

After eliciting this comparative data, the defendant should stress this data during the summation: "What do these facts tell us, ladies and gentlemen? They tell us two things. They first tell us that the plaintiff was an experienced oldtimer in this industry and he should have realized the truth. The other thing they tell us is that Ms. Jacobs was an inexperienced beginner. In her case, it's perfectly understandable that she wouldn't realize the error. She trusted the plaintiff, she knew that he was an old hand in this business, and she acted reasonably in relying on what he told her."

6. The misrepresentation related to a material part of the contract. The courts are eager to find materiality when the plaintiff is guilty of intentional wrongdoing. The courts are understandably more reluctant to find materiality in the case of mistake and negligent misrepresentation. Present expert testimony showing the dollar impact of the misrepresentation—both in absolute numbers of dollars and in relation to the size of the transaction: "The expert's testimony shows that this house is worth $15,000 less than it would be worth if that representation had been true. $15,000 is a lot of money for my client—especially when you consider that the purchase price was only $35,000. Ladies and gentlemen, that's close to half the purchase that Mr. Simms agreed to pay."

d.   Breach of an Express Warranty

Uniform Commercial Code 2-313 governs the creation of express warranties by affirmation, promise, description, and sample. The breach of an express warranty is a species of misrepresentation; the seller represented that the goods would have a certain quality, and that representation proves to be false. In one respect, it is easier to prove this type of misrepresentation. Proof of fraud requires evidence of knowledge and intent accompanying the misrepresentation, and proof of negligent misrepresentation necessitates evidence that the plaintiff's conduct fell below an objectively reasonably standard. A breach of express warranty is a strict liability misrepresentation; the defendant need not prove the plaintiff's scienter or negligence.

However, you should remember that it is usually unnecessary to treat breach of warranty as a misrepresentation defense. In most mercantile contracts, the seller's warranty becomes one of the conditions to activating the buyer's duty to pay. Rather than arguing that the breach of warranty is a defense to the buyer's liability, the buyer can argue that there is no liability to begin with; since the plaintiff seller breached the warranty, a condition to the buyer's duty failed, and the duty never became a duty of immediate performance.

LEGAL RESEARCH REFERENCE:
White & Summers chs. 10-12

Sec. 13-5. Duress or Compulsion

a. Physical Duress

Given the strong tradition of freedom of contract, the early common-law courts were reluctant to set aside agreements. However, even those courts would not tolerate the plaintiff's use of physical force or threats of force to obtain a contract. If the defendant proved that the plaintiff used or threatened to use criminal or tortious force to induce the defendant to enter the contract, the courts refused to enforce the contract. The modern commercial litigator rarely encounters cases of physical duress.

b. Economic Duress or Business Compulsion

However, economic duress is relatively common. The foundation for economic duress includes proof that

1. The plaintiff committed or threatened an illegal act. As under the physical duress doctrine, all jurisdictions treat the act as "illegal" if the act would violate Crimes or Tort law. Most modern courts treat a breach of contract as an "illegal" act. A few courts have asserted the power to apply economic duress whenever the act strikes them as "immoral" or "wrongful." However, the defendant should pause and research local law carefully before relying on that broad proposition; in most of the decided cases using the broad, "wrongful" language, there was a threatened breach of contract by the plaintiff.
2. The illegal act placed the defendant in a dire economic situation. The economic duress doctrine does not prohibit the plaintiff from driving a

hard bargain or exploiting the defendant's weak economic situation caused by the gods or the defendant's own stupidity. The economic duress doctrine applies only when the plaintiff's illegal act causes or seriously aggravates the defendant's position.

3. The plaintiff attempted to exploit the defendant's economic position by making a demand on the defendant. The demand might be that the defendant enter a new contract with the plaintiff or modify an existing contract in the plaintiff's favor without additional consideration.

4. The plaintiff's illegal act induced the defendant to accede to the plaintiff's demand. The act or threat overcame the defendant's free will; subjectively, the defendant agreed to the demand because of the threat. At trial, the defendant can testify directly to his or her state of mind at the time. Moreover, the defendant's prior statements may fall within the state of mind hearsay exception under Federal Evidence Rule 803(3).

5. The defendant acted reasonably in acceding to the plaintiff's demand. The commentators have urged the courts to abandon this requirement; analogizing to the elements of intentional fraud, the commentators argue that here again the plaintiff is guilty of bad faith wrongdoing. However, most courts continue to demand that the defendant act as a "constant person" and exercise "ordinary firmness" in resisting the plaintiff's demand.

6. The defendant had no reasonably adequate, available means of avoiding the economic loss other than by yielding to the plaintiff's demand. Many courts continue to list this element as a separate requirement for economic duress, but there is a growing understanding that element #6 is simply a factor to be considered in applying element #5; if there was a reasonably adequate, available alternative, the defendant did not act reasonably in yielding.

   Either under element #5 or #6, the defendant should testify that he or she did not have an opportunity to obtain independent advice and assistance. It is also helpful if the defendant can show that the technically available legal remedies (such as temporary restraining order and declaratory judgment) were too uncertain or time-consuming. At the very least, the defendant should testify that he did not realize that there were any legal remedies such as a T.R.O. immediately available.

Our hypothetical is based on the facts of an infamous, leading business compulsion case, *Thompson Crane and Trucking Company v. Eyman*.[1] The plaintiff is a tax attorney. The Internal Revenue Service has notified the defendant that he is being assessed an additional $50,000 in taxes. The notice states that if the defendant does not mail in a protest by 5:00 p.m. June 25th, he will have to pay the $50,000. The defendant contacts the plaintiff. The plaintiff agrees to represent the defendant for $4,000. The plaintiff promises to prepare and mail in the protest by 5:00 p.m. on June 25th. June 25th is a Saturday. The defendant testifies:

Q   What did you do on the morning of Saturday, June 25th?

A   I went down to the plaintiff's offices on Grant Place.

Q   Why did you do that?

A   He told me to stop by and sign the tax protest before he mailed it in to meet the deadline.

Q   What happened when you reached his offices?

A   He showed me the protest he had drafted for my signature.

Q   What did he say about the protest?   (1)

A   He said that he was seriously considering not mailing it in.

Q   What did he say about his reason for not mailing it in?   (1)

A   He said that it had been so much work preparing it that he didn't think $4,000 was enough pay.

Q   What did you tell him about mailing in the protest?   (1)

A   I told him that he had promised to do that, and I expected him to do it.

Q   What did he answer?   (1)

A   He said it was just tough.

Q   What did you think would happen if he didn't mail in the protest?   (2)

A   I figured that I was going to get socked for $50,000.

Q   Why did you think that?   (2)

A   That's how I interpreted the letter the I.R.S. sent me.

Q   What did the plaintiff say would happen if he did not mail in the protest?   (2)

A   He said something like, "Look. Remember what's at stake here. If I don't mail in this protest, you're going to have to dig into your pockets for $50,000 to pay the government."

Q   Under what circumstances did he say he would mail in the protest?   (3)

A   He demanded that I pay him $6,000.

Q   What did you do then?   (4)

A   I argued with him for a while. But then he got up and put the protest in his office safe. At that point, I gave in and signed a note for $6,000.

Q   Why did you give in?   (4)

A   Because I believed what he said about me getting stuck for $50,000. Pay $50,000 or $6,000—it's really no choice.

Q   At the time of this conversation, what legal training had you had?   (5)

A   I've never been to law school or anything like that. I'm a plumbing contractor.

Q   What experience have you had with tax law?   (5)

A   I pay my taxes, but this assessment was the first real problem I had had.

Q   How familiar are you with the procedures of the Internal Revenue Service?   (5)

A   They're Greek to me. The only procedure I know about is making out my own tax form. I relied on the plaintiff for everything else.

Q   Whom did you talk to before signing the $6,000 note?   (6)

A   No one.

Q   Why didn't you talk to somebody else like an attorney?   (6)

A   In the first place, it was Saturday. I didn't think I could reach anybody. Secondly, there I was in the plaintiff's office, and he was telling me that I had to sign this thing before I set foot outside the office.

Q   What did the defendant say he would do if you left without signing the note?   (6)

A   He said he'd rip up the protest.

Q   What sort of legal action did you think you could take against the plaintiff before 5:00 p.m. that night?   (6)

A   I didn't think there was anything I could do.

Q   What is a temporary restraining order?   (6)

A   It beats me. I guess I've gotta plead ignorance, as they say.

LEGAL RESEARCH REFERENCE:
Murray §351

Sec. 13-6.   Illegal Contracts

As a general proposition a court will not enforce an illegal contract. The defendant should usually rely on this proposition only as a last resort. In many cases, the evidence will show that both the plaintiff and the defendant realized the contract's illegality. The evidence proving the contract's illegality may taint the plaintiff, but it may just as easily damn the defendant in the jurors' eyes. Unless the defense has corroboration that the defendant was unaware of the illegality, illegality is a dangerous defensive theory. However, when there is corroboration or there is simply no other defense, the defendant can attack the contract's legality. A contract may be illegal in itself or because of its relationship with an illegal transaction.

a.   Contracts Illegal in Themselves

A contract is illegal in itself if its terms offend Criminal law, Tort law, or a strong public policy. The simplest case is the situation in which the contract's terms violate a statutory mandate. For instance, suppose that the state usury law provides that the maximum legal rate of interest on personal loans is 10%. A personal loan contract calling for 11% interest is unenforceable as illegal.

However, by far the most common illegality problem in modern Contract litigation is the legality of contracts in restraint of trade. When the seller conveys a business to the buyer, the seller may promise not to compete with the buyer in a specified geographic area for a certain period of time. Similarly, when an employer hires an employee, the employer may obtain the employee's promise that when the employment ends, the employee will refrain from competing with the employer. These promises are in restraint of trade; and even before there was national and state antitrust legislation, the common-law courts imposed restrictions on these promises.

GENERAL RESTRAINTS

The defendant can show that the promise was illegal by proving it was a *general* covenant not to compete. The key distinction is between general and *ancillary* restraints. An ancillary restraint is incident to a legitimate business transaction such as the sale of a business or the hiring of an employee. A general covenant does not accompany any other transaction; the other party simply pays the covenantor a sum of money in exchange for the promise not to compete. General restraints are *per se* illegal:

Q When you made this promise to the plaintiff, what else did you promise her?

A Nothing.

Q At that time, what employment was the plaintiff offering you?

A None.

Q At that time, what business, if any, were you selling to the plaintiff?

A None.

Q What did you give the plaintiff in exchange for the $30,000?

A The only thing I gave was my promise not to compete in the interior design business in Manhattan for a period of five years.

ANCILLARY RESTRAINTS

Even ancillary restraints are not *per se* legal. An ancillary restraint must have a reasonable scope; if the scope is overbroad, the contract is illegal. The defendant can attempt to prove overbreadth in three respects.

First, the defendant can show geographic overbreadth. The defendant should initially describe the geographic scope of the convenant itself:

Q Under your agreement with the plaintiff, in what counties couldn't you practice dentistry?

A I agreed not to practice dentistry in any county in California.

The defendant should then introduce the plaintiff's own records to show that the plaintiff did not have any customers or a substantial number of customers in some of the counties covered by the restraint. The plaintiff's records can be introduced as admissions under Federal Evidence Rule 801(d) (2). It is ideal if during discovery, the defendant can uncover reports documenting the plaintiff's expansion plans; the defendant wants to show that in the foreseeable future, the plaintiff does not even contemplate expanding into some of the areas covered by the covenant. The plaintiff's reports reflecting expansion plans also fall within Rule 801(d) (2). To help the jury visualize the proof, use two maps: one map showing the area covered by the restraint, a second map depicting the location of the plaintiff's clientele—and perhaps a third map reflecting the plaintiff's expansion plans.

Second, the defendant can show temporal overbreadth. Courts are reluctant to uphold lifetime covenants. The defendant should contrast the length of the covenant with (1) the length of time the defendant worked for the plaintiff and (2) the length of time the plaintiff's business has been in operation. The defendant has an appealing argument when the duration of the restraint exceeds both the number of years the defendant worked for the plaintiff and the number of years the business has been in existence. You might cross-examine the plaintiff in this fashion:

Q   Isn't it true that in exhibit two (the contract), you required my client to stay out of the druggist business for 15 years?
A   That's right. That's what it says.
Q   But you hired him for only one year. Isn't that true?
A   Yes.
Q   And at the time you hired him, you had been in business for only 16 months. Isn't that a fact?
A   That's correct.
Q   So you had been in business less than a year and a half?
A   Right.

Third, the defendant can show occupational overbreadth. Suppose that the plaintiff's medical clinic specializes in orthopedic problems but the plaintiff exacted a promise from the defendant that when the defendant quit the plaintiff's employ, the defendant would refrain from practicing "medicine" within the same county for five years. The defendant can attack the promise's occupational scope by presenting expert testimony that

—medicine includes many specialties,
—the defendant is qualified to engage in general medical practice or a specialty other than the specialty the defendant practised in the plaintiff's employ, and
—if the defendant engaged in general practice or another specialty, there is little risk that the defendant's practice would take clientele away from the plaintiff. There is some risk of diversion if the defendant shifts to general practice, but there is minimal risk when the defendant plans shifting to another specialty.

b.   Contracts Tainted by Their Close Relationship to Illegal Transactions

1.   Contracts tainted by their relationship to a past illegal transaction

The contract may be illegal because of its close relationship to a prior illegal transaction the plaintiff engaged in. When the defendant employs this theory, the defendant must be prepared to show that

1. Before forming the contract, the plaintiff engaged in an illegal act or transaction. One unfortunately frequent example is commercial bribery. In many jurisdictions, it is a crime for employer #1 to bribe employer #2's employee.
2. There is a close relationship between the plaintiff's prior illegal act and the present contract. The clearest case is the situation in which the bribed employee is employer #2's contracting agent; employer #1 biibes employer #2's employee to award a contract to employer #1. The simplest method of proof is the direct evidence of the employee's courtroom confession to the bribery and award. The admission of the employee's out-of-court statements is a thornier problem. If the employee made the statements to a third party during the employee's conspiracy with employer #1, the statements are admissible; the

statements arguably fall within Federal Evidence Rule 801(d) (2) (D) (the hearsay exception for agents' statements) and definitely within 801(d) (2) (E) (the exception for coconspirators' statements). If the employee refuses to testify at trial—perhaps on fifth amendment self-incrimination grounds, another theory of admissibility is possible; the employee declarant is now unavailable under Federal Rule 804(a) (1) or (2), and the statement amounts to a declaration against interest under Rule 804(b) (3). Absent direct evidence, the defendant will have to rely on circumstantial evidence of the conspiracy's existence such as proof of clandestine meetings between employer #1 and the employee and unexplained payments by em ployer #1 to the employee.

3. The illegality doctrine does not require proof that the defendant suffered economically because of the plaintiff's prior illegal act, but it is advisable to present that evidence when it is available. The defendant wants to be able to argue during summation not only that the plaintiff committed an illegal act; the defendant also wants to be in a position to portray himself or herself as the "victim" of the plaintiff's illegality. Suppose that employer #1 bribed the employee to sell employer #2's property to employer #1 for $100,000. Present a real estate appraiser's testimony that the property's fair market value was $130,000. Show that the plaintiff's illegality was part of a scheme to harm and defraud the defendant. Proof of the harm to the defendant motivates the jurors to want to find against the plaintiff.

2. Contracts tainted by their relationship to a future illegal transaction

The illegal transaction tainting the contract may be a future transaction. The plaintiff may have entered into the contract of purchase with a view to putting the material purchased to illegal use. The plaintiff may have ordered chemicals to be used in the manufacture of contraband drugs, or the plaintiff may have bought a firearm with the intention of employing the firearm in a series of armed robberies. It is clear that the plaintiff can be prosecuted for putting the property to those illegal ends. But when is the contract itself illegal because of the purpose the plaintiff had in mind? To defend on this theory, it is ideal if the defendant can show:

1. The plaintiff intended to use the subject matter of the contract in an illegal scheme. The plaintiff's statements evidencing this intention can be admitted under Federal Evidence Rule 801(d) (2) (admissions) and Rule 803(3) (declarations of state of mind). Lacking such statements, the defendant will have to prove the intent circumstantially. Federal Evidence Rule 404(b) is relevant here too. If the plaintiff has committed this crime in the past, Rule 404(b) authorizes you to prove the plaintiff's past, similar crimes as evidence of the plaintiff's intent at the time of contracting. If the plaintiff has been convicted of the crime in the past, Evidence Rule 803(22) sanctions the introduction of the judgment of conviction as substantive proof of the plaintiff's commission of the crime. First invoke 803(22) to prove the act, and then argue that the act is logically relevant to show intent under 404(b).

2. The scheme involved a serious crime. The most serious crimes are offenses such as homicide and rape that are both *malum in se* and life endangering. The least serious crimes are *malum prohibitum*, social welfare offenses, including the innocent merchandising of unwholesome food.

3. At the time of contracting, the defendant knew that the plaintiff had the illegal scheme in mind. The attorney should pause and deliberate before advising the defendant to raise this defense. In most jurisdictions, the foundation for the defense includes proof that your client knew of the plaintiff's illegal purpose. Raising the defense may implicate your client in a crime; depending upon the substantive Criminal law of your jurisdiction, the facts necessary to raise this Contract defense may make your client a coconspirator or an accessory before the fact. Your client may choose to forego the Contract defense and pay the contract damages rather than risk a conviction and imprisonment. The choice is your client's, and you should *never* plead this defense without your client's express, informed consent. By pleading this defense without the defendant's informed consent, you may be acting incompetently and breaching your duty of confidentiality.

4. The contract contained special provisions to facilitate the future commission of the crime. Suppose that the plaintiff intended to export illegally. The contract might well call for special packaging to facilitate concealing the true nature of the goods inside the box or crate:

Q   Under your agreement with the plaintiff, how were you supposed to box the firearms?   (4)

A   He wanted them boxed in plain, unmarked crates.

Q   How do you ordinarily box firearms shipped from your plant?   (4)

A   For safety's sake, we ordinarily box them in crates with "Danger—Firearms" painted in large red letters on every side of the box.

Q   Why did the contract call for boxing the firearms in plain, unmarked crates?   (4)

A   I explained what our normal procedures were to the plaintiff, but he insisted that we do it this way. He said that he didn't want the crates to give any indication of their contents.

LEGAL RESEARCH REFERENCE:
Murray §§334-49

Sec. 13-7.   Unconscionability

By way of case or statutory law, the American courts have finally recognized the unconscionability doctrine. One of the boldest provisions in the Uniform Commercial Code, Section 2-302, proclaims:

> If the court as a matter of law finds the contract or any clause of the contract to have been unconscionable at the time it was made, the court may refuse to enforce the contract, or it may enforce the remainder of the contract without the unconscionable clause, or it

may so limit the application of any unconscionable clause as to avoid any unconscionable result.

The unconscionability issue is tried to the judge rather than the jury. In most American jurisdictions, to prevail on this defense, the defendant must convince the judge that the contract or clause is both *procedurally* and *substantively* unconscionable.

LEGAL RESEARCH REFERENCE:
Murray §§350-54
White & Summers ch. 4

a.   Procedural Unconscionability

The defendant must initially show that the defendant's assent was apparent rather than real. The defendant can show that the assent was unknowing or involuntary.

1.   Unknowing assent

The defendant can show unknowing assent in three different ways.

First, the defendant can show that he or she did not realize that he or she was entering into a contract at all. The defendant should prove that this belief was both genuine and reasonable. Suppose, for example, that the attendant at a parking lot hands the car owner a receipt for the car as the car owner walks off the lot after parking. There is a disclaimer of liability on the back of the form:

Q   What did you think the form was?
A   I assumed that it was just a receipt for my car so that I could pick it up later.
Q   What, if anything, did the attendant say to you to call your attention to this disclaimer language on the back of exhibit three (the form)?
A   He didn't say anything about it. He just handed it to me as I walked by the booth.
Q   What signs, if any, were posted calling your attention to this disclaimer language?
A   If there were any signs like that, I sure didn't see them.
Q   When did you first notice the disclaimer language?
A   I didn't notice it until the next day. I reported the theft of my car to the attendant, and the next day I get this phone call from their insurance company. This lady from the insurance company points out that there's this limitation or disclaimer or whatever you call it on the back of the form. I never noticed it until then.

Second, the defendant can show that the clause in question was physically inconspicuous. A persuasive showing of physical inconspicuousness may require several witnesses. Your client should testify directly to the fact that he or she did not notice the clause. Then call a printer to testify about the size of the type:

Q   What is the size of the type of the front of this form?

A   It's regular reading size—12-point type.

Q   What is the size of most of the type on the back of this form?

A   It's much smaller, six-point type.

Q   Now please focus on the clause which begins, "The parking lot hereby disclaims. . . ." What is the size of that type?

A   It's quite small. My judgment is that that's only five-point.

Consider calling a reading psychologist to testify on the question whether print of that size is likely to catch the attention of the typical consumer.

Third, the defendant can prove that the clause's language was too sophisticated to be understood by the defendant. You should call the defendant to testify that he or she did not understand the true import of the clause. Corroborate your client with expert testimony. Have the reading expert analyze the level of reading skill a person would need to understand the clause:

Q   What level of reading skill would a person need to understand that this clause meant you were giving up your right to sue for personal injuries?

A   There are at least ten words in this clause that require 12th grade reading skills. Eight of those words are keys to understanding the clause; they are the subject or verb in the sentence. My opinion is that you would need 12th grade level reading skills.

Show that the average consumer could not understand this language:

Q   What is the average reading skill level of adults in the United States?

A   About the tenth grade.

Have the witness add that he or she tested the defendant to evaluate the defendant's reading skills:

Q   What is the defendant's reading skill level?

A   It's a bit below average. I'd estimate that it's a 9th grade level of skill.

2. *Involuntary assent*

Even if the assent was knowing in all three senses, the defendant can establish procedural unconscionability by proving involuntary assent—a "contract of adhesion." The defendant can prove involuntary assent in two ways.

First, the defendant can prove that the plaintiff has vastly superior bargaining power. When the market condition approaches monopoly, a business person enjoying the virtual monopoly has such bargaining power:

Q   Why did you buy the seed from the plaintiff?

A   I had little choice.

Q   What do you mean by that?

A   This seed was just being imported from Brazil, and my understanding was that the plaintiff was the exclusive representative of the consortium of Brazilian producers.

Q   Where else in the United States could you buy this seed?
A   To the best of my knowledge, there was no place else to go. You dealt on
    the plaintiff's terms, or you didn't deal at all.

The second method of proving involuntary assent is establishing that
there is no competition among the various producers with respect to the
clause in question. For example, even if American auto manufacturers otherwise compete against each other, they may all use the same disclaimer
clause. The effect is the same as that of a monopoly: If the consumer wants
the goods at all, the consumer is coerced into accepting the terms. As your
witness, call an economist who has prepared a study of competition within
the industry:

Q   How many of the auto dealers in the United States use this same dis-
    claimer clause?
A   Six of them do. A word or two may vary, but it's essentially the identical
    clause.
Q   What percentage of the total auto production in the United States do
    these six manufacturers account for?
A   Over 93% of the total production in any given year.

You can corroborate the witness' testimony by having the witness authenticate trade publications stating these statistics. Once your expert authenticates the trade publication, the text falls within the special hearsay
exception stated in Federal Evidence Rule 803(17).

LEGAL RESEARCH REFERENCE:
White & Summers §§4-3, 4-7

b.   Substantive Unconscionability

It is not enough for the defendant to show procedural unconscionability; the defendant must also demonstrate substantive unconscionability—the
clause has a harsh, oppressive effect. The defendant must persuade the judge
that if sustained, the clause will dramatically change the normal allocation
of risks under the contract. The manufacturer ordinarily bears the risk of
personal injuries caused by defects in the products marketed; the manufacturer may be liable in negligence, strict tort liability, or warranty. If the
manufacturer is permitted to disclaim that liability, the disclaimer shifts the
risk from the manufacturer to the consumer. In the United States, there is
such strong sentiment against the disclaimer of that risk that Uniform
Commerical Code 2-719(3) announces a general rule that "(l)imitation of
consequential damages for injury to the person in the case of consumer
goods is prima facie unconscionable. . . ." When the defendant does not
have the benefit of a statutory presumption, the defendant can show substantive unconscionability in two ways.

The defendant can initially show that the clause would have an unconscionable effect on the typical consumer. The defendant could call an insurance company executive with experience in automobile claims. After qualifying the executive as an expert, the defendant would ask:

Q What is the last year for which there are available national statistics on personal injuries caused by auto accidents?
A You're in luck. We've just received the statistics for the last calendar year.
Q During that year, how many persons suffered personal injuries because of traffic accidents?
A Slightly over a quarter of a million persons.
Q How many were killed in traffic accidents last year?
A 48,000 persons died in traffic accidents in the U.S. last year.
Q How many persons who survived the accidents suffered permanent injuries?
A 75,000 is the number, I believe.
Q What was the average amount of medical expenses that the persons who survived the accidents incurred?
A It was just under $3,000.

The defendant should continue the direct examination in this vein to show the judge that the clause in question can have a harsh effect on a large number of persons.

The defendant should next show that the clause had an unconscionable effect on this defendant. The defendant should prove the economic loss the defendant will suffer if the judge sustains the clause. In some cases, the defendant will lose the right to compensation for personal injuries if the judge sustains the clause. An insurer or manufacturer might be suing for a declaratory judgment that the clause is valid and that the defendant consumer has no right to compensation for personal injuries. The defendant can use the techniques discussed in Section 9-4 to establish the extent of the economic loss and personal injuries. After proving the defendant's own losses and injuries, the defense attorney can argue that the defendant is a victim of the plaintiff's unconscionable conduct and the defendant's plight illustrates the injustice that thousands of other consumers will suffer if the judge does not invalidate the clause.

LEGAL RESEARCH REFERENCE:
White & Summers §§4-4-7

CHECKLIST FOR THE SECOND LINE OF DEFENSE

____ The Statute of Frauds bars enforcement of the contract.

  ____ The contract is within the Statute's purview.
          and
  ____ The parties did not comply with the Statute.

OR

____ The contract is voidable or void because of mistake.

      ____ Unilateral mistake known to or caused by the plaintiff.
                  or
      ____ Mutual, material mistake.

OR

____ The contract is voidable or void because of misrepresentation.

      ____ Fraud in the factum.
                  or
      ____ Fraud in the inducement.
                  or
      ____ Negligent misrepresentation.
                  or
      ____ Breach of warranty.

OR

____ The contract is void or voidable because of duress.

      ____ Physical duress.
                  or
      ____ Economic duress.

OR

____ The contract is illegal.

      ____ The contract is illegal in itself.
                  or
      ____ The contract is closely related to a past illegal transaction.
                  or
      ____ The contract is closely related to a future illegal transaction.

OR

____ The contract is unconscionable.

      ____ Substantive unconscionability.
                  and
      ____ Procedural unconscionability.
            ____ Unknowing assent.
                        or
            ____ Involuntary assent.

FOOTNOTE

[1] 123 Cal.App. 2d 904, 267 P.2d 1043 (1954).

CHAPTER 14

The Third Line of Defense—The Techniques of Establishing Defense to Breach

Sec. 14-1. Introduction

The first two lines of defense relate to the formation of the contract. The next line of defense is the argument that even if the parties formed a contract, the defendant is not guilty of a breach. To disprove breach, the defendant can merely dispute the plaintiff's evidence that all the plaintiff's conditions were fulfilled or excused and that the defendant did not perform. If the defendant attempts to disprove breach in that fashion, the defendant is essentially relying on a simple defense.

However, there are affirmative defenses that can be raised—the discharge doctrines. The defendant can employ the theory that the contract duty was discharged by the parties' act or operation of law. This chapter discusses the evidentiary techniques the defendant may use to invoke the discharge doctrines.

> **LEGAL RESEARCH REFERENCE:**
> Murray §§197, 250

Sec. 14-2. Discharge by Act of the Parties

The first set of discharge doctrines rests upon the parties' mutual assent to the destruction of the contract duty.

a. A Contract of Rescission Negatively Destroying the Old Contract Duty

The parties entered into contract #1, for example, a contract for the sale of goods. At a subsequent point in time, they decide to terminate contract #1. They can terminate contract #1 by entering into contract #2, a contract of mutual rescission. The thrust of a rescission contract is essentially negative; it is an agreement to end the first contract and destroy all the duties under that contract. If the plaintiff later attempts to sue on contract #1, the defendant can deny the plaintiff recovery by proving the contract of rescission; even if the defendant at one time had a contract duty and did not perform that duty, the rescission contract destroyed the duty and precludes a finding of breach.

The parties' agreement for a mutual rescission is a contract. As such, the agreement must satisfy all the normal requirements for a contract. Hence, like the plaintiff in Chapter 5, the defendant must prove that

1. There was mutual assent for the contract of rescission. The key to proving mutual assent for a rescission contract is establishing that the parties agreed to *completely* terminate *all* the duties under contract #1:

    Q   When you made this proposal to the plaintiff, what did you tell him you wanted to do to your April agreement?   (1)
    A   I told him that I wanted to end it.
    Q   To the best of your memory, what were your precise words?   (1)
    A   I think I said something like, "I want to call the whole thing off."
    Q   Which parts of the agreement, if any, did you tell the plaintiff you wanted to continue in existence?   (1)
    A   None. I made it clear to him that I wanted to entirely end our business relationship.

2. The defendant gave the plaintiff legally sufficient consideration for the plaintiff's promise to release the defendant from contract #1. If at the time of the rescission the agreement is still executory on both sides, both parties still have rights under contract #1. Their mutual surrender of the remaining rights under contract #1 is legally sufficient consideration:

    Q   When you made this proposal to the plaintiff, what did you request from the plaintiff?   (2)
    A   I didn't ask for any money. All I wanted from him was for him to release me from the employment contract.
    Q   What was the plaintiff supposed to do under the original employment contract?   (2)
    A   He was supposed to make six $1,000 payments direct to my checking account.
    Q   When you made this proposal to him, how many of the payments had the plaintiff made?   (2)
    A   He had made three of the six payments.
    Q   What did you tell the plaintiff about the remaining three payments?   (2)

A   I told him that he could forget about the other three if he let me out of the deal.

Q   How did he respond to your proposal?   (2)

A   He said that was fine. He told me that he'd let me out of the contract if I forgot about the last three payments.

Q   What did you say then?   (2)

A   I said that that was great, and we shook on the bargain.

LEGAL RESEARCH REFERENCE:
Murray §252

b.   Contracts Affirmatively Replacing the Old Contract Duty with New Duties

Discharge by rescission is a negative technique; in the second contract of rescission, the parties terminate the first contract without creating new duties. The second discharge technique is affirmative; the parties discharge the prior contract by subsequently forming a new contract entailing positive duties of performance.

The threshold question of interpretation is this: Did the parties intend that the mere formation of the second contract would discharge the first contract? Or did they intend that the first contract would be discharged only when the second contract was performed? To answer that question, the courts consider three factors:

—Whether the parties formed the new contract before any breach of the first contract. If the parties form the new contract before any breach, the court is more likely to hold that the first contract was immediately discharged. After a breach, the innocent party is less likely to trust the breaching party—and less likely to immediately surrender his or her rights under contract #1.

—If the parties formed the new contract after a breach, whether the breach was disputed. If the breach is undisputed, the court is less likely to hold that the first contract was immediately discharged. If the breach is undisputed, the innocent party has a stronger bargaining position and is less likely to immediately surrender his or her right to recover for the breach.

—If the parties formed the new contract after a breach, whether the amount of the claim for the breach was liquidated. If the breach was liquidated, the court is less likely to hold that the first contract was immediately discharged. When the claim is unliquidated, the innocent party is much more likely to be willing to immediately surrender the claim in exchange for new contract duties.

1.   *Substituted contract*

When the parties form the new contract before any breach of the old contract, the courts usually label the new agreement "a substituted contract." The normal intention of the parties is that the formation of the substituted contract immediately discharges the duties under the old contract. If the plaintiff attempts to sue on the old contract, the defendant can rejoin by proving the formation of the substituted contract. To do so, the defendant should show that

1. There was mutual assent to the new contract. *See* Chapter 5.
2. The defendant gave the plaintiff legally sufficient consideration for the new contract. *See* Chapter 5.
3. The parties intended that the new contract would immediately discharge the duties under the old contract. The defendant should show that the parties reached the new agreement before there was any breach of the old agreement:

Q   Before you reached this new agreement, how much of the old agreement had you performed?   (3)
A   I made all the payments that the contract called for to that date.
Q   In what respects had you failed to perform the old agreement?   (3)
A   To my knowledge, none. I did everything that I was supposed to do to that point in the agreement.
Q   How much of the old agreement had the plaintiff performed?   (3)
A   He'd made all the deliveries he was supposed to.
Q   In what respects had he failed to perform the old agreement?   (3)
A   Just like me, none. As far as I could tell, he had lived up to the bargain.

Next show that the parties regarded the new contract as a replacement for the old contract:

Q   As you were discussing this new agreement, what references, if any, did you make to the April agreement?   (3)
A   We referred to it all the time because we were making the new agreement to replace it.
Q   Why do you use the expression, "replace it"?   (3)
A   Well, that was the whole point of our new agreement. For different reasons, we were both unhappy with the old deal. We were calling that deal off and putting together a whole new package.

Ideally, elicit testimony that the parties manifested an intention to immediately discharge the old contract:

Q   After you reached this new agreement, what did you do with the old written contract?   (3)
A   We tore it up.
Q   Who tore it up?   (3)
A   Actually the plaintiff did it.
Q   Why did you do that?   (3)
A   That deal was off, and we didn't need that contract any more.
Q   When you reached this agreement, what rights under the old agreement did you tell the plaintiff you were reserving?   (3)
A   I didn't say anything like that. We tore up the paper, and I was giving up all my rights under that contract.

Q What rights did the plaintiff say that he has reserving under the old agreement? (3)

A None. We both gave up the rights we had under the April bargain.

2. *Immediate accord and satisfaction*

When the parties form the new contract after an alleged breach but intend that the new contract's formation will instantaneously discharge the old contract, the courts label the new agreement "an immediate accord and satisfaction." Like a substituted contract, an accord and satisfaction is a defense when the plaintiff sues on the original contract. The foundation is very similar to the foundation for a substituted contract:

1. There was mutual assent to the new contract.
2. The defendant gave the plaintiff legally sufficient consideration for the new contract. If the claim under the original contract was disputed or unliquidated, the defendant's consideration can consist in surrendering the right to go to court to have the court resolve the dispute or fix the amount of the claim.
3. The parties intended that the new agreement would immediately discharge the duties under the old contract. It is ideal if the defendant shows that the claim arising from the breach of the prior contract was both disputed and unliquidated; if the claim is of that uncertain a character, the innocent party is more likely to be willing to immediately surrender the claim. Suppose that the original contract between the plaintiff and defendant called for the defendant to deliver several items of antique furniture to the plaintiff. The defendant delivered five items, but the plaintiff claimed that one item, a chair, did not conform to the contract:

Q What did you say when the plaintiff told you that she did not think that the chair lived up to the contract? (3) [DISPUTED]

A I told her she was wrong.

Q Why did you tell her that? (3) [DISPUTED]

A It's true that the contract said that the furniture had to be in "first-rate condition." But, as I tried to explain to her, that doesn't mean "without scratches." You've got to expect that in antique furniture.

Q How much greater would the value of the chair been if there had been no scratches on it? (3) [UNLIQUIDATED]

A That's impossible to say. In the minds of some antique dealers, the value might be less; without scratches, the furniture really doesn't look antique. Even if the value would be more, it's tough to name a dollar figure.

Q Why is it so difficult to come up with a dollar figure? [UNLIQUIDATED]

A Antiques are very individualized. They're not mass produced like modern furniture. And, to make matters worse, a lot depends upon the style preferences of the buyer. When you put those factors together, it's difficult to pull a figure out of the air.

Then, if possible, have the defendant testify that the parties manifested an intention to immediately discharge the original contract. The testimony would be exactly the same as in the case of a substituted contract. Prove that the parties ripped up the old contract or at least tore the signatures off the document. If the defendant's statements to the plaintiff manifested that intention, the defendant's statements may be admitted as nonhearsay under Federal Evidence Rule 801(c). The plaintiff's own statements will fall within Rule 801(d) (2) (admissions) and 803(3) (declarations of state of mind).

3. Executory accord

The courts use the label "executory accord" for the new agreement when (1) the parties form the new agreement after an alleged breach and (2) the parties intend that the old contract will be discharged only upon the new contract's performance. The court is likely to hold the new agreement to be an executory accord when the claim for breach of the old contract was undisputed and liquidated. Assume that the old contract called for the defendant to make loan payments in a specific amount on a particular schedule, for example, $150 every first of the month. The defendant breached by defaulting on a payment. The defendant acknowledged the default, and the claim was thus undisputed. Moreover, since the breach was the failure to pay a specific sum of money, the claim was liquidated. In this situation, it is unlikely that the plaintiff lender would immediately surrender his or her rights under the original loan contract. The plaintiff might be willing to adjust the payment schedule (reduce the amount of the monthly payment and increase the length of the loan), but the plaintiff might not want to lose his or her rights under the original contract until the defendant had performed the new contract.

The foundation for an executory accord includes proof that

1. There was mutual assent to the new contract.
2. The defendant gave the plaintiff legally sufficient consideration for the new contract. If the claim under the original contract is undisputed and liquidated, the defendant has no right to go to court to litigate the claim. The defendant will have to identify some consideration other than the surrender of that right. The defendant should testify that the parties changed some term of the agreement to the apparent benefit of the plaintiff. By way of illustration, the defendant could establish that in exchange for the reduced monthly payment, the defendant promised to pay a higher interest rate on the loan:

Q   What did you promise to do in exchange for the reduced monthly payment?   (2)
A   I agreed to pay 12% interest.
Q   What was the interest in your original loan agreement?   (2)
A   10%.

Q What interest rate did you agree to pay under the new agreement? (2)

A As I said, I agreed to 12%.

3. The parties intended that the new contract would "replace" the old contract:

Q What did you tell the plaintiff you wanted to do with the $150 monthly payments? (3)

A I told him that I wanted to discontinue them.

Q What did you tell the plaintiff about the amount of the payments you wanted to make? (3)

A I told him that I thought I could handle a $130 monthly payment.

Q How did the plaintiff respond when you said that to him? (3)

A He said it was agreeable to end the $150 payments and substitute a $130 monthly payment on two conditions.

Q What were the conditions? (3)

A The interest rate was going up from 10 to 12%, and consequently I'd have to make the monthly payments for 14 months beyond the original term of the loan.

Q What did you say when the plaintiff mentioned these conditions? (3)

A I told him that they were O.K. with me, and then we shook hands on the deal.

At early common law, the distinction between an immediate accord and satisfaction and an executory accord was critical. Although the defendant could use an accord and satisfaction as a defense to a suit on the old contract, an executory accord was absolutely unenforceable—it was no defense to the plaintiff's suit. Today, the courts enforce the executory accord in various ways. In some jurisdictions, the courts treat the accord as an affirmative defense; in others, the courts will enjoin the plaintiff from suing on the first contract; and in still others, the courts award the defendant money damages for the plaintiff's breach of the executory accord. You must research your local law to determine the status of an executory accord in your jurisdiction. You may have to plead the accord as an affirmative defense or counterclaim in your answer to be able to rely on the accord at trial.

LEGAL RESEARCH REFERENCE:
Murray §§253-56

c. Releases and Covenants Not to Sue

1. Releases

In subsections *a* and *b*, we discussed bilateral agreements between the contracting parties to discharge a prior contract; rescission and substituted agreements are bilateral contracts. The defendant's duty under the prior contract can sometimes be discharged without a bilateral agreement; the plaintiff can discharge by a unilateral act. The plaintiff can do so even if the defendant does not give the plaintiff any consideration for the act. This type of discharge is usually termed a *release*. To prove a release, the defendant should lay the following foundation:

1. The plaintiff prepared a writing. The defendant must authenticate the writing as the plaintiff's. The defendant can use any of the authentication techniques discussed in Chapter 5. Hence, the defendant could testify to observing the plaintiff's execution of the writing or recognizing the plaintiff's handwriting style.

2. The writing manifested the plaintiff's intention to immediately discharge the defendant's duty. A release is an executed transaction; as soon as it becomes effective, the release destroys and extinguishes the defendant's duty under the old contract. The defendant should point to the writing's language suggesting immediate discharge:

Q   Please read to the jury the sentence in exhibit B (the release) that begins with, "I, the undersigned. . . ."   (2)

A   Yes. It says, "I, the undersigned, hereby release, extinguish, demise, convey, quitclaim, and transfer any claim I have against Jane Powers under our contract dated April 3, 1981 to the said Jane Powers."

Most judges will permit the defendant to introduce the plaintiff's statements indicating that the plaintiff intended an immediate discharge:

Q   What, if anything, did the plaintiff say when he handed you exhibit B? (2)

A   He said that he was letting me go and that I was free of the employment contract.

3. The writing complies with the formalities requisite for a release. At early common law, the requisites were a writing, signature, and seal. In most jurisdictions, the seal has lost its common-law efficacy. However, because the seal was so useful, many jurisdictions have created statutory substitutes for the seal. Uniform Commercial Code 1-107 is illustrative:

Any claim or right arising out of an alleged breach can be discharged in whole or in part without consideration by a written waiver or renunciation signed and delivered by the aggrieved party.

To invoke this statute, the defendant would testify:

Q   Who prepared exhibit B?   (3) [WRITING]
A   The plaintiff did.
Q   How do you know that?   (3) [WRITING]
A   I was present in his office when he wrote it out.
Q   Whose signature appears on the bottom of the exhibit?   [SIGNATURE]
A   The plaintiff's.
Q   How do you know that this is the plaintiff's signature?   [SIGNATURE]
A   For a couple of reasons. I'm familiar with the style of his hand, and I also saw him write this paper out longhand.
Q   What did the plaintiff do with the writing when he finished writing it out? [DELIVERY]

A   He handed it to me.
Q   What, if anything, did he say when he handed it to you?   [DELIVERY]
A   He said he wanted me to have the writing.
Q   How did he describe the writing?   [DELIVERY]
A   He said it was a release that ended my obligations under our employment contract.

LEGAL RESEARCH REFERENCE:
Murray §259

2. *Covenant not to sue*

The courts use the expression *release* when the plaintiff's discharge of the defendant is immediately executed; the plaintiff does not merely promise not to sue on the contract duty—the plaintiff purports to immediately extinguish the duty. If the plaintiff's statement is merely a promise not to sue to enforce the duty, the statement is a *covenant not to sue*.

May the defendant rely on the plaintiff's covenant not to sue as a defense? You should first research the local law to determine whether in your jurisdiction, (1) the seal retains its common-law efficacy, or (2) the seal has been replaced by a statute with language broad enough to apply to both immediate discharges and promises not to sue on a contract duty. If there is and the plaintiff complied with the procedure, the plaintiff's unilateral covenant not to sue is enforceable; and if you have properly pleaded the covenant, it is a complete defense at trial. If there is no local procedure for enforcing a unilateral covenant or the plaintiff did not comply with the procedure, the court will enforce the covenant only if you prove that it is an enforceable bilateral contract. You will have to prove that

1. There was mutual assent to the covenant; and
2. The defendant gave the plaintiff legally sufficient consideration such as a lump sum settlement payment for the covenant.

LEGAL RESEARCH REFERENCE:
Murray §260

d.   Novation

The term "novation" is ambiguous. It is sometimes used loosely to describe any new agreement between the original contracting parties. In this sense, all the agreements discussed in subsection *b* are novations. However, the more precise and technical meaning of the term is an agreement in which either or both of the original contracting parties are replaced by new parties. For example, assume that *A* and *B* enter into a contract. *B* wants to be released from the agreement, and *C* is willing to take *B*'s place. There is a novation when *A*, *B*, and *C* agree to the substitution of *C* for *B*. If *A* later attempts to sue *B* on the original contract, *B* may prove the novation as a defense.

To prove the novation, the defendant must establish:

1. All three parties manifested their assent to the novation. Suppose that Mr. Adams hired Ms. Bennett as a computer programmer at his data processing center. Ms. Bennett receives a better job offer and wants to move to Providence. Mr. Carlton is interested in replacing Ms. Bennett. Ms. Bennett arranges a meeting with Messrs. Adams and Carlton. She is testifying about the meeting:

Q Who was present? (1)
A I was there, and so were Mr. Adams and Mr. Carlton.
Q What did you tell Mr. Adams about your agreement to work for him as a computer programmer? (1)
A I told him that I wanted to be let off the hook. I explained that I had a once-in-a-lifetime opportunity in Rhode Island and didn't want to pass it up.
Q What did you tell Mr. Adams about Mr. Carlton? (1)
A I told him that Mr. Carlton and I had attended the same computer training program and had the same qualifications. I said that Dave, that is, Mr. Carlton, was willing to take over my job.
Q How did Mr. Adams respond to your request to be released from your employment contract? (1)
A He said it was fine with him so long as Mr. Carlton agreed to take over the position.
Q What did Mr. Carlton say? (1)
A Dave said that he was not only willing but eager to work for Mr. Adams.
Q What happened then? (1)
A Mr. Adams took out my contract and destroyed it.
Q How did he destroy it? (1)
A He tore it up.
Q What else did he do? (1)
A He told Dave to go straight to personnel and they'd get him on the payroll with the same job description and salary that I had.
Q What did Mr. Carlton say when Mr. Adams said that? (1)
A He said something like, "That's great." He then left, saying that his first stop was going to be personnel.

If you anticipate that the plaintiff will seriously controvert the novation, you should present as much corroboration of assent as possible. During the discovery stage, search for the following corroboration:

—The plaintiff gave the old written contract to the defendant or destroyed the old written contract.
—The plaintiff issued a new written contract to Carlton.
—The plaintiff's personnel records struck the defendant's name. The records will qualify as prior inconsistent statements under Evidence Rule 613, admissions under Rule 801(d) (2), and business entries under Rule 803(6).
—The plaintiff's personnel records substituted Carlton's name.
—The defendant sent the plaintiff a letter mentioning the novation, and

the plaintiff did not respond and deny the novation. The defendant should argue that the plaintiff's failure to respond is an adoptive or tacit admission under Federal Evidence Rule 801(d) (2) (B). The parties' prior business relationship would make a response expectable if the statement about the novation in the defendant's letter were false.

—With the plaintiff's knowledge, Carlton began performing the same employment duties as the defendant had. The plaintiff's business records and the testimony of the plaintiff's employees can be used to prove this. The defendant may call the plaintiff's employees as hostile witnesses under Evidence Rule 611(c):

Q   Isn't it true that Mr. Carlton used the office that Ms. Bennett formerly used?

A   Yes.

Q   Isn't it a fact that Mr. Carlton had the same job title as Ms. Bennett had?

A   Yes.

Q   Isn't it correct that he worked the same hours as Ms. Bennett did?

A   Yes.

Q   Isn't it a fact that his immediate superior was Mr. Grant, the same superior that Ms. Bennett reported to?

A   Yes.

Q   Isn't it true that he supervised the same three employees that Ms. Bennett had supervised?

A   Yes.

2. The defendant gave the plaintiff legally sufficient consideration for the plaintiff's promise to release the defendant. If the plaintiff still had executory duties under the contract at the time of the novation, the defendant's surrender of the correlative rights is sufficient consideration:

Q   How many payments was Mr. Adams supposed to make to you under your employment agreement?   (2)

A   A total of 24. I was supposed to work for a full year, and he was going to pay me twice a month.

Q   When you had this meeting with Messrs. Adams and Carlton, how many payments had Mr. Adams already made to you?   (2)

A   I think the number was four.

Q   During this meeting, what, if anything, did you tell Mr. Adams about the other 20 payments?   (2)

A   I told him that if he agreed to substituting Mr. Carlton, Adams wouldn't have to make any of the remaining payments or give me any severance pay.

Q   How did Mr. Adams respond to your statement?   (2)

A   He said that the offer was fine and that we had a deal.

LEGAL RESEARCH REFERENCE:
Murray §258

Sec. 14-3.   Discharge by Operation of Law

The discharge techniques discussed in the last section require the voluntary act of at least one contracting party. Sometimes the defendant's duty can be discharged without any voluntary act by the parties; the law itself will discharge the duty. The most obvious example of discharge by operation of law is the operation of the statute of limitations. If the plaintiff does not file suit for breach of contract within the period of limitations, the statute bars the claim. Uniform Commercial Code 2-725(2) defines when a cause of action "accrues," and subsection 2-725(1) mandates that any "action for breach of any contract for sale must be commenced within four years after the cause of action has accrued." There are six other doctrines that can discharge a defendant's duty by operation of law.

LEGAL RESEARCH REFERENCE:
Murray §§197, 205-06
White and Summers §3-9

a. Discharge by Impossibility—The Death or Serious Illness of an Essential Person

If a particular person's action is necessary for the performance of the defendant's duty, that person's death or serious illness automatically terminates the duty. The foundation for this doctrine includes proof that

1. The person was "essential" to the performance of the defendant's duty. If an employee has entered into a personal services contract, the employee is an essential person. On the other hand, the death of an employer will not necessarily discharge the contract; whether there is a discharge depends upon how closely and personally the employer was to supervise the employee. The death of the sole proprietor of a large business will usually not discharge the sole proprietor's personal services contracts with the employees at the lowest operational level. In contrast, if an employer band leader was to direct and train the employee band members, the employer's death will probably effect a discharge.

2. At the time of contracting, it was unforeseeable that the essential person would die or become seriously ill during the contract's performance. When the defendant is the essential person who became seriously ill, the defendant himself can testify in person or via a deposition. Assume that the defendant's physician has already testified that the three symptoms of the illness' onset were a rash, blurred vision, and hoarseness in the throat. The defendant should affirmatively testify that he felt in good health and negatively deny having those symptoms:

Q   When you signed this agreement with the plaintiff, what was the state of your health?
A   I felt fine.
Q   What rash, if any, did you have at that time?

A   None. My skin was clear. The rash didn't develop until about three months later.

Q   How good was your eyesight at the time?

A   It was excellent. I had no problems at all. I started experiencing the blurring in my vision at about the same time the rash appeared.

Q   What was the condition of your throat when you signed the agreement?

A   Great. Everything, including the hoarseness, happened later. It was only then that I went to the doctor and discovered that I had this rare type of flu.

If the illness is still disabling the defendant at the time of trial, the defendant would be unavailable under Evidence Rule 804(a) (4); and the defendant's deposition would be admissible under Rule 804(b) (1). The defendant should testify that he or she felt in good health at the time of contracting. The defendant could also testify that during recent physical examinations, the physicians had told the defendant that he or she was in good health. The physicians' statements to the defendant are admissible as nonhearsay under Rule 801(c); the statements are logically relevant to show their effect on the hearer defendant's mind, namely, the creation of the reasonable belief that he or she was in good health.

If the essential person dies and the employer sues the decedent's personal representative, the representative should introduce circumstantial evidence of the decedent's state of mind. The decedent's family members and friends can testify about the decedent's apparent, generally good health; general health is a proper subject for lay opinion testimony under Evidence Rule 701. The same witness could testify that during the decedent's lifetime, he or she rarely became ill. The representative could also introduce the testimony of a physician who administered an annual or employment physical examination to the decedent before the decedent entered the contract:

Q   At the end of this examination, what did you tell Ms. Simpson (the decedent) about her health?   (2)

A   I told her that as far as I could tell, she was in fine shape.

As previously stated, this testimony is offered for the nonhearsay purpose of proving the statements' effect on the hearer's state of mind.

3.   During the performance of the contract, the essential person died or became so seriously ill that he or she could not perform his or her contract duties. A properly attested copy of the death certificate falls within the hearsay exception in Rule 803(9) and is self-authenticating under Rule 902(4). A hospital record reflecting the person's illness can qualify as a business entry under Rule 803(6). Rule 803(6) expressly authorizes the admission of "opinions or diagnoses" within the report.

However, it is best to present the live testimony of a physician. First call a witness to describe the defendant's employment duties. Next, the physician should be called to recite his or her qualifications, describe the person's symptoms, and diagnose the person's illness. Then include both the defendant's illness and employment duties in a hypothetical question, concluding:

Q   Doctor Thompson, given Ms. Simpson's illness and her employment duties, what would have been the effect on her health if she had continued to work as the plaintiff's general manager for the next six months? (3)

A   Her condition would have deteriorated badly. There's a risk that she would have died before filling out those six months.

Q   How great would that risk have been?   (3)

A   I have to add the caveat that it's always difficult to estimate this sort of risk, but my best, considered judgment is that it would be better than a 50% risk of death. Her condition was that serious.

4. The defendant's negligence did not contribute to the causation of the death or illness. The defendant can testify that he or she had a regular annual checkup after entering the contract and that the checkup did not disclose the illness. Then the defendant can describe how suddenly the illness came on:

Q   When did you first feel the pain in your chest?   (4)

A   It was August 13th, the day before I went to see Doctor Thompson.

Q   Before the 13th, what pain or discomfort did you feel in that part of your body?   (4)

A   None that I remember.

Q   Before the 13th, what unusual physical problems such as bleeding or dizziness did you have?   (4)

A   None. It just came on real sudden and unexpected.

Have a physician corroborate the defendant's testimony:

Q   Doctor Thompson, in this sort of illness, what early warning signs does the patient usually get?   (4)

A   I'm afraid that there are almost none. The deterioration occurs very gradually—it's hardly noticeable. Then one morning you wake up and, without any prior warning, you can be in terrible pain.

Q   How easily can a layperson recognize the onset of this illness?   (4)

A   I don't think that an untrained layperson could. The signs are quite subtle, and you need an intensive examination by a trained physician to detect the early symptoms.

Based on this testimony, you can argue during summation that the defendant had no early warning signs and, hence, was not negligent in failing to consult a physician before the illness became disabling.

LEGAL RESEARCH REFERENCE:
Murray §200

b.   Discharge by Impossibility—The Destruction or Unavailability of an Essential Object

Like a person, an object can be essential to the performance of the defendant's duty. Just as the person's death can release the defendant, the object's destruction can effect a discharge. Before rushing to an analysis of this discharge doctrine, though, the defense attorney should first consider risk of loss. If under Uniform Commercial Code 2-509, the risk of loss had already passed to the plaintiff buyer, the defendant seller is not guilty of any breach; the defendant seller not only has a defense but also may be able to recover on a counterclaim against the buyer. The defendant seller must resort to this discharge doctrine only if the destruction occurs before the risk of loss shifts to the buyer. U.C.C. 2-613 governs discharges based on "casualty to identified goods," and on its face that statute applies only when the casualty occurs "before the risk of loss passes to the buyer. . . ."

When the defendant must resort to the discharge doctrine, the defendant should prove that

1. The object was "essential" to the performance of the defendant's duty. U.C.C. 2-613 uses this language: "(T)he contract requires for its performance goods identified when the contract is made. . . ." The defendant may testify directly that the parties agreed on a particular object or quote the written contract's language specifying a particular object.
2. At the time of contracting, it was not reasonably foreseeable that the supervening event would occur. The defendant should testify that he or she did not foresee the event:

Q When you entered into the repair agreement with the plaintiff, what, if anything, did the plaintiff say about the possibility that lightning would strike the warehouse? (2)
A I don't recall him mentioning that.
Q What did you say to him about that possibility? (2)
A I know that I didn't say anything to him about that possibility.
Q Why not? (2)
A Who would have thought that that would happen? I just didn't foresee it.

Try to corroborate the defendant with an expert's testimony that the supervening event was extraordinary. If the event was a flood, put a weatherman on the witness stand:

Q What is your occupation? (2)
A I'm a weather observer here in Kentucky.
Q Whom do you work for? (2)
A I work for the U.S. Weather Service.
Q Where do you work? (2)
A I'm stationed here in Lexington.
Q How long have you been stationed in Lexington? (2)
A For the past 15 years.
Q What are your duties as a weather observer? (2)
A I maintain a constant watch of weather conditions in the area and broadcast alerts of dangerous, approaching conditions.

Q   What recordkeeping responsibilities, if any, do you have?   (2)

A   I have to record the important observations that I made, and I'm the records custodian for our office.

[At this point, have the witness authenticate official weather service records. If you do not want to call a live witness, introduce an attested copy of the records. The records fall within the public records hearsay exception in Evidence Rule 803(8), an attested copy is self-authenticating under Rule 902(4), and there is an excuse for the non-production of the original under Rule 1005.]

Q   According to defense exhibit D, what was the amount of rainfall on February 4th of this year (the date on which the essential object was destroyed)?   (2)

A   It was 13.4 inches of rain.

Q   According to defense exhibit E, what is the average amount of rainfall that has fallen on that date in this century?   (2)

A   Only 0.8 inches.

Q   When was the last time that Lexington had that much rain on a February 4th?   (2)

A   Well, you have to go all the way back to 1907 to find a comparable February 4th.

3. The object was destroyed or became unavailable. There are numerous methods of proving this element of the foundation. If a person witnessed the object's destruction by fire or flood, that person can testify directly to the event. The defendant's business records describing the event and destruction can qualify under Rule 803(6), and there may be an official, public report admissible under 803(8). If the fire or flood attracted wide publicity, the event may be judicially noticeable under Rule 201(b). There may even be a newspaper report of the event; the newspaper is self-authenticating under Rule 902(6); and by invoking Rule 804(b) (5) and analogizing to the general history exception in Rule 803(20) the judge may admit the newspaper report as evidence of the event's occurrence.

4. The defendant's fault was not a contributing factor to the occurrence of the event. It is easy to prove this element of the foundation when the event was an act of God. To be on the safe side, though, the defendant should testify that he or she had such little advance notice that there was no time to take preventative measures:

Q   When did you first learn that there was a flash flood warning?   (4)

A   As best I remember, it was about 8:30 in the morning.

Q   What did you do when you learned of the flash flood warning?   (4)

A   I called the whole staff together and told them that we should try to move the inventory to higher ground before the flood hit our area.

Q   When did the flood waters arrive?   (4)

A   They hit us at about ten minutes to nine.

Q   By that time, how much of your inventory had you been able to move to higher ground?   (4)

A Almost none of it. It took us some time to get the trucks ready to load; and by the time we had begun to load the trucks, the whole area was under seven feet of water. There was just no time.

The above facts are the elements of the common-law discharge doctrine. The Code adds a new allocation procedure to the common-law doctrine. Under U.C.C. 2-615(b), when the supervening event affects "only a part of the seller's capacity to perform," the seller may allocate among the buyers in a "fair and reasonable" manner. The seller must notify the buyers under 2-615(c), and the buyers then have the choice of accepting the allocation or terminating the contract under 2-616(1).

LEGAL RESEARCH REFERENCE:
Murray §198

c. Discharge by Impossibility—The Destruction or Unavailability of the Contemplated Means of Performance

The performance of a contract duty may involve the defendant's use of several objects. One object, the end product to be delivered to the buyer, may be absolutely essential to the duty's performance. However, there can be other objects that the defendant contemplates using but that are only incidental means of performance. For example, the defendant may contemplate using particular delivery trucks or railroad cars to ship the goods to the buyer. What is the legal consequence if it becomes impossible for the seller to use those contemplated, incidental means of performance? Uniform Commercial Code 2-614(1) answers that question:

> Where without fault of either party, the agreed berthing, loading, or unloading facilities fail or an agreed type of carrier becomes unavailable or the agreed manner of delivery otherwise becomes commercially impracticable but a commercially reasonable substitute is available, such substitute performance must be tendered and accepted.

To invoke this doctrine, the defendant must lay the following foundation:

1. At the time of contracting, both parties contemplated that the defendant would use these means of performance. The defendant should testify that during the negotiations preceding the formation of the contract, he or she mentioned the specific facilities to the plaintiff.

    Q How were you going to dig out the canal?   (1)
    A I was going to use a special dredger that I had purchased from a Belgian firm.
    Q What did you tell the plaintiff about the way you were going to dig out the canal?   (1)
    A I told him that I was going to use this dredger that was specially equipped for sandy bottoms.

Q   What did the plaintiff say?   (1)

A   He said that was fine. He said he's had some difficulty finding someone who could do the job, and he was glad that I had the right equipment.

Q   What objection, if any, did the plaintiff have to your use of that special dredger?   (1)

A   He didn't make any objection whatsoever. As far as I could tell, he was perfectly happy with the arrangement.

If the contract refers to the facilities, quote that reference to the jury. Alternatively, the defendant may be able to rely on a prior course of dealing under U.C.C. 1-205(1) or trade usage under 1-205(2) as the basis for an implication that the defendant would use those means of performance.

2. At the time of contracting, it was not foreseeable that the contemplated means would be destroyed or become unavailable. The defendant proves this element in exactly the same fashion as element #2 of the discharge doctrine for essential objects.

3. The contemplated means of performance were destroyed or became unavailable.

4. The defendant's fault was not a contributing factor to the occurrence of the event.

If the defendant establishes these four elements, the defendant obtains a *partial* discharge; the court will relieve the defendant from the duty of using the contemplated means of performance, but the defendant will still have to perform by "commercially reasonable" substitute means. To obtain a *complete* discharge, the defendant must establish a fifth element:

5. There is no commercially reasonable, alternative means of performance. The defendant may attempt to prove that there were no alternative means in existence:

Q   What happened after the tornado destroyed your dredger?   (5)

A   I had to discontinue work.

Q   Why couldn't you get another dredger?   (5)

A   You need specially designed equipment to dredge with the kind of sandy bottom in the plaintiff's canal. I purchased my equipment from a Belgian firm three years ago; and to my knowledge, I'm the only one in the southern United States with that type of equipment.

Q   What efforts did you make to obtain new specially designed equipment? (5)

A   I phoned my Belgian supplier, but he said that it would take at least nine months to have one ready for shipment to me.

    [*The Belgian's supplier statement can be admitted for a nonhearsay purpose under Federal Evidence Rule 801(c). One issue is whether the defendant acted reasonably, and the court must judge the defendant's reasonableness in part in light of the statements made to the defendant.*]

Or the defendant may attempt to prove that although alternative means existed, they were unavailable to him:

Q   What happened after the fire destroyed your railroad cars?   (5)

A   I phoned the plaintiff to tell him that I wouldn't be able to deliver on time.

Q   Why couldn't you deliver on time?   (5)

A   Not only couldn't I use my own railroad cars, I couldn't rent any.

Q   What efforts did you make to rent other railroad cars?   (5)

A   I phoned all the railroad freight departments in Topeka.

Q   What did they tell you?   (5)

A   They all said that there were no cars available for rental. This was the height of the grain shipping season, and there were no railroad cars to be had.

Finally, the defendant may attempt to show that although there were existing, alternative means of performance, they were prohibitively expensive. An alternative that is prohibitively expensive is not "commercially reasonable." The defendant would have to prove the excessive expense in the same manner in which the defendant would establish financial impracticability, discussed in subsection e, *infra*.

LEGAL RESEARCH REFERENCE:
Murray §199

d.   Discharge by Impossibility—Legal Impossibility

In Chapter 12, we discussed the termination of offers by supervening illegality; if the law changes and a material term of the offer becomes illegal, the offer automatically terminates. An analogous rule governs the situation in which the law changes after the contract's formation. The defendant can be discharged on the ground of supervening legal impossibility if the defendant proves that

1.   At the time of contracting, it was unforeseeable that the law would change. In some cases, it is foreseeable. For example, administrative agencies often circulate proposed regulations for public comment; receipt of a proposed regulation would certainly put the defendant on notice that the law was about to change. The defendant should testify to negate such notice:

Q   What notice, if any, did you have that the Food and Drug Administration was going to ban this chemical from the market?   (1)

A   None.

Q   What had you read about the proposed regulation in the trade papers before September 1st (the date of contracting)?   (1)

A   Nothing.

Q   What copies of the proposed regulation had you seen before September 1st?   (1)

A   None. That's what's so strange. The agency ordinarily does circulate proposed rules, but I can't recall seeing one this time.

Q   When did you first learn of the regulation banning the chemical?   (1)

A   It wasn't until November 5th.

Q   What happened on that day?   (1)

A   The plaintiff phoned me and angrily asked me how I intended to fulfill the bargain in light of the new regulation.

2. The "law" went into effect after the formation of the contract. There are three questions concerning the type of "law" that can effect a discharge.

The first question is whether a judgment or decree against the defendant as an individual can discharge. The courts are in agreement that laws of general application (public statutes, judicial decisions involving other parties, and administrative regulations) can lead to discharge. However, the traditional view is that a judicial order aimed only at the defendant cannot discharge. The traditional view insists on objective rather than subjective impossibility and argues that an order directed against the defendant alone is merely subjective impossibility. The trend is to the contrary. For example, U.C.C. 2-615(a) refers to orders as well as regulations.

The second question is whether the foreign law can effect a discharge. The courts unanimously hold that any domestic law (national, state, or local) can discharge. However, until recently, most courts denied discharges based on foreign law. Again, the trend is away from the traditional view. 2-615(a) mentions foreign law as well as domestic law.

The final question is what evidentiary techniques may the defendant use to prove the new law. Several techniques are available to prove domestic law. In many states, the defendant may request judicial notice of the law. A properly attested copy of the law such as municipal ordinance would be self-authenticating in a jurisdiction that has adopted Evidence Rule 902. In addition, under Rule 902(5), the defendant could resort to "(b)ooks, pamphlets, or other publications purporting to be issued by public authority."

The defendant has a similarly wide choice of evidentiary techniques in proving foreign law. With a proper chain of attesting and authenticating certificates,[1] a foreign public document is self-authenticating under Rule 902(3). On its face, the language of 902(5) is broad enough to encompass law books purportedly issued by foreign public authority. Federal Rule of Civil Procedure 44.1 liberally provides that in determining foreign law, the judge "may consider any relevant material or source, including testimony, whether or not . . . admissible under the Federal Rules of Evidence." When the defendant is relying on foreign decisional law, it is quite common to call as an expert witness an attorney or law professor familiar with the foreign law.

3. The new law affects a material term of the contract. In the words of U.C.C. 2-615(a), the new law must undermine a "basic assumption" of the contract. Changes affecting the goods the seller can deliver or the price the buyer can pay are almost always deemed basic. Thus, if a new rationing system prohibits the seller from manufacturing the goods or a new price control regulation prohibits the buyer from paying the agreed price, there will be a discharge.

4. The defendant's fault was not a contributing cause to the supervening illegality. There is usually no difficulty when the law change takes the form of a new statute or administrative regulation of general application. The problem arises when the law change is a judgment, decree, or order against this particular defendant. If the court entered the adverse judgment because of the defendant's intentional wrongdoing or negligence, the defendant will be denied a discharge. However, if the basis of the adverse judgment was a strict liability doctrine, the defendant can still obtain the discharge.

To show the basis of the prior judgment, the defendant may introduce attested copies of the pleadings and record of trial in the prior case; with a proper attesting certificate from the court clerk or reporter, the documents can be treated as self-authenticating under Evidence Rule 902. If the prior case arose in the same trial court jurisdiction as the present case, the present court may be willing to judicially notice the contents of the court file. By introducing the pleadings, jury instructions, and verdict, the defendant can show that the gravamen of the prior action was strict liability rather than true fault.

LEGAL RESEARCH REFERENCE:
Murray §201

e. Financial Impracticability

Even if it is physically and legally possible for the defendant to perform, in some jurisdictions the defendant may be discharged by financial impracticability. This is a minority discharge doctrine; most common-law courts have balked at recognizing the doctrine. However, the doctrine received a major boost when the draftsmen of the Uniform Commercial Code incorporated the doctrine in U.C.C. 2-615(a). To trigger this discharge, the defendant must lay this foundation:

1. The performance of the defendant's contract duty necessitates certain work. In some cases, the necessity will be evident to the jurors. In other cases, it is best to have an expert explain the necessity. For example, a contract may require a defendant builder to erect a building without explicitly imposing a duty to excavate. An expert, sometimes the defendant himself or herself, should explain why the performance of the express contract duty necessitates the other work.
2. After contract formation, an unforeseen event occurred. Sometimes the unforeseen event is the discovery of a physical condition making performance more difficult and costly. The defendant could testify:

Q   What happened on the third day of excavating?   (2)
A   We hit solid rock.
Q   What had you thought you would find when you began excavating?   (2)
A   We thought that the subsoil would be as soft and easy to remove as the topsoil.
Q   Why did you anticipate soft subsoil?   (2)

A   That's what our test borings led us to expect.

Q   What test borings?   (2)

A   Before we even bid on this project, the soil experts on my staff and I visited the work site. We wanted to find out what sort of subsoil conditions we would run into if we got the project.

Q   How many test borings do you usually make on a work site of this size? (2)

A   We'd usually make five or six borings at various spots at the site.

Q   How many test borings would it be customary for an experienced contractor to make on a site of this size?   (2)

A   A lot depends on the individual contractor, but our practice is probably average or typical.

Q   How many test borings did you make at this site?   (2)

A   We erred on the side of caution and made ten.

Q   How do you know that?   (2)

A   I accompanied my soil people to the site and was present while they did the borings.

Q   How far did you go down?   (2)

A   We went down five feet deeper than the bottom of the anticipated foundation.

Q   How far do you usually go down?   (2)

A   The same distance.

Q   What was the result of the borings?   (2)

A   Each time the drill sliced through the subsoil almost like butter. It's hard to believe; but even with ten borings, we must have just hit outside the edge of solid rock every time. That's the only way I can explain what happened.

In other cases, the unforeseen event will be a price increase for raw materials or finished goods needed to perform the contract duty. In an age of scarcity marked by energy and materials shortages, sudden, dramatic price increases are occurring more frequently. To prove that the price hike was unforeseen, the defendant should establish that the market price was stable for a substantial period before the defendant entered into the contract with the plaintiff. Assume that the parties executed their contract on December 20th. The contract required the defendant to deliver end products, and the defendant needed a particular raw material to manufacture the product. A week after the parties executed their contract, the price per ton of the material shot up to $200.

The defendant is testifying. The defendant should first authenticate copies of trade journals reporting market prices. After the defendant identifies the exhibits as popular trade journals, they can be authenticated under Evidence Rule 902(6); and the market reports in the journals are admissible as substantive evidence under Evidence Rule 803(17) and U.C.C. 2-724. The defendant continues to testify:

Q   According to defense exhibit D, what was the market price per ton on December 20th?   (2)

A   The price was $40 per ton.

Q   According to exhibit E, what was the highest price per ton paid on any day during that whole year?   (2)

A   Let's see. It says $51 per ton was the top price for the whole year.

3.   After the formation of the contract, the cost of performance increased. The defendant should show the increase in absolute numbers. When there is a reported market price, introduce the market reports. If there are no readily available market reports, have an expert testify to the cost increase. Expert testimony will usually be necessary when the unforeseen event is the discovery of a physical condition making performance more difficult. For instance, in the excavation hypothetical, have an experienced contractor or civil engineer testify to the anticipated cost of removing the rock.

4.   The cost increase is prohibitive. To show how excessive the price increase, the defendant should first show how the new cost compares to the anticipated cost. The defendant can use the evidentiary techniques discussed in Section 9-5d, analyzing the contractor's proof of Z. The defendant's expert should cost out the performance on the assumptions that (1) as anticipated, the subsoil was relatively soft; and (2) as it turned out, the subsoil was solid rock. To discharge, the cost increase must be astronomical. Even the courts recognizing this doctrine apply it cautiously. In one of the landmark cases, *Mineral Park*,[2] the cost increase exceeded 1,000%.

In addition to comparing the new cost of performance to the foreseeable cost, the defendant should show the new cost's effect on the defendant's business. It is true that the defendant may not "plead poverty" as a defense to a Contract lawsuit. However, when the issue is whether a cost increase is prohibitive, it is logically relevant to show the increase's impact on the defendant's business. Under Evidence Rule 403, the judge has discretion to limit the defendant's proof of the effect, but the defendant should attempt to detail the effect. Suppose that the defendant has already established that the increased cost of performance due to subsoil conditions will be $100,000. The defendant can dramatize that increase's effect impact on the defendant by comparing the $100,000 figure with the anticipated profit on the contract:

[*Assume that the defendant has already testified to C and, as an expert, costed out Z on the assumption that the subsoil was soft.*]

Q   What would have been your profit on this project?   (4)

A   Only $15,000.

Q   How do you arrive at that figure?   (4)

A   Well, the contract price was $150,000. If you assume that the subsoil was soft, the total cost of performance would have been only $135,000. Just subtract one from the other, and you get the $15,000 profit figure.

Q   What effect does the discovery of the rock have on that profit?   (4)

A   The cost of excavating jumps from $20,000 to $100,000. That's an increase of $80,000 in the cost of performance. It wipes out the profit entirely; now I have to suffer a $65,000 loss on a project that I thought was a gainer for me.

and with the defendant's profit for the entire year:

[*Assume that the defendant's bookkeeper authenticates the defendant's business records for prior years, describes the records as voluminous under Evidence Rule 1006, and now proffers a summary of the records.*]

Q   For the preceding year, what was the defendant's net profit?   (4)
A $130,000.
Q   What would have been the effect in that year if the defendant had had to pay this increased cost of excavating?   (4)
A   Another $80,000 would have eaten up well over half the profit for the entire year.
Q   What was the defendant's profit the year before that?   (4)
A   That was a pretty lean year. He made only $95,000 in profit.
Q   What would have been the effect in that year if the defendant had had to pay this increased cost of excavating?   (4)
A   That loss alone would come close to putting the defendant into the red. There'd hardly be any profit left worth talking about.

If the judge is very liberal, the judge may permit you to prove that the amount of the cost increase exceeds the defendant's cash on hand, that the defendant has substantial short-term debt, and that the defendant has unsuccessfully attempted to obtain loans to meet this debt. This evidence is logically relevant, and its introduction will indisputably help the defense; the evidence shows that cost increase is so prohibitive that it may drive the defendant out of business. However, exercising their discretion under Rule 403, most judges exclude this evidence. The judges fear that the evidence will tempt the jury to decide the case on an improper basis, namely, sympathy for the defendant.

5. The defendant's fault was not a contributing cause to the financial impracticability. The defendant's conduct is rarely the cause of an economy- or industry-wide price increase. However, the issue may be whether the defendant negligently delayed procuring the raw materials. The price increase may have occurred one month into the contract's performance; if the defendant had purchased the raw material immediately after entering into the contract, the defendant would not have had to pay the increased price. The defendant should explain any delay. Several explanations are plausible:

Q   Why didn't you buy all the grain you needed as soon as you signed the contract with the plaintiff?   (5)
A   Well, the contract called for me to store the grain at my bins. When I signed that contract, my bins were already packed full with grain to be shipped to other buyers. I had no choice; I had to get those shipments out first to make room before I could buy any more grain.

Or the defendant could testify:

Q Why did you delay buying the grain? (5)
A The market was a little unsettled then. In fact, it even appeared for a while that prices might go down. I thought that if I waited, I could get the grain at a more reasonable price.

When the defendant offers this explanation, the defendant should corroborate the explanation with reports of market prices or the testimony of a person familiar with the market.

LEGAL RESEARCH REFERENCE:
Murray §§203-05
White & Summers §3-9

f. Frustration of Purpose

The last discharge doctrine is frustration of purpose. This doctrine applies even when the performance is physically possible, lawful, and economically feasible. The essence of the doctrine is that an unforeseeable event has made it actually or virtually impossible for the parties to achieve a "foundational" purpose that they both had in mind at the time of contracting. The foundation for a frustration discharge requires these elements:

1. At the time of contracting, the parties had a "foundational" purpose in mind. Unfortunately, no court has been able to formulate a clear, neat definition of "foundational" purpose. However, the decided cases indicate that the court will find a purpose foundational when the defendant demonstrates that

—*The defendant had the purpose in mind at the time of contracting.* Suppose that the defendant wanted to rent an apartment in Washington, D.C. for a day to view and photograph the President's Inauguration Parade. The defendant was an avid supporter of the newly elected President and was willing to pay a substantial price to rent an apartment overlooking the parade route:

Q Why did you want to rent the apartment? (1)
A The apartment overlooked the Presidential Inauguration Parade route.
Q Why did you want to see the parade? (1)
A I've been a fan of the newly elected President for a long time. In fact, I contributed a bit to his campaign. I thought it would be the thrill of a lifetime to see it. I wanted to take lots of photographs. My two young children were going to come along as well.

—*The defendant communicated this purpose to the plaintiff:*

Q What, if anything, did you tell the plaintiff about the reason you wanted to rent his apartment for the day? (1)
A I explained to him what I just told you. I even showed him the letter I had received from the President during the campaign—the letter thanking me for my campaign contribution.

—*The plaintiff charged the defendant an enhanced price because of the defendant's special purpose.* The defendant should show that the plaintiff charged an increased price because of the foundational purpose:

Q   Why did you approach the plaintiff rather than any other apartment owners along the route?   (1)
A   He had a little ad in his window.
Q   What did the ad say?   (1)
A   It said something like, "Want to view the Inauguration Parade? Apt. for Rent on Inauguration Day. Inquire Within."
Q   What did you do after you saw this poster in the window?   (1)
A   As the poster said, I inquired within. I rang the doorbell, and the plaintiff came out.
Q   What did he say?   (1)
A   After I told him I'd seen the poster, he quoted me a price of $1,000 to rent the apartment on Inauguration Day.
Q   What did you say then?   (1)
A   At first I told him that the price was awful, but then I reluctantly agreed.

The defendant should also show the normal rate charged for such apartments. The defendant could call the manager of the plaintiff's apartment and prove the plaintiff's monthly rent, or the defendant could call a real estate agent familiar with local rental rates.

—*The defendant paid the enhanced price to achieve the foundational purpose*:

Q   Why were you willing to pay $1,000 to rent the apartment for a single day?   (1)
A   Viewing the parade meant that much to me.
Q   What, if anything, did you tell the plaintiff about your willingness to pay the $1,000 rental?   (1)
A   I told him that under normal circumstances, I wouldn't pay anything approaching that. I may even have said that it was highway robbery. But then I finally agreed.

The defendant must convince the judge that the plaintiff realized that but for the defendant's special purpose, the defendant would not have entered the contract and agreed to pay the enhanced price.

2. A supervening event occurred. The defendant may use the typical evidentiary techniques to prove the event's occurrence: testimony of an eyewitness, business records admissible under Evidence Rule 803(6), and public records admissible under 803(8). In our hypothetical, assume that the President became ill, forcing the parade's cancellation. In the case of such a well-publicized event, the defendant could request judicial notice under Rule 201(b). A newspaper report of the event would be self-authenticating under Rule 902(6); and analogizing to Rule 803(20), the judge may be willing to admit the newspaper report as substantive evidence under the residual, catch-all hearsay exception, 803(24).

3. At the time of contracting, the event was unforeseeable. The defendant should testify to his or her lack of foresight:

Q When you signed the contract with the plaintiff, what indication did you have that the President was ill? (3)

A None.

Q What newspaper or magazine articles had you seen suggesting that the President was in poor health? (3)

A None.

Q What indication did you have that the parade might have to be canceled? (3)

A None.

Q When did you first learn about the parade's cancellation? (3)

A I read about it in the *New York Times* two days before they were supposed to hold the parade.

4. The supervening event totally or substantially frustrated the defendant's foundational purpose:

Q Where were you on Inauguration Day? (4)

A We stayed home in St. Louis.

Q Why didn't you go to Washington and take possession of the plaintiff's apartment? (4)

A There was no reason to. The only reason I wanted to rent the apartment was to view the parade, and there wasn't going to be any parade. They swore the President in in the Oval Room. It was on television, and I could watch television as well in our own living room as I could in the plaintiff's apartment.

5. The defendant's fault was not a contributing cause to the occurrence of the supervening event.

LEGAL RESEARCH REFERENCE:
Murray §202

CHECKLIST FOR THE THIRD LINE OF DEFENSE

___ The conditions to the defendant's duty were neither fulfilled nor excused.

   ___ The plaintiff did not fulfill the conditions.
            and
   ___ There is no applicable excuse.

OR

___ The defendant performed the duty.

OR

___ The duty was discharged by the parties' voluntary acts.

____ A contract of mutual rescission

or

____ A substituted contract

or

____ An immediate accord and satisfaction

or

____ An executory accord

or

____ A release

or

____ A covenant not to sue

or

____ A novation

OR

____ The duty was discharged by operation of law.

____ Impossibility

or

____ Financial impracticability

or

____ Frustration of purpose

FOOTNOTES

[1] In an attesting certificate, the signatory usually certifies that (1) he or she is the custodian of certain official records and (2) the attached document is a true and accurate copy of the original official record in the signatory's custody. If the court can judicially notice or presume the authenticity of that signature, an attesting certificate is enough to authenticate the attached copy. However, sometimes the signatory is a foreign official or a low-ranking domestic official, and the court is unwilling to treat the attesting certificate as self-authenticating. The proponent of the document must then attach an authenticating certificate. In an authenticating certificate, the signatory usually certifies that (1) he or she has a certain official position (a high-ranking, domestic position), (2) he or she is familiar with the position of the person who signed the attesting certificate, and (3) the signature affixed to the attesting certificate is the authentic signature of the holder of that position. This chain of attesting and authenticating certificates makes the copy self-authenticating.

[2] Mineral Park Land Co. v. Howard, 172 Cal. 289, 156 P.458 (1916) ("10 or 12 times as much.")

CHAPTER 15

The Last Line of Defense—How to Establish Theories of Defense to Damages

Sec.

Sec. 15-1. Introduction

The last line of defense is a theory attacking the remedy the plaintiff seeks. The last line is often the most important; even if the plaintiff convinces the jury that a contract was formed and breached, the plaintiff's victory is hollow when the jury returns a small verdict. In most cases, a small plaintiff's verdict represents a defense victory. To achieve that victory, the defense can invoke both general and contractual limitations on damages.

> **LEGAL RESEARCH REFERENCE:**
> Murray §§219-20
> White & Summers §§6-1, 7-1

Sec. 15-2. General Limitations on Damages—The Five Basic Defense Attacks

Under the common law and most statutory schemes, the Contracts defendant has five basic theories for limiting the plaintiff's recovery. These five arguments serve as a checklist for defense attacks on damages.

a. Attack #1: The Plaintiff Did Not Suffer Any Economic Loss

This argument is the most palatable to the jurors. The defense can virtually concede formation and breach but argue during summation that the breach is "only technical."

In most cases, this argument is relatively simple to present. Present your own evidence of the market price to show that the market price equalled the contract price and, hence, that damages were zero. You can call an expert real estate appraiser to show that the market price equalled the contract price and, hence, that there were no damages. Or call your expert real estate appraiser to show that the deviations from the construction contract's plans and specifications did not diminish the property's fair market value. In most cases, the attack is straightforward disproof of the events and conditions the plaintiff relies on to show damages. The defense presents its disproof of the events and conditions in roughly the same evidentiary fashion as the plaintiff presents the proof.

The most complex type of case for the defense is a case where an expansible seller is seeking lost profits as damages. We analyzed this recovery in Section 9-7b. There are at least two ways in which the defense can disprove a loss of profits. First, the defense can show that the plaintiff's supplier could not have filled the plaintiff's order for an additional product. Suppose that the breach occurred in July. The defendant calls the general manager of the plaintiff's supplier. After identifying himself, the general manager testified:

Q   How many new orders did you accept in July?
A   None.
Q   Why not?
A   It turned out that we overextended ourselves in the first part of the year.
Q   What do you mean "overextended"?
A   We fell behind in our production schedule.
Q   How far behind did you fall?
A   By the end of June, we were about a month behind.
Q   How did you catch up?
A   We had to tell all our retailers that we wouldn't take new orders during July. We'd fill the orders that were already in, but we had to put everything else off until August.

Evidence of the supplier's inability to fill a new order disproves the loss of profits; if the plaintiff's supplier could not have filled the order, the plaintiff would not have been able to make an additional sale that month.

Second, the defense can show that demand slackened. Evidence of decreased demand also disproves a loss of profits; if there was no demand, the plaintiff could not have made a second sale. The best evidence of decreased demands is the plaintiff's own business records. The records can be introduced under Federal Evidence Rule 801(d) (2) (admissions) or 803(6) (business entries). It is best to show not only a general decline in demand but, moreover, the plaintiff's inability to resell the product the defendant contracted to buy. Check the plaintiff's records for several months following the alleged breach to trace the demand level and search the records to determine when, if ever, the plaintiff resold the specific product the defendant had contracted to buy. You could cross-examine the plaintiff in this fashion:

Q You agreed to sell this car to my client in January. Is that correct?
A Yes.
Q And the car's identification number was 1447981?
A Right.
Q Isn't it true that before the end of January, my client told you that he wouldn't accept the car?
A I think it was the 28th or 29th of January. It was right near the end of the month.
Q Isn't it a fact that you weren't able to sell that car during February?
A Right.
Q And you couldn't sell it in March. Could you?
A You're right.
Q Nor could you find a buyer in April. Could you?
A Yes. We just couldn't get it off our hands.
Q Isn't it a fact that in May, you sent the car back to the manufacturer in Detroit?
A That's correct.

b. Attack #2: The Defendant's Breach Did Not Cause the Plaintiff's Economic Loss

Even if the plaintiff sustained an economic loss, the defendant is liable only if the defendant's breach caused the loss. The defendant should negatively attack causation and, whenever possible, offer an alternative explanation of the loss' cause.

1. An attack on causation

The attack on causation does not have to be completely negative in tone. Quite to the contrary, the attack sometimes gives the defendant an opportunity to present affirmative evidence, portraying the defendant in a better light. For example, suppose that plaintiff sues for breach of warranty. The defense is that although the goods are now defective, the goods were in the warranted condition when they left the defendant's plant; the defect developed later when some other cause came into play.

To support this defense, some judges permit the defense to show the defendant's customary quality control procedures.[1] Proof of the defendant's safety and inspection procedures is logically relevant to diminish the probability that the defendant's manufacturing procedures caused the defect. Under Federal Evidence Rule 406, evidence of the defendant's customary inspection procedures is competent to show that the product the defendant delivered to the plaintiff was inspected and checked before delivery. The defendant's quality control chief could testify:

Q How many of your generators are checked when they come off the assembly line?

A   All of them. We inspect 100% of them when they come off.

Q   Who conducts the inspections?

A   My quality control people.

Q   What is their background?

A   Each of them has at least a B.S. degree, and they've all worked for me for at least four years.

Q   How do they inspect the generators?

A   They have a checklist of tests to run when the generator comes off the assembly line.

Q. How many tests are there?

A   There are a total of 15.

> [*The defense attorney should show that the checklist includes tests for the very quality the plaintiff claims the product lacked. The defense attorney should question the witness in detail about those tests to create the inference that the defect would have been discovered if it had existed.*]

The plaintiff may argue that under Evidence Rule 403, the judge has discretion to limit or exclude the defense's quality control evidence. However, if the defense offers to prove that the quality control inspection includes tests for the very defect the plaintiff claims, the defense evidence has substantial probative value under Rule 402; and on its face, Rule 403 authorizes exclusion only when the probative dangers "substantially outweigh" the probative value. Make an explicit offer of proof under Rule 103(a) (2); make it crystal clear to the judge that the quality control procedures included tests specifically tailored to detect the defect the plaintiff alleges.

2. Offer an alternative explanation for the loss

Standing alone, a defense attack on causation rarely satisfies the jury. The jurors will naturally be curious about the cause of the plaintiff's loss, and they usually will not be content with an attack on the plaintiff's theory of causation. In addition to launching an attack, the defense should offer the jury a plausible, alternative explanation of causation. If the defense fails to do so, the plaintiff will argue during closing: "Ladies and gentlemen, it's undisputed in this case that my client suffered a loss. The defendant has never denied that. The defendant has suggested that his breach didn't cause the loss, but note that the defendant hasn't even attempted to identify another cause of the loss. It's undeniable that the loss occurred, and there's only one possible cause that's been proven—the defendant's breach. The defendant hasn't even suggested another cause, and we all know that the defendant would tell us all about that other cause if that cause existed. The defendant hasn't told us anything about that other cause because it doesn't exist."

GENERAL ECONOMIC CONDITIONS

The defense can point to a general economic downturn as the cause of the plaintiff's loss. Suppose that the plaintiff alleges that the defendant breached a covenant not to compete and that the defendant's competition caused the plaintiff's volume to decline by 10% in 1981. Call a forensic economist as a witness and qualify the economist as an expert under Evidence Rule 702. Then have the economist authenticate market reports for the entire industry or, better still, for the industry within the local geographic area. These reports should fall within the special hearsay exception in Evidence Rule 803(17). The witness then testifies:

Q How does the industry's volume of business in 1981 compare with its volume for 1980?
A As these market reports indicate, there was a sharp downturn.
Q How sharp was the decline?
A Nationally, volume fell off by about 11%.

The expert should show that the decline was widespread throughout the industry:

Q What was the decline for transistor manufacturers in the Northeast?
A They did a little better than average. They dipped only 9%.
Q What about manufacturers in the West?
A They were hard hit. Their volume went down 13%, but all the losses are grouped around 10 or 11%.
Q How did the size of the firm affect the decline?
A Not much. The biggest manufacturers weathered it perhaps a bit better than most, but all the way up and down the line there was a 10 or 11% decline.

Finally, if possible, show that the plaintiff lacked the characteristic that best enabled companies to resist the downward market trend. Assume, for example, that through cross-examining the plaintiff's witnesses and introducing the plaintiff's records, you have already established that the plaintiff exports only 2% of its products. Your expert testifies:

Q Which transistor manufacturers were best able to maintain their volume during 1981?
A These market reports indicate that the only manufacturers who were able to avoid the decline were those with large export markets.
Q What do you mean by a large export market?
A Companies that sold 15 or 20 percent of their products overseas.

CAUSES PERSONAL TO THE PLAINTIFF

Even if there was no general economic downturn, the defendant may be able to point to an alternative cause personal to the plaintiff. Suppose that the plaintiff buyer seeks resale profits. During the plaintiff's case-in-chief, the plaintiff testified that he intended to resell to Graham Company in August and that the defendant's breach prevented him from making the resale. The defendant could call as a witness Graham's chief purchasing agent:

Q What dealings, if any, have you had in the past with the plaintiff?

A   Until about the middle of last year, he used to supply us with transistors for our receivers and radios.

Q   Why do you say "until about the middle of last year"?

A   Well, that's about when our dealings ended.

Q   Who ended them?

A   We terminated the relationship.

Q   Why did you do that?

A   I made the decision because of their constant delays in delivery. They'd quote you delivery in one day, and their trucks would show up three days later. We needed products delivered on time so that we could schedule our production facilities.

Q   When did you make this decision to stop buying from the plaintiff?

A   As I recall, it was in late July. I think our last purchase from the plaintiff was about the middle of that month.

It would be just as effective if the witness testified that the plaintiff gave the witness' firm poor maintenance service—like delivery delays, poor maintenance both provides an alternative cause and portrays the plaintiff in a less favorable light in the juror's eyes. If possible, elicit testimony that the customer informed the plaintiff of its decision to terminate and the basis for its decision. That testimony is not only relevant to attack the plaintiff's damages claim; the jury may infer that the plaintiff's damages claim was knowingly false and discount the plaintiff's general credibility.

CAUSES PERSONAL TO THE PLAINTIFF'S CUSTOMER

Finally, the defendant may be able to premise an alternative cause on a reason personal to the plaintiff's customer. Rather than calling the customer's purchasing agent, the defense could call the customer's general manager:

Q   What was your firm's financial situation in July and August of last year?

A   I'm afraid that we were in pretty bad shape.

Q   What do you mean by that?

A   Our cash flow situation was real bad, and we had to slow things down. As I recall, we temporarily laid off one quarter of our work force.

Q   How did this affect your transistor purchases during August?

A   Saying that it affected them would be a real understatement. We didn't make any purchases at all. We used up what we had in inventory, and we didn't start ordering transistors again until September.

Here too you should establish that the plaintiff knew that the plaintiff could not resell to the customer:

Q   What, if anything, did you tell the plaintiff about your decision not to buy transistors?

A   I personally phoned the plaintiff and told him point-blank about our decision.

Q   When did you make this phone call to the plaintiff?

A   I think it was late in the month of July.

Q   How do you know that it was the plaintiff you spoke with?
A   I've known him for over 12 years. I recognized his voice.

This testimony has the dual effect of rebutting the damages claim and impeaching the plaintiff's truthfulness.

c.   Attack #3: The Plaintiff Neglected to Mitigate the Economic Loss

The plaintiff may not recover damages the plaintiff could have reasonably mitigated. In some cases, reasonable action on the plaintiff's part can completely prevent any loss. In other cases, the plaintiff can reduce the amount of the loss. The foundation for a mitigation defense includes proof that

1. After the alleged breach, there was action the plaintiff could have taken. Suppose that the plaintiff was the buyer, and you want to prove that the plaintiff could have covered. The defense can present documentary evidence that cover was possible. For example, one of the defendant's employees can authenticate a publication as an accepted market report. Then, under Evidence Rule 803(17), the defense may use the report's contents as substantive proof that the supply situation would have permitted cover. Assume that the alleged breach occurred in early March:

    Q   According to defense exhibit A, how did the supply in March compare with the supply in February?
    A   It was about the same. The factories' production had been steady for several months.
    Q   How did the supply in March of this year compare with supply in March of the previous year?
    A   Supply increased a bit. By weight, the production this March was about 7% greater than the production in March of the previous year.

    The most convincing proof is the testimony of someone similarly situated to the plaintiff. The defense should call as a witness someone in the same line of business as the plaintiff. The defense should show any striking similarities between the plaintiff's business and the witness' business. Of course, the first step in this argument is to elicit selected characteristics of the plaintiff's business during cross-examination of the plaintiff: located 100 miles south of Chicago, $160,000 in annual sales, and 5 assembly line employees. Later, conduct the direct examination of your witness to highlight the similarities:

    Q   Where is your plant located?   (1)
    A   It's approximately 70 miles to the south of Chicago.
    Q   How many employees do you have working on your assembly line?   (1)
    A   We usually carry about 6 assembly line workers on our payroll.
    Q   What was your total for sales last year?   (1)
    A   I think that the ballpark figure was $150,000.

Some judges will permit you to preface your questions with declarative sentences, reminding the jurors of the plaintiff's testimony:

Q   Now the plaintiff has testified that he has 5 assembly line workers. How many employees do you have working on your assembly line?   (1)
A   We usually carry 6 assembly line workers on our payroll.

However, most judges will sustain an objection to these prefatory sentences. Finally, after establishing the similarities between the plaintiff's and witness' firms, elicit the witness' testimony that the witness' firm was able to obtain adequate supplies in March:

Q   What difficulty, if any, did you have getting steel for your manufacturing operations during March?   (1)
A   I can't recall any problems that we had.
Q   How many of the orders that you placed for steel in March were filled?   (1)
A   As I recall, all of them were.
Q   How quickly was the steel discovered?   (1)
A   At the latest, we got the steel a week after placing the order.

2. The action the plaintiff could have taken would have eliminated or reduced the plaintiff's loss. The defendant must make certain that the record reflects the price at which the plaintiff could have resold or recovered. If the defense evidence is in documentary form, read the price data into the record as well as the supply data. If the evidence is the oral testimony of a witness in the same line of business as the plaintiff, have the witness testify to the prices the witness paid or obtained and use the witness to authenticate market reports admissible under Evidence Rule 803(17).

LEGAL RESEARCH REFERENCE:
Murray §§227, 229

d.   Attack #4: The Plaintiff's Damages Are Uncertain and Speculative

Some jurisdictions apply the certainty requirement to both the amount and the fact of damage. The defendant can point to three different sources of uncertainty in the amount of damages.

1.   The lack of an established market price for the product

One way to show the uncertainty in the damages' amount is to establish that there is no ascertainable market price for the product. Antiques and classic artwork are good examples. As your witness, call an experienced antique dealer. After qualifying the witness as an expert under Evidence Rule 702, question the witness along these lines:

Q   How do you determine the value of a piece of antique furniture?
A   It's an awfully subtle type of determination. You've got to weigh many factors, including the stylistic preferences of the buyer.

Q   What formula can you use to determine the market value?

A   There isn't any. You can't just take the original purchase price and subtract depreciation, if that's what you mean by a formula. Quite to the contrary, many of these antiques have appreciated well above their original purchase price. Their current value may be many times their original purchase price.

Q   What trade magazines, if any, report the market value of antiques?

A   There are magazines for dealers and collectors, but they really don't report market prices. They report the prices paid for individual pieces, but that's no guarantee that any other piece of the same description can command the same price. If it's in somewhat different condition and the buyer has different tastes, the price would be much different.

Q   What market places are there for antiques like the New York Stock Exchange?

A   They don't exist. You go to a store or an auction, but you don't have an established market for antiques the way you do for stocks or gain or cars. Antiques are too individual for that.

2. *The newness of the plaintiff's business*

Some jurisdictions still religiously adhere to the new business rule that the profits of a new business are too uncertain to be recoverable as damages. If the defendant chooses to rely on this rule, the defendant should lay this foundation:

1. The length of time the plaintiff had been in business before the time of the alleged breach. The defendant may be able to use the plaintiff's own records to prove the time period. Jurisdictions vary on their definition of "new business," but you may assume in most jurisdictions following the rule that a business will be treated as new if it had been in existence less than one year. You should research local law to determine how strict or liberal your courts are in defining "new business."

2. Present a forensic economist's testimony that in this industry, profits are unpredictable in the first few years of a business' operation. Unpredictability is especially common in service industries in which the venture's success in developing goodwill and attracting clientele can depend on personal factors. Suppose that because of the defendant contractor's delay, the plaintiff had to delay opening her realty office. As your witness, call a forensic economist who has studied the real estate industry. After qualifying the economist as an expert, ask:

Q   How easily can you determine the probable profits of a real estate office in its first year of operation?

A   Gee. That would be virtually impossible to do.

Q   Why?

A   There's a qualitative difference between manufacturing industries and service industries, especially real estate.

Q   What is the difference?

A   So much of the firm's success depends upon the personalities of the people in the firm. If you're talking manufacturing, your steel beams either will or will not stand up under so much stress. But it's much tougher for a seller to objectively decide which realty firm to hire to sell his house. As I said, a lot depends on how you hit it off with the real estate agent on a personal level.

Q   What data would you need to make a prediction, based on reasonable economic certainty, of a real estate agency's first year profits?

A   I don't care how much data you give me. There's still the heavy reliance on the personal element, and I couldn't honestly give you a prediction in terms of certainty.

Q   What data would you need to make a prediction, based on reasonable economic probability?

A   I could give you a prediction, based on probability, after the agency has been open for about three years. That seems to be a make or break point in the realty business; the studies show that if you haven't hit an average profit margin by then, you're probably going to be closing your doors soon. But until you're that far into the history of the business, I can't even give you a probabilistic prediction. There are too many variables involved.

3.   The terms of the contract

A third source of uncertainty in the damages' amount is the terms of the contract. The defendant should show that

1.   There is an indefinite term in the contract. Requirements and output contracts are classic illustrations of this problem. Rather than naming a specific quantity, the contract defines the quantity as the seller's output or the buyer's needs. If the contract was oral, the defendant can testify directly that the parties agreed only to the requirements or output rather than a specific number. If the contract is written, quote the quantity term to the jurors.

2.   Show that there is no external standard of reference the court can refer to to remove the indefiniteness. If this is the seventh year that the parties have executed a requirements contract, the defendant seller could establish that the quantity the plaintiff ordered varied greatly from year to year:

Q   What was the maximum quantity you delivered in any year to the plaintiff?   (2)

A   115,000 units.

Q   What was the smallest quantity the plaintiff has ordered in any year? (2)

A   Quite a bit under the max. The smallest quantity was 35,000 units.

and that there was no pattern from year to year:

Q   How did the quantity in the second year compare with the quantity in the first year?

A   The second year the order increased in quantity.

Q   How did the third year compare with the second?

A This time the quantity ordered went down.
Q How did the fourth year compare with the third?
A Down again. This was the smallest year.
Q How did the fifth year compare with the fourth?
A This time it went way up. This year it hit the top.
Q How did last year compare with the fifth year?
A It dropped again.

When there is an erratic pattern, the defense can effectively use an audio-visual aid. The chart, depicting sharp increases and declines, is graphic proof of the uncertainty in the quantity amount.

You should not automatically make an uncertainty argument whenever the facts support the argument. By establishing the damages' uncertainty, you are proving the inadequacy of the plaintiff's remedy at law—and playing into the plaintiff's hands if the plaintiff wants specific performance. Make this argument when

—specific performance is impossible, for example, when the object you contracted to deliver to the plaintiff is no longer in existence,
—the court lacks equity jurisdiction to decree specific performance, or
—the plaintiff did not pray for equitable relief, and under the local pleading rules it is now too late for him or her to amend the prayer.

Further, remember that the courts almost never use the certainty requirement as a basis for denying the plaintiff all relief. Rather, they usually employ the requirement as the rationale for awarding damages on a more certain basis such as reliance damages. In a given case, particularly when the contract was going to be a losing proposition for the plaintiff, the plaintiff's reliance damages (out-of-pocket expenditures) may exceed normal expectation damages. In this situation, the defendant may well prefer that the court award the plaintiff normal expectation damages. Before urging an uncertainty argument, make certain that it is tactically advisable for you to raise the argument.

LEGAL RESEARCH REFERENCE:
Murray §226

e. **Attack #5: The Plaintiff Is Seeking Special Damages, and at the Time of Contracting the Defendant Could Not Reasonably Foresee These Damages**

As previously stated, when the plaintiff seeks special damages, the rule of *Hadley v. Baxendale* applies: The plaintiff must prove that at the time of contracting, the special damages were "within the parties' contemplation"—that is, given the special circumstances the defendant was aware of, the defendant should have foreseen that a breach would cause this type of damage. The defense approach to this argument is strikingly similar to its approach to argument #2 on causation. As we stated when we were discussing causation, the jurors are usually not satisfied with a negative attack on causation; they want to hear an alternative, plausible theory of causation from the defense. In a similar vein, the jurors rarely accept the defendant's flat denial that he or she could foresee the type of loss the plaintiff suffered. The jurors will want affirmative testimony that the defendant should have foreseen a state of affairs in which the loss would not have occurred. Thus, the foundation should include:

1. The defendant's denial that he or she foresaw the plaintiff's loss. If the plaintiff buyer is suing for lost resale profits, the defendant should emphatically deny foreseeing that in the event of a breach, the plaintiff would be unable to buy substitute goods to make the resale. Suppose that the defendant promised to supply the plaintiff's requirements during a six-month period. The defendant testifies:

   Q   What did you think the supply situation would be during these six months?   (1)
   A   I assumed that the supply in our part of the country was going to be pretty steady.

   If the defendant communicated that belief to the plaintiff, the defendant may describe his or her statement to the plaintiff:

   Q   Before you signed exhibit three (the contract), what, if anything, did you tell the plaintiff about the probable supply situation during these six months?   (1)
   A   The plaintiff told me that he was relieved to have a guaranteed supply of quality materials. I responded by saying that I was also happy with the deal. I told him that I thought there was a good possibility of a bumper supply in the next couple of months and I was as happy with his price as he was with my guarantee.

   The defendant's statement is not subject to a hearsay objection. It is arguably admissible as a declaration of the defendant's state of mind under Evidence Rule 803(3). Alternatively, the defense can argue that it is logically relevant to show its effect on the plaintiff's state of mind —the plaintiff's belief and, hence, a mutual assumption that supply would be adequate during the coming six months. If the statement is logically relevant for that purpose, it is admissible as nonhearsay under Evidence Rule 801(c).

2. The defendant should corroborate his or her belief by showing that the defendant's only reasonable assumption was to foresee a state of affairs in which the loss would not have occurred. The situation causing the loss was a sudden decline in supply. Take the converse of the situation which caused the loss. Prove that the converse was foreseeable. As a witness, call an experienced member of the industry and have that witness authenticate reports of supply data for the past few years. The reports' contents will then fall within the hearsay exception

in Rule 803(17). Assume that the plaintiff and defendant entered their contract in July:

Q According to these reports, what was the total production in July of this year? (2)

A That month total production for the U.S. was 75,000 units.

Q What was the average monthly production over the preceding two years? (2)

A It was real steady. It averaged out about 70,000 units a month.

Q What was the highest monthly production during that two year period? (2)

A 90,000 units.

Q What was the lowest monthly production during that period? (2)

A 60,000.

Q Before last July, what was the last time that monthly production has been below 15,000 units (*the production the month the plaintiff unsuccessfully attempted to buy goods for the resale*)? (2)

A You'd have to go way back to 1963 to find a month with production that low.

3. It is ideal if you can pinpoint the cause of the unforeseen event and illustrate how unexpected that event was. The jurors are naturally curious, and they will be much more inclined to accept your unforeseeability argument after you have identified the cause of the unforeseeable events. Have the experienced member of the industry testify:

Q Why did production decline so sharply in September? (3)

A It was a combination of things.

Q What things? (3)

A You see, other than the defendant, there are three big producers. And it just so happened that all three were temporarily put out of production at the same time.

Q How did that happen? (3)

A As best I recall, one was hit by a strike, the second had to shut down its plant because of a gas explosion, and the third closed temporarily because of a tornado that went through the town where the plant is located.

Q When was the last time that all three of these manufacturers were closed at the same time? (3)

A Even as far back as I go, I can't remember when that's even happened before.

Q How long have you been in this industry? (3)

A Almost thirty years now, and I can't remember that ever happening before.

LEGAL RESEARCH REFERENCE:
Murray §§224-25

Sec. 15-3.   Contractual Limitations on Damages

Even if the defendant cannot capitalize on any common-law or statutory restriction to preclude or limit the plaintiffs' recovery, there may be a restriction built into the contract. Contractual restrictions can take several forms. First, a contract provision may exclude any recovery for certain types of injury. For example, Uniform Commercial Code 2-719(3) deals with contract provisions totally excluding damages for personal injuries. Second, the contract may exclude damages but substitute another remedy such as repair and replacement of the goods. U.C.C. 2-719(1) (a) governs substituted remedies. Third, the contract clause may limit the amount of damages recoverable. U.C.C. 2-718(1) relates to such stipulated damages provisions.

When the plaintiff attacks a contractual limitation the defense is relying on, the defendant should prove compliance with the U.C.C. and common-law doctrines such as illegality; negatively, show that you did not violate any of these doctrines. However, it is a serious mistake to go on the defensive and permit the plaintiff to capture the psychological initiative in the suit. Go on the offensive and show the jurors affirmatively that the contractual limitation is procedurally and substantively fair. More specifically, your foundation should include proof that

1. The plaintiff's assent to the limitation was knowing.
2. The plaintiff's assent was voluntary.
3. The limitation is substantively fair; the defendant had a special reason for imposing the limitation, and the plaintiff received a *quid pro quo* for assenting to the limitation.

a. Knowing Assent

The evidentiary techniques that can be used to establish procedural unconscionability apply here as well. The plaintiff presumably introduced the contract (exhibit two) during the plaintiff's case-in-chief. The defendant should use the exhibit to show that the limitation was conspicuous:

Q   What is the title of the tenth clause in exhibit one?
A   It says "Limitation of Remedies."
Q   What color is most of the lettering on the exhibit printed in?
A   Most of it is in plain black.
Q   What color is "Limitation of Remedies" printed in?
A   It's red.
Q   How does the size of the print of "Limitation of Remedies" compare with the size of the rest of the print on the page?
A   I don't know the technical terms like six-point type, but I can see that the print is at least twice the size of the rest of the print on the page.

Under U.C.C. 1-201(10), language is "conspicuous" if it is "in capitals" or "in larger or other contrasting type or color." When the provision would strike an ordinary person as conspicuous, use audio-visual aids. Prepare exact copies for all the jurors, or mount a photographic enlargement for their view, or convert that page into a transparency and use an overhead projector. Use the same audio-visual aid during summation when you argue that "business people have to walk into deals with their eyes open, and any reasonable people with their eyes open would have seen the fifth clause of this contract staring them right in the face."

When the contract clause is plainly worded, stress that. The ideal wording for the defense includes such common expressions as "as is" and "with all faults," mentioned in U.C.C. 2-316(3) (a). The defendant should read that language aloud to the jurors during his or her testimony, and the defense attorney should underscore that language during closing: "Ms. Aubright (the defendant) didn't try to hide this clause from the plaintiff. The clause isn't buried under a lot of fancy expressions and lawyer talk. The clause comes right out and says that you buy 'as is.' Nothing could be clearer. You don't even have to be a business person to understand what 'as is' means."

b. Voluntary Assent

During summation, you also want to be in a position to argue that "no one forced the plaintiff to enter into this bargain. Nobody held a shotgun to his head. The plaintiff entered it on his own accord—completely freely and voluntarily." To have the factual ammunition for that closing argument, you can prove that the plaintiff is a good-sized business establishment with obvious bargaining power. On cross-examination of the plaintiff, ask:

Q Isn't it true that your company has been in existence for more than 23 years?
A Yes.
Q Isn't it a fact that you have over 1,700 employees?
A That's right.
Q Isn't it correct that last year, your gross sales exceeded seventy million dollars?
A Yeah.

If the defendant's firm is smaller, elicit the corresponding statistics during the direct examination of the defendant:

Q How long has your company been in business?
A Three years.
Q How many employees do you have?
A 650.
Q Last year, what were your gross sales?
A As I recall, they were slightly over $3,900,000.

If a plaintiff is a consumer rather than a business house, show that the plaintiff could have gone elsewhere to buy the product. Have an experienced member of the industry list other nearby stores that sell the same product. Request judicial notice of the bus or subway lines in the community to lay the groundwork for the argument that there was convenient transportation to the other stores. Consider calling as witnesses the other proprietors to testify that they had the product available and that they would have delivered to the plaintiff's residence.

c. Substantive Fairness

Your procedural fairness argument should satisfy the businesspeople and rugged individualists sitting on the jury; they expect the plaintiff to look out for the plaintiff's own interests, and they will have little sympathy for a plaintiff who knowingly and freely entered the contract. However, consumerism has been on the rise in the United States for well over a decade, and you should expect that some of your jurors will have pronounced pro-consumer sentiments. To win over these jurors, you must establish substantive as well as procedural fairness. To establish substantive fairness, you ideally prove two things.

THE NEED FOR THE CONTRACT LIMITATION

First, show that the defendant had a special reason for the contract limitation—a special need for the protection the limitation afforded:

Q   Why did you include this clause in your contract?
A   I had it written that way on the advice of Mr. Philips.
Q   Who is Mr. Philips?
A   He's the business consultant I hired when I was setting up the firm.
Q   What reason did he give you for including that clause in the contract?
A   He told me that I'd have to limit my liability for warranties on the drugs for at least the first couple of years of the firm's existence. He said the big, established drug firms had such a hold on the market that in the first few years, I'd be lucky to make any profit at all. In his opinion, if I opened myself up to paying lots of money on warranties, my firm would never have a chance to get off the ground.

   [*This testimony is not subject to a hearsay objection. Under Federal Evidence Rule 801(c), the evidence can be admitted for the nonhearsay purpose of showing its effect on the defendant's state of mind, that is, the creation of the belief that the contractual limitation was necessary.*]

Then call the business consultant to corroborate the defendant's testimony. In some cases, the defendant's special reason will be very appealing to the jury. For example, the consultant or the defendant may have read an insurance study that a particular type of fraudulent claim is often made and that the fraudulent claim is difficult to unmask. The jurors will readily accept protection against fraudulent claims as a legitimate reason for inserting a contract limitation.

THE QUID PRO QUO

Second, show that the plaintiff received a *quid pro quo* for assenting to the limitation:

Q Before he signed the contract, what, if anything, did the plaintiff say about the tenth clause?

A He asked me why I had included that clause. He said that he's been in this line of business for several years and couldn't remember seeing any clause like it.

Q What did you say then?

A I told him that he was certainly right but that in other respects, I was giving him a better deal than he could get elsewhere.

Q In what respects was that true?

A As I mentioned to him, because I had lower warranty expenses, I was able to offer a slightly lower price than usual and better installation service.

Q How much lower was your price?

A I usually set it at about 3% below the going rate in the county.

Q In what respects was your installation service better?

A During installation, most of the firms in our area use a paint that's guaranteed for only two years. The paint we use is warranted for ten years.

Q What did the plaintiff say then?

A He said that he was happy with the deal and that he thought it was a pretty good trade-off, especially the lower price.

Have an experienced member of the industry corroborate the defendant's testimony that the prevailing market price was higher and that the customary practice was to use inferior paint during installation. Now you are in a position to argue that "Acme didn't ask something for nothing. It's true that the plaintiff agreed to the limitation on damages, but it's just as true that we gave him something—a lower price and better installation. There was nothing unconscionable, illegal, or unfair about the bargain that Acme made with the plaintiff."

The plaintiff may cite Federal Evidence Rule 403 and argue for the exclusion of this evidence as prejudicial. However, you have a strong argument for the admission of the evidence. If the plaintiff has expressly attacked the contract limitation as unconscionable, the evidence is highly relevant. Under U.C.C. 2-302(2), when deciding a clause's conscionability, the court should consider evidence of the clause's "commercial setting, purpose and effect." Alternatively, the judge may accept the argument that the plaintiff has impliedly attacked the clause as unconscionable or a breach of the obligation of good faith under U.C.C. 1-203. In addition, remember that if the judge characterizes the issue as an unconscionability question, the judge decides the issue rather than the jury. A Rule 403 objection has much less force at a bench hearing than it does at a jury trial.

LEGAL RESEARCH REFERENCE:
Murray §§234, 340
White & Summers ch. 12

CHECKLIST FOR THE FOURTH LINE OF DEFENSE

____ The plaintiff did not suffer any economic loss.

OR

____ The defendant's breach did not cause the plaintiff's economic loss.

    ____ A negative attack on causation.
           and
    ____ Offer an alternative explanation for the loss.

OR

____ The plaintiff neglected to mitigate the economic loss.

OR

____ The plaintiff's damages are uncertain and speculative.

    ____ The lack of an established market for the product.
           or
    ____ The newness of the plaintiff's business.
           or
    ____ The terms of the contract.

OR

____ At the time of contracting, the defendant could not reasonably foresee the damages.

OR

____ A provision of the contract precludes recovery of the damages.

    ____ The plaintiff's assent to the provision was knowing.
           and
    ____ The plaintiff's assent was voluntary.
           and
    ____ The provision was substantively fair.

FOOTNOTE

[1] Pulley v. Pacific Coca-Cola Bottling Co., 68 Wash.2d 778, 415 P.2d 636 (1966); Bernstein, *Evidence of Producer's Due Care in a Products Liability Action*, 25 Van.L.Rev. 513 (1972).

PART IV

The Post-Evidence Stages of the Trial

CHAPTER 16

Jury Instruction Tactics—How to Get the Trial Judge's Seal of Approval on Your Theory and Theme

Sec. 16-1. Introduction

At this point in the trial, the parties have presented all their evidence, but the attorneys have not yet delivered their summations. In most major cases, the judges and attorneys now adjourn into the judge's chambers for an informal instruction conference. Note that the court reporter is usually absent; if anything occurs at the conference that you may want to challenge on appeal, make certain that the judge calls the reporter in and has your objection noted for the record.

The conference is a neglected advocacy tool. Most counsel use the conference for the obvious purpose of hammering out the final charge to the jury. However, as we shall attempt to point out in this chapter, there are several other useful objectives an imaginative counsel can pursue at the instructions conference.

Sec. 16-2. Determining the Content of the Jury Instructions

The first function performed at the conference is deciding which instructions to read to the jury during the final charge. The judge often lists the instructions he or she intends to give and then asks the attorneys whether they have any objections, modifications, or additions. The instructions ordinarily cover such topics as the respective responsibilities of the judge and jurors, the governing substantive law, evidentiary matters, deliberation procedures, and any special finding procedures. How can the attorneys shape the instructions to their clients' advantage?

a.   General Considerations

To help unify your case and set up your closing argument, request instructions on your theory and theme.

THEORY INSTRUCTIONS

The *theory* instructions will be the instructions on the substantive law. In a jurisdiction with pattern or standard instructions, even before trial began you should have been able to anticipate the approximate wording of the substantive law instruction on your theory. You should have been paraphrasing this instruction whenever you stated your theory during the trial— during the voir dire, opening statement, and direct examination; if you have, the jury will hear a familiar echo when the judge reads the final charge to the jurors. Tender a modified pattern instruction with the parties' actual names substituted for "the plaintiff" and "the defendant." If you personalize the substantive law instruction on your theory, that instruction will stand out when the jurors hear it; its concrete diction will contrast sharply with the abstract terms in most of the other jury instructions.

You occasionally will not have the opportunity or duty to use a pattern instruction. Some jurisdictions do not have standard instructions; other jurisdictions treat their pattern instructions as mere guidelines and give the trial judge discretion to use other instructions; or your theory may relate to such a novel Contract doctrine (*e.g.*, promissory estoppel as a hybrid cause of action) that your jurisdiction's pattern instructions do not cover the doctrine. In these cases, you should submit a special instruction to the judge. Submit the special in writing and accompany it with a memorandum of law. The memo will ideally include two things: (1) substantive Contract law decisions accepting the proposition of law stated in your special instruction; and (2) an indication that other jurisdictions have approved the wording of your proposed special. When you are searching for approved instructions from other jurisdictions, consult E. Devitt & C. Blackmar, Federal Jury Practice and Instructions—Civil and Criminal (3d ed. 1977) and California Jury Instructions—Civil (Book of Approved Jury Instructions) (6th ed. 1977). Both texts contain an extensive set of well-written Contract instructions.

THEME INSTRUCTIONS

In addition to theory instructions, you will want at least one or two instructions highlighting your *theme*. Your theme may be the fact that although the defendant denies forming a contract, the defendant prepared goods for shipment to your client—something the defendant habitually does not do until after accepting an offer. Request instructions on prior inconsistent conduct and the value of habit evidence. Remember that in a minority of jurisdictions, including the federal courts, the trial judge retains the common-law power to comment on the evidence and identify permissive inferences for the jury. If your theme relies upon circumstantial evidence, it would be most helpful if the judge agreed to comment on the evidence and inform the jury that if they believe circumstances *A*, *B*, and *C*, they may draw inference *D* supporting your theme. These are evidentiary instructions that you can integrate into the discussion of your theme during summation. You can strengthen your theme argument by citing the instruction placing the judge's *imprimatur* on the theme.

b. Special Strategies for the Plaintiff and Defendant

1. Strategy for the plaintiff

The plaintiff wants a set of instructions that is short and simple. Most of us struggled in law school to grasp abstract legal concepts. Imagine how difficult it is for laypersons to understand those concepts when their "education" consists of a single lecture by the judge. The longer and more complex the jury instructions, the more likely the jury is to become confused; and if they are confused, they may resolve doubt against the plaintiff with the burden of proof. If you were urging several theories at trial but one proved unexpectedly weak, consider abandoning the theory at the instructions conference; request that the judge not even instruct on that theory. Further, to counter defense attempts to make the final charge lengthier and more complex, the plaintiff should be ready to urge the various objections discussed in subsection C, *infra*.

The plaintiff also prefers instructions worded affirmatively: "You *may* find for the plaintiff if. . . ." Affirmatively worded instructions set a positive tone for the jury charge, and they are easier for the jurors to understand.

The plaintiff finally desires generally worded instructions. The more generally worded the instruction, the more room the jurors have to maneuver during deliberations. If the instruction requires only that the plaintiff "notify" the defendant of a breach of warranty, during deliberation the jurors can find alternative methods of notice. The jurors may not accept the specific notice theory the plaintiff argued during summation, but the generally worded instruction permits the jurors to develop their own notice theory during deliberations.

2. Strategy for the defense

If the defense's primary thrust is either confusion or the weakness of the plaintiff's evidence, the defense attorney should request instructions with four qualities.

First, the set of instructions should be lengthy and complex. The defense should request an instruction on all the theories of liability and defense raised by the facts. Multiple instructions not only tend to confuse the jurors; they often set up strawman plaintiff's theories that the defense can easily knock down during summation.

Second, the instructions should be negatively worded: "You *cannot* find for the plaintiff unless. . . ." It is ideal if at the end of this sentence, the judge enumerates a long list of facts the jury must find before returning a plaintiff's verdict: "unless the plaintiff satisfies you by a preponderance of the evidence that

1. On July 1st, the plaintiff and defendant entered into a contract to buy the plaintiff's house;
2. The plaintiff fulfilled the condition of having the house in clean condition by July 11th;
3. On July 11th, the plaintiff fulfilled the condition of tendering a deed for the property to the defendant;
4. On July 11th, the defendant refused to tender a check for $4,000 to the plaintiff; and
5. On July 11th, the difference between the contract price for the plaintiff's house and its fair market value was $10,000."

The more negative the wording and the longer the enumeration, the heavier the plaintiff's burden of proof will sound to the jury.

Third, the instructions should highlight the plaintiff's burden of proof. A burden of proof instruction is very helpful when the plaintiff seeks equitable relief such as a decree of specific performance. In that situation, the plaintiff may have to satisfy a stricter burden of proof such as clear, positive, and convincing evidence. It is usually to the defense's advantage if the judge amplifies on the instruction on burden of proof.

Finally, the instructions should be worded as specifically as possible. The more specific the instructions, the easier it is for the defendant to convince the jurors that the plaintiff has not sustained the burden of proof. For example, the defense should resist a generally worded instruction that to qualify as an offer, a proposal must have "definite terms." The defense should request an instruction requiring that the jury find "an identification of the parties, a description of the subject matter, a price term, a quantity term, a quality term, and a delivery term."

c.   Objections to Proposed Instructions

The following objections can be made to instructions proposed at the conference:

—*There is no factual support in the record for the proposed instruction.* Suppose that the defense introduced evidence suggesting that the defendant was mistaken at the time of contracting, but there was no evidence that the plaintiff induced or knew of the mistake. The plaintiff may raise this objection against a defense request for a mistake theory instruction.

—*The proposed instruction misstates the facts.*

—*The proposed instruction misstates the law.*

—*The proposed instruction is argumentative.* An argumentative instruction invades the jury's province by applying the law to the facts. This objection often arises when the central issue in the case is the application of a legal standard such as whether a good was "fit for ordinary purposes" under U.C.C. 2-314. The plaintiff may request an instruction tracking U.C.C. 2-314 and using the language, "fit for the ordinary purposes for which such goods are used." However, it would be objectionable if the plaintiff overreached and sought an instruction that the lack of a safety latch was "a good indication" or "strong evidence" that the saw the defendant sold the plaintiff was unfit. That instruction not only states the law; it applies the law—and thereby usurps the jury's function.

— *The proposed instruction is cumulative.* To confuse the jury, the defense often requests special instructions amplifying on the pattern instructions. The plaintiff should resist these requests on the ground that the special would be cumulative.

— *The proposed instruction would be confusing to the jurors.* Instructions that contain undefined, technical terms or double negatives are often subject to this objection.

Sec. 16-3. Other Functions of the Instructions Conference

Although deciding the jury instructions is the foremost purpose of the conference, the conference has other significant uses.

a. Deciding Which Exhibits Will Go into the Deliberation Room with the Jury

An exhibit's admission does not guarantee that the jury will have the exhibit during deliberations. In most jurisdictions, the judge has discretion to determine which exhibits will go to the jury room.

You should certainly request that the judge send the jury exhibits that are important in themselves, for example, the contract itself. Moreover, you want the judge to send the jury exhibits you used as memory aids during the trial. Some trial attorneys try to introduce at least one exhibit during each witness' testimony. They display the same exhibit during closing when they discuss the witness' testimony. Finally, they request that the exhibit go to the jury. The exhibit's presence in the deliberation room will help remind the jurors of the witness' testimony. Do not assume that the judge will automatically send your best exhibits into the deliberation room; make a specific request during the conference.

b. Obtaining Permission to Use Audio-Visual Aids During Summation

During closing, you may want to use demonstrative evidence in addition to the exhibits introduced during trial. For instance, you may want to use a chart listing all the elements of damage or an enlargement of a key jury instruction. It is quite embarrassing if you attempt to use the exhibit without advance permission and the judge interrupts, admonishing you in front of the jury. Clear your audio-visual aids with the judge during the conference.

c. Obtaining Permission to Quote the Jury Instructions During Summation

Some judges absolutely forbid quotation from their instructions. Again, your summation will lose much of its momentum if the judge cuts you off in mid-sentence and chastises you in the jury's hearing. If you have not appeared before this judge before and do not know the judge's practice, ask point blank for permission during the conference.

d. Disposing of Anticipated Objections to Statements During Summation

At the conference, you can request an advance ruling that the opposing counsel may not make a certain remark during closing. You may have appeared against this attorney before, and you know that he likes to make repeated references to the wealth of corporations such as your client even when punitives are not in issue. If you expect that argument and consider it objectionable, raise the objection at the conference. If the judge sustains your advance objection and the opposing counsel nevertheless makes the objectionable statement, you are much more likely to win a mistrial motion. By disregarding the judge's advance ruling, the opposing counsel has demonstrated subjective bad faith—and, more importantly, angered the trial judge.

The other side of the coin is that you may want an advance ruling that you may permissibly make a certain remark during closing. You want to make a particular statement, but you want to avoid the risk of mistrial. Your safest course of action is to seek an advance ruling that your contemplated remark is permissible.

e. Miscellaneous Matters

At the conference, you may make or renew motions such as motions for a nonsuit or mistrial. As we previously stated, in many jurisdictions, to preserve the issue of the legal sufficiency of the plaintiff's evidence for appeal, the defendant must renew the motion at the close of all the evidence. The conference is held after the close of all the evidence. The conference is the most convenient time for renewing the motion.

The instructions conference is one of the most neglected areas of advocacy in trial work. Few trial attorneys realize the full potential and utility of the conference. Some of the most difficult substantive law issues come to a head at the conference when the judge must draft the instructions. Moreover, as we have seen in this chapter, there are several tactics you can employ at the conference to increase the effectiveness of the climax of your case —the closing argument or summation.

CHECKLIST FOR THE INSTRUCTIONS CONFERENCE

____ Request favorable instructions.

    ____ Request
        ____ substantive law instructions on your theory
        ____ evidentiary instructions on your theme.
    ____ If you are the plaintiff, request instructions that are
        ____ short
        ____ simply worded
        ____ worded affirmatively
        ____ generally worded.
    ____ If you are the defendant, request instructions that
        ____ are rather lengthy
        ____ are complex
        ____ are negatively worded
        ____ are worded specifically
        ____ stress the plaintiff's burden of proof.

____ Oppose the other counsel's request for instructions on the grounds that:

    ____ There is no factual support in the record for the proposed instruction.
    ____ The proposed instruction misstates the facts.
    ____ The proposed instruction misstates the law.
    ____ The proposed instruction is argumentative.
    ____ The proposed instruction is cumulative.
    ____ The proposed instruction would be confusing to the jurors.

____ Request that the judge send your exhibits into the deliberation room.

____ Request advance permission to use audio-visual aids during summation.

____ Request advance permission to quote favorable jury instructions during summation.

____ Request an advance ruling forbidding the opposing counsel from making a particular, objectionable comment during summation.

____ Request advance permission to make a particular comment during summation.

____ Renew motions such as motions for a directed verdict.

CHAPTER 17

Delivering a Closing Argument That Hits Hard at Your Theory and Theme

Sec. 17-1. Introduction

The last step in presenting your case to the jury is delivering the closing argument or summation. Many trial attorneys believe that this is the most critical juncture in the trial—when victory can be snatched from the jaws of defeat! That belief probably overstates the role of the summations in most cases. It is difficult to win a case with weak facts during summation although you can easily lose a case with strong facts by delivering a sloppy summation. The summation is usually critical only when the case is very close on the facts. Nevertheless, given the principle of recency, it is important to leave the jurors with a favorable impression just before they retire to deliberate.

The function of the closing argument contrasts with the function of the opening statement. In the opening, you tell the jury *what* your evidence will show. During closing, you tell the jury *why* they should believe your witnesses, make the inferences you desire, and draw the legal conclusions necessary for your verdict. The summation should not be a rerun of the opening statement.

Sec. 17-2. The General Contents and Structure of a Closing Argument

What then should you include in your closing? Many practitioners have found the following structure to be optimal.

a. The Introductory Amenities

At the outset, thank the jurors for their patience and attention during the trial. Briefly explain the role of closing argument: "Ladies and gentlemen, the opposing counsel and I are now going to deliver what are called the closing arguments in this case. This will be our last chance to talk to you before you go into the deliberation room and decide the case. This is my last chance to convince you that the only just verdict in this case is a decision in favor of Mr. Hartman. I'm going to show you why that is the verdict you should return in this case."

b. Restate the Theory of Your Case

Next echo your opening statement: "As you will remember, during my opening statement, I explained Mr. Hartman's position to you." Reiterate your theory of the case. If the judge permits, immediately after restating your theory of the case, quote the judge's instruction on your theory: "In a few moments, her honor will give you the instructions for deciding this case. One of the instructions she will read you states Mr. Hartman's position. I'd ask you to pay special attention when her honor is reading that instruction and especially this wording: . . . ." If the instruction is lengthy or complex, consider placing the instruction in large letters on a chart; the judge has discretion to permit you to do so, and the chart will help the jurors understand the key instruction.

Review your theory and the instruction on the theory slowly for the jurors. You have to enable the jurors to reason to a verdict for your client. As Lawrence Smith states in *Art of Advocacy: Summation* §1.44 (1978):

> Psychology studies show that appeals to reason are better than appeals to emotion. They are more important and more lasting. It appears that the reason for this conclusion is that very strong emotions block out almost entirely the ability to reason. So that if a person is caught up in a storm of emotion, he will have very little memory of what was said. He remembers his feelings about the subject matter, but he will not be in a position to defend those feelings in the jury room. Appeals to emotion, while effective at the time they are given, are not lasting. Thus, if you give an argument which appeals strictly to emotion and if the jury could render its verdict immediately, you might win. But after the judge has charged the jury, and they have probably been to lunch, the appeal to emotion fades and they return to logic, looking for reasons to find in your favor. If your argument has given them no reasons to give you a verdict, you will certainly lose. The emotional appeal of your argument will have faded away.

Even if your closing has aroused some jurors' emotions, the emotional appeal alone will not guarantee a favorable verdict. The judge will cool the jurors' emotions by reading them the final charge, and there will ordinarily be enough conscientious jurors on the panel that there will be a genuine deliberation and an attempt to rationalize the verdict the jurors prefer. This is especially true in jurisdictions in which the jury receives a written copy of the instructions. Explain your theory clearly to aid the jurors in rationalizing a verdict for your client.

c. Simplify the Case for the Jurors

As we stated in the very first chapter, one essential characteristic of a winning case is simplicity. Tell the jurors that this case is relatively simple: "Ladies and gentlemen, I know that you listened to five long days of testimony in this case, but this is really a very simple case." In your next breath, list the elements of your theory that are not in real dispute: "All the witnesses agreed that Mr. Hartman and the defendant entered into an agreement to buy Mr. Hartman's plane"; "It's undisputed that. . . ."; "The plaintiff never denied. . . ."; or "The defendant even conceded that. . . ." Briefly relate the law to the facts and show the jurors that the factual evidence unquestionably establishes most of the elements of your legal theory. It is especially important for the plaintiff and defendants asserting affirmative defenses and counterclaims to simplify their case as much as possible.

d. Identify the Key Disputed Element of Your Theory

After negatively telling the jurors what issues are not in dispute, affirmatively tell the jurors what the key issue is: "There's one real question in this case: Did the defendant make a positive, unconditional statement that he didn't intend to live up to his agreement with Mr. Hartman?"; "This case boils down to one, simple question. . . ."; or "There's only one real dispute between Mr. Hartman and the defendant. . . ." This key issue, of course, is the most controverted element of your theory—and the issue your theme relates to.

e. Argue the Disputed Element of Your Theory by Hammering Away at Your Theme

The nature of the theme argument you make depends on the nature of the key issue in the case. The issue can fall into one of three categories.

1. A credibility issue

The key issue can be which witnesses the jury should believe. For example, suppose that the disputed issue in the case is whether the defendant made an unequivocal anticipatory repudiation. The testimony is direct evidence. The plaintiff testified that the defendant said flatly that he would not perform while the defendant gave contradictory testimony that he said "there is an outside chance" he would not meet the delivery schedule. The case turns on whether the jury believes the plaintiff or defendant. How do you argue a credibility issue?

Begin by *positively bolstering the credibility of your witnesses*. Point out that

—many of your witnesses are "disinterested with no stake in the case,"
—there are "physical facts" supporting your witnesses' version of the incident,
—your witnesses' version is more "plausible" and "consistent with common, everyday experience," and
—the opponent's witnesses "conceded," "admitted," or "never denied" many of the facts your witnesses testified to.

After bolstering your witnesses' credibility, *impeach the opposing witnesses' credibility.* As Professor Younger has pointed out, when a case turns on a credibility issue, you must take the gloves off during closing and hit hard at the opposing witnesses' credibility. A complete, ideal impeachment argument includes five elements:

—Cite the impeaching evidence: "Remember, ladies and gentlemen, that on cross-examination we caught the defendant in no less than six inconsistencies between his testimony today and what he said at the deposition." "The plaintiff's key witness is a convicted felon."
—Explain the significance of the evidence; explain *why* the evidence should lower the witness' credibility in the jurors' eyes: "You heard the evidence that only four months ago, the plaintiff's key witness told an outright lie on his employment application for IBM. A lie—a false, deceitful act. That act gives us some real insight into Mr. Nelson's character. And with that insight, we know that he's not the type of person we can trust." "The defendant's key witness admitted her long friendship with the defendant. They've been close friends ever since high school. We're not saying that she consciously lied today. But it stands to reason that your friendship with a person is going to bias you in that person's favor. It'll affect you subconsciously. When in doubt, you call the question in favor of your friend. That's a natural, human reaction."
—Third, quote or paraphrase any instructions relevant to the impeaching evidence. "In a few minutes, Judge Wilson will give you the instructions in this case. One of those instructions tells you that in deciding whom to believe, you should consider whether a witness has a bias or prejudice." The jury attaches much more weight to the judge's statement than to yours; they discount your statements because they know that you are an advocate—a hired gun. The impeaching evidence will have more impact if the jurors realize that the judge says they may treat the evidence as impeaching. (In some jurisdictions, out of courtesy to the judge, counsel always state that they "believe" that the judge will give a certain instruction.)
—Give the jury an analogy illustrating why the evidence is impeaching.[1] Analogies are useful during closing for several reasons.
    A skillful attorney will use the analogy to bolster his or her own credibility in the jury's mind. Many attorneys preface analogies with such statements as, "This reminds me of a story my father used to tell me when I was a young boy," or "When I was a child, my grand-

mother used to read me a story. . . ." The analogy helps the attorney demonstrate to the jurors "the sort of basic values that make us accept the lawyer as a decent, credible person."[2] The analogy evokes "[t]he reverence for the family relationship" and enhances the jurors' image of the attorney.[3]

The analogy also helps the jurors to understand the impeachment on a more concrete, human level. Suppose that you disproved one aspect of an opposing witness' testimony and the judge is going to give a *falsus in uno, falsus in omnibus* instruction. You could use the famous analogy of the child accompanying the father to dinner at a restaurant: "When they brought out his plate of stew, it looked terrific. But the very first bite he took, the meat was spoiled—rancid. Now what did he do? Did he pick all through that plate, looking for a good piece of meat? Or was he entitled to call the waitress over and ask her please to take it back because it was rancid? What are you entitled to do with the testimony of Mrs. Norman?"[4]

—Finally, and most importantly, integrate *your theme* into the impeachment argument. Mention the theme at least once during your argument. Suppose that you impeached the defendant by prior inconsistent conduct; the defendant denies forming a contract, but the defendant prepared boxes for shipment to the plaintiff and the defendant's practice is not to ready goods for shipment until after forming the contract. In addition to using the tools of the jury instruction and an analogy, remind the jurors of your capsulized theme: "As I said during the opening statement, ladies and gentlemen, the defendant's actions speak louder than words. The defendant's words may deny that he had a contract with Mr. Farrel, but that's not the way the defendant acted."

2. An historical inference issue

A second type of key question is an historical inference issue. You are relying on circumstantial evidence, and you want the jury to draw an inference from the circumstantial evidence that is necessary for your case. For example, in a breach of warranty action, the plaintiff may allege that a defect in the generator the defendant sold the plaintiff caused the fire that destroyed the plaintiff's plant. There was no eyewitness to the start of the fire, and the plaintiff must rely on circumstantial evidence. Or the defendant denies contract formation, and the plaintiff's employee who negotiated with the defendant is now unavailable. As circumstantial proof, the plaintiff has evidence that the defendant shipped some goods conforming to the alleged contract to the plaintiff; but the defendant claims that the goods were sent as samples rather than a delivery under a contract. How do you argue an historical inference issue? There are two basic methods.

One method is to rely on expert testimony. A person qualifies as an expert precisely because the person's knowledge or skill enables the person to draw inferences beyond a layperson's ability. An expert on fires and explosions may have testified that a generator malfunction was the most likely cause of the fire. In this situation, explain to the jury that the historical inference question turns into a *credibility* question: the competence and impartiality of the expert. Then argue this type of case in roughly the same fashion as you would argue any credibility issue. To bolster your expert's credibility, highlight the respects in which your expert's credentials are superior to those of any opposing expert. In addition, stress the factual bases your expert cited for his or her opinion. Tell the jury that your expert did not testify to "some theoretical opinion"; your witness expressed "an expert opinion that has a common sense basis in hard fact."

The second method is to convince the jurors that your inference is more consistent with common sense and ordinary human experience. That is precisely the standard the jurors will resort to when they retire to deliberate. A complete historical inference argument will include these elements:

—Cite the facts that you think are implausible. Emphasize that the opposing party or an opposing witness volunteered these facts on direct by the opposing attorney: "On direct examination by his own attorney, the defendant came up with the story that out of the blue, he just decided to send my client some free samples for inspection."

—Assert that those facts are "implausible," that they are "inconsistent with common human experience," and that "that's just not the way things happen in the real world." Try to put an incredulous tone into your voice when you make these statements.

—Third, quote or paraphrase any relevant instruction. In many jurisdictions, the judge gives the jurors an instruction counseling them to consider their "experience in life and knowledge of the ways of the world" in evaluating the evidence. Almost all jurisdictions have instructions on the value of circumstantial evidence.

—Give the jury an analogy illustrating the value of circumstantial evidence. There are innumerable circumstantial evidence analogies. Circumstantial evidence footprint analogies are quite common—footprints in snow and Robinson Crusoe first seeing Friday's footprints in the sand.

—Last, work *your theme* into your historical inference argument. In the opening statement, you may have dubbed the defense theory "the free sample story." Repeat your theme, and put a disbelieving tone in your voice whenever you say "the free sample story."

3. *A legal standard issue*

The third type of key issue is a legal standard question. There may be little or no question about the historical facts in the case. However, given the historical facts, the jury must decide whether the consumer goods the defendant delivered were "fit for the ordinary purposes for which such goods are used" under U.C.C. 2-314(2) (c); or the judge must decide whether the contract clause was unconscionable under U.C.C. 2-302. The jurors or judge must essentially decide how the legal standard applies to the facts; there is little dispute over either the wording of the legal standard or the facts the standard applies to. How do you argue a legal standard issue? An ideal argument includes these elements:

—First a general call to duty. Mo Levine, the great New York trial attorney, once remarked that the best strategy is to remind the jurors that they are the conscience of the community and that they must render a verdict they can be proud of—a verdict they could describe to their neighbors with pride.

—Next tell the jurors specifically that their basic task is setting a standard in this case. The plaintiff may contend that the saw the defendant sold the plaintiff was so dangerous that it was unfit under U.C.C. 2-314. In that case, tell the jurors "you have to decide whether that saw was fit for its ordinary uses. And in doing that, ladies and gentlemen, you are helping to set the safety standards for this community."

—Third, quote or paraphrase the judge's instruction fixing the legal standard the jury must use.

—In general terms, discuss the effects of a verdict for your side and the opposing side on community standards. "If you find for Mr. Schwartz, you're voting for safety. You're telling every businessperson in this community that when consumers buy dangerous products like saws, they expect those products to be safe. But what message will you be giving the business community if you return a verdict for the defendant? What standards are you setting then?"

—If possible, integrate an analogy into your argument. You might use a story about how, when you were a child, you always accompanied your father to the hardware store. Your father told the store owner about the household project he was working on, and the store owner then carefully selected the tools your father needed. You always liked the store manager; he was a good man—and a good businessman. The jury should signal the business community that they want all merchants to use the same kind of care in selecting goods for their customers.

—Work *your theme* into your argument. In the opening statement, you told the jury that you would present a safety expert's testimony that a knob costing 20¢ could have prevented the accident. Your theme is "The knob would have cost the defendant 20¢. The accident cost my client his arm." Put an accusatory tone in your voice when you repeat that theme during closing.

f.   Concluding Remarks

Just before concluding your argument, restate the theme. If you have especially strong facts supporting the theme, convert one or two of the facts into rhetorical questions: "Is it plausible, is it believable that the defendant all of a sudden decided to send Ms. Jamison some free samples?" Do *not* answer the question; pause, and let the jurors answer the question in their own minds. The jurors will cling to the answer much more tenaciously if they discover it for themselves. Then continue, verbalizing the verdict you want the jurors to return: "We all know the answer to that question. And, ladies and gentlemen, I think we all know that the only just verdict in this case is a verdict in favor of Ms. Jamison and in the amount of $31,000."

Sec. 17-3. Specific Strategies for the Plaintiff and Defendant

In most jurisdictions, there are three summations: the plaintiff's opening summation, the defendant's summation, and the plaintiff's rebuttal summation. Since the plaintiff has the ultimate burden of proof, the plaintiff has the privilege of opening and closing. Having the first and last words is obviously an advantage; the plaintiff can capitalize on the principles of primacy and recency. When the only real defense is going to be an affirmative defense, the defense should consider stipulating to prima facie liability. In some jurisdictions, by doing so, the defendant gains the right of opening and closing.

a. The Plaintiff's Opening Summation

1. The content

The plaintiff ordinarily devotes most of the opening summation to liability rather than to damages. Some trial attorneys prefer to say nothing about damages in the opening summation and then hit hard at damages in the rebuttal summation; they reason that delaying the damages discussion increases its impact and limits the defense's opportunity to respond.

This "sandbagging" tactic is dangerous in the extreme. The scope of the plaintiff's rebuttal argument is limited to true rebuttal, meeting arguments raised for the first time in the defense summation. If the plaintiff attempts this tactic against an experienced defense counsel, that counsel may outsmart the plaintiff. Before beginning the defense summation, the defense counsel may approach the bench; point out that the plaintiff did not mention damages in the opening summation; state that he or she does not intend to discuss damages; and seek an advance ruling that if he or she does not mention damages, the judge will sustain a scope objection when the plaintiff tries to mention damages for the first time in the rebuttal summation. If the judge is willing to sustain the scope objection, the plaintiff's gamesmanship backfires: the jury will never hear argument on damages, and they may return a wholly inadequate plaintiff's verdict. To be on the safe side, devote some of the opening summation to damages. Review all of the elements of damages, cite a dollar figure for each element, and tell the jury the total amount of the desired verdict.

2. *The style*

The plaintiff should deliver the opening summation in a low-key, businesslike tone. Save most of your emotional appeals until the rebuttal summation. A little bit of emotional appeal goes a long way, and too much of it will turn mośt jurors off. During the opening summation, your diction and demeanor should be calm and restrained.

Be visual during closing—just as you should be during opening and the case-in-chief. Use charts enlarging key jury instructions on your theory and theme. Pick up exhibits introduced during your case-in-chief and display them to the jurors. Use the exhibits as memory joggers; a display of the exhibit will help the jury recall the testimony of the witness associated with the exhibit. Shift into the first person, and act out crucial passages of testimony.

b. The Defense Summation

1. *The content*

There are two schools of thought about the heart of the defense summation.

One school urges the defense counsel to try to confuse the jury. Make the jury think that the case is very complex. List all the elements of causes of action and defenses and mention all the weaknesses in all the elements. This school has more adherents in criminal cases than in Contract lawsuits. Its popularity in criminal cases is understandable; because of the fifth amendment, the prosecution has a heavy burden of proof (beyond a reasonable doubt), cannot call the defendant as a witness, and cannot even comment on the defendant's failure to testify. The Contracts plaintiff does not face the same problems; the plaintiff has a relatively light burden in most cases (a preponderance of the evidence), can call the defendant as an adverse witness, and can damn the defendant's failure to testify. Because of the differences between criminal cases and Contract suits, more experienced commercial litigators reject this school of thought.

The second school is the predominant view among experienced commercial litigators. Focus the jury's attention on your theory of the case (the weakest link in the plaintiff's case or the strongest argument for your affirmative defense or counterclaim), and do battle on your theory. Argue for your theory in much the same fashion as the plaintiff would, depending on whether the central issue is a credibility, historical inference, or legal standard question.

DISCUSSING DAMAGES

Should the defendant discuss damages? There are two situations in which the defense should not. We have already mentioned the first situation: The plaintiff neglected damages in the opening summation, and the judge has indicated or you are confident that the judge will sustain a scope objection when the plaintiff attempts to discuss damages for the first time in rebuttal. In this situation, discussing damages plays into the plaintiff's hands and gives the plaintiff an opportunity to discuss damages under the guise of rebuttal. If you avoid discussing damages, there is a good chance that any plaintiff's verdict will be a hollow victory in an inadequate amount.

The second situation is the case in which you think that you have an excellent chance of winning the liability issue. If you spend a good deal of time discussing the plaintiff's damages, some jurors may interpret your discussion as an admission of liability: Why would she devote so much time to talking about damages if she really thought that her client had not breached the contract? In this situation, the boldest defense attorneys make no mention at all of damages.

Others use more cautious strategies. Some initially tell the jury confidently that the jury will not have to reach the damages issue in this case. After all, the only reasonable conclusion is that the defendant did not breach. Next, they give the jury the impression that the judge is forcing them to discuss damages: "However, his honor has to give you instructions on damages, and for that reason I feel obliged to say a few words about damages in this case." Finally, without citing a specific figure to the jury, the defense attorney tries to point out weaknesses in the plaintiff's proof of damages, especially obvious exaggerations. In this way, the defense attorney can hedge against a plaintiff's verdict with little risk that the jurors will interpret the damages discussion as an admission of liability.

Professor Mauet also counsels a cautious strategy. He recommends that the defense attorney use the following language:

> Now, I am going to talk for a moment about damages. I'd be derelict in my duty to my client if I didn't, but I don't want you to think we owe the plaintiff money. However, the plaintiff spent some time on this issue, and I feel there are some things we should answer.[5]

He also recommends that the defense counsel discuss damages before liability; that sequence permits the defense counsel to end on a high note, flatly and vigorously denying the defendant's liability near the end of the summation.[6]

2. The style

In large part, our remarks about the plaintiff's style apply to the defense. Like the plaintiff, the defendant should be as visual as reasonably possible.

And like the plaintiff, the defendant should deliver most of the defense summation in a calm, low-key tone. An understated tone is especially effective on the defense when the plaintiff has used an overly emotional appeal in the opening summation. Point out that the defense will not use such tactics, and with temperate diction and demeanor review your theory and theme.

However, near the end of the defense summation, it is appropriate for the defense attorney to wax tactfully emotional. Without calling the plaintiff a liar, emphasize the facts impeaching the plaintiff's credibility. If you have an affirmative defense such as the plaintiff's fraud or duress, point out that your client is the real victim in the case. If you have a counterclaim, argue that in reality, it is the plaintiff who broke his word and breached your client's trust. End on a high note by reciting your most offensive theme argument and delivering that argument in an accusatory tone.

c.   The Plaintiff's Rebuttal Summation

1.   *The content*

The worst temptation in the plaintiff's rebuttal is to go on the defensive and to deliver your last speech to the jury as a point-by-point rebuttal of the defense summation: "The defense attorney says . . . , but the facts show. . . . The defendant next contends that . . . , but the truth is that. . . ." By structuring your rebuttal in this negative fashion, you surrender the psychological initiative to the defendant. Rather, integrate the defense attacks into a review of your theory of the case. Repeat the first element, and then rebut the defense attacks on that element. Mention the second element, and then meet the defense arguments relating to that element. Impose your theory and your structure on the jury deliberations.

Unless your liability case is so weak that it needs substantial shoring up, devote most of the rebuttal summation to damages. Discuss the elements of damage one by one in the same sequence in which the judge will mention them in the jury instructions. As you mention each element, write its title and dollar figure on a chalkboard or easel; explain why you are using that dollar figure; and then total for your verdict. Make it seem as if the verdict that you want is simple arithmetic.

2.   *The style*

The rebuttal summation is the time for the plaintiff's emotional appeals. Humanize your client and dramatize the facts of the case: When the contract was formed, your client "trusted" the defendant; when the defendant breached, your client was "shocked and disappointed"; the defendant breached "intentionally and in bad faith"; and because of the breach, your client suffered "severe" and (when appropriate) "crushing" economic losses. Make the jurors dislike the defendant—and motivate them to want to return the verdict you have asked for.

Sec. 17-4.   Objections During Summation

There are several objections you can make to the opponent's summation. The etiquette of closing argument is that counsel rarely make objections even when the objections are well-founded. Attorneys usually make objections only when (1) the error is egregious, perhaps warranting a mistrial, or (2) the opposing counsel's summation is flowing smoothly and forcefully, and the objection will interrupt its flow. The most important objections are:

The opposing counsel has misstated the facts. There may be no evidence in the record to support the attorney's statement, or the attorney may be misstating the evidence. In many cases, the judge's only response to this objection is an admonition to the jurors, "The jurors will remember the evidence that they have heard in this case."

The opposing counsel has misstated the law. Be especially attentive when the opposing counsel is paraphrasing one of the jury instructions. It is quite easy for the counsel to slip and misstate the law. For example, after quoting the jury instruction on the burden of proof, the defense counsel may attempt to amplify and explain the expression, "a preponderance of the evidence." The explanation may be a distortion, making the burden sound heavier than it is.

One of the most common misstatements by the plaintiff is a violation of the so-called Golden Rule:

> For example, take the "golden rule" followed in many states. * * *
> It got its name from its function. The rule forbids asking the jurors
> to put themselves in the shoes of one of the parties to the action. It
> is called the "golden rule" because you are not permitted to ask
> the jury to do unto the parties the way they would want things
> done unto themselves.[7]

Hence, in a breach of warranty action under U.C.C. 2-314, the plaintiff may not ask the jurors, "Would you have accepted a saw in that condition?" That question misstates the law; the issue is not whether the jurors would have accepted the good but rather whether the good was acceptable, judged by an objective standard of reasonableness.

The opposing counsel's statement was inflammatory and prejudicial. A statement during summation is objectionable if it is both inflammatory and prejudicial. "Inflammatory" means that the statement naturally tends to arouse the jurors' emotions. However, even as so defined, not all "inflammatory" statements are improper. Thus, although it is usually inadvisable to call an opposing witness a "liar," it is permissible to do so.

To be objectionable, an inflammatory statement must also be "prejudicial." What does "prejudicial" mean in this context? The term has the same technical meaning here that it has in an evidentiary context under Federal Evidence Rule 403: A statement is "prejudicial" if it naturally tends to tempt the jury to decide the case on an improper basis. Calling the plaintiff a "liar" is permissible because it is proper to decide the case on the proper ground that the plaintiff is lying about the historical merits. However, in most cases it is impermissible to call the defendant a "rich industrialist"; except when punitive damages are in issue, the defendant's relative wealth or poverty is immaterial.

In short, the opposing counsel can object and disrupt the momentum of your summation whenever you are desperate or foolish enough to make an inflammatory, prejudicial statement. However, quite apart from the technical law of summation, there is a more substantial reason for refraining from such statements. The overwhelming majority of trial judges and jurors are decent, fairminded people. They will usually resist and resent emotional invective. Modern commercial litigation has a decidedly businesslike atmosphere, and it is a serious mistake to place your faith in impassioned pleas and histrionic oratory. Most modern Contract lawsuits are not won by dramatics and epithets. The whole point of this text is that Contract suits are won by artistry with facts—facts creatively sculpted into persuasive theories and themes.

CHECKLIST FOR STRUCTURING A CLOSING ARGUMENT

____ Attend to the introductory amenities.

 ____ Thank the jurors for their patience and attention during the trial.
 ____ Briefly explain the function of closing argument.

____ Restate your theory of the case.

 ____ Echo the reference to your theory in the opening statement.
 ____ Restate the theory.
 ____ Mention the jury instruction on your theory.
 ____ List the elements of your theory.

____ Simplify the case for the jurors.

 ____ Show the jurors which elements of your theory are in reality undisputed.
 ____ Identify the key element of your theory that the opposing party disputes.

____ Argue the disputed element of your theory by hammering away at your theme.

 ____ If the dispute is a credibility issue,
  ____ positively bolster the credibility of your witnesses
    and
  ____ impeach the opposing witnesses' credibility:
   ____ Cite the impeaching evidence.
   ____ Explain why that evidence should lower the witness' credibility in the jurors' eyes.
   ____ Quote or paraphrase any instructions relevant to the impeaching evidence.
   ____ Give the jury an analogy illustrating why the evidence is impeaching.
   ____ Integrate your theme into the impeachment argument.

OR

    ___ If the dispute is an historical inference issue,

       ___ rely on expert testimony:

          ___ Highlight the respects in which your expert's credentials are superior.

          ___ Stress the factual bases for your expert's opinion.

            or

       ___ argue that your inference is more consistent with ordinary human experience:

          ___ Cite the facts that you think are implausible.

          ___ Assert that those facts are inconsistent with common human experience.

          ___ Quote or paraphrase any relevant instruction.

          ___ Give the jury an analogy.

          ___ Work your theme into your historical inference argument.

OR

    ___ If the dispute is a legal standard issue,

       ___ make a general call to duty

       ___ tell the jurors specifically that their task is setting a standard

       ___ quote or paraphrase the instruction fixing the legal standard

       ___ discuss the effects of a verdict for your side and the opposing side on community standards

       ___ integrate an analogy into your argument

       ___ work your theme into the argument.

___ <u>Make your concluding remarks.</u>

    ___ Restate your theme.

    ___ Convert one or two of the strongest facts supporting your theme into rhetorical questions.

    ___ Verbalize the verdict you want the jurors to return, including the amount of damages.

FOOTNOTES

[1] McElhaney, *Trial Notebook—Analogies in Final Argument*, 6 Litigation 37 (Winter 1980).

[2] *Id.* at 38.

[3] *Id.* at 39.

[4] *Id.* at 40.

[5] T. Mauet, Fundamentals of Trial Techniques 350 (1980).

[6] *Id.* at 310.

[7] McElhaney, *Trial Notebook—Analogies in Final Argument*, 6 Litigation 37, 42 (Winter 1980).

CHAPTER 18

A Final Note on the Winning Strategy

Like an attorney's presentation to a jury, a book needs a theme. The theme of this handbook is that a Contract litigator must strive for the qualities of brevity and simplicity in trial work. The experience of the master litigators shows that the trial attorney can best achieve those qualities by the strategy of developing and using a theory and theme at trial.

FORMULATING THE THEORY AND THEME

During the course of this handbook, a large number of multi-element, substantive Contract doctrines were reviewed. Given those doctrines, constructing *your simple theory* may seem to be a formidable task. In truth, whether you are the plaintiff or the defendant, the formulation of the theory is relatively easy. As we pointed out in Chapters 5 through 9, almost all plaintiffs' theories are reducible to five basic elements: The parties formed a contract (Ch. 5); the contract should be construed as creating certain conditions for the plaintiff to fulfill and a duty for the defendant to perform (Ch. 6); all the conditions were fulfilled or excused (Ch. 7); the defendant materially breached the duty (Ch. 8); and the plaintiff is entitled to the remedy he or she prays for (Ch. 9). These will be the fundamental elements of your theory whether the agreement in dispute is a realty, construction, personal service, or sales contract.

Formulating a defensive theory should be just as simple. Chapters 12 through 15 pointed out that almost all defense theories are variations of four straightforward arguments: The parties did not form a contract (Ch. 12); the contract was unenforceable (Ch. 13); the defendant did not breach (Ch. 14); or the plaintiff is not entitled to the remedy prayed for (Ch. 15). Whatever the type or subject matter of the contract giving rise to the lawsuit, your defensive theory will be reducible to one of these four lines of defense.

After developing your theory, frame *your theme*. Predict the most disputed element of your theory, frame your strongest argument on that element, and reduce that argument to a short, catchy expression—an expression you can repeat and hammer away at during the trial. We have noted several examples of themes in this text. When the defendant denied contract formation but had boxed the goods for shipment to the plaintiff, the plaintiff opted for an "actions speak louder than words" theme. When the plaintiff alleged contract formation but there were numerous differences between the letters the parties exchanged, the defendant chose the theme of "the disagreement written on the face of the letters." If you force yourself to use your creativity, you can construct a short, attention-getting theme for every case you try.

PRESENTING THE THEORY AND THEME

At trial, you must singlemindedly develop your theory and theme. You must have the courage and discipline to hold all of your other relevant evidence in reserve—regardless of the time and money you expended to acquire that evidence in pretrial discovery.

Everything you do at trial should purposefully contribute to the presentation of your theory and theme. During the preliminary remarks before voir dire questioning, briefly state your theory to the jurors in two or three sentences. During the questioning itself, insinuate the theme.

In your opening statement, give the jurors an expanded discussion of all the elements of your theory. Devote more time to the element your theme relates to than to any other element. At this point, do not simply insinuate the theme; state the theme to the jurors explicitly at point-blank range.

Begin your case-in-chief with the witness who can give the jurors the best overview of your theory. End the case-in-chief with your most convincing witness on the theme. Hold your other evidence in reserve, and make every direct examination question contribute to the development of the theory and theme.

When you are in the instructions conference, keep the theory and theme foremost in your mind. Try to get the judge's *imprimatur* on the theory and theme; before the conference ends, get the judge's assurance that he or she will give a substantive law instruction on your theory and an evidentiary instruction or two on your theme.

Finally, bring the theory and theme to a successful denouement during summation. At the outset of the summation, remind the jurors of your theory; and simplify the case for them by showing them that most of your theory's elements are undisputed or admitted. Then identify the pivotal, disputed element of the theory that your theme relates to. The heart of your summation is powerfully arguing the theme to prevail on that element of your theory. Review the evidence supporting your theme, cite the pertinent jury instruction, give the jury a helpful, common-sense analogy, and reiterate the catchy label for your theme: "actions speak louder than words" or "the disagreement written on the face of the letters."

Perhaps the most helpful parallel is a Hemingway novel. The best Hemingway novels drive forcefully toward a single moral, and their manuscripts have been pared down to the bare minimum. The novels are so short and simple that you fear that by adding or deleting even a single word, you might disturb the natural order of things. However, the seeming simplicity of these novels is in reality the product of meticulous editing—months of agonizing over every word and sentence to make certain that each one contributed to the development of the literary theme. The trial attorney planning the theory and theme is a Hemingway, relentlessly striving for simplicity and continuity.

The old Shaker hymn tells us that simplicity is both a virtue and a gift. The first part of that remark certainly applies to trial work; there too simplicity is an important virtue. However, simplicity does not come easily as a gift to the trial attorney. In trial work, unfortunately, simplicity comes grudgingly through hard work. It is hard work to wade through a small mountain of pretrial discovery material to sort out the ammunition for your theory and theme. It is even harder to resist temptation and to exercise the discipline to stick to that theory and theme at trial. The trial attorney's task is unquestionably hard work; but the task is doable—and your case is winnable—if you have a sound grasp of the fundamentals of developing and presenting a theory and theme. These fundamentals hold true whether the contract in question is a simple, $1,000 bargain for the sale of goods or a complex, $10,000,000 construction agreement. It is my sincere hope that reading this handbook has given you a sense of those fundamentals.

Index